FUNDAMENTALS OF SUSTAINABLE DEVELOPMENT

The impact of development needs to be considered beyond the narrow focus of economic, ecological or social concerns. This new and expanded edition builds upon the first edition's accessible and comprehensive overview of the challenges linked to striving for a sustainable, holistic approach to development. Providing a multifaceted approach to the subject in order to encompass what is referred to as 'people, planet and profit', this second edition provides a complete update of the text, with increased coverage of new and major topics including the Sustainable Development Goals and the circular economy.

An interactive and complete educational tool, the book comes with a companion website (www.routledge.com/cw/roorda) containing exercises, learning goals and summaries for each chapter as well as over forty video clips. It also offers a 'lecturer section' which includes a PowerPoint to accompany every chapter, and answers and explanations to the exercises.

This stimulating book is an invaluable resource for students and lecturers in all disciplines who have an interest in the sustainability of our planet, and our human society and economy.

Niko Roorda works as a senior consultant on sustainable development, corporate social responsibility and change management for companies and universities in several countries. Based on more than 20 years of experience in these topics, he received his PhD title at Maastricht University in 2010. For his achievements Roorda received the Dutch National Award for Innovation and Sustainable Development.

Comments on the first edition

'There is an ever increasingly large number of books on the market dealing with sustainable development, so any new book has to offer something new. *Fundamentals of Sustainable Development* by Niko Roorda offers just that in a very innovative way. The book really is interdisciplinary and while challenging in places it is truly accessible to readers of all backgrounds. The presentation of the book is excellent and the format makes this a very attractive paperback, and it is not too big for students (and lecturers) to carry around. This is a colourful and intriguing textbook which I highly recommend. It is the sort of book you wish you had written yourself, but Niko Roorda has done just that and in the process added a remarkable edition to the sustainability library.'

Professor Nick Gray, *Trinity College Dublin*

'The particular strength of *Fundamentals of Sustainable Development* lies in bringing together issues of equity (among people) arising from insufficient recognition of ecology (around the planet) in the economy of growth (as irresponsible profits). We strongly recommend careful reading – not just by federal and provincial bureaucrats and legislatures but also by organisations of employers and labour.'

Dr A. Ercelan and Muhammad Ali Shah, *The News on Sunday*

FUNDAMENTALS OF SUSTAINABLE DEVELOPMENT

Second edition

Niko Roorda
with Peter Blaze Corcoran and Joseph P. Weakland

SCIENTIFIC ADVISORY COUNCIL:

TH. A. M. BECKERS
J. GRIN
J. L. A. JANSEN
P. MARTENS
R. RABBINGE
M. A. SLINGERLAND
J. F. D. B. WEMPE

Routledge
Taylor & Francis Group

LONDON AND NEW YORK

from Routledge

First published 2017
by Routledge
2 Park Square, Milton Park, Abingdon, Oxon OX14 4RN

and by Routledge
711 Third Avenue, New York, NY 10017

Routledge is an imprint of the Taylor & Francis Group, an informa business

First edition published by Routledge in 2012

British Library Cataloguing-in-Publication Data
A catalogue record for this book is available from the British Library

Library of Congress Cataloging-in-Publication Data
Names: Roorda, Niko, author.
Title: Fundamentals of sustainable development / by Niko Roorda.
Description: Second Edition. | New York : Routledge, 2017. | Revised edition
    of the author's Fundamentals of sustainable development, 20152.
Identifiers: LCCN 2017004159 | ISBN 9781138714182 (hbk) |
    ISBN 9780415345880 (pbk) | ISBN 9780203726099 (ebk)
Subjects: LCSH: Sustainable development—Study and teaching. |
    Environmental education.
Classification: LCC HC79.E5 R648 2017 | DDC 338.9/27—dc23
LC record available at https://lccn.loc.gov/2017004159

ISBN: 978-1-138-71418-2 (hbk)
ISBN: 978-1-138-09265-5 (pbk)
ISBN: 978-0-203-63961-0 (ebk)

Typeset in Bembo
by Apex CoVantage, LLC

Visit the companion website at www.routledge.com/cw/roorda

CONTENTS

FIGURES

TABLES

ABBREVIATIONS

AOFG	Agriculture and Organic Farming Group
AU	African Union
B2B	Business to Business
Bt	Bacillus thuringiensis
C2C	Cradle to Cradle
CFC	Chlorofluorocarbon
CH_4	Methane
CCS	Carbon capture and storage
CHP	Combined Heat and Power
CITES	Convention on International Trade in Endangered Species of Wild Fauna and Flora
CO_2	Carbon Dioxide
COP	Conference of the Parties
CSD	Commission for Sustainable Development
CSP	Concentrated Solar Power
CSR	Corporate Social Responsibility
CSS	Carbon Capture and Storage
DFD	Design for Disassembly
DJSI	Dow Jones Sustainability Index
ECOMOG	ECOWAS Monitoring Group
ECOWAS	Economic Community of West African States
EEA	European Environmental Agency
EEC	European Economic Community
EIR	Environmental Impact Reporting
ESG	Environmental, Social and Governance
ETS	Emissions Trading System
EUA	EU Allowance
EU	European Union
EU ETS	EU Emissions Trading System

EU-MENA	Europe, Middle East and North Africa
FAO	Food and Agriculture Organization
FSC	Forest Stewardship Council
G20	Group of 20
G8	Group of 8
GDP	Gross Domestic Product
GE	Genetically engineered
Gha	Global hectares
GHG	Greenhouse gas
GM	Genetically modified
GRI	Global Reporting Initiative
GTS	Green Tobacco Sickness
HCFC	Hydrochlorofluorocarbon
HDI	Human Development Index
HFC	Hydrofluorocarbon
HIF	Health Insurance Fund
HITEC	Hyderabad Information Technology Engineering Consultancy
ICC	International Criminal Court
IFC	International Finance Corporation
IFOAM	International Federation of Organic Agriculture Movements
IGO	Intergovernmental Organization
ILO	International Labour Organization
ILUC	Indirect Land Use Change
IMF	International Monetary Fund
IPCC	Intergovernmental Panel on Climate Change
ISMUN	International Youth and Students Movement for the United Nations
IT	Information Technology
ITER	International Thermonuclear Experimental Reactor
IUCN	International Union for Conservation of Nature and Natural Resources
LCA	Life cycle analysis
MA	Millennium Ecosystem Assessment
MDG's	Millennium Development Goals
MSC	Marine Stewardship Council
MSR	Market Stability Reserve
NER	New Entrants Reserve
NGO	Nongovernmental Organization
NSSD	National Strategy for Sustainable Development
O_3	Ozone
OECD	Organisation for Economic Co-operation and Development
ODP	Ozone depletion potential
PCB	Polychlorinated biphenyl
PPP	(1) People, Planet, Profit or People, Planet, Prosperity
	(2) Purchasing Power Parity
	(3) Public-private partnership
R2P	Responsibility to Protect
RDA	Recommended Daily Allowance

REDD	Reducing Emissions from Deforestation and forest Degradation
RESFIA+D	Responsibility, Emotional intelligence, System orientation, Future orientation, personal Involvement, Action skills + Disciplinary competences
SDG's	Sustainable Development Goals
SEEA	System of integrated Environmental and Economic Accounting
SF	Science fiction
SME	Small or Medium sized Enterprises
SSA	Sub-Saharan Africa
SUV	Sports Utility Vehicle
TREC	Trans-Mediterranean Renewable Energy Cooperation
UN	United Nations
UNAIDS	United Nations Programme on HIV/AIDS
UNCED	United Nations Conference on Environment and Development
UNDP	United Nations Development Programme
UNEP	United Nations Environmental Programme
UNESCO	United Nations Educational, Scientific and Cultural Organization
UNFCCC	United Nations Framework Convention on Climate Change
UNFPA	United Nations Population Fund
UNICEF	United Nations Children's Fund
USA	United States of America
UV	Ultraviolet
VSO	Voluntary Service Overseas
WBCSD	World Business Council for Sustainable Development
WCED	World Commission on Environment and Development
WHO	World Health Organization
WSCSD	World Student Community for Sustainable Development
WTO	World Trade Organization
WWF	World Wildlife Fund for Nature

ACKNOWLEDGEMENTS

The author is grateful for the voluntary and valuable contributions made by a large number of people:

The two co-authors

Joseph P. Weakland, University of Florida, and Peter Blaze Corcoran, Florida Gulf Coast University, for doing a splendid job in making all kinds of adaptations and improvements, rendering the book highly suitable for an international orientation.

The members of the scientific advisory council

Theo Beckers, Tilburg University; John Grin, University of Amsterdam; Leo Jansen, Delft University of Technology; Pim Martens, Maastricht University, Open University of the Netherlands, Nederland, Zuyd University of Applied Sciences; Rudy Rabbinge, Wageningen University and Research Center; Maja Slingerland, Wageningen University and Research Center; Johan Wempe, Erasmus University Rotterdam.

The members of the evaluation group: professors, senior lecturers and lecturers in many universities

Ramon Alberts, Peter van der Baan, Reijer Boon, Frank Braakhuis, Theo de Bruijn, Elena Cavagnaro, John Dagevos, Kees Duijvestein, Luud Fleskens, Ruud Folkerma, Huub Gilissen, Wim Gilliamse, Huib Haccou, André de Hamer, Sieuwert Haverhoek, Marjan den Hertog, Ludo Juurlink, Peter Ketelaars, Josje van der Laan, Daan van der Linde, Edith Louman, Jeroen Naaijkens, Marco Oteman, Yolanda te Poel, Marcel Rompelman, Bert Schutte, Rien van Stigt, Timo Terberg, Joke Terlaak Poot, Sytse Tjallingii, Windesheim Paul Vader, Jan Venselaar, Ton Vermeulen, Niek Verschoor, Gerben de Vries, Kees Vromans, Nick Welman, Fred Zoller.

Experts in NGOs, companies, governments and other organisations

Paul Bordewijk, Daan Bronkhorst, Matty van Ewijk, Mark Goedkoop, Heleen van den Hombergh, Douwe Jan Joustra, Xantho Klijnsma, Alison Kuznets, Martijn Lampert, Bram van der Lelij, Peter Lindhoud, Joep van Loon, Piet Luykx, Chris Maas Geesteranus, Jan Diek van Mansvelt, Roel van Raaij, Margreet Schaafsma, Gerard Steehouwer, Anne Stijkel, Cees van Straten, Johan Vermeij, Merel van der Wal, Auke van der Wielen, Martin van Wissen, Hans van Zonneveld.

The author wants especially to thank his son, Michiel Roorda, who read the text with a critical eye and introduced additional questions.

INTRODUCTION

Sustainable development is an important subject. One can see this on TV and in the newspapers, where the issue makes headlines every day, whether or not with the phrase 'sustainable development' being included literally. It is evident in expenditure by the authorities and by companies, who annually spend billions of euros on sustainable development and on corporate social responsibility. It is no longer possible to think the subject away, while it is quickly becoming – just like the idea of 'quality' a few decades ago – a permanent core concept for *all* companies and organisations.

A grand opportunity

This is no wonder, for two reasons: because sustainability offers a major chance, while *un*sustainability is a serious threat. If we proceed in the unsustainable manners of the past and partly still of the present, the human society is under threat, as we nowadays know that we humans are able to destroy large parts of our planet, e.g. through climate change, through destruction of nature or through massive wars. At the same time, we now possess the science and technology and – in many cases – the political will to solve all those major problems, and if we do, we can make our world more sustainable, more fair and a better place to live. This grand opportunity is now available, more than ever before.

In order to grasp that opportunity, society, governments and the corporate world consequently require professionals in all fields who possess knowledge of sustainable development and who can do something with that knowledge, as is evidenced by the growing number of companies that simply require staff with these abilities. This is why this book was written.

Aim of the book: all disciplines

Fundamentals of Sustainable Development focuses on students at the bachelor's or master's level in universities. The book has some unique characteristics.

In the first place, it focuses on *all* disciplines, including those in technical, economic, social, environmental, agricultural, educational and art courses. To all of them, it offers a broad and well readable introduction to the complicated concept of sustainable development.

Consequently, the book does not go into each and every detail. It is not intended for those who want to become high-level experts on sustainability. For them, other books exist that go into the deep, offering many details at a high level of abstraction. Instead, *Fundamentals of Sustainable Development* can be well understood by everyone who is able to follow a university course in whichever discipline.

A book like this is highly relevant. As we need society to develop in a sustainable direction, it is essential that not just some, but *all* professionals with a high level of power and responsibility – in every company, government department, NGO, etc. – are able to think and act in a sustainable way. So, an introduction to sustainable development at a basic level should be a compulsory element in the study programs of each discipline in every university. Such an introduction is exactly what this book offers.

Balanced and systemic

As it is to be applied in all disciplines, the book naturally outlines sustainable development in a balanced manner, taking into account aspects of the social sciences (such as people, cultures, social cohesion, empowerment, education and health), nature and the environment, and prosperity and the economy. Together these subjects are often described as *people, planet* and *profit*. Furthermore, the balanced approach extends to the facets of *space* and *time*, meaning that the global side ('development') and the future aspects thereof ('sustainability') are treated as equally important. The topics are discussed at a systems level, helping the readers to understand the fundamental reasons for the present unsustainability. This holistic viewpoint is made understandable with the aid of many realistic case studies, some of which are based on the work of students.

This balanced and systemic approach is a second unique characteristic of the book, as most books about sustainable development tend to focus either on economic, ecological or social issues.

Not just a book

The third 'unique selling point' is that it is *not just a book*. Actually it's a complete educational methodology, consisting of many different items, with the book as its core element. All other materials and accessories are to be found on the website that goes with the book. For the students, the website contains elements like e.g. the learning goals for each chapter (described in terms of knowledge, insight, skills and attitude), a summary for each chapter and a glossary of all important terms and concepts. Also included: a large amount of ca. 200 exercises and tasks, making use of many different educational approaches, such as discussions, problem-based learning, projects, research tasks, serious games. The required tools for this, such as computer programs, spreadsheets, tables and graphs, and 40 movie clips, are all available on the website.

For those who want to have some more detailed information, the website contains extra course materials, one extra informational text for each chapter.

For the lecturers, there is more – well hidden behind a password – the answers and explanations of many of the exercises, for example. And a PowerPoint is included for each chapter, containing all or most of the images in the chapters, enabling the lecturers to easily discuss the contents of the chapters with their students.

Many lecturers themselves, while being prepared and eager to teach sustainability topics to their students, are themselves finding it difficult to understand the concept. That is why the book has been used, even before its publication, as a tool for postgraduate education to university lecturers in several countries.

Validation and credits

This book was validated at three different levels. The scientific verification of the contents was undertaken by an advisory council, consisting of seven scientists of international renown, each of whom are authoritative in a specific area of sustainable development. Besides, cases and texts were added, and the entire book was checked again by the two co-authors, who are also highly learned experts on sustainable development: Joseph Weakland and Peter Blaze Corcoran.

The societal aspects were evaluated and improved with the help of many representatives of NGOs. And the educational qualities were overseen by a group of around 30 higher education lecturers and their students.

All those who helped in this or other ways to create this book are thanked in the Acknowledgments. To all of you: I owe you deeply.

For the second edition

Since the first edition of *Fundamentals of Sustainable Development* was published in 2012, many things have changed. A lot of sustainability issues have passed through important developments, and it became essential to write a new edition.

The structure of the second edition is equal to the first; as a consequence, educators using the book with their students don't have to drastically adapt their curricula.

Some topics underwent serious alterations. The most important changes are:

- The introduction in Section 4.8 of the Sustainable Development Goals (SDGs, 2015–2030), preceded by an evaluation of their predecessors, the Millennium Development Goals (MDGs, 2000–2015). The SDGs together form the globally accepted agenda for sustainable development, and they are of course essential for an introductory textbook on that topic.
- The discussion about the ECOWAS in Section 5.4 has a more optimistic conclusion than in the first edition. Many severe problems yet have to be solved in this African region; but there are strong indications that the ECOWAS members are improving significantly, which is a hopeful sign.
- Another hopeful sign are the current developments around climate and energy, discussed in Chapter 7. Major parts of this chapter have been rewritten altogether, as the current situation differs significantly from the one when the manuscript for the first edition was completed. The two most relevant developments are the Paris Agreement on Climate Change of 2015 and the growing competitiveness of sustainable sources of energy, compared with fossil fuels.
- A final major change in the second edition is the treatment of the 'circular economy' in Section 8.3. This topic is quickly becoming more relevant, which again is a hopeful sign, as it may contribute to a transition of the worldwide economy towards sustainable development.

Besides these major changes, nearly all tables and graphs have been updated. Many cases have been renewed too or even replaced with others that have become more relevant. Hundreds of smaller changes have been made in the text of the eight chapters.

All in all, the second edition is fit to be used in the years before and after 2020. Naturally, during those years more changes will occur; it is up to the reader to use the information with care, and to compare the contents with the most recent developments reported in the news media and the scientific journals.

Niko Roorda, Tilburg, 2017

PART 1

SWOT analysis

This book consists of two parts. The first part, from Chapters 1 through 4, analyses the situation in the world with respect to sustainable development, while the second part, from Chapters 5 through 8, provides a range of strategies and methods for solutions in terms of sustainable development. In other words, the first part of the book poses questions; the second part provides answers.

The analysis in Part 1 starts with an overview of the subject, and basic concepts are introduced.

Chapters 2 and 3 proceed with analysing a number of so-called *flaws in the fabric* – weaknesses and threats that together constitute the reasons why people around the world are working for sustainable development.

The resources for doing this are outlined in Chapter 4, in which a series of 'sources of vigour' – the strengths and opportunities that are the counterparts to those flaws – are dealt with.

An analysis of the strengths, weaknesses, opportunities and threats is often abbreviated as a 'SWOT analysis', which is why the first part carries that name.

Through the SWOT analysis, it will be possible, by the end of Chapter 4, to formulate 12 objectives for sustainable development – ones that at the very least will have to be attained in the decades to come. These comprise the agenda for selecting strategies for the solutions that will be discussed in Part 2.

Part 1 is made up of the following chapters:

1   Sustainable development, an introduction
2   Flaws in the fabric: people and nature
3   Flaws in the fabric: people and society
4   Sources of vigour

1

SUSTAINABLE DEVELOPMENT, AN INTRODUCTION

In this chapter the following topics and concepts will be discussed:

1.1   Man and nature
1.2   Rich and poor
1.3   Problems and success stories
1.4   Two dimensions: here and there, now and later
1.5   The definition of 'sustainable development'
1.6   The Triple P
1.7   Top-down and bottom-up

A glossary containing all the terms in this chapter and others is available on the website of this book.

Case 1.1   The Dutch river dykes

On 30 January 1995 the Dutch authorities made the decision to evacuate the river areas around the Maas and the Waal rivers. Tiel, Hedel, Kerk, Kerkdriel, Zaltbommel, Kesteren and more than ten other villages were evacuated. In a section of the major city of Nijmegen thousands of inhabitants were even forced to abandon their homes. Companies shut down. Speed was of the essence, with the threat existing of a major flood. In total, a quarter of a million people abandoned their homes, finding food and accommodation in other places such as the Autotron car museum and the events centre in Rosmalen (Figure 1.1).

FIGURE 1.1 The Maas floods, 1995

Source: https://beeldbank.rws.nl, Rijkswaterstaat/Bart van Eyck.

It had been raining heavily throughout December in Europe, and rivers in France and Germany had swollen to unprecedented levels. A huge volume of water came barrelling down the Rhine and Maas rivers towards the Netherlands, with water pouring over the river dykes in Limburg, while Venlo and Borgharen were flooded. Meanwhile, another fear arose for other dykes – because they had soaked up so much water, they could weaken and be washed away. If that happened, a disaster would have been unavoidable.

When the dyke near the town of Ochten was pushed 50 centimetres sideways on 29 January, the situation became too dangerous. On that same day the mass evacuation started.

But the dykes did not give. They held their ground, reinforced by thousands of truckloads of sand. Once the water levels gradually sunk in the first week of February, the inhabitants were permitted to return to their homes, and damage was limited to a few thousand homes and factories in Venlo and Borgharen and in the washlands.

The Netherlands had escaped certain disaster, and this for the second time, for in 1993 the situation had been just as precarious.

Chapter 1 first investigates the meaning of sustainable development through exploring the manner in which the Netherlands deals with the waters of the many rivers that flow through its country. This manner includes both the sustainable and less sustainable facets.

A second example covers another very serious problem – the fact that millions of children have become blind as a result of a vitamin A deficiency. It will be possible, through examining this problem from various angles, to form an opinion on various sustainable solutions. Meanwhile, studying other complex issues such as environmental pollution, poverty and overpopulation gives rise to an understanding of the complicated relationship between all these problems, as well as to the necessity of tackling them in a comprehensive and sustainable manner.

Using these scenarios as a foundation, the concept of sustainable development is introduced from an intuitive perspective, and is subsequently compared to the 'official' definition thereof – the one most commonly used.

Sustainable development involves the distribution of prosperity between the various parts of today's world, and also the distribution of that prosperity between humans today and humans of tomorrow. So as to make these two facets comprehensible, this chapter employs the much-used phrases of 'here and there' and 'now and later'. They will be practiced through a number of case studies.

A second approach that is frequently used for categorising sustainable development is that of 'people', 'planet' and 'profit', with the latter also sometimes called 'prosperity'. The cases in this chapter are used to examine this three-way categorisation.

A third approach for distinguishing between types of sustainable development involves 'top-down' and 'bottom-up'. Countries, governments or multinational companies can all focus on sustainable development, this being the top-down approach. But individuals can also devote themselves to the cause of sustainable development, either on their own or in groups; this being the bottom-up approach. These concepts are likewise illustrated through the cases.

1.1 Man and nature

Case 1.1 details the Dutch people's age-old battle with water. There have been many deluges over the last thousand years, both from the sea and from rivers, and there is a good reason why the Netherlands is renowned around the globe for its dykes.

In the wake of the great flood of 1953, which saw over 1,800 people lose their lives, the Delta Works were constructed, with dykes raised and storm-surge barriers installed across the river deltas of south-west Netherlands. Once the entire project was completed, it was thought the country would now be permanently secured against flooding. However, this turned out to be untrue.

The major rivers of the Low Lands provided an unpleasant surprise in both 1993 and 1995, with flooding occurring two times in a few years. That's twice in a row – a striking occurrence, given that the last time the rivers burst their banks was in 1926. What was going on?

In the course of 1995 much work was done investigating the causes, and it emerged from studies and debates that there were a number of reasons.

One of these was that the rivers have been canalised (see Figure 1.2).

In other words, the winding and twisting – the meanders – that originally constituted parts of the rivers were straightened. This was done to facilitate shipping and dyke-building, but it also means that the water flows through the rivers at a greater speed and that the rivers contain a smaller volume of water. Though this is not noticeable under normal circumstances, in the winters of 1992–1993 and 1994–1995 there was an extraordinarily high rainfall in Europe, and a large proportion of that rain flowed through the Netherlands into the North Sea.

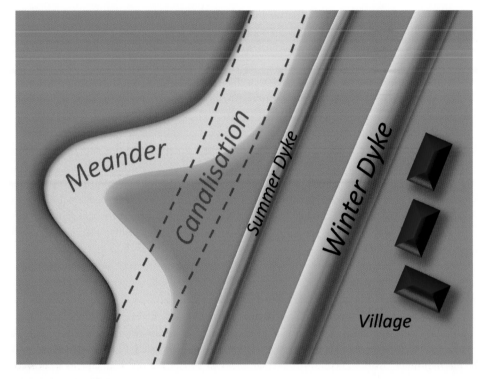

FIGURE 1.2 Canalising a river

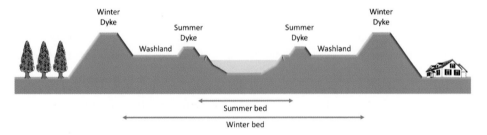

FIGURE 1.3 A riverbed in summer and winter

There was simply not enough space for that mass of water. The situation was further exacerbated by the fact that the floodplains, a natural feature of rivers, were no longer available because of the dykes. Though the washlands – the area between the summer dykes and winter dykes – still existed, houses and farms had been built on them (see Figure 1.3).

There was yet another cause for the floods. Forests alongside the river had been felled on a large scale, not just in the Netherlands but in other countries too – in the regions where the water flows down from the mountains and gathers. And towns and cities were also built. Forests are able to retain water for some time in their soil, so that the rainwater does not all flow into the rivers at once, but cities actually decrease the ground's ability to absorb water. With forests absent and cities present, the water quickly swelled into a large mass that suddenly placed the river channels under a great deal of pressure. The Netherlands was not the

FIGURE 1.4   The washlands near Olst

Source: Gerhard Aberson, Wikimedia.

only victim, and in France and Germany there were 25 fatalities in 1995. These causes aside, in 1995 much thought was naturally also given to why there was suddenly such a high rainfall during those years. Could it have been the result of rising temperatures due to global warming? This was certainly possible, but it was no simple task to prove it, with data from a great many years required. The book will return to this matter in Chapter 7.

The struggle between the Dutch people and the water that surrounds them serves as an example of the relationship between people and the natural environment. "We can utilise the natural environment," was the feeling. "We can even adapt it to serve our purposes – canalising rivers, felling forests, building towns, all for the purposes of safety, economic interests and the need for space to live and work in." Even more: "We can trust the technology for controlling water – to the extent that homes are to be built in the washlands" (Figure 1.4).

The river alterations are only one example of how the natural environment has been modified to serve the purposes of the population. Polders and marshes have been drained, and forests have largely been decimated in past centuries. The landscape is covered by meadows, roads, greenhouses and cities. All these changes were made for the sake of profit, safety or the welfare of the people. The landscape has been drastically altered, possibly in the Netherlands more so than in any other nation in the world. Should one examine the country from the air, it is striking that the whole of the Netherlands is divided up into sections, with scarcely any piece of it where nature exists in its original state. Not a spot goes unused, it seems (Figure 1.5).

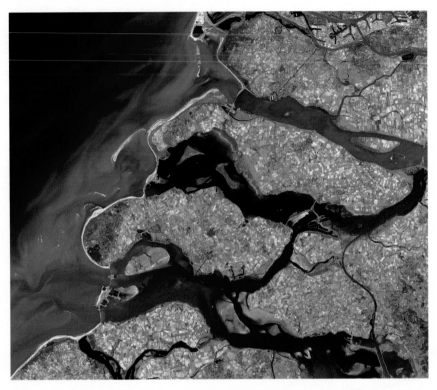

FIGURE 1.5 Not a spot goes unused, it seems. From space one can clearly see that in the Dutch province of Zeeland, just like in the rest of the Netherlands, almost every piece of available land is used. The massive dykes and constructions to keep the water under full control – the Delta Works – are also visible

Source: NASA Earth Observatory/GSFC/METI/ERSDAC/JAROS, and U.S./Japan ASTER Science Team.

In 1993 and 1995 the rivers demonstrated that if you radically alter the environment, nature can turn against you. This is primarily due to a combination of reasons that would not cause any issues should they exist on their own. For the rivers, this combination was that of canalisation, deforestation, urban development and perhaps global warming – each of these changes might not have caused floods of such magnitude on their own, but the combination of them proved disastrous.

Questions

- Do you know what type of natural environment once existed where your home now stands? Was it forest or marsh, heathland or open water?
- Do you presently live below sea level? If not, have you ever been in a place below sea level?

We are easily able to modify the natural environment, on the condition that we carefully weigh up the various interests involved against each other, such as the safety of people, the surface area used by people, the economic benefits and the power of nature and the environment. In the case of river management, this weighing up of the interests went too far in the direction of human modifications. The balance was tipped to benefit safety and the economy, with the interests of the natural environment being underestimated. The ultimate result of this was that the exact opposite of what was intended was achieved, and in 1993 and 1995 safety came under threat and the economy was damaged by the flooding and evacuations. This is known as the **rebound effect**, which occurs when the success of a certain action results in unintended side effects that decrease the positive consequences of the action or even cause the exact opposite to happen.

Room for the river

The Dutch have been engaged in battling the waters that surround them since the Middle Ages. After a number of dykes and dunes in what are today the provinces of Holland and Zeeland were washed away in 1421, resulting in the loss of over 2,000 lives, bundings and groynes were constructed in the sea, with a dyke built at a later stage. In the following centuries more and increasingly stronger sea and river dykes were constructed, with an inland sea dammed in 1932. In response to the great flood of 1953, killing again around 2,000 people, the Delta Works were built, the final parts of which were completed in 1997.

These types of solutions are all focused on controlling the natural environment and a confidence in our own power. But the events of 1993 and 1995 made it clear that this approach has its own limits. It took a long time before the engineers and policymakers realised that the problem could not be tackled by further reinforcing the dykes even more. The solution could not be found through attempts to use an increasing amount of our own force to control the natural environment, but rather through adapting ourselves to the forces of nature itself. And so, the '**Room for the River**' programme was born.

One of its many-part projects was completed by the end of 2002, when the dyke of the Lower Rhine near the city of Arnhem was shifted 200 meters, creating a washland beside the river that could be flooded when the waters rose.

In this manner 45 hectares of land were returned to the river. An additional bonus was the fact that the region became a part of the national '**ecological network**' of the Netherlands, an interconnected network of extant and yet to be created nature reserves in the country, focusing on the restoration of biodiversity and the resilience of the natural environment. Thanks to 'Room for the River', natural wetlands were linked up for the benefit of river fauna.

The same approach was employed to develop quite a number of other flood regions, such as the 700-hectare Millingerwaard near Nijmegen that was returned to the river, turning it into a major nature reserve containing channels, islets and sandbars. Another example can be seen in Figure 1.6. In various places old meanders on the river were either restored or side channels were dug. In many areas the rivers were returned to a more natural course. This was all undertaken to give the rivers more space, required when floods arise. The power of the water is now accepted and employed instead of fought – within limits, of course.

The tide turns

The turning of the tide of thought that resulted in 'Room for the River' is a fine example of sustainable water management, one which it is expected can be maintained for a long time, even when climate change results in temperatures rising even further over the course of the twenty-first century. This also accounts for the word 'sustainable' in the sense of 'able to continue existing for a long time' – the old policy, based on attempts to fully control the forces of nature, could no longer be pursued, as it was unsustainable.

FIGURE 1.6 *Room for the River.* The Westervoort Hondsbroecksche Pleij is a former wash-land on the banks of the Nederrijn and the IJssel. The dyke has been shifted, giving the river (shown at the top at its normal level) a wide course when its level rises (top)

Source: https://beeldbank.rws.nl, Rijkswaterstaat, Dutch Government.

The word **control** is a concise way to sum up the old policy in a single word. A suitable term for the new, sustainable water management is **adaptation**, i.e. accepting and to a certain extent modifying the forces of nature. Such a term, which in one word represents an entire way of thinking, is called a '**paradigm**', and the turnaround in considering control to that of considering adaptation is a **paradigm shift**, which is characteristic of many forms of sustainable development – more examples of paradigm shifts will appear throughout this book.

The introduction of the 'Room for the River' programme has signified a dramatic change for the infrastructure of the wetlands in the Netherlands. Together, the old and new natural regions along the rivers make up an extremely complex **system**, consisting of numerous constituent parts. This change was necessary, given that the system contained a '**flaw in the fabric**' – it was poorly designed to tackle the developments that people were faced with in the twenty-first century. More room for the rivers is still being created at full speed, and the process is in the middle of an enthralling **transition**, a fundamental change to the system based on a paradigm shift.

This new approach is an example of *sustainable development*, a development that leads to an environment in which the interests of humanity, the economy and the natural environment are balanced with each other. What this means is that it is not only people who have sufficient space, but also forests and other natural areas, with no overexploitation of these natural areas, in which the natural resources will not be exhausted. Such a development leads to a country where people and nature can live together in a sustainable manner.

Sustainable development can best be tackled on an international scale, as demonstrated by the example of the rivers. The underlying causes of the problems encountered in the rivers in the Netherlands can be found in at least four other European nations. Alone, the Netherlands can resolve some of those causes, but not all of them.

The following section deals with another example of sustainable development, in which it becomes much clearer that this is an international process.

1.2 Rich and poor

The preceding section dealt with the relationship between humanity and the natural environment, and the book will regularly return to that topic. But first now, a different relationship will be examined – the relationship between people themselves. The following case involves the unequal distribution of prosperity between people in different parts of the world, between 'rich' and 'poor'.

Case 1.2   Rice and vitamin A

It's called golden rice, thanks to its colour. And for millions of children it could mean the difference between sight and blindness, or even between life and death – quite literally.
But opponents say that golden rice is unnecessary, maybe even dangerous.

Some 250 million young children around the world suffer from the consequences of vitamin A deficiency, with 250,000 being struck with incurable blindness every year. Others get measles or the flu, thanks to their immune systems being weakened by a lack of vitamin A. Around half of them die from these diseases.

In the developed world, it is almost unheard of to suffer from a vitamin A deficiency. It exists in abundance in our foods, such as eggs and fish, while many fruits and vegetables contain beta-carotene (β-carotene), which our bodies convert into vitamin A. Carrots contain a great deal of β-carotene, giving them their orange colour. ("Carrots are good for your eyes," it is often said, and it is true too.)

In the poorer regions of the world (primarily southern Asia and Africa), the average diet contains little vegetables, fruits, eggs and similar products. The primary food for a few billion people is rice, which contains no vitamin A.

A number of large, multinational companies have now found a way to deal with this problem. They are developing a new variety of rice, one that does contain β-carotene, using genetic technology that involves a flower: a yellow daffodil (Figure 1.7). The daffodil is able to create β-carotene because it has the proper genes to do so, and these genes were transferred in a laboratory to rice cells. The rice grains harvested from the plants cultivated from this experiment turned out to indeed contain β-carotene. Thanks to the yellowy-orange colour – or maybe just thanks to marketing reasons – this variety has been named 'golden rice'.

In the case of the golden rice, there has been a meeting of two very different cultures. On the one hand there are a few billion ordinary people, frequently poor, living in developing countries and suffering from serious diseases as a result of malnutrition, whereas on the other hand there is a group of modern, Western-oriented companies with profits stretching

FIGURE 1.7   Yellow daffodil, source of genes for golden rice

Source: Marc Ryckaert (MJJR), Wikimedia.

into the billions that state that they can solve the problems these people suffer from with the aid of technology.

The question naturally arises – is it true? Is it really true that the genetically changed ('**genetically modified**' or '**GM**'; also called '**Genetical engineering**' or '**GE**') golden rice can solve the problem of vitamin A deficiency? Opinions are divided, which is hardly strange, given how extraordinarily complicated the situation is.

Biotechnology is expensive, and it costs a great deal of money to develop a new crop. The companies occupied with this task do not perform it out of a sense of charity, but because they expect to generate profits. This could easily lead to the seeds for these new plants being more expensive than normal seeds. Meanwhile, Third World farmers have little money, and so the question remains whether they would be able to afford such seeds.

The researchers that created golden rice sold their rights to it to a couple of major companies, Syngenta and Monsanto. In the sale, these companies promised that they would not include their patents in the price charged for the seeds to farmers in poor countries. That is great, of course, but it also raises questions, one of which is: why would the companies do that? Is profit suddenly no longer a priority, or will the farmers henceforth be compelled to buy their seeds annually from Syngenta and Monsanto, rendering them permanently dependent on the companies? Furthermore, the two companies are not the only ones involved, as methods were used in the development of golden rice to which many other companies hold legal rights. For golden rice alone, a total of 70 different patents were involved, owned by 32 different companies in a complex legal network of combinations. And so it is still an open question as to how expensive these seeds will be, and whether the farmers will be able to afford them. However, even if the rice is ultimately affordable, it remains to be seen whether the farmers will be prepared to abandon crops they are used to and move to other ones.

Biotechnology is not without its risks, and there exist issues such as the chance of an unwanted distribution of genes. This means that the introduced genes end up in the open fields amongst other crops, brought there by insects or by other means. What this will mean for the natural balance cannot be predicted. Or the introduced genes might have unexpected side effects on the rice, resulting in unknown effects on the metabolism of a person that consumes it or in the poisoning of insects in the rice fields.

These are the reasons why the environmental organisation Greenpeace has declared itself an opponent to genetic modification. Attempting to stop the cultivation of golden rice, the movement calculated that it contains a vastly insufficient quantity of β-carotene to make a meaningful difference to vitamin A deficiency. Proponents of GM foods counter by stating that the rice does not have to be the *only* source of vitamin A, and that experiments are still ongoing for increasing the β-carotene content of the rice even further. The website www.goldenrice.org states that it is expected that the β-carotene concentration can become sufficiently high to satisfy the recommended dietary allowance (RDA) for vitamin A in children that likewise consume the RDA of rice.

A fundamental objection by opponents to golden rice is that the "technological" approach to the problem of vitamin A deficiency obscures the underlying cause of that problem, which is – they assert – the poverty that is rife in large parts of the world. This leads to people in these regions having an imbalanced feeding pattern, and so they miss out on essential nutrients. In other words, the real cause is the enormously unequal distribution of prosperity between the various parts of the world. As long as this inequality exists at such high levels, issues such as vitamin A deficiency shall likewise continue to exist.

Questions

- Why do you think certain companies are prepared to withhold including their patents on golden rice in the price charged to poor farmers?
- And why do you think Greenpeace calculated that golden rice contains far too little β-carotene to be meaningful?

Rice is not the only plant being subjected to experiments involving genetic modification. Maize is another one (see figure 1.8), as well as cotton. Bt cotton, also known as Bollgard, is cotton into which the genes of the bacteria 'Bacillus thuringiensis' have been introduced to increase the plant's resistance to the cotton worm ('pink bollworm'). This increased resistance is of significant benefit to the environment, as fewer pesticides need to be used. When it comes to maize, which has become vulnerable due to the fact that extensive selective breeding has dramatically diminished the genetic diversity, experiments are being undertaken to introduce greater diversity. Soy has been genetically modified (GM) to increase resistance to herbicides; already in 2007, 60 percent of the worldwide soy harvest consisted of GM plants. Soy is incorporated into many foodstuffs, and it is almost certain that every reader of this book regularly consumes genetically modified soy. However, it has been posited that pregnant women who eat GM soy might harm their unborn babies – studies have apparently demonstrated this in rats. In short, GM is the subject of intense debate, and shall remain so for some time yet.

FIGURE 1.8 The Germplasm Enhancement for Maize (GEM) project is an attempt to increase the genetic diversity of North American maize through incorporating genes from exotic varieties, such as the oddly shaped or coloured crops from Latin America shown here

Source: GM corn: Keith Weller, US Department of Agriculture.

Case 1.3   The battle continues: Greenpeace vs. 111 Nobel Laureates. . .

Greenpeace, November 2015: twenty years of failure

www.greenpeace.org/international/en/publications/Campaign-reports/
Agriculture/Twenty-Years-of-Failure

Why GM crops have failed to deliver on their promises

Myth 1: GM crops can feed the world

Reality: There are no GM crops designed to deliver high yields. Genetic engineering is ill adapted to solve the problems underpinning hunger and malnutrition – it reinforces the industrial agriculture model that has failed to feed the world so far.

Myth 2: GM crops hold the key to climate resilience

Reality: Genetic engineering lags behind conventional breeding in developing plant varieties that can help agriculture cope with climate change. Climate resilience heavily depends on farming practices that promote diversity and nurture the soil, not on the oversimplified farming systems that GM crops are designed for.

Myth 3: GM crops are safe for humans and the environment

Reality: Long-term environmental and health monitoring programmes either do not exist or are inadequate. Independent researchers complain that they are denied access to material for research.

Myth 4: GM crops simplify crop protection

Reality: After a few years, problems such as herbicide-resistant weeds and super-pests emerge in response to herbicide-tolerant and insect-resistant GM crops, resulting in the application of additional pesticides.

Myth 5: GM crops are economically viable for farmers

Reality: GM seed prices are protected by patents and their prices have soared over the last 20 years. The emergence of herbicide-resistant weeds and super-pests increases farmers' costs, reducing their economic profits even further.

Myth 6: GM crops can coexist with other agricultural systems

Reality: GM crops contaminate non-GM crops. Nearly 400 incidents of GM contamination have been recorded globally so far. Staying GM-free imposes considerable additional, and sometimes impossible, costs for farmers.

Myth 7: Genetic engineering is the most promising pathway of innovation for food systems

Reality: Non-GM advanced methods of plant breeding are already delivering the sorts of traits promised by GM crops, including resistance to diseases, flood and drought tolerance. GM crops are not only an ineffective type of innovation but they also restrict innovation due to intellectual property rights owned by a handful of multinational corporations.

Washington Post, June 29, 2016: Letter from 111 Nobel Laureates

To the leaders of Greenpeace, the United Nations and governments around the world

The United Nations Food & Agriculture Program has noted that global production of food, feed and fiber will need approximately to double by 2050 to meet the demands of a growing global population. Organizations opposed to modern plant breeding, with Greenpeace at their lead, have repeatedly denied these facts and opposed biotechnological innovations in agriculture. They have misrepresented their risks, benefits, and impacts, and supported the criminal destruction of approved field trials and research projects.

We urge Greenpeace and its supporters to re-examine the experience of farmers and consumers worldwide with crops and foods improved through biotechnology, recognize the findings of authoritative scientific bodies and regulatory agencies, and abandon their campaign against "GMOs" in general and Golden Rice in particular.

Scientific and regulatory agencies around the world have repeatedly and consistently found crops and foods improved through biotechnology to be as safe as, if not safer than those derived from any other method of production. There has never been a single confirmed case of a negative health outcome for humans or animals from their consumption. Their environmental impacts have been shown repeatedly to be less damaging to the environment, and a boon to global biodiversity.

Greenpeace has spearheaded opposition to Golden Rice, which has the potential to reduce or eliminate much of the death and disease caused by a vitamin A deficiency (VAD), which has the greatest impact on the poorest people in Africa and Southeast Asia.

The World Health Organization estimates that 250 million people suffer from VAD, including 40 percent of the children under five in the developing world. Based on UNICEF statistics, a total of one to two million preventable deaths occur annually as a result of VAD, because it compromises the immune system, putting babies and children at great risk. VAD itself is the leading cause of childhood blindness globally affecting 250,000–500,000 children each year. Half die within 12 months of losing their eyesight.

WE CALL UPON GREENPEACE to cease and desist in its campaign against Golden Rice specifically, and crops and foods improved through biotechnology in general;

WE CALL UPON GOVERNMENTS OF THE WORLD to reject Greenpeace's campaign against Golden Rice specifically, and crops and foods improved through biotechnology in general; and to do everything in their power to oppose Greenpeace's actions and accelerate the access of farmers to all the tools of modern biology, especially seeds improved through biotechnology. Opposition based on emotion and dogma contradicted by data must be stopped.

How many poor people in the world must die before we consider this a "crime against humanity"?

Sincerely,

119 Nobel laureates, initiated by Sir Richard J. Roberts

http://supportprecisionagriculture.org/nobel-laureate-gmo-letter_rjr.html

1.3 Problems and success stories

Our planet is faced with other problems of a magnitude equal to that of vitamin A deficiency. Climate change, child labour, mountains of waste, problems involving immigration, the depletion of natural resources, refugees, soil pollution, hunger, war, epidemics and terrorism are but a few examples. On the face of it, these are all issues that might have little to do with each other. Yet they can all be traced back to a few underlying causes.

One of these is an *excess* of certain things. This is often a problem facing richer nations. A wealth of food could, for example, lead to an excess of calories, and thus to typical problems experienced in the more prosperous countries, such as obesity and cardiovascular diseases. Abundant opportunities for travel lead to traffic jams and aircraft noise, while an excess of money for buying whatever one pleases leads to excess refuse, excess greenhouse gas emissions and excessive exploitation of nature and the environment. Other problems arise from a *deficiency*, a problem naturally encountered in the poorer regions. This is expressed as a shortage of money and (consequently) a shortage of food, education, medical care, safety and liberty. In many cases, this also entails a deficiency in terms of democracy and respect for human rights.

An excess in one place, a deficiency in another – in many cases the primary issue is thus poor distribution. Many of these issues are subsequently not solely related to the rich or to the poor countries, but rather pertain to the differences between them. This interaction is evident from a couple of examples:

- The influx of immigrants into the rich countries is due to the poverty and insecurity elsewhere as well as to the expectation that life will be better in the rich nations.

- Terrorism perpetrated in rich countries is – in part, at the very least – connected to the disadvantageous position of citizens in other nations, as well as to feelings of jealousy and resentment.
- Child labour in developing countries is, to some degree, an issue because of the demand for cheap luxury goods from the rich West.
- Even development aid can have unintended side effects. There have been cases in many countries in which free products, donated as aid, rendered local small companies unable to compete, further damaging an already fragile economy.

The preceding examples demonstrate that many of the major problems with which the world is faced are interrelated in a complex way. It is frequently possible to come up with a solution for tackling one of these problems, but it will always emerge that this solution will have consequences that could invoke or exacerbate other problems. One of these is the introduction of golden rice, which might cause unexpected environmental or health problems.

Another example: to decrease the greenhouse effect, one could use wind turbines. But windmills disrupt the landscape and kill birds. Or one could build dams in the rivers to generate hydropower; but dams result in the further evaporation of fresh water, a resource that is very scarce in many areas.

What this boils down to is that there is no such thing as a simple solution. The various major problems influence each other, and it seems as if they are all connected in an inextricable complexity (Figure 1.9). The only way any of the issues can be solved is if great achievements are simultaneously realised in a wide array of other issues. In other words, if you want to solve one problem, you must address them all.

FIGURE 1.9 The various major issues are all interconnected in near inextricable complexity. If you want to solve one of these problems, you must simultaneously address them all

Source: Eric Bajart: Gunung Kawi Temple (Bali, Indonesia), Wikimedia.

One might think there is reason enough to be pessimistic about the chances of improving the situation, and to do nothing – simply leaving things as they are. But this is not necessary, and many successes have been achieved in the past. A small selection of these success stories:

- **Health:** Smallpox has been eradicated worldwide, with other epidemic diseases set to follow.
- **The environment:** Chlorofluorocarbon (CFC) is a gas used in aerosol cans and fridges, amongst others. But it has also attacked the Earth's ozone layer. An international treaty, the Montreal Protocol, was signed in 1989 for reducing usage of CFC and related substances, and this figure was cut to 3 percent by 2013 (see Figure 1.10). Details about the Montreal Protocol are discussed in Section 6.4, in Part 2 of this book.
- **The economy:** The **Gross Domestic Product** (**GDP**, the grand total of everything earned in a year in a country) in Asia and Oceania rose between 1960 and 2013 from $991 per inhabitant to $6,236. An increase was even witnessed in sub-Saharan Africa, one of the poorest regions, from $680 to $1,016 (these figures have been adjusted for inflation and are expressed in 2005 US dollar values).
- **Poverty:** In 1981, 52 percent of people living in developing countries were in a state of absolute poverty. By 2010, this figure had shrunk to 21 percent, according to the World Bank.

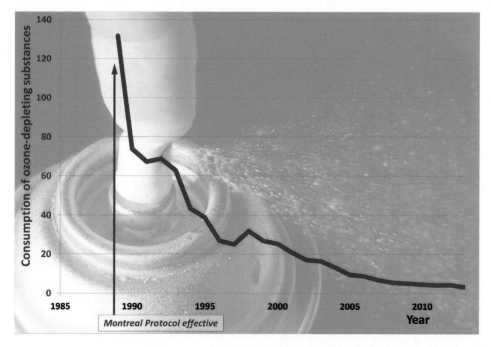

FIGURE 1.10   Worldwide use of CFCs between 1989 and 2013. The vertical axis unit is in 'ODP Metric Tons' (times 10^4). ODP stands for 'Ozone depletion potential', the ability to degrade ozone

Source: Background photo: Andrew Magill, Wikimedia.

Questions

- Are you familiar with any other "major" problems not outlined earlier? Do these include ones that relate to the differences in prosperity between the richer and poorer nations, or to the relationship between humans and the natural environment?
- What would you consider a success when it comes to tackling these types of issues, one that is truly worthwhile pursuing? Do you know any examples of such success stories that have actually (in full or in part) been achieved?

Aside from the previously mentioned advances, and numerous others, we are also faced with situations that are deteriorating. Moreover, one can also question many of these advances. An example of this is the fact that increasing prosperity leads to the environment being placed under increasing pressure.

Is the world a better place than it was 10, 20 or 30 years ago? Or rather, can real advances be expected in the next 10, 20 or 30 years? Or should we actually worry that the problems will worsen and the world will descend into a wretched place?

Some people are decidedly pessimistic about the state of affairs, fearing that things will become very troublesome in the course of the twenty-first century. Some of them even believe it is conceivable that mankind shall cease to exist before the century's end. And then there are those who are optimistic, who believe that the major problems will solve themselves, to a greater or lesser extent. The truth lies somewhere between these two extremes. The *pessimists* are half correct – it is true that things will end badly for humanity *if* we continue on our current path. We are ruthlessly exploiting nature, attacking the environment and maintaining an unequal distribution of poverty that can never lead to a stable world. But the *optimists* are also half correct – there is every chance that in reality things will not go so badly at all. The only thing is that it will not happen of its own accord, and an extraordinary effort will be required. Many people will have to work towards this goal over a long period, and the result will not be a world free of issues, one that is beautiful for all eternity. Many of the solutions to current problems will, should they be implemented, undoubtedly lead to fresh problems. That has been the recurrent theme throughout history, and it will certainly continue to be so. However, there is every reason to expect that the whole magnitude of the issues will decrease, and that as a result the world will be subjected to true improvement.

Should we succeed in solving, to a large extent, the primary issues, the world will be a healthier, safer and more attractive place for many people than it is now. The shift towards this goal is called **sustainable development**.

According to the dictionary the word '**sustainable**' basically means: 'able to keep going over time'. It is used in reference to, for example, manufactured objects such as electrical equipment. If an advertisement mentions a sustainable washing machine, it probably refers to the fact that the washing machine will work properly for years, and will not wear out rapidly.

In the same way, we can speak of a 'sustainable **society**', which is a society that is able to continue existing for a lengthy period. Society at present cannot be considered as being particularly sustainable, given the overexploitation of the environment, the unequal distribution of prosperity, etc. But should we succeed in introducing real improvements to society, the world could be transformed into an increasingly stable and sustainable one.

A confusing addition to this is that sustainable objects (objects that do not wear out quickly) do not always contribute to a sustainable society. From the perspective of sustainable development, it is sometimes better if certain things are not made to last. Indeed, it can only be considered as positive that most of the gas-guzzling cars from the 1950s are now worn out and have been replaced.

Furthermore, the idea of a sustainable society does not mean we can look forward to a rigid and unchanging world. As stated previously, the solutions to the problems we are presently faced with will certainly lead to other problems arising, albeit ones which are hopefully less extensive. Over and above these changes, new developments in science and technology, as well as in culture and communication, will always continue to provide change. 'Sustainable' consequently does not mean 'static' or 'rigid' and it is clear that a perfect world in which all our major problems are solved will never become a reality.

For this reason, the term 'sustainable development' is preferable to 'sustainable society', with the former indicating that what is at issue is a process of continuous, unceasing improvement towards a society that is becoming evermore sustainable.

1.4 Two dimensions: here and there, now and later

Sustainable development leads to a world in which an increasing number of people are able to lead decent lives for many generations to come.

This means that there are two sides to sustainable development:

1   A decent life for an *ever-increasing part of the population*.
2   This decent society is *sustained* for a lengthy period.

An ever-increasing part of the population refers to the distribution of prosperity amongst an increasing number of people. One could call it the distribution of prosperity from *here* to *there*. *Sustained* in turn covers the future, which one can consider as the relationship between *now* and *later*. One deals with '**space**', while the other deals with '**time**' – the two dimensions of sustainable development (see Figure 1.11).

The preceding description is not particularly accurate when it comes to defining the concept of 'sustainable development', and the terms that are used are relatively vague. What is a *decent life* anyway? Could it be the same as living life with dignity? Or having a prosperous or healthy life? *An ever-increasing part of the population* – how many people, and how rapidly should the number of them increase? And what about a society that is *sustained* for a lengthy period? How long a period – 20 years, a century, a thousand years? Until the end of the world?

As a minimum, a *decent life* would entail sufficient food, healthy food, clean drinking water, only a small chance of exposure to infectious diseases, and security – being safeguarded from war, terrorism and natural disasters. And for most cultures, at least in modern times, also: a good education with a reasonable chance of finding suitable employment and a good salary. Besides: freedom, including the freedom of expression, thus also democracy and human rights.

An *ever-increasing part of the population* – a reasonable goal could be to halve the percentage of people that are truly poor – living on less than 1.25 dollars a day – over a 25-year period. An alternative goal might be for all children to be attending school. This is not such a crazy objective, as it was the exact goal the United Nations set in its so-called Millennium Development Goals, which were designed for the years 2000 till 2015. They are now replaced with the UN Sustainable Development Goals (SDGs, 2016–2030) that you will read more about soon.

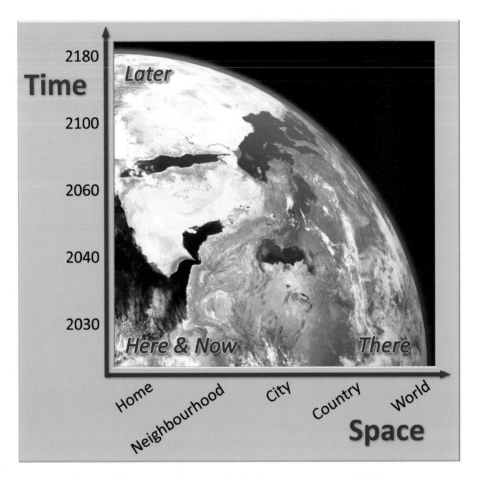

FIGURE 1.11   The two dimensions of sustainable development: space and time

Source: Background photo: NASA Headquarters - Greatest Images of NASA (NASA-HQ-GRIN).

Finally, what about *sustained for a lengthy period*? There is certainly not much point in a profound consideration of a world that will continue to exist for all eternity. Nobody could possibly think that far ahead. But if one considers the issue in reverse, it becomes possible to make some sense of it. Possible reasons might be explored that could lead to society reaching an unpleasant end or to reaching a distressing level of prosperity – the causes of **unsustainability**. These might include: an ice age or a period with a very tropical climate, three billion refugees, a giant meteorite, or the complete destruction of the natural environment. A worldwide epidemic, maybe triggered by a released laboratory virus, could be the cause, or it could be World War III. Once these possibilities are raised, methods for countering them can be conceived.

Questions

* Think about what the minimum requirements would be for you in terms of what you would consider to be a 'decent life'.

- Is it important to you that, aside from yourself, other people can also lead a decent life? If so, who would you include – your friends and family, all the inhabitants of your town, of your country or the whole world? Would you include animals?
- If you consider a society that must be sustained 'for a lengthy period', what time span would you consider a reasonable one to focus on – ten years, or until your death? Until your grandchildren die, or even longer?

Space and time aspects can be stipulated in both of the cases just detailed. A few examples are included in Table 1.1.

1.5 The definition of 'sustainable development'

All things considered, the definition of sustainable development provided in the previous section is relatively vague. The objectives to which sustainable development is supposed to lead are not clearly stipulated, nor is the pace at which this must take place. This is hardly surprising, given that the world is extremely complex, as is sustainable development. The future can barely be predicted, so how could one determine to any degree of exactitude what the path of sustainable development must be? That is completely impossible.

But there have been scientists and politicians who have endeavoured to find a more precise definition of sustainable development. Actually, there have been very many of these, but they

TABLE 1.1 A few space and time aspects for two cases

	Case 1.1 The Dutch river dykes	*Case 1.2 Rice and vitamin A*
Space	• Floods in the Netherlands are caused by deforestation and urban development in other countries, amongst other things • The great need for space in the Netherlands means that floodplains and even washlands are used for agriculture, housing and industry	• The problem affects poor nations, and the proposed solution is offered by companies based in rich countries • The underlying cause of vitamin A deficiency is an imbalanced diet, which is the result of the unequal distribution of prosperity
Time	• It is expected that rain in the mountainous regions will, thanks to the greenhouse effect, increase and thus so will river levels • The need for space will grow even further in the Netherlands (see Case 1.4), resulting in it becoming increasingly difficult to make the additional room for the rivers available	• Until this problem is solved, hundreds of thousands of people will become blind every year; for the rest of their lives they will be a hurdle to their nation's economic improvement • The issue might be cheaply and effectively solved through future technology, rendering golden rice unnecessary • Should economic conditions improve in the poor countries, the citizens could afford better foodstuffs and golden rice will become unnecessary

generally could not agree amongst themselves on the definition, which is why we have *over a hundred* definitions of the concept today.

There is one definition that most people do consider authoritative. It dates back to 1987 and was devised by a commission set up by the United Nations, the World Commission on Environment and Development (WCED). The body is generally referred to by the name of its chairwoman, Gro Harlem Brundtland (at that time Prime Minister of Norway), as the **Brundtland Commission**. It defined sustainable development as a development that:

> . . . *meets the needs of the present without compromising the ability of future generations to meet their own needs.*

This definition corresponds to that stated earlier, as the same two issues are covered:

1 *the needs of the present generation* (= a decent life for an ever-increasing part of the population: **Space**)
2 *the needs of future generations* (= a decent society continues to exist for a lengthy period: **Time**)

Unfortunately, this "official" definition is still as vague as the previous one. Here too, the goals that sustainable development should focus on are not sharply defined, nor is the desired pace.

But is it such a bad thing that sustainable development remains such a vague concept? To be honest, it is, because misunderstandings can easily arise. Even worse, there are people that will misuse the term. The word 'sustainable' has gradually become quite 'in' – a hype, as it were – which is why companies and advertising agencies often employ it as recommendation. "This is a very sustainable car!" one might hear. But, as stated previously, a car that is sustainable, that will last for a long time, is not per se a positive thing in terms of sustainable development.

This aspect aside, the lack of a highly exact definition for sustainable development is not disastrous, and it certainly does not pose a problem in the field. A good way to discover how to do that is to consider first the opposite – *un*sustainability. The following case deals with this.

Case 1.4   The lack of space in the Netherlands

The Netherlands has no space left, it is sometimes said. Of course, this is not true in the sense that another person could not be fitted in, but it is true in the sense that all the inhabitants use the available space quite intensively. Not a spot goes unused, it seems.

The reason for this is not primarily the large population, nor even the high population density. The major reason is the *prosperity* of the Dutch people.

Prosperity means that collectively the Dutch have a great need for space. They all want a house, preferably a big one, and some even want two or more homes.

They want recreational activities, and so they need football fields and golf courses, lakes for sailing and beaches for surfing, as well as camping sites and holiday parks. If possible, it would be great if a little more space was also devoted to the natural environment, but large industrial parks are needed for the factories and distribution centres for manufacturing and distributing all the country's goods. And traffic congestion (at least one car for everyone!) means that additional roads must constantly be built.

This is in no sense disgraceful – it is entirely human to want things like that – nor would it pose a problem if the Netherlands had limitless land available. But that is not the case, and the Dutch are forced to make do with a little more than 41,000 km^2.

Until now, everything the people have wanted still fits into that little country bordering the North Sea. But this is set to change, unless great care is taken. In 2000, the Dutch Ministry of Housing, Spatial Planning and the Environment launched a study into space usage over the next three decades. The ministry distinguished between seven different applications (or "functions") for the available area (see Table 1.2).

The first step was to examine the recent (1996) situation, after which it was examined how the need for space was expected to change for each of the seven functions. Various scenarios were employed, based on diverse forecasts for population growth, economic growth, etc. This resulted in high and low estimates for most of the seven functions.

For six of the seven functions, it emerged that the need for space will grow, with a decreasing need expected for only one of them – agriculture. For one other, water, the increase was due to, amongst other things, widening the rivers as a safety measure (see Case 1.1).

The total result is that the total requirement for land will rise by between 600,000 and a million hectares – 15 to 24 percent of the present surface area! To put it differently, the Netherlands is becoming too *small*.

TABLE 1.2 The need for space in the Netherlands until 2030

Function	In use in 1996	Estimated increase through to 2030	
		Low scenario	*High scenario*
Homes	224,231	39,000	85,000
Work	95,862	32,000	54,000
Infrastructure	134,048	35,000	54,000
Sport and recreation	82,705	144,000	144,000
Water	765,269	490,000	490,000
Nature and landscape	461,177	333,250	333,250
Agriculture	2,350,807	– 475,000	– 170,000
Total	**4,114,099**	**598,250**	**990,250**
% of total		15%	24%

Note: *Figures in hectares (ha)*

The term '**infrastructure**' in Table 1.2 refers to: roads, railways, dykes, bridges, airfields, harbours, windmills, electric cables and power stations, natural gas networks, sewers, broadcasting masts and so on.

This shortage of, let us say, (an average of) 800,000 hectares poses a difficult problem. One could naturally turn a blind eye to it and think: "Oh well, it will automatically sort itself out, 2030 will come of its own accord." But then there is the chance of being 'automatically' faced with unpleasant consequences, ones that could assume gigantic proportions. It would be more sensible to consider possible solutions now, and to take steps on the grounds of these.

One could, for example, consider not building any new roads, or freezing the construction of new industrial areas or residential areas. But taken all together this would still not provide sufficient space-saving. Another, very drastic, option would be to open up the nature reserves that still exist, or sacrifice large tracts of agricultural land to urban development.

Another approach is to attempt to enlarge the country. It would not be the first time this has been done, with the entire province of Flevoland, with an area of 240,000 hectares, created through reclaiming sections of the former inner sea. Other lakes have been similarly turned into land. But even Flevoland constitutes less than a third of the expected shortage by 2030, and so areas amounting to three times the province's size would have to be created. The remains of the inner sea are simply not big enough, and so the new land would have to be built in the North Sea.

The problem is that every solution to this issue will raise fresh issues. Table 1.3 shows some examples of this.

One solution to which much attention is devoted is that of **multifunctional use of space**, through which areas are simultaneously used for multiple purposes. This could be done using layers, with a parking garage, power station or factory beneath the surface, and residences or recreational areas above them. Another option would be to have these adjoining each other, such as a business park with homes scattered between the commercial buildings. But this could also lead to odours and noise pollution, or even to hazards if dangerous substances are used by the businesses. Additional investments would be required to combat these hazards. Railways and highways could be beneath the surface, located in tunnels, but this idea has lost some appeal since a number of major fires have broken out in European tunnels, in the years after 2000. And so, the multifunctional use of space could certainly contribute to the lack of space in the country, but it also creates new problems in turn.

TABLE 1.3 A few possible solutions to the future shortage of space

Possible solution	New problems
Enlarge the Netherlands – new land	Major, incalculable environmental damage, enormous financial outlay
No new roads	
No new residential areas	Congestion worsens further
Drastically reduced agriculture	Housing shortage
Drastically reduced recreation	Major damage to agricultural industry, extreme reliance on food imports
Drastically reduced nature areas	
Decreased economic growth	Major damage to tourist industry, consumer dissatisfaction
Fewer people through e.g. emigration	Major environmental damage, consumer dissatisfaction
Multifunctional use of space	Less money for the environment, consumer dissatisfaction
	Fewer working people, unacceptable regarding the aging population
	Additional investments, unsafe, nuisance created by other functions

---

Questions

- If you had to choose between drastically reduced agriculture, nature areas, roads, recreational space or urban space, which would you opt for?
- Imagine you were offered a house surrounded by large factories, and it was 50 percent cheaper than elsewhere. Would you buy it?

Of course, the preceding overview of possible solutions is far from comprehensive, and one can come up with plenty of other options. The shortage of space is a thorny issue, and difficult decisions will have to be made and billions of euros spent on it in the years to come.

1.6 The Triple P

The three cases covered in the preceding sections all relate to sustainable development – rivers, golden rice and shortage of space. On the face of it, it might seem as if these examples have little to do with each other, yet they do share common ground.

One such match is the *environment*. The floods were caused in part by deforestation and in part by the changing climate. Opponents to golden rice have warned of potentially serious environmental consequences if the genes are accidentally introduced into other plants in the wild or should the rice turn out to be poisonous to certain insects. Meanwhile, the growing shortage of space in the Netherlands can lead to the environment being damaged in a variety of ways, including the construction of new land in the North Sea and cutting back on space for the natural environment.

A second common theme is that of *people*. The floods and the threat of the dykes breaking constitute a threat to the safety of people. Houses must be demolished in order to extend and raise the river dykes, and the occupants are forced to move. In the case of golden rice, the theme pertains to the health of people, including blindness and skin afflictions as a result of vitamin deficiency. Another factor is the culture of the people, the things they are accustomed to – farmers might not be willing to start growing a new type of rice originating from a (to them) unknown company.

When it comes to the shortage of space in the Netherlands, people are acting in a slightly different role, that of the *consumer*. The consumer will have to be satisfied, to a greater or lesser extent, with future developments and will want to be able to expand freely. In all these cases (rivers, rice and space), the *welfare* and the *culture* of people are at issue. And there is also a third match between the cases, the *economic interest* involved and the *prosperity* of the people – the financial system. One of the reasons why the rivers were canalised was to facilitate shipping. The evacuations in the wake of the floods shut down factories, resulting in a serious financial setback, while the alterations to the dykes and the creation of new wetlands cost many billions of euros. One reason why the introduction of golden rice is such a complex issue is that the interests of so many international companies are at stake, with the upshot being that the seeds might come at a price that the farmers in the poorer regions of the world simply cannot pay. Meanwhile, with regard to shortage of space in the Netherlands, the economic interest of the agricultural companies and the recreational industry come into play, as do employment and economic losses as a result of congestion.

And so the three aspects are raised that play a role in all the cases – *people, planet* and *profit*. Books and articles on sustainable development frequently consider these to be the three primary areas of attention for sustainable development, also called the 'three pillars' of

FIGURE 1.12 The Triple P: the three primary aspects of sustainable development

Source: Background photo: NASA Headquarters–Greatest Images of NASA (NASA-HQ-GRIN).

sustainability. These are usually called **people**, **planet** and **profit**. However, during a major UN conference on sustainable development in Johannesburg, South Africa, in 2002 (see Chapter 4), it was proposed that 'profit' be replaced with the broader concept of '**prosperity**', which not only covers the profitability of companies, but also the economic and financial interests of individual people and of countries.

Together the three words are labelled the '**Triple P**' (see Figure 1.12). Corporations often use the phrase '**Triple bottom line**', which refers to the same three Ps.

Table 1.4 returns to two of the cases described earlier, and a number of aspects are shown, classified according to the three Ps. The table is far from complete, as both the cases are extremely complex.

1.7 Top-down and bottom-up

Two ways were discussed for grouping the topics of sustainable development. The first involves the two dimensions of space and time, the second involves the Triple P.

There is a third way for grouping sustainability topics, as shown in the following two cases. Case 1.5 deals with waste or, to be more precise, with the question of how to prevent a very large amount of useful materials being simply chucked out.

TABLE 1.4 A few *People – Planet – Profit* aspects in two cases

	Case 1.2 GM crops	*Case 1.4 Shortage of space in the Netherlands*
People	• Health (blindness, skin ailments, immune system) • Lack of certainty about the health consequences of GM foodstuffs • Are farmers willing to move to golden rice (Figure 1.13), GM maize or Bt cotton?	• Consumer demands compete with each other • Risk of a housing shortage • Emigration presents issues for the aging population • Nuisances and risks in the event of multifunctional use of space
Planet	• Advantage – fewer pesticides • Risk – unwanted spread of genes • Unexpected side effects of genetic modification, such as poisoning insects	• Major environmental damage in the North Sea if new land is constructed • Risk – less space for the natural environment
Profit	• Investments and patents from a large number of companies • Can farmers afford the seed? • Farmers' continuing dependence on multinational companies?	• Losses for agricultural and recreational companies, etc • Multifunctional use of space requires excessive financial outlay • Economic losses from traffic congestion

FIGURE 1.13   See Table 1.4. Will golden rice cost the farmers or not? Will they be willing to move to a genetically modified crop? At the summit of Pha Pon Golden Mountain in Laos it seems as if they are, as seen in the photo. The perfect solution to VAD (Vitamin A Deficiency), or too good to be true?

Source: Hank Leung, www.flickr.com/hleung

By way of a preamble, we will first define a few terms:

White goods = domestic appliances such as dishwashers, washing machines, coffee machines, microwave ovens, mixers, fridges, etc.

Brown goods = appliances present in the 'living room', such as televisions, video recorders, CD players, amplifiers, mp3-players, etc.

Electronic waste = also called e-waste, equipment used in information technology (IT) processes, such as computers, printers, calculators, games computers, telephones, fax machines, etc.

Case 1.5   Waste disposal fee

Switzerland enjoys one of the highest per capita incomes globally. Not surprisingly, the country is also among the world's most technologically advanced, with the average Swiss consumer spending nearly 3,600 USD on new gadgets each year. What you may not know is that Switzerland was the world's first country to create a national system for managing its electronic waste. Consumers who purchase items such as a television or a coffee maker pay a small additional sum at the checkout counter. This levy is a **waste disposal fee** *and it is required by Swiss law.*

In 1998, 'The Return, the Taking Back and the Disposal of Electrical Appliances' (ORDEA) ordinance came into force in Switzerland, which meant that the manufacturers of all electrical appliances (white and brown goods) were obliged by law to take back their products that were discarded by users. In this procedure, the manufacturers were responsible for an environmentally sound way of processing them. The idea behind this is, of course, that the manufacturers are and remain responsible for the products that they sell – society is not burdened with a mountain of waste, and everything is returned to the manufacturer. Also, because the appliances contain valuable material, or maybe even usable parts, the manufacturer is encouraged to do something useful with them, and a closed cycle is created through recycling and reuse. A cycle such as this one does not only shrink the amount of waste, it also means that fewer new raw materials are required.

Buyers are compelled to contribute to this closed cycle with a surcharge payable on certain appliances, which is intended to cover the costs of disposal and recycling. Two producer responsibility organizations help manage the waste stream, 'SWICO', the unit of the Swiss Association for the Information, Communication and Organisational Technologies (ICT) handles mainly waste ICT and consumer electronics (CE) such as personal computers. 'SENS,' the Swiss Foundation for Waste Management, handles mainly waste electrical and electronic equipment (WEEE) such as refrigerators and computers. According to the organization Swiss E-waste Competence, "In 2005, some 42,000 tonnes of used equipment were professionally recycled. This means more than 75% of the material was returned to the raw materials cycle." In 2014, the rate had increased to nearly 100 percent.

There is a subtle difference between recycling and reuse. **Recycling** involves recovering materials from discarded products and using them as a raw material for a new product. **Reuse** involves recovering complete components from discarded products and (once they are cleaned, checked and, where necessary, repaired) reusing them.

Questions

- A manufacturer's products are returned to it, and the company can reuse the components and raw materials. If the manufacturer takes a smart approach, additional profits can be gleaned from the used products over time. Do you think it is right that the buyer must pay an additional sum for this process?
- Under what circumstances would you be willing to purchase or use an electric appliance that contains reused components?

Case 1.6, like Case 1.5, deals with reuse, but in a very different way indeed.

Case 1.6   eBay.com

On offer

10-gram gold bars in original packaging
Strapless turquoise and blue cotton romper juniors size 11/13
Rare India antique 1-rupee note signed by Dr Manmohan Singh
Bridgeville, Calif.
My children's favourite toys, for them to pay for ruining my bathroom
    [Figure 1.14]

Wanted

My complete set (1–15) of ER for your complete set (1–10) of NCIS even up
MICE Christmas fabrics/Panels
Bold statement necklace beads and connectors
Vicki Pettersson
Rear wheel for a Schwinn or someone very handy who can respoke the wheel.

Have you ever bought or sold something on eBay or any other website devoted to second-hand goods?

It's easy to do, cheap and fun. Many agree, and online auction sites are visited by millions of users each day.

This form of reuse is easy on a buyer's wallet, thanks to the fact that such a vast array of used products is cheaper than when bought new. It is great for the seller, who receives something in exchange for his discarded things instead of having to pay to get them to the rubbish dump. It is good for the environment, as the process saves on raw materials and energy consumed in manufacturing unneeded new items, and it also keeps the levels of waste down. It puts people in touch with each other in an unexpected manner.

And then it is also a success story from a commercial point of view. Thus, eBay and similar online auction sites represent all three of the Ps, and they demonstrate that sustainable

FIGURE 1.14 My children's favourite toys, for them to pay for ruining my bathroom

Source: levelord on Pixabay.

development is not just about the problems with which we are faced. It can also simply be fun and exciting.

The online market place also demonstrates something else. Earlier in this chapter, we dealt with studies and measures by the authorities (raising the dykes, shortage of space in the Netherlands, a waste disposal fee), as well as issues revolving around foodstuffs in faraway countries where multinational companies are involved (golden rice). All of these activities are set up by large and powerful countries and companies. This is a **top-down** approach: decisions are made at a high level and affect many people. But Case 1.6 covers transactions by normal individuals, like selling used toys or a romper. Vast companies or governments do not have to play a part in this, and it is person-to-person, **bottom-up**.

As a rule, sustainable development is tackled top-down, especially when huge and global issues are at stake – the future of humanity, the natural environment, the planet itself. But when individual people or small groups are involved, a bottom-up approach can often be equally effective. Another example is Case 1.7, which shows that a bottom-up approach that generates a following can lead to major results.

Case 1.7 *Vanua domoni*

For as far back as Fijian history can go with its folklore, the coral reef has had an important part in it. There are reef passages with individual spirit guardians who are offended if provoked in such situations as rubbish being thrown or scattered in the ocean. Some reefs in Fiji are still sacred to this day.

The concept of *vanua domoni*, "our beloved land," is deeply instilled in Fijians. *Vanua* includes the land, the ancestors, the spirits, the waters and the people. The notion of *vanua domoni* includes responsibility to all of life and an understanding that all life is interrelated. This includes responsibility to ancestors and to generations to come.

In the past decades, ecologists, environmental scientists and marine biologists have arrived at the same alarming conclusion. They discovered that 35 percent of Earth's coral reefs have already been damaged. According to the Coral Reef Alliance, a non-profit organization dedicated to protecting coral reefs worldwide, approximately another 10 percent will be gone in the next decade. The cause is human manipulation of the environment and pollution.

Situated along the Fijian Coral Coast on the island of Viti Levu is the Tagaqe Village. The chief of the village, Ratu Timoci Batirerega, has worked with villagers to create a "marine protected area." He has planted mangroves on his shore with the help of his people, mostly the youths. The protected area stretches to the nearby Hideaway Resort. In a program established in 2002, the Village and Hideaway Resort worked with Walt Smith International, a business that exports coral and is a world-renown pioneer of coral farm development. Moreover, the award-winning resort is the very first hotel in the world to plant corals on its shores. The resort organizes educational ecotourism opportunities for visitors – even allowing them to sponsor and plant corals. Hideaway Resort welcomes interested parties who want to visit the coral nursery and gardens. The University of the South Pacific coordinates with the village chief to host marine biology students from around the world who are interested in researching and surveying Fiji waters.

Chief Ratu Timoci's commitment to the restoration project is singular. He continually impresses upon the people of his *tikina* (district) the reality and importance of this project. Children and youth participation is greatly encouraged because they will learn from it and continue to be involved in years to come. A Fijian Islander's daily life is bound by three types of laws and tradition; namely, *vanua*, *lotu* (church), and *matanitu* (government). Ratu Timoci was careful to blend the restoration strategies with local protocol. In most Pacific Islands, chiefs and elders are the only people who can pass restrictions on fishing grounds. Final decisions made by the chief are honoured and respected. The Chief said he has witnessed the negative change in his *qoliqoli* (fishing grounds) from when he was a young child to when the project started. Now, years later, the chief and his people are reaping the rewards of restoring the coral reef. Manta rays, lobsters, octopi and reef sharks have returned to the shallow waters at the shore. The Chief believes that time and understanding is what it takes to heal the environment.

The islanders were wrestling with the problem of the degradation of coral reefs as a result of pollution and anthropogenic climate change. Using a top–down approach, it is exceedingly difficult to make any progress. But the coral reef restoration project on the Island of Viti Levu demonstrates that excellent results can be achieved, on the basis of initiatives launched by ordinary people, from the bottom-up.

The two different approaches – top-down and bottom-up – are both important, and they complement each other. This can be witnessed when local initiatives by citizens are supported by the authorities or by a company. More of these examples are detailed throughout this book. They give hope, as they demonstrate that every individual is able to make a positive contribution to the sustainable development of our world.

Summary

Sustainable development focuses on improving the living conditions of people throughout the world as well as on intensifying the natural environment, creating a society that can be sustained for a lengthy period. This approach requires a number of paradigm shifts, such as the move from control to adaptation. Simply by examining the actual circumstances using new approaches such as these, it becomes possible to correct the flaws in the fabric that are deeply ingrained in our human systems.

In order to understand the broad field of sustainable development, a number of classifications have been created, including

* The Triple P
* The two dimensions of space and time
* Top-down versus bottom-up

A more detailed summary can be found on the website of this book, where you can also find other tools designed to help process this and other chapters, including

* An overview of the learning goals for each chapter
* A series of exercises and assignments (and for lecturers: solutions or discussions of them)
* Supplementary materials for exercises, including software, movie clips and spreadsheets
* For lecturers: PowerPoint presentations containing the images from every chapter

2

FLAWS IN THE FABRIC

People and nature

In this chapter the following topics and concepts will be discussed:

2.1 One-way traffic: no cycles
2.2 Positive feedback: moving up or down without inhibitions
2.3 Overexploitation: a gigantic footprint
2.4 Clean water: all for mankind, but still not enough
2.5 Agriculture and stock farming: excessive efficiency and yet still too low
2.6 Consequences for the natural environment

A glossary containing all the terms in both this chapter and others is available on the website of this book.

Case 2.1 Animal feed

Everyone eats. Some of us might only eat vegetables, but most of us eat meat too. Meat consumption varies widely between developed and developing countries, as well as between cultures. People in Vietnam, for example, each eat around 28.6 kilograms of meat annually, while the average American consumes 125 kilograms of animal protein. In both countries, the flesh of cattle, pigs and chicken are primary sources of meat. These animals are, together with the people that eat them, a part of the food chain.

This chain starts with the vegetables that the animals consume. Besides grass, this animal feed consists of maize, tapioca, soy and copra (dried coconut), amongst other things. This material – animal feed or fodder – was once grown locally, frequently by the same farmer that had the livestock on a mixed farm. But times have changed, and today many countries ship an increasing amount of their animal feed from abroad. Vietnam, for example, imports around 80 percent of its animal feed from suppliers in other parts of the world, with the United States, Brazil, and Thailand being some of the biggest suppliers.

A disadvantage of this import is that one-way traffic from these countries to Vietnam – and to other countries, e.g. in Western Europe – becomes an issue. Valuable nutrients in the soil of the supplying nations are used to cultivate fodder, which is subsequently shipped to Vietnam. On arrival, it is consumed by the livestock and in turn by people. Ultimately, a large proportion of the nutrients end up, via fertiliser (manure), in the agricultural land – in Vietnam! And so it is not returned to the fields where the fodder was originally grown.

This is a poor state of affairs for both ends of the chain. In Vietnam the nutrients are piling up, an 'over-fertilisation' that results in increasing levels of nitrate in the groundwater and the surface water. The result is a green 'soup' of algae in lakes and rivers, acidification of nature reserves and a decrease in **biodiversity** (diversity of species), amongst butterflies and mushrooms in particular, which struggle to grow in an acidic environment. Over-fertilization also reduces the quality of drinking water and even contributes to acid rain in the region. Meanwhile in the countries supplying the animal feed, the consequences are even worse. They are suffering from the opposite problem – the loss of valuable nutrients. Soil fertility declines and erosion increases, irreparably damaging the land. Where irrigation is required, much valuable fresh water is used, and a great deal of land is also required, resulting in the loss of tropical rainforests in Thailand and Brazil. It takes much agricultural land to grow animal feed, which could have been used to develop agriculture for the local population – a problem that is of particular concern in India.

Many of the issues that make sustainable development a necessity have arisen from fundamental errors in the way in which humanity has arranged its world. The various unsustainability problems are inextricably linked in the fabric of the global human system: see Figure 2.1.

This chapter deals with a series of such 'flaws in the fabric of the system'. An example of these is the fact that valuable natural resources, such as the fertile soil in Case 2.1, are used but are not replenished – in other words, the absence of a closed cycle. Another flaw is the continuing exploitation of the natural environment, and there are other flaws that concern the economic structure, the growth of the world population, the distribution of prosperity and many more.

These flaws in the fabric constitute the primary causes of the major problems in the world. Fortunately, these flaws are countered by a large number of 'sources of vigour' that can be used to tackle them. Chapter 4 will deal with those sources of vigour. Here, a number of flaws in the fabric will be examined.

2.1 One-way traffic: no cycles

A large proportion of Vietnamese animal feed comes from abroad, and this is a thorny problem. It is a relatively new issue – the livestock used to simply eat plants that were grown locally, which thrived thanks to the fertiliser derived from that same livestock, forming a **cycle**. And therein lies the core of the problem, for in the present system the problem is (in part) the **one-way traffic**. See Figure 2.2.

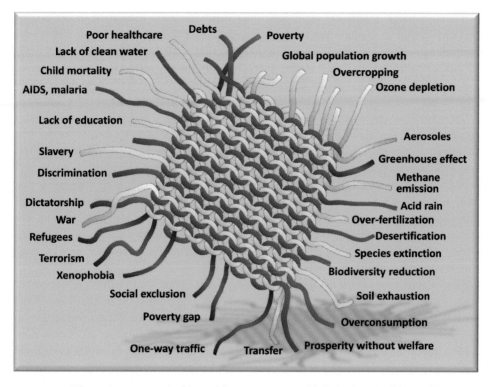

FIGURE 2.1 The various unsustainable problems are inextricably linked in the fabric of the global human system

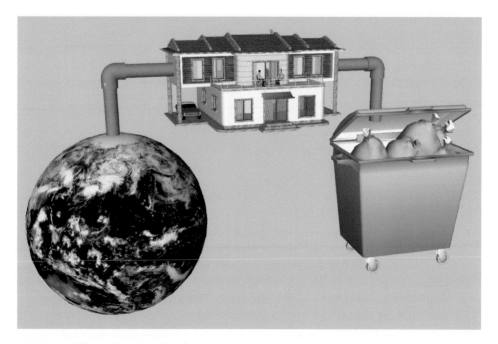

FIGURE 2.2 The cycle is not closed

It seems a simple solution to close that cycle – send a portion of the fertiliser, the surplus, back to the countries where the fodder was grown. People have experimented using this approach before. In order to cut weight and volume, the fertiliser was processed into dry pellets that were shipped out. But it turned out to be economically unfeasible – too expensive.

A response might then be: why do we continue on this path, when the logical conclusion is that it cannot continue like this forever?

But it is not an easy task to break one-way traffic. There are a number of reasons for this, one of which is that there are so many stakeholders. Imagine that the Vietnamese farmers collectively decide to stop using animal feed imported from abroad. That would cause them serious problems, because the sole use of feed grown in Vietnam would force costs up dramatically, and this when agriculture in the country is already struggling to compete against Western countries with access to the latest agricultural technology. Many farmers would go bankrupt. But this issue aside, moving to domestic feed is difficult for yet another reason. The present number of cattle, pigs and poultry means that Vietnam would have to allocate sufficient agricultural space to grow all the animal feed required – no easy task in one of the most densely populated countries in the world.

So to whom would it fall to change this system based on one-way traffic? The importers? Importing feed is their livelihood, or at least a part of it. Maybe then the foreign farmers that cultivate the animal feed? For many farmers in developing countries, this is the only way to earn sufficient money to survive.

How about the Vietnamese authorities? On their own, they cannot do much, for it is not only Vietnam that is involved, but also numerous other countries that import large quantities of their animal feed. Should Vietnam go alone in trying to break the system, the farming industry in the country would collapse as a result of foreign competition. And meanwhile, the system will simply continue. But let's say that a group of nations did decide to stand together – what would their governments do? Prohibit the import of feed, or maybe levy high import tariffs? That would bankrupt thousands of farmers in both Vietnam *and* in other developing countries. And finally there is the consumer, the man or woman in the street in Vietnam (and elsewhere) who buys meat and other animal products. What could they do? What could *you* do?

Alone, very little. You could become a vegetarian, of course. But although most vegetarians do not eat meat they usually do consume eggs and dairy products such as milk and cheese. So you would have to become a **vegan**, and shun everything of animal origin. The only problem is that there would only be a noticeable result of this when a significant proportion of the population made the switch to veganism, which is not very likely in the immediate future.

Questions

- (If you're not a vegan:) Do you think you should feel pangs of conscience about the fact that, every time you eat meat or drink milk, you make a small contribution to the decimation of tropical rainforests in Asia or South America?
- Whose fault is it that the one-way traffic of animal feed continues to exist? The multinational companies that import the fodder or the farmers who use it? The people who eat meat and cheese? You yourself? In a nutshell, who shoulders the blame?

One-way traffic – a flaw in the system

It is an extraordinarily difficult task to change the animal feed importing system. This is because it is deeply rooted in a much larger system, one that consists of food supply in Vietnam and other countries, as well as of agriculture in large segments of the world. The system is fundamentally flawed, one could call it a flaw in the fabric, a flaw upon which the entire system is constructed.

This inherent flaw related to animal feed can be easily graphically represented, such as Figure 2.3.

Figure 2.3 shows the word **resource**. Everything one might extract from the natural world, from the Earth or from the air is a resource. Ore is a resource, as is oil and natural gas. Clean water, plants, nutrients extracted from the soil, wind (as a source of energy) and sunshine are also all resources. In a broader sense, the landscape is also a resource – a source of beauty and tranquillity.

Figure 2.3 demonstrates the flaw in the fabric: if one-way traffic exists from a resource to a location where it is discharged, it is only logical that within a period of time there will be a shortage in one place and a surplus in another.

This flaw can, in principle, be easily remedied by closing the cycle, as can be seen in Figure 2.4, where the resources are returned (or recycled) to their source after consumption. An easy task *in principle*, but generally not in practice, given that the system is often extremely complex, and that there are many different stakeholders.

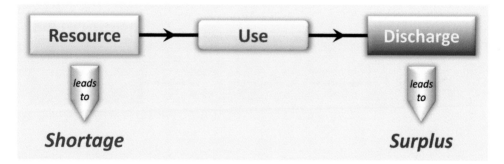

FIGURE 2.3   One-way traffic, or a cycle that is not closed

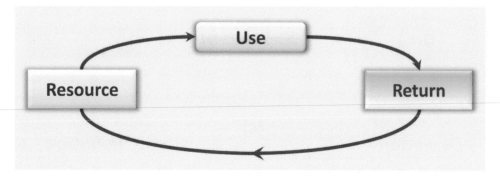

FIGURE 2.4   Closed cycle

This particular flaw in the fabric – one-way traffic – can be found in many instances. It is what is causing the greenhouse effect, for example. Figure 2.5 shows (a) animal feed and (b) the one-way traffic that leads to the greenhouse effect. In the latter case the resource is oil and natural gas (and other products, such as coal and lignite) – fossil fuels that have been in the Earth for hundreds of millions of years and that are now being extracted and burnt at a high rate of knots. The 'discharge' referred to in this case involves the emission of greenhouse gases into the atmosphere, with the primary gas being carbon dioxide, or CO_2. The one-way traffic of these greenhouse gases is likewise deeply rooted within the system as a flaw in the fabric, given that almost the entire global economy is based on oil and natural gas. The solution to this flaw does not lie in closing the fossil fuel cycle. Although it is partly possible to collect the CO_2 and pump it back into the ground, the largest part still escapes into the atmosphere. This is why the solution to this issue must (at least in part) be found in other energy sources, ones that can be a part of a cycle such as energy derived from biofuels, or in wind, water or sunlight.

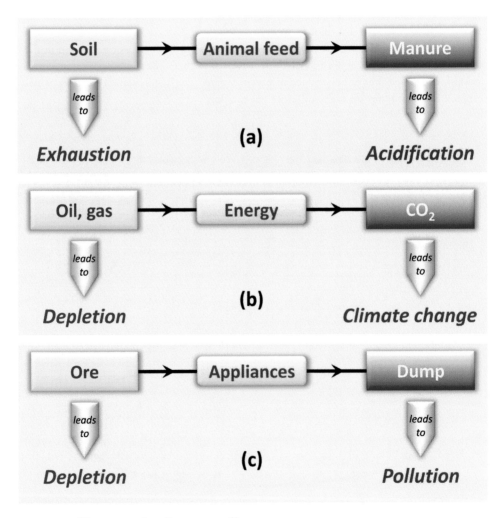

FIGURE 2.5 Three examples of one-way traffic

Climate change resulting from the greenhouse effect as a result of CO_2 emissions is a world-wide problem that, of all the forms of unsustainability, could well be the most serious threat to our future. For this reason, a separate chapter in this book (Chapter 7) has been devoted to it.

And then there is ore-extraction, such as iron, aluminium and other metals (the 'c' in Figure 2.5). Here we are again dealing with resources that will one day be depleted, as every kilogram removed from the ground will never be replaced. The waste disposal fee, discussed in Case 1.5 in the previous chapter, is a highly successful attempt at closing this cycle by reusing or recycling parts or materials.

The question for every unclosed cycle is: which problem is worse, the shortage on the side of the resource or the surplus on the side of the discharge? When it comes to animal feed, the biggest problem is probably on the side of the resource, with enormous damage being caused, particularly in the developing countries. For fossil fuels, the opposite holds true, with the discharge being the most severe. The emission of greenhouse gases cannot continue unabated for decades, even though oil and natural gas can probably still be extracted for much longer at acceptable costs.

Each of the previous examples of one-way traffic is a way of transferring the negative consequences of our economic prosperity onto others. With regard to animal feed, Vietnam cannot grow the fodder required to feed its livestock. So instead of solving their problem, the Vietnamese transfer it to people in other countries. When it comes to the CO_2 discharged into the atmosphere, we transfer the damage our energy consumption causes onto the natural environment and onto future generations (Figure 2.6). The same holds for rubbish dumps. In Chapter 3, this mechanism of *transferring the problems* is discussed in further detail.

FIGURE 2.6 One-way traffic: oil is extracted from the ground, CO_2 is lost to the atmosphere

Source: Le Havre, Wikimedia.

Flaws and transitions

One-way traffic is not the only flaw in the fabric of the system of our civilisation, although it is one of the gravest. More examples are provided throughout this chapter and the next. The summary of these issues might make the reader feel dejected or even fearful of the future. One might gain the impression that there are so many flaws rooted in the global system that it will be simply impossible to improve the situation – to develop the world in a truly sustainable manner. The good news, for those readers who may feel this way, is that Chapter 4 deals with a whole series of 'sources of vigour': strengths and tools for bettering the situation. This means that only once that chapter has been concluded, will one be able to gain a realistic impression of both the weaknesses in the system and its strengths, allowing for a balanced consideration of the whole. In doing so it will emerge that there is every reason not to succumb to the negatives, but rather to address them with energy and enthusiasm.

Sustainable development is a necessity because of the deeply rooted flaws in the fabric. Should all the issues be simple mistakes that could easily be solved, preferably independently of each other, we would never have to deal with sustainable development. But for the very reason that these are profound and interlinked questions, sustainable development is a very slow process that can only be achieved step by step. It takes decades at the very least. In the years to come we are set to see drastic changes in our world, more than many are able to imagine.

The term for such a drastic change, 'transition', was already outlined in Chapter 1. The move to sustainable agriculture can only happen through such a transition, given that the agriculture and food system contains real and deeply rooted flaws. The same applies to the global energy system, which is at present largely based on fossil fuels – another flaw, and consequently also only solvable through a transition.

Questions

- An example of a transition in recent years was the rise of modern electronics, such as computers, mobile phones and the Internet. Can you imagine what your life would have been like if this transition had not happened?
- Transitions are succeeding each other at an ever-increasing rate. Try to imagine what life will be like for you in 25 years.

2.2 Positive feedback: moving up or down without inhibitions

Everything that is alive has the tendency to grow. Should there be no checks or inhibitions on growth, this tendency could result in growth exceeding safe boundaries, and if that happens it could be disastrous – the natural balance disrupted, rampant growth, plagues, the ecosystem collapsing and species becoming extinct. In principle, this holds true for every species of plant and animal, and for humankind too. This section demonstrates that the relationship between humankind and the natural environment is not an antithetical one – as if humanity was not a part of the natural world – but that this natural environment still resides within people. The human nature is just as focused on growth as every other living thing, and it also leads to occasional catastrophes. The underlying mechanism in this is called *positive feedback*.

Case 2.2 Black Monday

It all started on Monday, 19 October 1987, in Hong Kong. Shares being traded on the stock market suddenly plummeted in value. Within hours the downturn had spread to Europe, reaching the United States six hours later. Panic-stricken dealers all thought that, with prices sinking, they had to shed their shares as quickly as possible. They offered them up for sale in huge volumes, causing the prices to drop even more. This caused the panic to worsen, and even more shares were put up for sale, resulting in prices sinking further. . . and so on.

In the space of one day stock markets sank by almost 23 percent – a value of 500 billion dollars simply vaporised.

It was a crash, the biggest stock market crash in years. To this day it is known as *Black Monday*.

FIGURE 2.7 A restless crowd gathers outside the New York Stock Exchange during the Great Crash of 1929

Source: Le Mémorial du Québec, Tome V, 1918-1938, Montréal, Société des Éditions du Mémorial, 1980. Photographer unknown.

A **crash**, a large-scale downturn of share prices, is a dramatic event. Banks, companies and individual investors can all suddenly find themselves bankrupt, whereas employees can find themselves out on the street.

The 1987 crash was neither the first nor the last of its kind. The biggest and most famous crash was in 1929 (Figure 2.7), which led to the Great Depression and was so severe that a number of people committed suicide in its wake. Another, less dramatic one, occurred in 1998; and just a decade later the world was hit again when the crisis in the American housing market, turning into a severe banking crisis, saw the economic world floundering in the worst crisis in many years (Figure 2.8).

A stock market crash is the result of the way in which the stock markets operate. Each share is a proof of ownership of a piece (or a share) of a company. The shareholders collectively own the company. What this means is that the value of a share should actually be determined solely by the value of the company, with share prices simply tagging along with the changing value of the company, based on profits and losses. But the reality is slightly different – the value of shares is primarily based on *expectations* of profit or loss, and consequently on levels of confidence in the economy.

So if, on a bad day, the dealers were to lose their confidence in the economy, they would try to ditch their shares. When they are offered for sale, en masse the share prices fall, causing confidence levels to decline further, and hence the stock market is faced with a vicious circle spiralling downward.

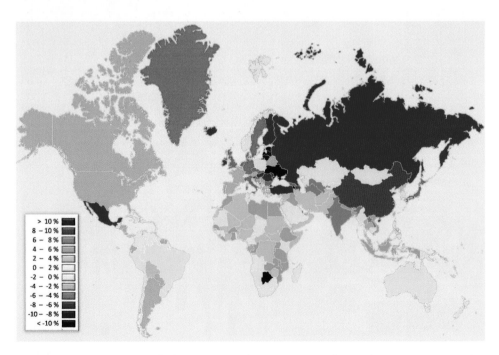

FIGURE 2.8 Many countries had a negative real GDP in 2009, due to the economic crisis that started in 2007 as a housing crisis

Source: CIA World Factbook, 2010.

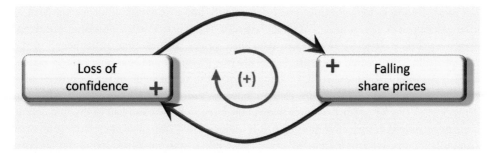

FIGURE 2.9   Loss of confidence in the stock markets causes positive feedback

To put it differently, event A (loss of confidence) creates and amplifies event B (falling share prices), after which event B in turn amplifies event A (Figure 2.9). The situation quickly gets out of control.

The stock exchange system is affected by so-called **positive feedback**.

Positive and negative feedback

Feedback is somewhat akin to cycling. The cyclist constantly checks whether he is on the correct path and, if not, he will correct his course, a process that is largely unconscious and automatic for a seasoned cyclist. The bicycle will always meander slightly, almost to an invisible degree, and that is the exact reason why the cyclist and his mount maintain the proper course. Everybody who cycles is able to do this, and these corrections are called 'feedback'. The cyclist must continuously check if he is on the right course, and immediately react to any deviations from it. This reaction is the *opposite* to the action of the bicycle – should the bicycle deviate to the left, the cyclist steers to the right, and vice versa. Because of these opposing directions, it is referred to as **negative feedback**. Negative feedback means a cyclist can stick to a stable course. *Negative feedback leads to stable systems.*

When it comes to stock exchange systems, feedback is also involved, as the system reacts to changes in the system itself. This time however, the two effects both point in the same direction – downwards – and that is why this is positive feedback. Most of the time the fluctuations are only minor, and the system remains in equilibrium. But it is an unstable equilibrium, comparable to a pencil standing upright on the table (as in Figure 2.10). Should the equilibrium be sufficiently disrupted, then confidence collapses and a small dip develops into a total meltdown. *Positive feedback leads to unstable systems.*

The words 'positive' and 'negative feedback' can lead to confusion. In everyday conversation 'positive' generally refers to something good while 'negative' pertains to less pleasant things. For feedback the terms are reversed, with negative feedback mostly favourable and positive feedback mostly unfavourable.

FIGURE 2.10   The stock market is like an upright pencil – just too far out of equilibrium and it will fall

Positive feedback does not only spiral downwards. Just as loss of confidence can lead to sinking share prices, a great deal of confidence lead to rising prices, in turn causing confidence to increase. This unfettered growth can send share prices skyrocketing, as happened in the years preceding 1987 when stock prices initially rose gradually and then increasingly rapidly to reach astronomical values, worth much more than the actual value of the companies they represented (see Figure 2.11). This is called a 'bubble', and it was such a bubble that burst in October 1987 (Figure 2.12). A comparable bubble burst in the second half of the first decade of the twenty-first century, after housing prices in the United States had risen far beyond their actual value. This gave rise to another crisis, and while it was not as sudden as the one two decades previously, it proved much more serious.

Questions

- What would it be like to cycle if your handlebars were subject to positive feedback instead of negative feedback?
- For the technically minded: could you design a bicycle like that? And would you be able to learn to ride such a bicycle?

The presence of positive feedback in the economic system means that it has a fundamental flaw. A flaw in the fabric that, as long as it continues to exist, will lead to instability that will not stop to seriously damage the economy from time to time.

There are more examples of positive feedback that give rise to structural unsustainability.

FIGURE 2.11　A bubble in 2007 led to the housing crisis, which generated into a financial one and finally into a general economic crisis across the globe

Source: Mila Zinkova, edited by Alvesgaspar, 2007, Wikimedia.

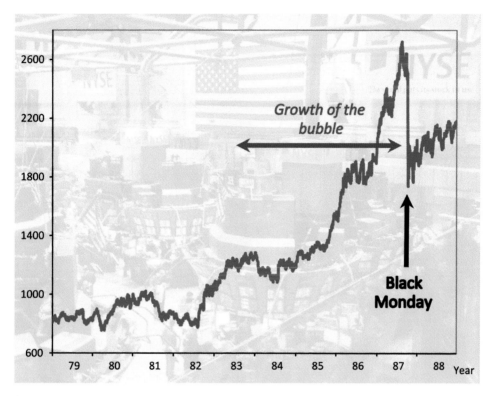

FIGURE 2.12   Dow Jones Index (closing prices) between 1979 and 1988

Background photo source: Ryan Lawler: New York Stock Exchange, 2008, Wikimedia.

Population growth

The number of people on this planet has been rising for centuries, a rise that is in part due to positive feedback. The cause of this will be examined here briefly, and the issue will receive greater attention in Chapter 6.

The world population has demonstrated a certain level of growth for tens of thousands of years. Initially, this growth was very slow. People lived from gathering food, with a little bit of hunting on the side, and agriculture had not yet come into being. The yield of food was relatively low in terms of lifestyle, meaning that few people could live off every square kilometre.

On occasion the number of people in a given area increased to such an extent that the land could not produce sufficient food to feed them, resulting in famine. In most cases, this would have led to wide-scale mortality, but sometimes people succeeded in moving to a new way of obtaining food. In one sense, this was actually a step backward, as the new lifestyle meant one had to work harder. But the food yield per square kilometre increased greatly.

Agriculture meant that food could be provided for many more people, and so the population increased greatly, as can be seen in Figure 2.13.

After some time (centuries or maybe millennia) there was once again a time when the population was too large. In some regions, famine was inverted thanks to improved agricultural techniques, such as the plough and, later, draught animals to pull the plough.

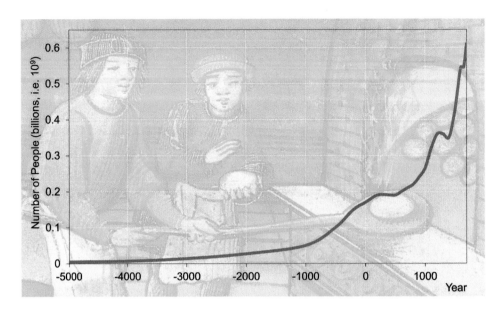

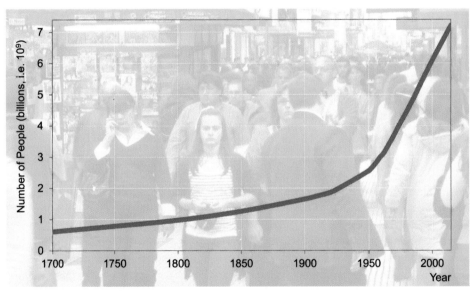

FIGURE 2.13 Size and growth of the world population until 1700 (above) and from 1700 to 2015 (below)

Background image source: (top) Maggie Black: The Medieval Cookbook, Wikimedia; (bottom) Niko Roorda: Buenos Aires, Argentina 2009.

And so, positive feedback was introduced: event A (population increase) gave rise to event B (improved food production), which in turn amplified event A once again.

A further step in this development started around 1600, when production increased greatly as a result of **mechanisation**, **industrialisation** and (in the twentieth century) **automation**. Production per worker increased by titanic proportions as a result of these developments.

Agriculture also billowed with the introduction of chemical fertilisers, while improved hygiene and healthcare contributed to the high population growth.

The uninhibited growth of the human population continued unabated for centuries, and actually accelerated in the 1950s, when the growth rate was so high that the world population doubled in the space of 35 years. To this day the population in many countries is still growing rapidly, but in certain other parts the pace has slowed and in some regions the growth rate is even approaching zero, including in Western Europe. This is because positive feedback is fortunately not the only determining factor for population growth, as Chapter 6 will show.

2.3 Overexploitation: a gigantic footprint

The increasing size of the world population has placed the natural environment under a great deal of pressure, and both nature and the environment have suffered greatly as a result. But population growth is not the sole reason for environmental issues. In rich countries the damage to the environment is exacerbated by the increased prosperity, while in the Third World it is the fact that people are living in poverty which compels people to live an unsustainable lifestyle that harms the environment.

An oft-used method for calculating damage to nature and the environment is the **ecological footprint**. The ecological footprint is the amount of land that a person or a country requires to support himself or itself. Every person requires a certain amount of land, with some of it devoted to a house to live in, another piece – somewhat larger – going to growing food and other sections for generating power, industry, processing waste and CO_2, recreation and so on.

The piece of land a person requires will increase in proportion to the level of prosperity he or she enjoys. The symbolic name for that piece of land is the ecological footprint and the measurement involves, as it were, the size of the foot a person requires for support.

On the face of it, it seems very simple to calculate the size that the average footprint can be per person. Just take the total surface area of the globe's land, which is 148,900,000 square kilometres, and divide that equally amongst all the people. In the year 2000 there were over six billion people, a figure that passed seven billion by 2011. Divide these figures by each other and the answer is that in 2002 there were 0.025 square kilometres, or 2.5 hectares, available per person – a patch of land of 250 by 100 meters each. In 2017 the world population passes 7.5 billion, and the same calculation results in only 2.0 hectares per person, given the increase in the population.

In reality, things are somewhat more complex. Firstly, an assumption was made in the previous calculation that every square meter of land is available for human use, which is naturally not the case, as a major portion is required for virgin fauna and flora if we want to retain at least some of the present biodiversity. Furthermore, some of the land is completely unsuited to human purposes – the ice fields of Antarctica and Siberia, the peaks of the Himalayas and the Rocky Mountains and the arid plains of the Sahara and Kalahari deserts come to mind. All these areas are not included, or can barely be included (Figure 2.14).

The flipside is that certain parts of the seas and oceans can be included because, for example, they are used to catch fish or to generate wind energy.

Another reason why this calculation must be more complex is that not all usable pieces of land are of equal benefit. On the one hand, that is because some lands are more fertile or have a more fertile climate than others (Figure 2.15), while on the other it is because people

FIGURE 2.14   When calculating the footprint or biocapacity, the Sahara may be counted as usable land, but with only a very low weighting factor

Source: Michael Martin: Sahara: Arakao, Niger, Wikimedia.

wish to undertake different things using the land. People require different things of a plot of land on which rice is grown than of a plot upon which a town is built or sports are played.

All these issues are taken into account when it comes to calculating the ecological footprint. Every piece of land that has a high beneficial value is multiplied by a large factor – a high 'weighting factor' – while all barren, dry and unusable pieces of land are multiplied by a small factor, which means they contribute little to the equation.

This results in an imaginary value, a symbolic representation of the number of hectares of useful land available for humans. These imaginary hectares are called '**global hectares**' (or **gha**). This available area is called the **biocapacity**.

The biocapacity of the planet is not a constant. Technological advances, e.g. in agriculture, have raised the planet's total biocapacity from 10 to 12 billion gha between 1961 and 2010. However, the world population increased faster, and so the space available to a person has gone down. In 2000 the space per person stood at 1.95 global hectares, an amount that shrunk

FIGURE 2.15 Tropical jungles, such as the rainforest at the foot of Mount Kilimanjaro in Africa, have a very high weighting factor when it comes to calculating the footprint or the biocapacity

Source: Chris 73, 2007: Mount Kilimanjaro, Wikimedia.

to 1.8 gha per person in 2006. By 2017, when the world population had increased even further, there was less than 1.7 gha per person left. This amount is labelled the **fair share** of land every person is entitled to.

Overexploitation

Those 1.7 global hectares are what each of us *can* use (in 2017). Should we not exceed that size, we will preserve the ecosystem and the environment will not be degraded. The reality is unfortunately very different, and it was calculated in 2016 that the total footprint of all human beings in 2012 amounted to an area of 20 billion global hectares being used – 64 percent more than the 12 billion that are available. In other words, we are using more land than we can permit ourselves to, causing damage to the environment and to nature. Waste products are piling up in the atmosphere, water and soil. Biodiversity is on the decline because plant and animal species are dying out. This is nothing short of **overexploitation**: we are living beyond our planet's means.

At this stage, the calculation of the footprint does contain a fair amount of uncertainties and assumptions, which means that the results cannot be taken all too literally. Alternative calculations have been designed in which the fertility of the soil, the climatic conditions and the other factors are taken into account in a different manner. But one thing still emerges from every approach – structural overexploitation is being perpetrated, as Figure 2.16 illustrates.

A good way of investigating this structural overexploitation is to examine cycles. Closed cycles, as detailed earlier in this chapter, were not invented by mankind but have been a part of the natural environment for millions of years. One example is the water cycle: water evaporates from the oceans and seas, rains down onto the land and flows through streams and rivers back to the sea. Then there is the fertile soil cycle, used by plants to grow and subsequently by the animals that eat the plants, after which the nutrients are returned to the soil by way of manure – the food chain.

People exploit these natural chains, for example through the consumption of rain and river water in agriculture, industry and households, which is returned to the natural cycle through the drains. We also tap into an extant cycle when it comes to food production, the same as we do for the consumption of timber and other natural construction materials. These materials are called **renewable resources** or **growth resources**, materials that grow continuously and naturally.

Things are fine as long as we link into natural cycles on a modest scale, but there is a risk that excessive infringement is occurring with extant cycles. This is overexploitation, as can be seen in Figure 2.17.

Overexploitation is at issue when more wood is used than is growing (in the same amount of time), leading to deforestation. Another example is the overly intensive use of fresh water for the purposes of irrigation, industry and drinking. This will lead to drought and **salinisation**.

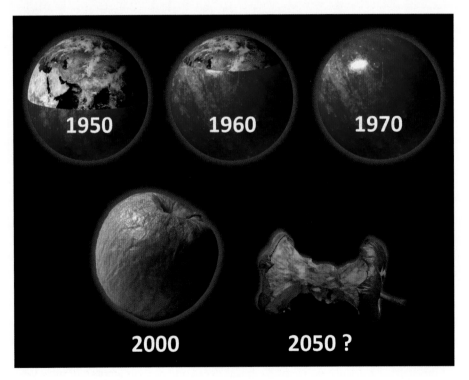

FIGURE 2.16 The global ecological footprint is far outstripping the biocapacity of the planet

Background photo source: NASA Headquarters - Greatest Images of NASA (NASA-HQ-GRIN).

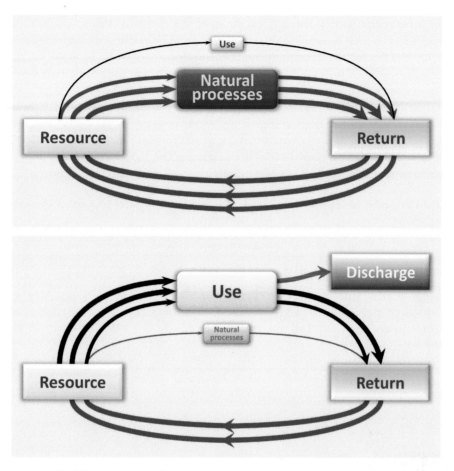

FIGURE 2.17   Linking into a natural cycle. Top: at a modest level. Bottom: ruthless exploitation

Fair share

People do not all contribute equally to the large footprint. As a rule of the thumb, it holds that the greater the prosperity, the bigger the personal footprint. Websites such as www.foot-printnetwork.org allow every person to determine his or her own individual footprint. If a person uses a great deal of electronic appliances, and consequently a high level of materials and energy, the footprint will be increased. Meat consumption also enlarges the footprint, as does travel, especially by airplane.

Questions

- What do you think the size of your own ecological footprint will be – is it larger or smaller than that of the average person living in your country?
- Do you expect your footprint to be larger or smaller than your fair share?
- What if your footprint is larger than your fair share? Are you prepared to shrink it, and how would you go about that?

Fair is fair – every person naturally has the right to a reasonable slice of the biocapacity of our world. But what is a reasonable slice? There could be varying opinions on that. One might suppose that it is fair when every individual, irrespective of where he or she might live, is entitled to an equally large portion – the worldwide average fair share. Table 2.1 is based on this assumption, with the results graphically represented in Figure 2.18.

Now, as an example, a look at the United States makes clear that the footprint of the average American is nearly five times as large as his or her fair share. On the other hand, Indians are very modest, using only 69 percent of the footprint to which they are entitled. This low figure reflects the fact that many Indians live in poverty. The right-hand column shows that the world population is occupying a 64 percent greater footprint than they should.

TABLE 2.1 Footprint per country. Assumption: all persons, irrespective of where they live, have an equally large fair share.

	USA	UK	Belgium	Argentina	China	Nigeria	India	World
Population (millions)	317.5	63.0	11.1	41.1	1,408	168.8	1,237	7,080
Fair share	**549**	**109**	**19**	**71**	**2,436**	**292**	**2,140**	**12,248**
Per inhabitant	1.73	1.73	1.73	1.73	1.73	1.73	1.73	1.73
Actual footprint	**2,604**	**309**	**82**	**127**	**4,787**	**203**	**1,484**	**20,107**
Per inhabitant	8.2	4.9	7.4	3.1	3.4	1.2	1.2	2.84
Fair share percentage	474%	283%	428%	179%	197%	69%	69%	164%

Source: Global Footprint Network (2016)

Data for 2012. Figures are in millions of global hectares, or (*per inhabitant*) in global hectares per capita.

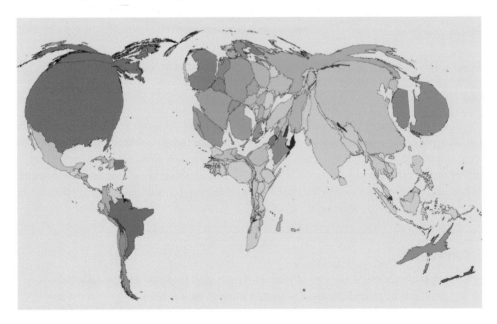

FIGURE 2.18 The countries in this map are enlarged or shrunk, with their size corresponding to their ecological footprint

Source: Global Footprint Network (2009). Updated versions of this and other types of maps can be found at http://www.viewsoftheworld.net.

However, whether the calculation used in Table 2.1 is fair is debatable. It ignores the fact that different countries have very different population densities. Belgium, for example, is amongst the most densely populated on the planet, and if you were to actually grant every Belgian person a piece of land that is just as large as the land you might give to the Finns in their sparsely populated country, it would mean that Belgium is 'entitled' to a large slice of Finland's area.

Another point of departure can also be employed, in which every country must make do with the biocapacity it possesses in its own territory. This calculation produces Table 2.2.

Table 2.2 tells us that the biocapacity of Belgium is 13 million global hectares, with a collective footprint more than six times the country's biocapacity. In this calculation, the Belgians score much higher than the Americans, who together have a footprint 'only' twice as large as the biocapacity of the US. This is due to the fact that there are proportionally fewer people in the United States, giving Americans much more land per hectare than the Belgians.

Questions

- Which is more fair – that every person, irrespective of the country in which he or she lives, can claim an equally large piece of land, the fair share (as in Table 2.1)?
- Or that every country limits itself to the area of that country, so that people in densely populated countries each have a smaller piece of land (as in Table 2.2)?

That the ecological footprint in Belgium is 6.17 times its biocapacity means that there must be tracts of land elsewhere in the world that are being used on behalf of the Belgian people, amounting to a total area several times larger than the country itself. It is not hard to guess where a part of this 'additional Belgium' can be found. For example: just as Vietnam, and just like several other countries in western Europe, Belgium imports a lot of animal feed, which is partly grown in the United States, Brazil, Argentina and Thailand, and that is where large parts of 'Belgium' are located. Other parts of the country can be found in nations where trees are grown for timber and coffee consumed in Belgium, where tropical forests are located that process Belgian CO_2 emissions, and so on. The calculation of the ecological footprint shows that Belgium, and all other rich countries, must drastically reduce its use of biocapacity in other parts of the world if their people hope to cease their overexploitation.

TABLE 2.2 Footprint per country. Assumption: every country must make do with its own biocapacity.

	USA	UK	Belgium	Argentina	China	Nigeria	India	World
Biocapacity	**1,207**	**82**	**13**	**284**	**1,267**	**118**	**619**	**12,248**
Per inhabitant	3.8	1.3	1.2	6.9	0.9	0.7	0.5	1.73
Actual footprint	**2,604**	**309**	**82**	**127**	**4,787**	**203**	**1,484**	**20,107**
Per inhabitant	8.2	4.9	7.4	3.1	3.4	1.2	1.2	2.84
Percentage of biocapacity	216%	377%	617%	45%	378%	171%	240%	164%

Source: Global Footprint Network (2016)

Data for 2012. Figures are in millions of global hectares, or (per inhabitant) in global hectares per capita.

2.4 Clean water: all for mankind, but still not enough

From space the Earth's gleaming blue colour is striking: see Figure 2.19. It is a sign that our planet holds huge oceans of liquid water. To be honest, it is an inconceivable amount of water – 1,386 million cubic kilometres, nearly 1.4 billion trillion (10^{21}) litres. The vast majority of this water, around 97.5 percent, is saltwater, while over two-thirds of the remaining 2.5 percent of **fresh w**ater is held in glaciers and other forms of permanent ice and is largely unavailable to humans. What remains is ten million cubic kilometres of groundwater and a 'mere' 135,000 cubic kilometres of surface water in rivers, lakes and marshes.

More than enough to ensure mankind is supplied with clean water, one might say. The entire world population uses 4,000 cubic kilometres of water per year, an average of 1,700 litres per person per day. Most of this water does not flow out of taps in homes, but is used in agriculture and in industry to provide for all our needs – food, clothing, transport, luxury goods, etc. Figure 2.20 provides further details on this.

FIGURE 2.19 From space the Earth's gleaming blue colour is striking. It is a sign that this planet contains large oceans of liquid water

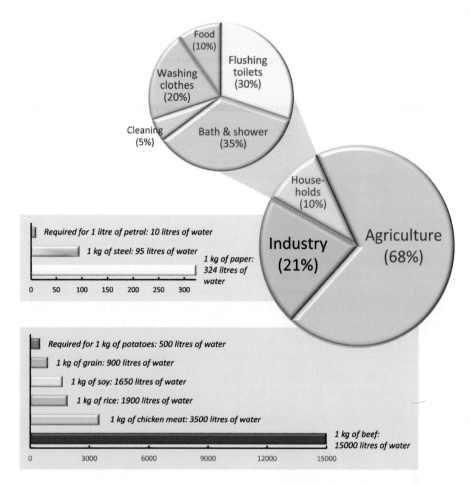

FIGURE 2.20 Clean water consumption by agriculture, industry and households, averaged out across all people

Source: Clarke and King (2004).

Question

- How many litres of water a day do you think you use?
- Do you occasionally shower longer than is necessary?

And yet, even though so much fresh water is available, there are still people who suffer drastic shortages. There are a number of reasons for this, one of which is that water is very unequally distributed around the world. Deserts receive but a fraction of the rainfall a country like the United Kingdom receives. Another reason is that the majority of the available fresh water may not be used for people at all, as otherwise nothing would be left for the natural environment and the entire world would die out. Then there are also regions where the fresh water is not potable, such as in Bangladesh where the groundwater is naturally contaminated with arsenic. In the year 2000, half a billion people (8 percent of the world's population) were living in a country grappling with chronic water shortages – see Figure 2.21, in which access to an improved water source refers to the percentage of the population with reasonable access to an adequate amount of water from an improved source, such as a household connection, public standpipe, borehole, protected well or spring and rainwater collection. Unimproved sources include vendors, tanker trucks and unprotected wells and springs. Reasonable access is defined as the availability of at least 20 litres a person a day from a source within one kilometre of the dwelling.

Compared to the situation in 2000, things have improved drastically, following a target set by the Millennium Development Goals (MDGs, see § 4.8). However, there is a serious risk that this development may change dramatically due to climate change. Further action is needed, as has been agreed in the follow-up of the MDGs 2000–2015), the Sustainable Development Goals (SDGs, 2015–2030; see also § 4.8).

Some of the things we are doing actually have the opposite effect of what we want – a 'rebound effect'. Water tapped from rivers and lakes is subjected to increasingly intensive use, and agricultural irrigation is the primary culprit in respect of water consumption. Meanwhile, the major dams that dot many rivers are responsible for increased evaporation, through which much precious water is lost. A country such as Egypt is confronted with both evaporation and irrigation, and the Aswan Dam on the Nile has increased evaporation while agricultural lands are irrigated with water from the same river. These combined aspects are so powerful that at certain times of the year the Nile does not even reach the Mediterranean Sea, with the current actually being reversed and seawater flowing upstream. The reversed current means the land has suffered grave salinisation and is becoming unfertile. Egypt's lands are already suffering from decreased fertility, thanks to the fact that the Nile has become a neat and predictable

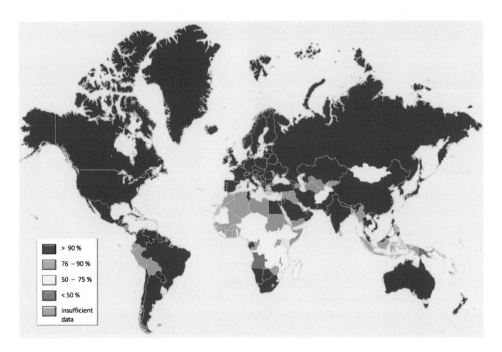

FIGURE 2.21   Access to clean water by country

Source: WHO Global Health Observatory (2015)

river since the dam was built, one that no longer floods, sparing potential victims of drowning, but no longer depositing fertile sediment along the river banks. Egypt is now reliant on chemical fertilisers, but this does not stop the salinisation.

Numerous rivers and lakes around the world are subjected to the same intensive use. Drought leads to a lack of drinking water and hygiene and consequently to very high child mortality rates. The land becomes scorched, and deforestation and desertification set in. In certain cases, lakes have even shrunk, one of the most frightening examples of this being the Aral Sea, shown in Figures 2.22 and 2.23, that borders the former Soviet republics of Kazakhstan and Uzbekistan. Around 1910 the saltwater lake was over 50 meters deep and covered an area of 450 by 290 kilometres – a gigantic body. From around 1960 onwards, the water of the lake and the inflowing rivers started to be used intensively for large-scale Soviet agriculture. The lake retreated rapidly, and around 2010 it was virtually non-existent. The bare ground that is now exposed is white from the salt, and fishing harbours like Aralsk and Mo'ynoq are ghost towns.

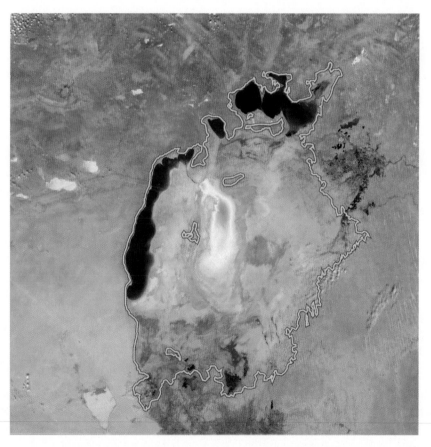

FIGURE 2.22   The once vast Aral Sea is now ten percent of its former size as a result of its rivers being diverted, and large sections of it have been transformed into a white salt field, clearly visible from space. The yellow outline shows the body of water's size in 1985; the photo shows what remained in 2009

Source: NASA Earth Observatory, 2009.

FIGURE 2.23   Rusting ship in what was once the Aral Sea, a symbol of unsustainability

Source: Staecker, Wikimedia.

Foreign dependence on clean water can easily lead to conflicts, and on numerous occasions countries have been brought to the brink of war over disputed use of water. This is hardly surprising when one looks at bodies of water such as the Jordan River. It borders the countries of Israel and Jordan, as well as a country in-the-making, Palestine. Israel has performed true miracles, with large portions of the southern Negev desert blossoming, and the sight of whole sand plains transformed into productive lands is a beautiful one. But it is all at a cost. Every year some 1.3 cubic kilometres of water flows down the Jordan River, and Israel draws off around 0.7 cubic kilometres of that – over half the annual flow. The Dead Sea, into which the river drains, is receiving far too little water and its water levels have dropped by dozens of meters while the salinity has risen proportionally – the Dead Sea is deader than ever. When compared to Israel, living standards in Jordan are significantly lower, as is drainage from the eponymous river. Imagine that Jordan was to consume just as much water as Israel – what would happen, particularly in political and even military terms? And what if Palestine also wanted to join in on an equally intensive scale?

The answer to that question was given at the end of 2013, when excellent news arrived from the Middle East. After years of negotiations, Israel, the Palestinian Authority and Jordan signed an agreement on the construction of a pipeline. The pipe of 180 kilometers will bring water from the Red Sea to an installation that is to be built in Jordan, where it will be desalinised. This clean water will then be used in Jordan, Israel and on the West Bank. Annually, 80 to 100 million cubic meters of water will become available. Whether this will be sufficient, will become clear later; the Dead Sea loses a billion cubic meters of water every year.

Other major rivers are also shared by countries with tense relations. Examples include the Euphrates and Tigris rivers in the region shared by Iraq, Turkey and Iran (see Table 2.3) and

TABLE 2.3 Consumption and renewable resources of fresh water.

Country	Consumption	All renewable sources	Internal renewable sources	Dependency on other countries	Data from (year)
Asia					
India	648	2,081	1,446	31%	2010
Pakistan	184	247	55	78%	2008
Bangladesh	36	1,227	105	91%	2008
Azerbaijan	12	35	8	77%	2012
Turkmenistan	28	47	1.4	97%	2004
Uzbekistan	49	82	16	80%	2005
China	603	2,840	2,813	1%	2013
Middle East					
Saudi Arabia	23	2.4	2.4	0%	2006
Kuwait	0.42	0.02	0	100%	2002
Iraq	66	90	35	61%	2000
Turkey	42	231	227	2%	2008
Iran	93	138	129	7%	2004
Syria	14	26	7	72%	2005
Jordan	0.87	0.94	0.68	27%	2005
Israel	1.4	1.8	0.75	58%	2004
Egypt	74	58	1.8	97%	2010
Libya	5.8	0.7	0.7	0%	2012
Africa					
Somalia	3.3	15	6	59%	2003
Sudan	27	103	4	96%	2011
Ethiopia	5.6	122	122	0%	2002
Eritrea	0.58	7	2.8	62%	2004
Europe					
Germany	33	154	107	31%	2010
Hungary	5.1	104	6	94%	2012
United Kingdom	8	147	145	1%	2012
Netherlands	11	91	11	88%	2012
Americas					
Brazil	75	8,647	5,661	35%	2010
Costa Rica	2.3	113	113	0%	2013
El Salvador	2.1	26	16	41%	2005
USA	419	3,069	2,818	8%	2010
Canada	39	2,902	2,850	2%	2009
World	**3,768**	**54,738**			

Source: FAO (2016): AQUASTAT Main Database, retrieved in September 2016. All figures are in km³ per annum. All renewable sources = accounted inflow of surface water + accounted inflow of groundwater + internal renewable sources. This indicator does not consider the possible allocation of water to downstream countries. Dependency on other countries = internal renewable sources / all renewable sources.

the Indus, which separates Pakistan from India. How long will it be before the first large-scale conflict breaks out due to the need of access to water resources?

Relations with neighbouring countries can also become strained in areas where war is less of a threat. The Netherlands might be a very wet nation, but 88 percent of that water enters the country in the Rhine and Maas rivers, making the country reliant on Switzerland and Germany in terms of the quality of the Rhine's water and on France and Belgium for the Maas' water. By the end of the twentieth century, this was painfully noticeable, with French potash mines daily discharging large amounts of salt into the Maas. The river's water became so saline that it cost the Dutch waterworks companies much work and expense to purify it to the extent that it was potable. It was only after years of negotiations between the Netherlands and France that the salt discharges decreased. This example demonstrates that discord does not only arise from the distribution of scarce water resources, but also when the quality of the water is affected.

In the year 2000, this fact hit home with a bang in Hungary, when the Aurul gold mine in Romania accidentally released around a hundred tons of extremely lethal cyanide into the Someş River, which flows into the Tisza River in Hungary. Almost everything living in the Tisza died and it was the worst environmental disaster ever in Hungary, causing huge problems for drinking water.

Another cause of water shortages involves irregular supply. Ethiopia and Eritrea are known for the large-scale famines that occasionally afflict the nations as a result of extreme droughts, and (partly due to these droughts) wars. Table 2.3 may not indicate that these two nations suffer from a shortage of clean water, but rainfall there is highly unpredictable and sometimes years go by without a drop falling from the skies.

Meanwhile, the unequal distribution of fresh water worsens due to climate change, which has increased precipitation in certain regions of the world (including Germany and Bangladesh) and decreased it in others (including large tracts of Africa).

Fortunately, there is much that can be done. As a start, water can be consumed with much greater care in many regions. Irrigation is frequently poorly employed, causing unnecessary evaporation while another portion of the water will drain off immediately, often taking fertile soil with it. By technically improving field irrigation, large quantities of water can be saved. The same applies to industry, where there is plenty of room for more efficient water consumption. Furthermore, a great deal more rainwater can be caught and used than is presently the case.

Cycles can also be better closed than they are now, especially in developing countries. If these nations extended their sewer systems, waste water could be collected, purified and reused as drinking water. This is the norm in most European countries. But in some other countries many people are horrified by the mere idea!

Case 2.3 Toowoomba says no

Sydney Morning Herald, 30 July 2006

Toowoomba says no to recycled water

Residents of drought-stricken Toowoomba have convincingly rejected the notion of drinking their own waste water. In a controversial referendum 62 percent of residents opposed the treating of sewage for drinking water in the inland south-east Queensland city.

The outcome was a resounding victory for the no campaign by a group calling itself Citizens Against Drinking Sewage.

Yes campaigners included Toowoomba Mayor Di Thorley, who had said recycling sewage for drinking water was the most economically and environmentally effective way to fix the city's critical water shortage.

The federal parliamentary secretary for water added recycling water was important for Australia as demand was expected to exceed supply from existing water sources in nearly all major Australian cities within the next 20 years.

Comment in an online forum, 26 July 2006

'I am not going to drink piss from God knows who, am I?'

Technological solutions are also available. One could, of course, convert salty seawater into fresh water, but the problem is that energy is required for the process. This means that the water problem could be partly converted into an energy problem – if we had unlimited sustainable energy we would in principle also have unlimited fresh water. In this there is some good news in the fact that the driest areas on the planet are also the areas where the most solar energy is available. It is thus conceivable that large regions of the Sahara and other deserts are decked out with solar panels that can aid in producing large quantities of fresh water from the oceans, as Chapter 7 explains.

In other parts of the world, biotechnology can lend a hand. Rice, the most popular food for a large portion of humanity, requires waterlogged soil to be planted (Figure 2.24), which involves a huge amount of water that is certainly not available in sufficient quantities in many areas. This is why scientists are working on different types of rice that require less water.

FIGURE 2.24   Rice needs waterlogged soil. Rice terraces, such as this one in the Chinese province of Yunnan, are built to hold the water that would otherwise flow down the incline

Source: Jialiang Gao, www.peace-on-earth.org, 2003.

2.5 Agriculture and livestock farming: excessive efficiency, but still not enough

This chapter started by establishing that raising livestock in Vietnam results in issues of unsustainability, as animal feed grown in other countries results in one-way traffic. But when it comes to stock farming, there are some more problems at hand.

Excessive efficiency

After the European Economic Community (the EEC, the precursor to the EU) was established in 1958, the body focused on agriculture in Western Europe. At that time the region did not produce enough food to sustain its population, and the threat of famine existed! Subsidies were introduced to stimulate agriculture. One result of this was that the cost of food production was artificially lowered, and consequently the prices in shops were likewise unnaturally low, which is still the case today. Debate has been ongoing for years about abandoning the farming subsidies, but it is not an easy task as the entire European agricultural system is based on them. If they are abandoned, European farmers will face wide scale bankruptcy and the dramatically climbing prices will raise consumer anger. But that is not all, for the system is further buttressed by trade barriers that ensure surcharges are levied on agricultural products imported from outside of the EU's borders. This means that farmers in Africa and South America have almost no chance of earning a reasonable income from exports to Europe – the system is upholding the unequal distribution of prosperity in the world. And so, to this day these subsidies and trade barriers form a flaw in the fabric that is a deep-seated part of the agricultural system.

In order to increase food production, efficiency was likewise upped. Machinery was introduced for plowing, sowing and harvesting. Agricultural consolidation created extensive fields on which a single crop was grown – monoculture. Stock farming was also subjected to the industrial approach, with plant and animal diseases combated and prevented through the mass introduction of pesticides and antibiotics. Control became the paradigm! Nothing was left to chance, aside from the weather. Actually, even that is not true, and gigantic greenhouses were built to exclude weather factors. Natural gas is used to heat those greenhouses, which means they make a significant contribution to climate change.

For many years the natural environment formed a balance of sorts to counter this intensive agriculture, a factor that, for a number of decades, the authorities only paid attention to when they had no other option. This might have changed in recent years, but the interests of the natural environment are still not always consistently taken into account – when the economic interests are big enough, nature must make way. This can be seen across the Atlantic in the Gulf of Mexico. In 2010, the BP oil spill threatened the fragile marine ecosystems of the Gulf. The risk to coastal estuaries was particularly significant, as estuaries are the breeding ground of many aquatic organisms – several species of which are either endangered or economically important to local fisheries. Famous for its pristine beaches, the region also feared the spill would have catastrophic consequences for Gulf's tourism industry. The Triple P is unbalanced in this case, where profit outweighs people and planet.

Problems gradually arose as a result of the intensive agriculture and livestock farming in the second half of the twentieth century, as did criticism. Monoculture meant that crops were vulnerable to plagues, and the use of pesticides harmed the natural environment. Moreover, what about animal welfare in **bio industry**? Starting in the 1990s the tightly controlled agricultural industry not only suffered from impending crises but from acute disasters too (see Table 2.4). BSE, or mad cow disease, swine flu, bluetongue, Q fever and

TABLE 2.4 Disasters and crises in agriculture and nature management since 1945

Cause	Consequences
Farming subsidies	Third World development impeded; unnatural price changes for agricultural products
Monoculture	Vulnerability to plagues
Pesticides	Natural environment and health damaged
Importing animal feed	Deforestation and overexploitation in Brazil and elsewhere
Bio industry	Animal suffering
Acid rain * due to a surplus of fertiliser	Forests, moors and surface waters impaired
1996: Mad cow disease	150 deaths in Western Europe
Genetically modified (GM) food	Mistrust by consumers; possible damage to health and to nature
1997: Swine flu	12 million pigs 'culled'
Phasing out European farm subsidies	Bankruptcy amongst farmers
2003: Bird flu (H7N7)	31 million chickens 'culled'
Aerosols*	Health damage, construction of roads and suburbs frozen
2006: Bird flu (H5N1)	Fear of a pandemic
2007: Bluetongue disease	Millions of sheep put down
2010: Q fever	Pregnant goats and sheep 'culled' en masse; breeding ban

Agriculture is in part responsible, together with industry and traffic

multiple strains of bird flu, all successively led to livestock slaughter, bankruptcies amongst farmers and even to human mortalities. There is much fear for yet more disasters in the farming community. Foot-and-mouth disease or maybe leaf spot? Or will the corn root-worm bring the next plague?

Case 2.4   Fears over food borne pathogens. . .

Food and Agricultural Organization of the United Nations press release, 26 January 2003, Rome

Countries around the world should be concerned about 'Mad Cow Disease'

The UN Food and Agriculture Organization (FAO) today has urged countries around the world, not just those in Western Europe, to be concerned about the risk of *bovine spongiform encephalopathy* (BSE, see figure 2.25) and its human form, the *new variant Creutzfeldt-Jakob disease* (nvCJD). In a statement issued in Rome, FAO called for action to protect the human population, as well as the livestock, feed and meat industries. (. . .)

Within countries, FAO recommended applying the so-called Hazard Analysis and Critical Control Point system (HACCP) which aims at identifying potential problems and taking corrective measures throughout the food chain. Some of the issues include the production of animal feed, the raw materials used, cross-contamination in the feed mill, labeling of manufactured feeds, the feed

FIGURE 2.25 2008: protests in South Korea against the import of beef from the USA, by people who are concerned about BSE

Source: hojusaram, Wikimedia.

transport system, as well as monitoring imported live animals, slaughtering methods, the rendering industry and the disposal of waste materials.

"Strict controls have been implemented in the United Kingdom and are now being implemented in the rest of the EU," FAO said. "Countries outside the EU should adopt appropriate measures to protect their herds and to ensure the safety of meat and meat products. Legislation to control the industry and its effective implementation is required, including capacity building and the training of operatives and government officials."

It is becoming clear to an increasing number of people that endeavors to completely manage agriculture and the natural environment cannot be sustained. The entire system is in drastic need of an overhaul. This is why many consumers increasingly prefer more sustainable food alternatives. Some growers have responded by producing organic crops, adapting to the forces of nature, rather than attempting to control them. For example, this means that things such as chemical pesticides would, where possible, have to be replaced by natural substitutes. Ladybugs were introduced to combat the louse, while plants were brought in to counter other plagues by replacing monoculture with fields containing a variety of plant types, including those that kept insects at bay. These approaches allow for a dramatic decrease in the use of chemicals. Alongside these patterns, various options for ecological agriculture are also presently being developed – successfully, as can be seen in the supermarket, where sales of these products are increasing by a double-digit percentage every year.

Depending on the climate in which food is grown, greenhouses can in turn be set up so that natural gas is no longer required to heat them, using a combination of wind and solar energy with cold storage (in winter) and heat storage (in summer) deep below the surface. Thus, today we are even able to build greenhouses that require no energy at all, but actually feed power into the grid.

Eating locally is another alternative to the current unsustainable food system. The import of fruit and vegetables from far-off countries requires large amounts of energy and thereby contributes to the greenhouse effect. In voluntarily shunning these foods, consumers can reduce their carbon footprints. Whether they are prepared to do that remains to be seen – will many people change their behavior?

Insufficient efficiency

Efficiency might have been the primary goal of agriculture and livestock farming for years, but in spite of this the efficiency levels are still far too low. The reasons for this are as follows.

Meat and dairy constitute an important source of protein, but they are an inefficient source. Beef cattle, for example, eat grass, hay, soy and tapioca – plants that contain vegetable protein. They convert it into animal protein in their bodies – a process they are not particularly good at, given that every kilogram of animal protein in a cow's body requires *ten kilograms of vegetable protein*. Table 2.5 shows how much agricultural land is required to produce a given quantity of protein. Beans, soya beans in particular, lead the pack, with a mere quarter of a hectare required

TABLE 2.5 Agricultural land required for producing 20 kilograms of protein per annum

Food source	Land (hectares)
Beans	0.25
Grass	0.3–0.6
Grain	0.6
Potatoes	0.7
Dairy cattle	1–3
Chickens	3
Sheep	2–5
Pigs	5
Beef cattle	3–6

Source: Bender (1992).

to produce 20 kilograms of protein. Pigs are ill-suited, needing five hectares to produce the same amount of protein – 20 times the amount of land required for beans. Pigs not only need that land to walk around, and the largest part of it is actually devoted to growing pig feed.

It does not automatically follow from this that vegetables are always preferable to meat. The composition of animal protein is somewhat better for the human diet than that of vegetable protein, and furthermore, not all land is suitable for growing crops, with grass being the best choice for certain types of land. Agricultural waste can be used as animal feed, and the manure from the livestock can in turn be used to fertilise the soil for crops, closing the biological cycle.

In spite of this, when Westerners – the biggest meat-eaters on the planet – would start to rely on vegetable sources of protein for a significantly larger portion of their nutritional needs than today, the environment would benefit considerably, much less land would be used and the dietary costs would also be much cheaper. Meat production consumes 80 percent of agricultural land around the world, while meat makes up only 15 percent of all food consumed. Unfortunately, a significant change to this situation will not be easy, for eating meat has deep cultural roots.

Nutrition technology might contribute to any changes. Should it be possible to produce meat-like products using plants or fungi that are indistinguishable from real meat, it is conceivable that consumers convert en masse – and maybe unconsciously – to veganism. The final chapter will return to this issue, and show that we are well in the way to do this.

2.6 Consequences for the natural environment

For the natural environment, the consequences of worldwide overexploitation are dramatic. The following case serves as an example.

Case 2.5 The Tasmanian tiger

Tasmania is an island, equivalent in size to the American state of West Virginia, off the south coast of Australia with a natural environment all of its own.

In 1936 the *Tasmanian tiger* (Figure 2.26) was declared a protected species, with good reason too, as the number of Tasmanian tigers had dwindled rapidly in

FIGURE 2.26   The Tasmanian tiger

Source: Brehms Tierleben, 1929.

recent years. This was in part due to the fact that farmers hunted them, blaming them for killing sheep (which was probably not true). Between 1888 and 1914 they shot the animals in the thousands. The species then succumbed to a disease that killed most of the remaining animals. It was only later that biologists realised the species was threatened with extinction. In 1933 the last Tasmanian tiger to be captured in the wild was taken to a local zoo. It died in 1936 – the last Tasmanian tiger ever seen alive. The species was declared protected after its death – too late.

The Tasmanian tiger is not the only species of animal that has become extinct. Perhaps the most famous is the dodo, which died out on the island of Mauritius in the seventeenth century. Centuries earlier, the aurochs, mammoth and sabre-tooth cat also succumbed to extinction. Species have also become extinct in more recent years. On 6 January 2000 the very last Pyrenean ibex died, and later in the same year the Miss Waldron's red colobus was declared 'presumed extinct'. It is not only fauna that is threatened with extinction, with flora suffering the same fate too. A striking example is the Tambalacoque tree, also known as the Dodo tree. In 1973 it was claimed that only 13 of them remained, all of which were over 300 years old. It has been hypothesised that the tree has been unable to reproduce since the extinction of the dodo, as the seeds first had to be eaten and defecated out by the bird before they could germinate. Although this hypothesis has been contested, experiments are being conducted with turkeys to see whether they can replace the dodo and cause the seeds to sprout.

Questions

- So what? What does it matter that the dodo and the Tasmanian tiger are extinct?
- And what does it matter that other species will die out in the near future?

The extinction of species is not the only problem nature is confronted with. Another serious issue is **habitat loss**, the dwindling of natural environments or their total disappearance (Figure 2.27). Habitats make way for towns, roads, agriculture or recreational purposes. Or they might be managed in an unsustainable way, making the habitat's composition increasingly less natural and the biodiversity – the diversity of the species present – decreases. Habitats also suffer from external causes, such as poisons used in agriculture, acid rain or climate change. In industrialized areas, many natural environments are shredded by highways, and are consequently unable to sustain predators in particular, which require large contiguous regions.

With regard to extinction, it is wise to distinguish between '**locally**' and '**globally extinct**'. In the former case, a species dies out in a certain area, such as in the Gulf of Mexico. Should that be the case it will still be possible to obtain specimens of the species from elsewhere and re-release them into the wild. But should a species be subject to global extinction, it will be gone forever. There is also an intermediate phase, 'extinct in the wild', in which case there are still specimens in protected environments, such as zoos. It is then attempted to keep the species going through breeding programmes, hopefully introducing them back into the wild at a later stage. There is a danger involved in this approach when dealing with fauna (and not with flora) in that, although the species might be physically undamaged, its original behaviour is lost, which means the animals cannot live naturally in the wild.

FIGURE 2.27   Habitat loss: one of the causes being cities stretching beyond the horizon

Source: Jeremy Daccarett, flickr.

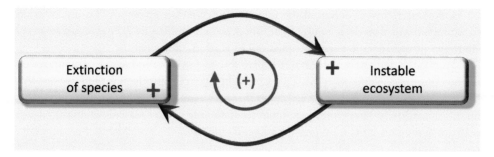

FIGURE 2.28   The extinction of species as a result of positive feedback

When species die out, the consequences could be unexpected. The example of the Tambalacoque tree illustrates that species of plant and animal are frequently dependent on each other to ensure their continued existence. Hundreds or thousands of species together form complex **ecosystems**. When a part of a breeding system (such as the Tambalacoque tree and the dodo) or a part of a food chain disappears, the entire ecosystem can be affected, with the result being that other species can also become extinct – a form of positive feedback, as shown in Figure 2.28. As was seen earlier in this chapter with regard to the economy, positive feedback here can also lead to unpredictable consequences, such as a sudden collapse of the entire ecosystem, with possible dire consequences for ourselves. To put it differently: *we do not know (quite literally) what we will be doing to ourselves if we destroy the natural environment.*

Positive feedback also comes into play as a result of deforestation, as shown in Figure 2.29. Natural forests in the tropical zones have suffered the greatest loss. The tropical rainforests are responsible for a large amount of evaporation, but when trees are felled, evaporation declines

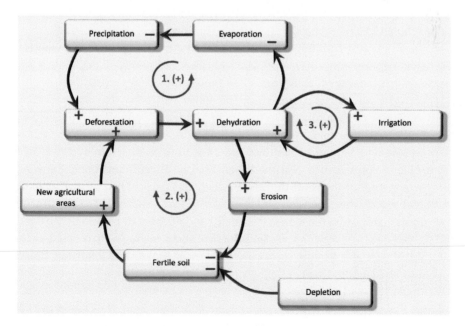

FIGURE 2.29   Various feedbacks as a result of deforestation

and local climate change occurs in the form of decreased precipitation. This results in the remaining forested areas drying out. This feedback is shown in Figure 2.29 as loop 1, with the minus signs (for evaporation and precipitation) indicating a decrease.

In loop 2, the deforestation leads to the bare soil drying out, resulting in erosion accelerated by the sun and wind. After this, the uppermost layer of soil, which is the most fertile, is blown as dust or washed away with rainwater that no longer subsides into the soil, but simply runs off immediately. These forests are often felled for the sake of agriculture, but the yields are disappointing once the most fertile land has disappeared. In consequence the agricultural activities produce little, especially once the land is further decimated through overly intensive farming (depletion). The dried out land is duly abandoned, which in turn leads to desertification while new tracts of forest are felled. Once again, positive feedback arises.

In some places agriculture has been responsible for yet a third feedback loop. Water is extracted from the ground for abundant irrigation, resulting in the groundwater level sinking and the soil further drying out. As a result, even greater irrigation is required.

An important underlying cause of the degradation of the natural environment is poverty. People in parts of Africa, Asia and South America are often compelled to act in an unsustainable manner. An example is the Sahel, the region to the south of the Sahara Desert. Cautious attempts are presently being made to plant new forests in the area, but the local need firewood for cooking and heating. They do not have the money to buy fuel, and so they are often fully reliant on the little wood they can find – to the detriment of the young trees. This process is amplified by the population growth, which is greatest in the poorest countries. But unexpected success stories are heard, even in the Sahel.

Case 2.6   The paradox of a green Sahel

The Sahel has been reputed for many years to be an insurmountable and dry desert region. Thanks to local farmers, this impression has been completely reversed.

In Africa's poorest country, Niger, an unprecedented success is being realised. The Sahel is green with trees. In the last two decades five million hectares of former forest has been sown with trees – 250 thousand hectares a year.

When Niger was strictly controlled by the authorities, every tree was owned by the state. This was of no concern to the citizens and, if the opportunity arose, they would cut down a tree for firewood. But in the 1990s, with control gone and political power waning, farmers began to consider the trees on their farms as their own property, and consequently cherished them. Under normal conditions, the wind cuts like a razor into the fields of the dry Sahel, and farmers had to sow three or four times a year when the sand and wind buried their seedlings. The trees act as a windbreak, and when there are between 20 and 60 trees to a hectare, the wind and sun have less free play. The seedlings survive, and it will suffice to sow just once.

Early this year at a summit in Lisbon, the African Union and European Union agreed to build a green wall in the Sahel from Senegal to Djibouti. However, this is no longer required, as farmers in Niger have already built their own green wall.

This is not only happening in Niger. People in Burkina Faso, the Dogon in Mali and the inhabitants of Senegal are all giving seed to similar initiatives.

Source: Volkskrant, 19 April 2008

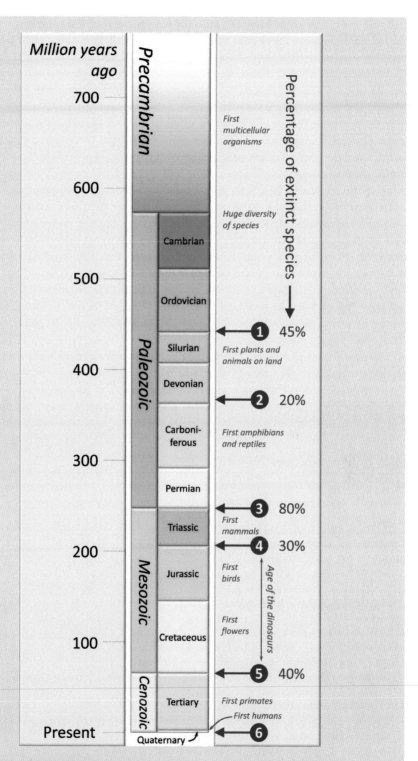

FIGURE 2.30 Six major extinction peaks

Sources: Leakey (1995), Stanley (2016).

Some people consider humanity as a 'cancerous tumour' for nature – a scourge that has spread throughout the world. Extinct animals? It's all humanity's fault. But this is not true – species of animals have disappeared and been replaced by new types for as long as life has existed. You might not see this if you are strolling through a forest, where everything appears to be calmly and peacefully coexisting. Such a forest is in a **natural equilibrium**, we say. But in reality there is no such thing as a natural equilibrium. We believe that equilibrium exists because the life of a human is so short when compared to the history of life. The maximum period a human might live to, around a century, is barely a snapshot in the natural world. Examine a period of ten or a hundred million years as a whole and you will see how nature changes continuously. Species come and species go. Even the continents themselves move, drifting on the surface of the Earth, colliding with each other and being ripped apart.

But what is special about the time we are living in is the fact that the rate at which animals and plants are currently dying out is very high. We are living in a period of mass extinctions. This has happened at least five times before in the history of our world, and Figure 2.30 shows the six **extinction peaks**, including the present one. The various geological eras are also shown. The end of the cretaceous period, 65 million years ago, is famous for marking the sudden end of the dinosaurs. The cause, or one of them, was presumably a giant meteorite collision. Though this may have been a shocking event, it was not the worst. It is estimated that at the end of the Permian period, some 250 million years ago, 70 percent of all species disappeared in a short time.

Some extinction peaks were due to the continents joining up to form a supercontinent, making the length of the oceanic coasts, which act as the breeding ground for many species (just as the Gulf of Mexico coast is today), much shorter. This has happened numerous times in the history of the Earth. Intense volcanic activity was another cause, with the discharged dust blocking sunlight and giving rise to ice ages.

TABLE 2.6 A few facts about extinction

All species together (*animals, plants, bacteria etc.*)[1]
- Circa 99.9% of all species that have ever existed have died out long ago
- Normal extinction rate: 1 in every million species per annum
- That means 10 to 100 species become extinct every year
- Presently around 27,000 species per year become extinct

Birds[2]
- Since 1850: circa 1 per 10,000 species have become extinct every year
- That is around 100 × normal rate
- Presently 12% of all species of birds are threatened

Mammals[2]
- There are 5,488 known species of mammals
- On average, species of mammals last for 1 to 10 million years
- So the normal extinction rate is 1 species every 200 years
- Last 400 years: 89 species have become extinct
- Presently 1,141 mammals are threatened (21%)

After previous mass extinctions[3]
- Recovery of the diversity of species: 5 to 10 million years
- That is 200,000 human generations or more
- Humans (*homo sapiens*) have existed for around 10,000 generations

---

Sources: (1) Wilson (1992), (2) Vié et al. (2008), (3) Kirchner and Weil (2000).

Species also become extinct between the extinction peaks, but at a slower rate. They are continuously replaced by new species, which arise through evolution. A present, our planet is undergoing a sixth extinction peak, and this time mankind is at fault. We cannot yet say what percentage of fauna and flora will die out this time, as we are still in the midst of the mass extinction. However, we do know a number of facts, as detailed in Table 2.6.

The consequences for humanity cannot be foreseen. It is possible, although unpredictable, that the ecosystem will suddenly collapse at either a local or international scale – an 'ecological crash', as it were. One of the causes of this could be climate change, which Chapter 7 will deal with. But even if this does not happen, humanity will suffer from large-scale economic and emotional damage.

Blog

Monday 8

We dealt with something different at school today. Animals! Well, I don't know what they are either. The teacher tried to explain, but I didn't understand any of it. I think they are like cars, because they can move of their own accord, but nobody can get in them! So I asked what the point of them was, but the teacher didn't know either.

And their wheels are not even round, they're long and thin, like poles. How is that possible? You can't drive on poles. So I asked: where are these animals? And the teacher said: they don't exist anymore, but they used to.

2 responses | Print | Disclaimer

Wednesday 10

The teacher told us more about animals today. Did you know that they used to have all sorts of brands? There were things like dogs and cats and cows. The cows had taps, and when you turned them some type of white cola came out and you could drink it.

5 responses | Print | Disclaimer

Thursday 11

We learnt about something else today. Plants. I think they are like little cupboards on one leg, because sometimes they contain food, and you can grab it and eat it. Were there also different brands? I asked. Yes, the teacher told me, you have normal plants and then you also have trees. Trees are very tall and they also stand on one leg but they don't fall over. I think they look like streetlights, but they don't light up. So they're utterly useless. No wonder they don't make them anymore!

1 response | Print | Disclaimer

Monday 15
 Today we learnt about something new at school. Humans. They are a type of animal with only two wheels. I asked the teacher: where are these humans then? But he didn't know.

0 responses | Print | Disclaimer

The Red List

For the last few decades, the IUCN (International Union for the Conservation of Nature and Natural Resources) has been keeping a list of threatened or extinct species of plants and animals. Table 2.6 contains a number of facts from the list concerning birds and animals. The photos on the following pages (Figure 2.31) are of a number of species on this **Red List**. The list is used around the world to determine protection programmes and can be consulted online by anyone.

Summary

In Chapter 2 we discussed the flaws in the fabric that upset the relationship between mankind and the natural environment. The primary flaws we dealt with are:

- One-way traffic, with examples being the use of animal feed, fossil fuels and ore. A good solution would be to close the cycles.
- Positive feedback. Examples include the stock markets and the worldwide population growth.
- Overexploitation of nature, thanks to an ecological footprint that is already larger than the biocapacity of planet Earth and is growing further. The consequences of this over-exploitation are further amplified by a very unequal distribution, with the rich nations having far more than their fair share...
- A special example of overexploitation is the use of clean water, a resource that will be in extremely short supply in the course of the twenty-first century if action is not taken.
- Agriculture and livestock farming also contribute to the excessive ecological footprint. Attempts to increase efficiency have had the unintentional consequence of leading to crises and disasters.

The consequences of these flaws continue. Species of animals and plants are becoming extinct on a mass scale, as can be seen on the Red List, biodiversity is declining and habitats are being lost. In part as a result of climate change, species are migrating and ecosystems are being disturbed.
 A more detailed summary can be found on the website of this book.

a)

b)

Endangered
or extinct

d)

c)

FIGURE 2.31 (a) The Moroccan damselfly, *Calopteryx exul*, is under threat. (b) Only 1,500 golden toads (*Bufo periglenes*, Costa Rica) remained, according to an estimate in 1987. Since 1989 it has not been seen, it is presumed extinct. (c) *Cephalanthera rubra*, the red helleborine, is an orchid that was last seen in northwestern Europe in 1985. It can still be found in France, but it is critically endangered. (d) The mountain gorilla (*Gorilla beringei beringei*, Central Africa) is likewise critically endangered, with some 700 left around the world, some of those in zoos. By way of comparison: around 7,391,378,120 of its relative, the human species (Homo sapiens sapiens) – were alive in May 2017 (see: www.census.gov/ipc/www/popclockworld.html)

Source: (a) Mroede, Wikimedia; (b) Charles H. Smith, U.S. Fish and Wildlife Service; (c) TKnoxB from Chemainus, BC, Canada, Wikimedia;

3

FLAWS IN THE FABRIC

People and society

In this chapter the following topics and concepts will be discussed:

3.1 PPP in imbalance: the economy first
3.2 Inequality: the lack of solidarity
3.3 Dehumanisation: alienation and exclusion
3.4 The lack of safety: terror, war, dictatorships
3.5 The fabric of man, nature and the economy

A glossary containing all terms in both this chapter and others is available on the website of this book.

Case 3.1 Malawian nicotine

Thirteen cents a day; that is what he earns on average for 12 hours of work in the tobacco plantations. Kirana Kapito is one of the many children in Malawi, Africa, who weed the fields, harvest tobacco and carry the bales. Kirana started working when he was eight. He is now 14 and, because his slight body absorbs the equivalent of 50 cigarettes a day, he has serious nicotine poisoning. He suffers from nausea, vomiting, headaches and difficulty breathing. It is called 'Green Tobacco Sickness', or GTS, which hinders brain development. He has never been to school.

In Malawi nearly all children work, and almost 80,000 of them are employed in the tobacco plantations (Figure 3.1). The law stipulates that heavy labour is prohibited for children up to the age of 14, but there are hardly any checks. This is not surprising, as the revenue from the plant is indispensible. Tobacco is extremely important for the penniless nation, making up no less than 70 percent of exports. The livelihood of two million Malawians depends on tobacco revenues.

FIGURE 3.1   Child labour: grading tobacco at an estate in Zeka Village, Kasungu, Malawi
Source: Plan/Eldson Chagara.

Malawi produces high quality tobacco, and it can be found in nearly all the tobacco melanges of all the big brands. All smokers smoke Malawian tobacco.

Kirana's health is deteriorating. Because his resistance has decreased he has suffered from malaria, diarrhoea and lung infection in recent months.

Child labour is an issue in many parts of the world. According to UNICEF, around 150 million children between the ages of 5 and 14 are working. Many of them do not have the opportunity to go to school and so they will probably remain illiterate for the rest of their lives, which also means they will never be able to make a proper contribution to society. In many cases one cannot hold their parents or bosses responsible, as economic circumstances often compel them to set children to work for starvation wages. People, working on behalf of profit.

This distressing scenario is just one of the many global flaws in the relationship between humanity and the economy. This chapter investigates a number of these flaws in the fabric, and examines what these mean for people in various countries – both far from and near to home.

3.1 PPP in imbalance: the economy first

In Chapter 1 the Triple P was introduced, the triumvirate of people, planet and profit (or prosperity) that are the three important aspects of sustainable development. In a sustainable world, each of these three aspects is taken into account in order to ensure that none of them lose out. If this were the case, then one could say that the three Ps are in mutual balance.

The previous chapter described that this balance does not presently exist. The environment is structurally overexploited around the world, which means that the interests of the planet are not sufficiently protected in our present state. Poverty in many parts of the globe is evidence that people are likewise underexposed. The Triple P is not balanced, with the profit aspect dominating. Money is often considered more important than human lives or nature conservation, as is symbolically represented in Figure 3.2; economic arguments are the dominant consideration in a wide array of plans and decisions.

Case 3.1 shows that this is not often merely due to ill will or carelessness – many times there are simply no conceivable ways to change the situation quickly, because the causes are deeply rooted in the economic system. This is evident in a number of ways.

The influence of the corporate sector

The following details, concerning the profits generated by a number of companies and the gross domestic product (GDP), are notable (see also Table 3.1).

- The ten biggest companies in the world generated collective revenues of over 2,856 billion dollars in 2015. That is more than the GDP of the United Kingdom (at 2,849 billion

FIGURE 3.2 The Triple P in imbalance: profit outweighs planet and people

Background photo source: NASA Headquarters–Greatest Images of NASA (NASA-HQ-GRIN).

TABLE 3.1 The ten multinational companies with the greatest revenue (in 2015)

Rank	Company	Country	Industry	Revenue (billion USD)
1	Walmart	United States	Retail	482.1
2	State Grid	China	Power	329.6
3	China National Petroleum	China	Petroleum	299.3
4	Sinopec	China	Petroleum	294.3
5	Royal Dutch Shell	Netherlands, United Kingdom	Petroleum	272.2
6	Exxon Mobil	United States	Petroleum	246.2
7	Volkswagen	Germany	Automobiles	236.6
8	Toyota Motor	Japan	Automobiles	236.6
9	Apple	United States	Technology	233.7
10	BP	United Kingdom	Petroleum	226.0
Total				**2856.6**

Source: Fortune Global 500 (2016)

dollars in 2015), which has the fifth largest GDP in the world after the United States, China, Japan and Germany.

- The 20 biggest companies in the world generated collective revenues of 4,556 billion dollars in 2015. That is more than the collective gross domestic products of 165 countries, with a combined population of nearly 1.5 billion people.
- Nigeria, a country with a population of 182 million, is endeavouring to use legislation to limit environmental damage resulting from oil production by Royal Dutch Shell, a company with 90,000 employees. Nigeria had a GDP per capita of 2,640 dollars in 2015. In the same year, the oil company generated a turnover of 272.2 billion dollars, which amounts to an average of three million dollars per employee. (Sources: IMF (2016); World Bank (2016); Fortune 500 (2016)

In itself, it does not have to be a sin that these companies generate a great deal of money and can use it to exercise much influence. Many companies aim to devote themselves to the interests of the environment and society. The furniture company Ikea, for example, is one company that is internationally recognised for its corporate social responsibility (CSR). But the fact that there is so much more money flowing through the corporate sector than through the hands of the average financial minister or treasury secretary has resulted in a situation where it is not easy for companies to refrain from ever abusing their position.

With regard to this, consider the fact that the governments of most wealthy nations are elected and are thus subject to democratic checks and balances. The managers of companies are not elected but appointed, and so they are free of these democratic checks and balances. To compensate for this, we have legislation, which exists to ensure that the companies act responsibly. But because the big companies are engaged in many countries, they deal with different types of laws, complicating both the checks and balances and compliance with these laws. Chapter 5 shows that a fair number of companies move their factories to countries where the environmental and working conditions legislation is lightweight.

The companies are of course accountable to their owners, the shareholders. The problem is that these people frequently put good financial results first, so that profit automatically takes precedence over people and planet. This situation is however slowly changing, and in an increasing number of companies the shareholders and clients are keeping a critical eye on the social and environmental consequences of business activities.

The GDP is not green

Gross domestic product, which was just discussed, is actually calculated in an incomplete way. It indicates how much a country earns in a given year, but it does not examine the real costs thereof.

Let us say that a certain quantity of iron ore is mined in a given country in a given year, which is in turn sold for a sum of ten million euros. This sale contributes ten million euros to the GDP. Sounds all right? On the face of it, this might well be the case, but don't forget that something was not only earned, some other thing was lost – iron ore, with a sales value of ten million euros. And that is *not* included in the GDP.

Here is another example: imagine that a factory manufactures goods to the value of 100,000 euros. This figure is included in the gross domestic product. But if that same factory, in manufacturing those goods, emitted greenhouse gases, polluted the soil, damaged a part of the natural environment and so on, all adding up to some 20,000 euros worth of damage, that latter figure is not deducted from the GDP.

So what we are faced with when dealing with the GDP is that the depleted ground resources are not taken into account, and nor is damage to nature and the environment. But the GDP is still employed everywhere as an important guideline for economic policy. Governments map out their political course on the basis of it, which means their plans are based on incomplete figures.

A growing number of experts and organisations consider the GDP to be an unreliable indicator, and alternative methods have been designed to calculate the GDP. This is known as **environmental accounting**, methods that include environmental damage and the depletion of stocks resulting in a **Green GDP**. The best-known method is the **System of Integrated Environmental and Economic Accounting** (SEEA), which was developed by a combination of various international organisations, including the United Nations, the European Union and the World Bank. In spite of this, all countries still use the traditional method for working out their GDP, the result of which means environmental interests and the shrinking stocks remain systematically underexposed.

Different visions

The relationship between the three Ps can be examined from a variety of ways. Many policy-makers and economists are inclined to perceive the relationship as it is shown in the upper-most half of Figure 3.3, a view in which humanity and the natural environment are two independent sections, which are bound to each other as a result of the economy, and with their value expressed in monetary terms. It is tempting, due to such a vision, to design the economic system as a kind of one-way traffic, which automatically creates a weaving fault.

A second disadvantage of this view is that the chance is greater that the three Ps are not in balance, and that the economy is considered more important than the other two Ps. This creates problems such as overexploitation and dehumanisation.

Another way of looking at this relationship is to consider the entire planet as a whole, with this view being labelled **holistic**. This is represented in the lower part of Figure 3.3.

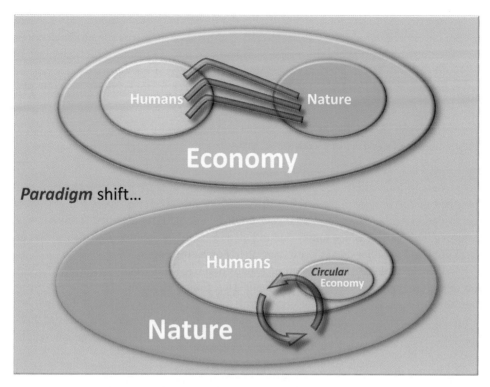

FIGURE 3.3   Different visions; the top image shows man and nature as a component of the economy, the bottom image shows economy as one of man's activities, which is in turn a part of the natural environment

The holistic concept sees humanity as being a part of the natural environment from which it originated, while the economy is a component of the human system. The green GDP is one way of expressing this connection. This vision makes it much more self-evident to create closed cycles. If this is done in a consistent way, it will lead to a *circular economy*, an important new paradigm which is increasingly dominant in current and future years. Chapter 8 discusses this topic in more detail.

Questions

- Do people exist for the sake of the economy, or does the economy exist for the sake of humanity? Or could it be that both are true?
- Or does the economy exist more for some people than for others?

At present the human system is arranged for the most part as is shown in the uppermost part of Figure 3.3. The Triple P is imbalanced, with the P for profit outweighing the P for planet and the P for people. International and national policy is greatly dominated by economic considerations, to the detriment of the natural environment and also, in a number of places, to the detriment of human well-being.

An improvement to this fundamental flaw in the fabric does not necessarily have to mean that the interests of the economy are neglected. On the contrary – true sustainable development is only possible if the economy plays a leading role, both to maintain the well-being of the wealthy nations and to improve the living conditions in poor ones. It is precisely because the economy is so dominant in our society that makes it necessary for economic forces to play a key role on the path towards sustainable development.

The necessity of continuous economic growth

The economies of most of the world's countries are growing. This factor is very positive in the poorer and moderately wealthy nations, as they have a great deal to catch-up on when compared to the wealthy countries. But the economy also continues to grow nearly every year in those wealthy countries – their **real GDP** (being the GDP adjusted for inflation) is increasing. This growth is not simply due to inflation (which would mean that there was no actual growth) but rather due to a real increase in purchasing power.

Economic laws dictate that such an increase is necessary, and when growth over a given year is low, a country is considered to be suffering from a recession, during which many companies struggle. Even worse, negative growth can occasionally occur, when the economy shrinks, as was the case in many countries in the years following the financial crisis of 2008. Then we are faced with a depression, and it is a safe bet in these times that people will be dismissed en masse.

Continuous growth is essential for maintaining our level of prosperity. But this is also a problem, as growth can never be sustained for all eternity. We can see that by examining what would happen if the economic growth really did continue in perpetuity. Imagine: economic growth stays at a constant 2.5 percent a year over the ages. This would mean that a nation's wealth would double around every 30 years. After 60 years, this wealth will be quadrupled, and after 90 years (three times 30 years) it has grown eightfold. Three centuries later the nation's wealth would have increased by a thousand times, and after 12 centuries it would be 1,000 billion times richer.

This is of course completely ridiculous. Not just because wealth reaches absurd proportions on this path but also because such a rise in prosperity would devastate the Earth within a few centuries or even earlier (see Figure 3.4). That is, assuming that economic growth is paired to material growth, which entails a rise in the consumption of natural resources, energy and other resources. In theory, it would be possible for economic growth to increase while material growth gradually subsides and eventually ceases. An example of this in real life is the fact that computers are capable of doing more every year (and consequently rise in terms of economic value) but do not require an ever-increasing amount of material or energy to do so. This disconnection of economic and material growth is referred to as **dematerialisation**. But even if the computer has proved to be a successful example, this does not mean that dematerialisation is generally easy. To date, economic growth has almost exclusively resulted in real material growth, and so the consumption of resources and the overexploitation of the natural environment likewise increases.

The economic necessity of a continuous economic growth that results in material growth is a flaw in the fabric, as such growth cannot be sustained in the long term. A society that wishes to exist for an extended period will over time have to learn to survive without economic growth, or at least without material growth.

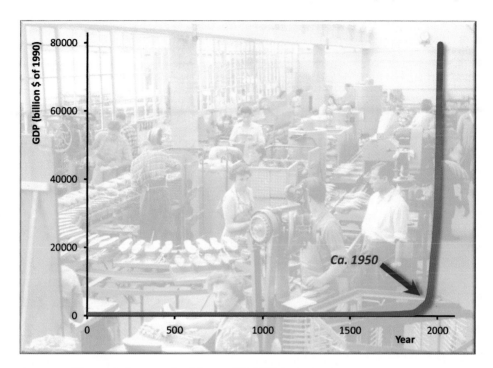

FIGURE 3.4   The explosive growth of the world's GDP in recent years

Background photo source: Oliver 1983: Angulus plant, Bad Soden am Taunus, Germany 1958.

Barriers and subsidies in international trade

The rich Western nations are generally champions of the free market system, in which companies and countries can freely trade amongst themselves. But the truth of the matter is that they do not entirely live up to this principle. An example of this is the trade barriers they maintain in the form of import duties.

Imagine that a farmer in a poor country grows sugar and wants to sell it in the EU. When the sugar is imported into the EU, the EU countries impose a duty – increasing the price by about 400 euros per ton (in 2012) – over and above the original price. This duty is pocketed by the EU. Its purpose is to protect the EU region's own farmers, as was mentioned already in Chapter 2, and the imported sugar becomes significantly more expensive for European buyers, while the farmer in the poor country finds it difficult or even impossible to sell his sugar.

The EU, as well as the USA and Japan, also favour their own farmers through agricultural subsidies, as can be seen in Figure 3.5.

The countries of the European Union annually donate an amount with a value of about 150 dollars per capita as development aid, in many places of the world. That is nice, but at the same time the EU countries subsidise their own agriculture annually with about 100 dollars per capita. Just like the import duties, the subsidies to the own agriculture make it harder for farmers in developing countries to export to the EU, and to the US and Japan as well, which partly cancels out the development aid.

The EU agricultural subsidies were not introduced in order to obstruct the poorer nations, but rather with the best of intentions in mind. They stem from a time when Europe was faced

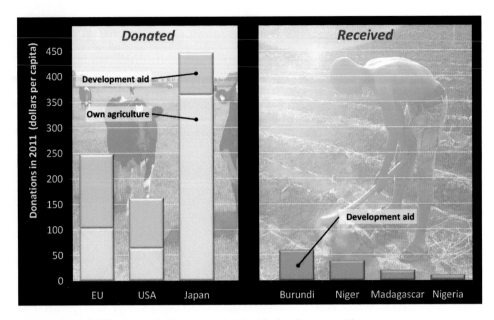

FIGURE 3.5   Subsidies on agriculture, compared with development aid

Source: World Bank 2016.

Background photo sources: (left) Bert Knottenbeld, Flickr; (right) Stephen Morrison/AusAID, Wikimedia.

with great food shortages in the wake of World War II. The subsidy system was extraordinarily successful and its goal that Europe would never be afflicted by famine again was quickly achieved. It is ironic that some time later the system actually contributed to the exact opposite in other parts of the world. This gives rise to an important observation: *A method that provides a solution at a specific time to a problem can, at a later time, actually constitute a (part-) cause of the same (or another) problem.* No one solution to a problem can be expected to be suitable forever.

Attempts are being made to cut these duties and subsidies, with some success. However, it has proved incredibly difficult to cut them to any significant degree, or even scrap them. This is because these subsidies, which have now existed for decades, have created an agricultural system of low prices and large quantities of livestock in the wealthy nations that, should comprehensive change be introduced, would result in many farmers going bankrupt and prices rising for the consumer. Here again we are confronted with a flaw in the fabric.

3.2 Inequality: the lack of solidarity

Questions

- Is your monthly income more or less than the average for all people across the world?
- Do you think you might earn a top salary over the course of your career? Do you want to?

Income is highly unequal amongst people, not only within countries but also between countries. In order to measure this factor, the GDP is generally used. The GDP of a nation divided by the number of inhabitants of the country is the average annual income per person, or the **per capita GDP**. You can see a few examples in Table 3.2, including Malawi, which was dealt with in Case 3.1.

Amongst the upper rows in Table 3.2 the GDP values are shown, expressed in US dollars per capita. For countries such as the United States, the average income per person is more than 100 times that for Malawi. To appreciate what that means, imagine dividing an amount of, say, ten dollars between an American person and a Malawian – the American would receive $9.90 thereof, with the remaining ten cents going to the Malawian. In all fairness, it must also be stated that it is not only the incomes that differ between nations – so do prices. In the US the income earned may be high; but the costs are also high, and with the same money you could buy a great deal more in Malawi than in the United States. In order to create a fair comparison of the prices, the **UNDP (United Nations Development Programme)** has converted each country's per capita GDP from "real" dollars into a type of imaginary currency, called **PPP dollars**. 'PPP' is an abbreviation of **Purchasing Power Parity**. These PPP dollars are designed to omit the price level differences.

Table 3.2 also includes these converted values for the per capita GDP, which are used as a measure for actual purchasing power. This actual purchasing power in the United States is 47 times that of Malawi.

Inequality in income is not the only way in which people and countries differ from each other, and there are many other indicators, such as the fact that people in some countries have a much greater chance of living a long life and of being healthy than in others. The lower section of Table 3.2 contains a number of figures that are characteristic of the health conditions and levels of education in a selection of wealthy and less wealthy countries. Unequal distribution (Figure 3.6) also pertains to freedom, and Table 3.2 also includes the **Human Freedom Index** for these countries. Many factors can limit freedom, including political oppression and the lack of prosperity. In India, there is little political oppression, and the country is the world's largest democracy, but thanks to the lack of prosperity many people are not able to live in an actual state of freedom. Taken together, there are many types of inequality – see Table 3.3.

Mutually reinforcing factors

As can be seen in Table 3.2, the unequal distribution is always to the advantage of certain countries and to the disadvantage of certain others. There is no scenario in which you will live longer and be healthier in one country while in another you will be richer. On the contrary, it is always the same countries that are advantaged, and this is no coincidence, given that the various advantages reinforce each other. If the economy is doing well, then money is available for good healthcare and education. Education in turn contributes to improved hygiene while, thanks to the fact the population is well educated and healthy, the economy can grow further. This is once again positive feedback – if things are going well, they will get even better. The converse of this feedback also holds. Take Brazil, for example, a country that is struggling with its issues. In 2015, it received development aid from wealthy countries to the tune of 910 million dollars, a tidy sum. But this form of development aid is generally granted in part in the form of *loans*, which must be paid off at a later stage. Even worse is the fact that an increasing amount of interest builds up year after year on that part of the loan not yet repaid. Brazil resultantly built a

TABLE 3.2 Data for select countries

	China	India	USA	Brazil	Nigeria	Japan	Netherlands	Malawi	Latvia
Population (in millions)	1371	1311	321	208	182	127	16.9	17.2	2.1
Economy									
GDP per capita (international $ of 2010)	6,416	1,806	51,486	11,159	2,548	44,657	50,925	494	14,244
GDP (PPP international $ of 2011)	13,400	5,730	52,549	14,455	5,639	35,804	46,374	1,113	22,628
Per capita GDP growth in 5 years (2011–2015)	46%	39%	11%	5.0%	26%	3.1%	3.1%	22%	19%
Income disparity [1]	13	9	16	41	16	4.5	9	11	10
Income < $1.25 per day	12%	33%	–	6%	68%	–	–	62%	–
Foreign debt (billion $)	1,680	486	17,911	428	68	2,861	2,527	1.2	10
Debt service [2] (billion $)	52	93	–	60	0.70	–	–	0.065	8
Development aid (billion $)	–	3.0	–	0.91	2.4	–	–	0.92	–
Health and education									
HDI (Human Development Index)	90	130	8	75	152	20	5	173	46
Life expectancy at birth (years)	75.8	68.0	78.9	74.4	52.8	83.6	81.3	62.7	74.2
Births per woman [3]	1.56	2.4	1.9	1.79	5.7	1.4	1.7	5.1	1.5
Doctors per 100,000 people	146	65	242	176	40	214	392	2	290
Access to clean water	95.5%	94.1%	99.2%	98.1%	68.5%	100%	100%	90.2%	99.3%
Literacy (15 years and older)	95%	63%	100%	90%	51%	100%	100%	61%	99.8%
Percentage educated [4]	65%	39%	95%	54%	28%	87%	89%	9%	99%
Child labour (5–14 years)	–	12%	–	9%	25%	–	–	27%	–
Access to the Internet	49%	18%	87%	58%	43%	91%	93%	6%	76%
Civil Liberties Index [5]	6	3	1	2	5	2	1	4	2
Military									
Military expenditure ($ per capita)	157	38	1854	118	11	322	524	3	145

Nations are categorised according to their population size.

(1) "R/P 10%", i.e. averaged income of the wealthiest 10% divided by the averaged income of the poorest 10% of the population

(2) In 2014. Debt service = total of all annual costs of a debt: repayment + paid interest

(3) Should no immigration or emigration exist, if the number of births per woman is circa 2.1, this will lead to a stable population

(4) Primary + at least some secondary education

(5) Civil Liberties Index: 1 = most free, 7 = least free (*ordinal scale*)

Sources: UNDP: Human Development Report (2015), UN Statistics Division (2016), World Bank (2016), Index Mundi (2016), Freedom House (2016), CIA (2016).

FIGURE 3.6   Unequal distribution

Source: Fritz Behrendt, with thanks to Mrs. Behrendt.

large level of debt in previous years, for which the nation paid the wealthy countries a sum of over *60 billion dollars* (nearly 300 dollars per person) in interest and repayments in 2015. In fact, in 2015, the destitute Brazil paid a gigantic *net* sum (that is, after deducting the received development aid) to the wealthy nations, and not the other way around! The accrued debts hang around the neck of a developing nation like a millstone. Staying with Brazil, its foreign debt in 2015 had grown to 428 billion dollars. The development aid, granted with good intentions, has over time had an extremely detrimental effect upon the economies of poorer countries. Fortunately, much attention has been focused on this **debt trap** in recent years, and sections of the debt are now being gradually cancelled. This process was accelerated since 2005 when the **G8** became involved. The G8 is the 'Group of 8', consisting of the seven most powerful industrial countries in the world (the United States, Canada, Japan, Germany, France, the United Kingdom and Italy) and Russia. They collectively decided, pressurised by public opinion, to cancel or decrease the debt of a few dozen countries. This type of international policy has more recently been determined by a larger group of nations, the **G20**.

The debt trap demonstrates that unequal distribution between countries is not simply a coincidence that shall disappear of its own accord in due course – it has rather become a component of the global system, a flaw in the fabric.

TABLE 3.3 Types of unequal distribution

Unequal distribution relates to:	I.e. it is about:
Life and health	life duration
	healthy food
	medical care
	safety
Prosperity	possessions
	income
	free of debts
	availability of resources
Access to knowledge	literacy
	education
	Internet
Power	military
	cultural
	political
	ideological
Freedom	democracy
	independence
	freedom of expression
	freedom of movement and settlement
	right to use one's own
	protection from discrimination
Environment	ecological footprint
	trading in emission rights

This flaw has further consequences too. Because the wealthy nations are able to spend money on things other than the basic needs, such as food, housing, education and health-care, they have much latitude to invest in military resources. The last line in Table 3.2 shows military expenditure per capita, from which it is evident how the United States, in particular, has become so militarily dominant in the world. In other words, unequal distribution also relates to *power*. The unequal distribution of power is not only visible in terms of military dominance, and the rich West, led by the United States, also outstrips the rest of the world in other respects. This includes the cultural influences, the 'Disney culture', the Western image of fashion, Western pop music and more (see Figure 3.7). And there is also the ideological and political dominance. An illustration of this is the fact that three of the five members of the Security Council, which is the most powerful body within the United Nations, are wealthy Western nations – France, the United Kingdom and the United States (the other two are Russia and China).

Questions

- Do you believe that Western culture (the culture of Europe and the US) is dominant in other parts of the world?
- Which is stronger, to your expectations: Asian cultural influences in the US or American cultural influences in Asia?

FIGURE 3.7   Cultural dominance: McDonald's in China

Source: Ian Muttoo, Wikimedia.

The poverty trap

Poverty can be found in all regions of the world, not just in Third World nations, but also in the wealthy ones. In England, for example, poverty exists amongst both the immigrant population and the native people.

Case 3.2 Special assistance

Mrs Littlebury is 67 years old and she has been living alone since her husband died two years ago. She lives off her state pension, but this is not enough to make ends meet, and her savings are rapidly dwindling. Her fixed monthly costs (rent, power, insurance, etc.) and payments toward an old debt leave her with almost no money to purchase necessities such as food, medication and clothing. Although she is entitled to housing benefits, she is not aware of this fact.

Ever since she had a car accident four years ago, she walks with difficulty. This means that she rarely goes out. Because she can no longer afford a telephone or newspaper, she has little contact with the outside world. Mrs Littlebury believed her situation was so hopeless that she recently attempted to end it. When her suicide attempt failed, she was admitted to the psychiatric division of a hospital.

In the hospital she came into contact with her municipality's social services. They investigated her situation, immediately ensuring that she received housing benefits. They also applied for special assistance on her behalf, allowing her access to the 'meals on wheels' program, which meant she would have a warm meal five times a week. An application for compensation for moving is still in the works. If it is approved, Mrs Littlebury will move to a ground floor apartment – she is no longer able to climb stairs. (Mrs Littlebury is not her real name.)

Poverty is defined in a variety of ways. **Absolute poverty** (Figure 3.8) indicates the inability of a person to maintain a certain minimum living standard, a minimum that includes the necessities of life such as food, clothing and shelter, as well as access to education and healthcare and the ability to maintain social contact. **Relative poverty** involves the prosperity (or lack thereof) of a person in comparison to other people or groups in the same environment or nation. From this point of view, somebody in a wealthy country can still be considered poor, even though that person has a greater income than a person with an average income in a poor country.

Questions

- If you could choose, in which country would you like to live?
- If you could have chosen before you were born, in which country would you have selected to be born?

Since a number of years, Norway leads the HDI ranking, followed by Australia, New Zealand, the US and several European countries. It is evident from the HDI that there are not only major differences in prosperity and income between nations, but also between individuals within those nations. Table 3.2 provides a sample of this disparity in income. The two types of inequality – within a country and between countries – are not independent of each other, and we can consider it in terms of a sort of poverty spectrum starting close and

FIGURE 3.8   Absolute poverty: born, living and dying in a slum in Jakarta, on top of a garbage dump

The UN development organisation, the UNDP, releases an annual report on the prosperity and standard of living in nations across the world. A gauge was created for this purpose called the **Human Development Index (HDI)**. The HDI shows the levels of poverty in countries and of the more or less unequal distribution of poverty within them.

Source: Jonathan McIntosh, Wikimedia.

Close by ←					→ Far away
Native poor	Immigrants in wealthy nations	Illegal aliens, in hiding or expelled	Refugees to wealthy nations	Refugees in Africa, etc.	Poverty in the Third World
⬆	⬆	⬆	⬆	⬆	⬆
Concealed poverty and exclusion	Discrimination, ghettoisation, underclass	Turn to criminality, prostitution	Boat refugees, exploitation, expelling	War, economic displacement	Hunger, child mortality, environmental destruction

FIGURE 3.9   Spectrum of poverty – from close by to far away

moving further away. In other words, from 'here' to 'there' (the 'space' dimension of sustainable development).

In Figure 3.9 one can see the poverty of the native population – the original inhabitants of a country – on the left. Mrs Littlebury, who appeared in Case 3.2, falls under this group. The other categories deal with the immigrant population, which are not only those people born outside of a country, but also the **second generation immigrants** who were born in England but have foreign-born parents. The distinction between native and immigrant populations is vague, as one could also consider third, fourth or tenth generation immigrants.

Questions

- For how many generations should your family live in your country before you could be called a native?
- In a way, *everybody* is an immigrant, of a certain generation. If you did not immigrate yourself, do you have any idea how many generations ago your ancestors entered the region where you live?

The African Americans in the United States seem to be something of an eternal immigrant group. Many of their ancestors have lived in the US for generations, but they are still treated by some sections of the white population as unwanted foreigners. The same is true for the Dalit, the untouchables in India. Prosperity and poverty in many countries are unequally distributed between the native population and the immigrant populations, as Figure 3.10 illustrates for the United Kingdom, and also between age groups and between the genders. Women are disadvantaged in regard to men, and the percentage of them who are poor is higher.

Some of the immigrants in wealthy nations are there illegally, and they are located in Figure 3.9 just to the left of the centre. Together with others, they have arrived in Western countries as refugees, or have been brought there by people smugglers. **Political refugees**, who are threatened in their homelands on account of their political convictions, their religion, race or their community, are generally admitted (especially in the EU and the US) more easily than **economic refugees**, who flee their homelands because they are seeking improved living conditions. The latter type is often thrown out of the country, irrespective of whether they then run the risk of succumbing to famine. All these refugees constitute a literal link between the poverty in Third World nations and the poverty in the wealthy ones, as Figure 3.10 illustrates.

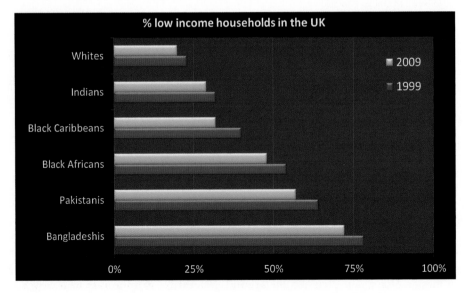

FIGURE 3.10 Percentage of low-income people in the United Kingdom by ethnic group

Source: The Poverty Site (2016).

Questions

- Would you view Case 3.2 differently if you knew that it did not concern Mrs Littlebury from England but Mrs Rahim, who followed her husband five years ago to England, after he arrived in the country eight years ago as a refugee from Bangladesh?
- Is Mrs Littlebury stupid because she did not know she was entitled to housing benefits? Is she alone in her ignorance?

The refugees and immigrants are not the only link between poverty at home and poverty elsewhere. Another connection is the fact that there are underlying causes, as a result of which poverty continues to exist instead of being gradually eradicated. These causes are for a large part identical in both cases – poverty here and poverty in far-off countries – and both involve positive feedback, as can be seen in Figure 3.11. Both wealth and poverty are amplified through this feedback, where severe poverty results in problems such as a low level of proper personal care (see loop 1 in Figure 3.11). A factor such as this might be due to the lack of clean water, poor hygienic conditions (like the lack of a sewer system), lack of knowledge of proper personal care or poor or unbalanced food sources. There is an additional issue in many nations in that the poor have little or no chance of taking out insurance against healthcare costs. All these factors mean that poor people are on average less healthy than their richer counterparts. Because of that, work absenteeism is greater, the jobs they hold are not as good and their income is lower – and so they have little opportunity to liberate themselves from their poverty. The lack of decent schooling, a great expense in many countries, also leads to lower income (loop 2), and the impoverished are furthermore frequently compelled to supplement their earnings with loans, so that debts mount until the interest due becomes untenable (loop 3). Mrs Littlebury provided an example of this in Case 3.2.

The sum of these feedbacks that keep poverty alive, even reinforcing it, is called the **poverty trap**. The poverty trap is not only an issue for individual poor people, but also for entire countries. The debt trap that Third World countries fall into is a part of this complex poverty trap at a national level.

The upper portion of Figure 3.11 shows how wealth can likewise reinforce itself. Loop 4 shows how it is possible, with capital, to invest in profitable enterprises and thus become wealthier – an impossible move if one is impoverished. Loop 5 is a mirror image of loop 2 – having money provides the opportunity for good education, which contributes to achieving a decent income. Loop 6 is of a slightly different nature, in that money also grants a certain form of power. This is true for both senior managers and for institutions, having many opportunities to influence both their own and each other's salaries. Thanks in part to this factor, the wage packets of the powerful can grow to dizzying proportions.

This type of feedback tends to make the rich richer and the poor poorer, and in reality this is often truly the case. Figure 3.12, for example, shows the development of purchasing power in Brazil. In a period of 32 years, the purchasing power of both the richest and the poorest 10 percent increased ca. 200 percent, so it seems that both groups fared equally well. But when the development is expressed in PPP dollars, a different image arises: while the annual income of the wealthiest increased by $32,000, that of the poorest increased by less than $800. Similar graphs can be made for many nations – rich as well as poor ones.

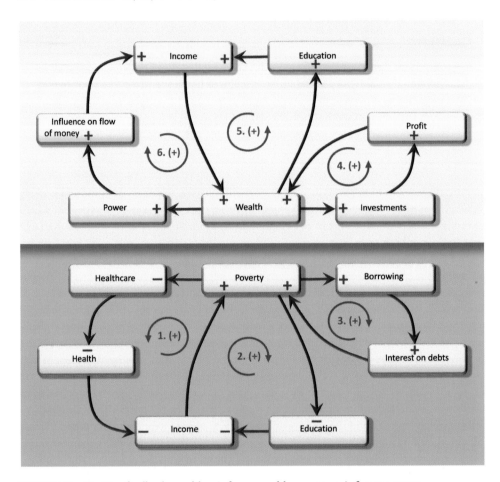

FIGURE 3.11 Positive feedback: wealth reinforces wealth, poverty reinforces poverty

This mirrors what happened to the gap between the wealthy and poor nations. The per capita GDP in sub-Saharan Africa grew by 85 percent between 1980 and 2015, while in that same period the per capita GDP in China grew by 2,700 percent (!) and in the United States by 170 percent. But in PPP dollars, this looks very different: The sub-Saharan average PPP income increased in those 35 years by $1,600, in China by $13,000, and in the USA by $33,000. What this means in real terms is evident in Figure 3.13, where the per capita GDP is shown in PPP dollars.

The graphics in Figures 3.12 and 3.13 provide a realistic picture of the changes to the actual purchasing power over the years. The dollars in both figures are PPP dollars (PPP = Purchasing Power Parity), and are thus adjusted for both inflation and for price differences in the various countries. Both the graphics demonstrate that the feedbacks for wealth and for poverty have resulted in the gap between rich and poor growing in recent decades, both between individuals and between countries. 'Money makes money' – wealth tends to amplify itself, and so does poverty.

This growing divide between rich and poor has consequences that reach deep into society. One of the most serious of these is the flow of millions of refugees, who live in

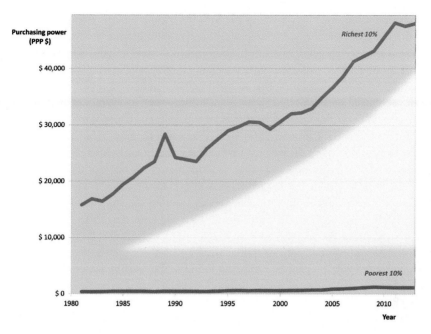

FIGURE 3.12 The growing gap between poor and rich in Brazil between 1981 and 2013: purchasing power evolution of the poorest and wealthiest 10 percent (in PPP dollars, corrected for inflation)

Source: World Bank (2016).

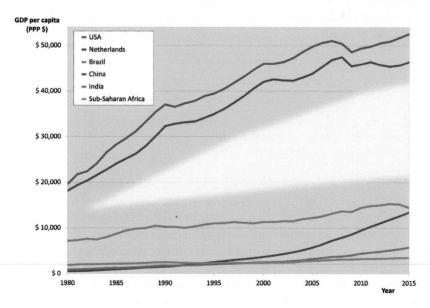

FIGURE 3.13 The growing international gap – real purchasing power evolution between 1980 and 2015, expressed in PPP dollars

Source: World Bank (2016).

degrading circumstances. This flow is in part headed for the wealthy nations, and countries such as the United States are confronted with massive immigration problems, especially the illegal aliens that try to get across the Mexican border from Central and South America. Western Europe is faced with the same problem of refugees from Africa and Asia in particular. In one year alone, 2000, some 360,000 people applied for asylum in the 15 countries that then made up the EU. In those years, future scenarios were sketched of groups of people trying to enter the wealthy countries in the millions, which could only be repelled using military force. Back around 2000 such a scenario seemed unlikely to most people; but in the second decade of the twenty-first century, things look differently, as huge masses of refugees try to reach Europe and other wealthy regions of the world, mostly from war-stricken countries in Africa and the Middle East.

But issues arising from refugees in the wealthy nations are still minor when compared to those in the poor nations. The latter group have far fewer resources to provide decent reception facilities for the refugees, and the flows even involve larger groups of people, with over 80 percent of displaced persons (refugees, asylum seekers, people dispelled within their own countries and stateless people) not being found in the wealthy nations but rather in the poor ones.

Questions

- What would you do if you lived on less than a dollar a day in Africa, your children were unable to attend school, you saw no chance for improvement at home, and you anticipated that things would be better in Europe or the US?
- Is such a person entitled to a decent existence?
- On the other hand, what would happen in Europe or the US if every economic refugee was admitted?

Transfer

In Chapter 2, agriculture in the country of Vietnam was discussed, which imports animal feed from other countries – a necessity, as Vietnam does not have the capacity to produce all the feed it requires. Because this is one-way traffic, a number of other nations are confronted with problems.

Another example is how Western countries handle the problem of electronic waste (commonly referred to as "e-waste"). These countries export their broken or obsolete computer equipment to poorer regions, such as the Chinese province of Guangdong – one of the largest e-waste dumping sites on Earth. In the city of Guiyu, impoverished labourers use archaic methods to mine the material for precious metals. In the process, these men and women (and often child labourers) are exposed to a health-threatening cocktail of chemicals. The surrounding environment is contaminated with an array of toxins. This is an example of a frequent issue, which is that wealthier nations are not able to solve a number of their own problems and consequently transfer the consequences thereof to other countries. The wealthy nation's economy blossoms thanks to this, stomachs are well fed, to the detriment of the economy and health of the poor nations. This phenomenon is called **transfer**.

Case 3.3   The ships of Chittagong

Forty years ago they were simply dismantled in Europe, and in the US and Japan, but environmental regulations were tightened up and it became more and more expensive. Mammoth supertankers, giants of the seas – every year hundreds of them reach the ends of their lives. When demolition became too expensive in the wealthy countries, the work moved to countries such as China. But the environmental legislation eventually also made it too costly there, and today India and Bangladesh do duty for ship breaking.

The coast of Chittagong, the second largest city in Bangladesh, is strewn with massive steel carcasses (Figure 3.14). They are dismantled almost entirely by hand and the steel is recycled, while all possible loose parts are sold on.

Ship breaking in the region provides a living to around 45,000 people. They have no protection whatsoever, given that Bangladeshi laws are lax. Each ship holds between ten and a hundred tons of paint, which contains poisonous metals such as cadmium, lead and mercury. The ships also contain arsenic, asbestos and PCBs, as well as flammable and explosive substances.

Workers dismantling smaller boats in Western countries wear protective clothing, including masks, required by law. This is not required in Bangladesh. It costs too much money.

FIGURE 3.14   Dismantling ships on the beach in Chittagong

Source: Stéphane M Grueso, Wikimedia.

The scenario outlined in Case 3.3 is a characteristic example of this transfer. Because it has become too expensive to demolish oceangoing vessels in Western countries, the work has been transferred to nations where it is cheaper. The rich countries thus export their hazardous waste elsewhere, successfully ridding themselves of the problem.

Transfer means that the consequences of a certain lifestyle, such as environmental damage, health risks and economic damage, are not borne by those that cause them but rather by others. Transfer can happen in different directions, with problems transferred to people elsewhere (from here to there) and problems transferred to yet unborn generations (from the present to the future).

One can find many examples of transfer problems to be faced in the future, one of which is the fact that barrels of chemical waste were dumped in the oceans until a few decades ago. It was believed that these barrels would remain intact for a lengthy period. This practice is now internationally prohibited, but those barrels are still there – 'time bombs' that could one day burst open.

Another example involves greenhouse gas emissions. Today's energy requirements will cause climate issues at a later date. These emissions also involve transferring the problem to another part of the globe, as the largest culprits (per capita), including the US and Europe, shall suffer relatively fewer consequences thereof, including rising sea levels, increasing bad weather and increasing droughts. When it comes to rising sea levels, it will primarily be those countries with low coastlines (such as the Netherlands, Bangladesh and a number of small island states) that will suffer. It is expected that countries with robust economies will be able to deal with the problem, but those with weak economies do not have the resources to follow suit and could be left holding the baby as the waters rise.

Staying with energy, nuclear power provides another example of transferring a problem to the future. Although the present generation benefits from a nuclear power station for a handful of decades, the radioactive waste must be securely stored for thousands of years afterwards (this will be more comprehensively covered in Chapter 7).

Even well-intentioned but naïve attempts to aid poor countries can bold down to this transfer. Old shoes are collected and sent to the Third World, but shoes contain chrome, which is used to tan leather. Old shoes are actually chemical waste, which the First World can easily rid itself of in this way.

Global attempts were made to impose restrictions on transfers, with the **Basel Ban** taking effect in 1995. Pursuant to this agreement, the wealthy nations that make up the membership of the OECD (the Organisation for Economic Cooperation and Development) are prohibited from exporting hazardous waste to non-OECD nations. In 2016, 181 countries have ratified the treaty; only 12 UN member states have not. Eleven of them are relatively small nations such as Grenada and Tuvalu; the only large country that is no party to the treaty is the United States of America. The ban does not apply to seagoing vessels, as can be seen by Case 3.3, or to airplanes.

3.3 Dehumanisation: alienation and exclusion

Case 3.4   End of the line for rail ticket offices?

Daily Gazette, *United Kingdom, 11 June 2011*

Eight train station ticket offices in Colchester and Tendring could close. A report commissioned by the Government recommends stations with one member of staff and annual ticket revenue of less than £1million do not need an office. Colchester Town, Wivenhoe and Harwich International are among those that fall into this category.

Rail users will have to buy tickets from a machine instead. Vacant offices could be replaced with shops, bringing in more cash for train companies. Stations with high numbers of commuters and revenue between £1 million and £2 million, including Marks Tey and Hatfield Peverel, could see a reduction in ticket office hours.

Mark Leslie, secretary of the Essex Rail Users' Federation, said: "This would be a great inconvenience to the rail travelling public. It's not just about buying tickets, it's information as well, especially for complex or combination tickets you might want to buy, such as buying for the next day. Also, if you remove staff at some of the smaller stations, it would make travelling along some lines a free service as there are no barriers. Often the machine is not working, so even those who want to buy a ticket might not be able to.

The revenue they would lose could be substantial."

The McNulty Study was commissioned by the government to review efficiency and value for money on the railways. The report suggests if the changes are adopted by rail companies, they should install more ticket machines. Larger stations, such as Colchester North and Clacton, could also see more ticket machines and fewer station staff, if the proposals are implemented.

Efficiency

The closing of counters by the English railway service is a symptom of a trend that has been observed for dozens of years in Western nations – the fact that the presence of flesh-and-blood people is on the wane. The reason behind this is almost always in order to pursue greater efficiency, so as to achieve the same result at a lower cost.

Some years earlier the conductors on many trams have also disappeared, followed in the 1980s by the introduction of ATMs for banks and post offices, where money could be withdrawn or transferred. Before these automatic cash dispensers, everyone withdrew their money over the counter.

Question

- Would our lives be more pleasant if vending machines could act a little more human?

If the ticket machine could speak. . .

"Good morning, sir! I'm your ticket machine. Can I help you?"

"Ok, I would like to buy a train ticket."

"With pleasure."

"Oh. I'm going to London; will it be expensive?"

"It will not cost British Rail anything, apart from a tiny piece of paper, worth about half a penny."

"No, I mean. . . for me?"

"You mean, the ticket is for you?"

"Yes! Of course!"

"All right, I see."

"So, do you have any idea what a trip to London would cost?"

"Certainly, Sir."

"Well?"

"Indeed, Sir."

"Well, what will it cost me?"

"The journey from Watford to London will cost £8.30. The journey from Brighton to London will cost £14.90. The journey from Croydon to London will cost £4.80. The. . ."

"I mean, from Canterbury, of course!"

"Thank you."

"So?"

"What?"

"Well, how much then will the journey cost?"

"I can only tell you the train fares at present, not then. My superior might have more information on future fares."

"I'm not interested in future fares. I only want to know what the journey will cost now."

"I understand."

"Look, forget it. I don't want to go to London anymore. I don't want anything anymore, not even to go home."

"Where is home?"

"Where my wife is. But she left me!"

"Where did she go?"

"To live with her new boyfriend."

"I'm sorry to tell you that her new boyfriend is not on our list of destinations."

"I don't want to go there anyway. I don't want anything anymore!"

"The price is zero pounds. Do you have a discount card?"

"I don't want a discount card; I want my wife back!"

"I do not know what the fare for that is. It might indeed be expensive."

"Just forget it. I'm going for a drink. You want to join me for a beer?"

"British Rail equipment is not permitted to consume alcoholic beverages during working hours."

"Oh. What time do you get off work?"

"I am switched off at 00.30."

"Should I pick you up then and we can have a few pints?"

"Sounds great!"

Around the same time, the local beat officer in many municipalities was replaced by cops in cars or (at a later stage) surveillance cameras. The municipalities themselves were merged into ever-larger units for financial purposes. In the country of Japan, for example, there were over 3,000 municipalities in 1999. Today, that number has been cut nearly in half. The Japanese authorities hope to use the mergers to reduce financial deficits and government spending. For the inhabitants of the dissolved municipalities, however, a merger often results in losses. Distances to community officials become larger; the contacts are less personal. People find it more and more difficult to identify themselves with the places they are living, as their villages become a part of neighbouring megacities, home towns no longer appear on a map, or the city's name is changed. A similar wave of mergers has been ongoing for years amongst companies, hospitals, universities, colleges and high schools. Cities around the world are growing, with over half of the global population now urbanised. Even countries are getting bigger. In antiquity, classical Greek society was dominated by states the size of a today's modest-sized city, the modern world is covered by countries the size of half a continent, or even an entire one, as can be seen in Figure 3.15.

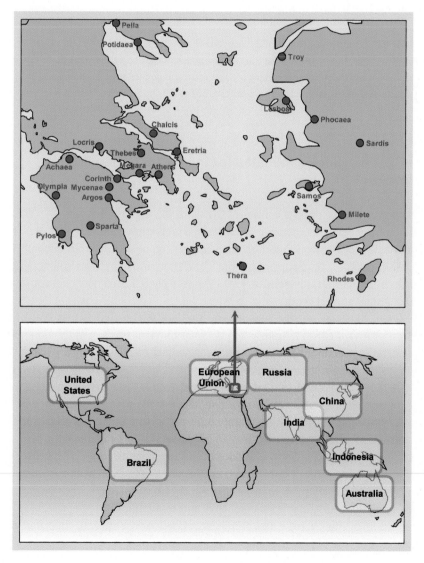

FIGURE 3.15   Countries are getting bigger. Top: a few leading city-states in Greece around 400 BCE. Bottom: a few leading countries in the twenty-first century

This evolution has a flipside – the distance between politicians and their electorate has grown, and a diminishing number of people bother to cast their vote in an election; social control on the streets and in public transport has decreased; violence, fare dodging and vandalism are growing problems. Occupants of nursing homes receive insufficient care, as a result of which they sometimes go days without being washed or have to wait hours to go to the toilet. Getting back to the train: a number of people, especially the elderly, no longer take the train as the ticket machine inspires so much fear amongst them.

All these issues can be summarised using the term '**dehumanisation**'. Surveillance cameras and vending machines replace contact between humans. People are treated impersonally, like objects instead of individuals, or even worse, not like citizens but like *safety risks*. In more and more countries, all citizens must be able to identify themselves on the street. Under certain circumstances, preventative frisking by the police has been legalised, even if there is no suspicion whatsoever that a crime has been committed. Passports now contain the bearer's fingerprints.

Personal data is recorded in digital files, which are then linked to each other or traded commercially, frequently without the citizen being permitted to peruse this data. This is great from a technical perspective, and efficiency levels are high. The state is increasingly involved, not to protect the personal living environment, but rather as a threat thereto.

Case 3.5 Facebook nominated for the Australian Big Brother Awards 2011

US company *change.org* is a winner of the 2016 Big Brother Award!

The globally operating company, owner of a well-known website with the same name, has a progressive reputation, as it appears to be a non-profit organization that allows people – or groups of people – to design and launch an online petition that can be signed on the website. However, it really is a commercial corporation, making a solid annual profit.

However, that was not the reason why the jury of the German edition of the Big Brother Award (BBA) (Figure 3.16) decided to grant the award to *change.org*, in the category 'Economy'. The company repeatedly ignored privacy issues and data protection laws. It sells private data of signatories to petitions, launched e.g. by Médecins Sans Frontières, Oxfam or Unicef, to third-party organisations, with prices of up to half a million dollars for one data list. Big data indeed! The way this is done is prohibited by laws in several countries and by EU laws; the prohibition cannot be overridden by the declaration of consent used by *change.org*.

Besides, even after the Court of Justice of the European Union (EUCJ) prohibited the unrestricted transfer of data, based on the so-called Safe Harbour Framework, from Europe to the US by companies like Facebook and Google, *change.org* continued to do so, thus violating several laws and regulations.

The report of the German BBA 2016 jury closed with a cynical: 'Heartfelt congratulations on the Big Brother Award 2016, *change.org*!'

FIGURE 3.16   The Big Brother Award

Source: Privacy International.

   The Dutch BBAs of 2015 were granted to the Secretary of State for the Home Department (or Minister of the Interior) of the Netherlands for his excessive plans for monitoring citizens, thus potentially criminalizing the entire Dutch population; and to the National Police for its use of 'predictive policing' based on big data, turning civilians into suspects due to deviant instead of criminal behaviour.

   In the US, a Big Brother Award was given in 2005 to Brittan Elementary School in California, because they attached an RFID tag to each of their students, in order to be able to know at all moments exactly where they were, "because it would streamline the taking of attendance", as the principal explained.

   Source: www.bigbrotherawards.de; www.privacyinternational.org; https://bba2015.bof.nl

In the meantime, offices are increasingly using flexible office space. Previously, desks in many office buildings were empty for part of the day – a waste of money! And so the modern office was thought up, where nobody has a fixed workspace. Come to work in the morning, armed with a case containing a laptop, choose a desk that is empty at that time, place a photo of your partner in the corner, log in wirelessly and get to work.

What all these developments have in common is that people are considered as economic objects. Efficiency is of overriding importance. If an ATM or vending machine is cheaper than a staffed counter, then that is the solution. What the effects on people are is difficult to assess. It is certainly easy to draw money, especially when in a hurry. But the sum of all these very easy and smooth impersonal contacts is that society becomes less human, less empathic. It ignores the fact that, aside from being rational entities, people are also biological beings, for whom behaviour is not only influenced by logic but also by hormones, not just by intellect but also by emotions. The compulsion towards efficiency has changed people slightly, and as a result affects the dignity and essence of human beings.

This loss of humanity is a characteristic example of the imbalance in people, planet and profit. Where the previous chapter demonstrates that profit generally beats planet, here we see that profit also prevails over people. The impression is created that people are here to serve the economic system instead of the other way around. Thus, to some extent all people become slaves. It is no surprise that an increasing number of people are alienated from society, while aggression and a lack of manners are on the rise, as illustrated by the fact that the streets are unsafe. Everything is increasing in size – countries, cities, companies, healthcare institutions, schools. The only thing not getting bigger is the individual. And so alienation spreads: the feeling people have that they no longer really belong.

Social exclusion

Various groups of people populate the lowest strata of society in the countries that make up Europe and North America. They are indigenous people, such as Mrs Littlebury, and frequently poorly educated. They are also some of those immigrants that are living legally in the country, or may even have been born there, and may hold a passport from the country in which they live. Then there are also those living illegally in the country. All these groups suffer from **social exclusion**, they have few opportunities for participating fully in society, as can be seen in Table 3.4. Amongst other things, this table deals with **normative integration** – the acceptance of generally applicable values and standards. This subject, which is primarily of concern in respect of immigrant populations, is a sensitive one as it involves clashing interests. On the one hand it is important that everyone is able, to a certain degree, to have their own system of values by which they live, while being respected by others. But on the other, the indigenous citizens have developed a number of values over the ages that they consider as fundamental, such as those relating to human rights, security and animal rights. This clash of values leads to intense societal debates, and a few examples of the current state of this debate in the West are detailed in Table 3.5. You don't have to look far to find very different standards among countries, however. In France, for example, the law prohibits students and pupils at standard schools from wearing headscarves, whereas other countries would not consider such a law.

Social exclusion, the poverty trap, different cultural backgrounds and customs together lead to **segregation** – separate groups within society. The physical manifestation of this is

TABLE 3.4 Characteristics of social exclusion

Characteristic	Examples
• Insufficient social participation	• Little social contact • Little social support • Large chance of unemployment
• Insufficient normative integration	• Rejection of generally applicable norms and values • Insufficient knowledge of language and culture
• Material deficiencies	• Insufficient money for basic needs • Unpayable debts • Lack of knowledge on subsidies
• Insufficient access to civil rights	• Insufficient healthcare, education, housing, social services • Little understanding of the right to vote

Source: Jehoel-Gijsbers (2004). A few examples have been added.

TABLE 3.5 Degree of acceptance of a few non-Western cultural elements in most Western countries

Degree of acceptance	Cultural elements
Universally rejected, prohibited by law	• Female circumcision • Calls for a Jihad • Ritual slaughter outside of an abattoir • Wearing a face veil (niqāb) at schools
Generally rejected, but not prohibited by law in most countries	• Freedom to have little knowledge of local language and culture • Wearing a niqāb in public
Officially accepted but under debate	• Islamic schools
Generally accepted in most Western countries	• Other public holidays (such as Eid ul-Fitr • Mosques, Hindu temples • Male circumcision
Universally accepted	• Oriental restaurants • Oriental medicine

'immigrant neighbourhoods' and 'immigrant schools', and more generally to a mutual lack of understanding and to discrimination. High unemployment and poverty amongst the under-privileged groups in turn leads to criminality, which leads to **stigmatisation**, where there is an impression that 'all' members of an immigrant group are criminals or that 'all' indigenous people might think this.

Questions

- Have you ever suffered from stigmatisation?
- Have you ever stigmatised anybody?

One consequence of this is a growing feeling of insecurity and dissatisfaction amongst the various population groups. The social middle class responds by calling for greater safety, with the politicians reacting by introducing measures that are to the detriment of civil liberties, including the obligation to carry identification and the installation of more surveillance cameras in public areas. The police and domestic intelligence service received wider authorities that can lead to constitutionally enshrined human rights being impaired – the state spies on its own citizens.

The various aspects of this scenario amplify each other, which is again a form of positive feedback. This creates a breeding ground for violence and terror, a situation that could easily explode.

3.4 The lack of safety: terror, war, dictatorships

People that are excluded, or feel as if they are excluded, do not feel at home in our society. And when people do not feel at home, they go in search of a place where they will feel at home – in search of other ideas, other ideals, which are sometimes radical. Ideas that may fundamentally contradict the principles of our open and democratic society. This is something we have also experienced in our city, and not just amongst those who feel excluded or are excluded due to poverty. We also see this amongst those who feel excluded on the grounds of their ethnicity because of their faith – Islam. Many of these people are neither poor, nor deprived, nor poorly educated. But they do feel excluded, and as a result some of them shall become radicalised. And radicalisation can become a source of rioting, or even worse problems.

The preceding quote is part of a speech delivered a few years ago by the mayor of a large European city. The fact that radicalisation can indeed lead to rioting or worse was demonstrated in 2005 in France, when rioting by immigrant youths in the suburbs (*banlieues*) of Paris spread to other French cities in a wave of violence that lasted weeks and saw 9,000 cars torched, amongst other forms of damage.

Violence had also erupted earlier in the Netherlands.

Case 3.6 School on fire

Theo van Gogh was murdered in November 2004, shot dead by an assassin in Amsterdam who then took a knife to him. The murder of the well-known film-maker was inspired by religious Islamic motives.

A week later a number of youths in the village of Uden, Brabant, avenged the attack by setting the Islamic elementary school Bedir alight, which burnt to the ground. Racist slogans were chalked on the walls, including 'fucking Muslims' and a 'white power' sign.

The incident made international headlines. 'Fire-fighters struggled Tuesday night to put out the fire at the burning Bedir school in the southern town of Uden, where someone had scrawled "Theo rest in peace" in the building,' said the broadcaster CBS in the US. 'Eine Moschee im friesischen Heerenveen wird angezündet, eine Koranschule im Brabanter Uden brennt ab,' ('A mosque in the Frisian city of Heerenveen was set to fire, a Quran school in Uden burned down') in the words of the German Frankfurter Allgemeine Zeitung. The mosque in Friesland and the school in Uden were not the only targets, as many other incidents occurred. A storm of violence had broken out, in which Christians and Muslims attacked and counterattacked. A brief overview of the first ten days follows:

2 Nov. *Amsterdam:* Theo van Gogh is murdered.

4 Nov. *Utrecht:* arson attack on mosque. *Amsterdam:* Moroccan office vandalised. *Huizen:* attempted arson attack on An-Nasr mosque. *Breda:* attempted arson attack on mosque. *Groningen:* arson attack on mosque.

7 Nov. *Rotterdam:* arson attack on Mevlana mosque. *Rotterdam:* mosque vandalised. *Amsterdam:* EMCEMO (Euro-Mediterranean Centre for Migration and Development) vandalised.

8 Nov. *Eindhoven:* bomb attack on Tarieq Ibnoe Ziyad Islamic school. *Utrecht:* arson attack on Triumfator church. *Amersfoort:* arson attack on Immanuel church.

9 Nov. *Rotterdam:* attempted arson attack on two churches. *Uden:* arson attack on Bedir Islamic elementary school. *Boxmeer:* arson attack on Paulus church.

10 Nov. *Heerenveen:* arson attack on Sefaat mosque. *Rotterdam:* arson attack on church. *Eindhoven:* arson attack on Van Eupen Catholic school.

11 Nov. *Veendam:* mosque and town hall vandalised.

FIGURE 3.17 Dehumanisation, alienation from society, discrimination and social exclusion – all lead to riots and uprisings

Source: Lausanne, 2007, Wikimedia.

Case 3.6 shows how segregation and discrimination can easily become a breeding ground for mutual hate, expressed through riots, uprisings and violence. When the state responds to this with a major display of power and the use of police violence, the hatred escalates further and could ultimately even adopt the form of terror (Figure 3.17).

'Rogue states'

A minority of human beings live with a reasonable degree of freedom. There is a partial relationship between the level of prosperity and the degree of democracy, as is illustrated by the freedom index in Table 3.2. The countries with the greatest wealth almost all have a high degree of freedom and democracy, with the only exceptions all being small states such as Singapore. China, which is experiencing strong economic growth, might eventually demonstrate that prosperity and a low degree of freedom and democracy are possible in a large country. But on the other hand, not all democracies are wealthy, as shown by Brazil and India.

What holds for the exclusion of individual people in the wealthy nations likewise holds for entire countries on the world stage. This entails the exclusion of countries and peoples that do not receive a real opportunity to seriously participate in the international society. The characteristics of such countries are strikingly similar to those of individuals that have been excluded (see Table 3.4):

• Poverty and debt

  • Low level of education
  • Language barriers through the poor command of international languages (especially English)
  • A different religion and culture from those globally dominant (Greco-Roman history, Christianity, humanism)
  • Lack of infrastructure and an economic structure
  • Minimal participation in international economic traffic as a result of trade barriers and subsidies for manufacturers in wealthy nations
  • Minimal access to communication through information technology (IT) and television
  • Scant influence within international bodies (such as the World Bank, Security Council, G20 and NATO)
  • Jealousy of the rich regions
  • Stigmatisation (like the label 'rogue state')

And, just like the exclusion of individuals, the exclusion of countries also leads to discontent, expressed through the rejection of the Western culture, the amplification of extremism and even terrorism and war. This situation gave rise to terrorist attacks, such as those on the Twin Towers in New York City on 11 September 2001 (Figure 3.18).

Western countries and a number of others react to such threats and attacks using comparable means – abusive language, threats and attacks (Figure 3.19). The enemies are labelled 'rogue states', as is the case with Iran and North Korea, and they are isolated, insofar as is possible, on the world stage through cultural, political or trade sanctions. This rarely achieves the desired result, and the global exclusion of these states is actually intensified by it, leading to a vicious circle that amplifies the entire process instead of quelling it. Other countries, such as Afghanistan and Iraq, are attacked and seemingly neutralised, in which overwhelming military

FIGURE 3.18 The attack on the Twin Towers in New York City, 9 September 2001

Source: Michael Foran.

force is used, rendering Western troops almost completely invulnerable. This leads to an alternative form of warfare, where resistance to the all-powerful armies moves underground, as it did in Vietnam in the 1960s and 1970s, and the fighters continue as guerrillas or terrorists. The war then changes into a civil war, resulting in many victims.

In other parts of the world, including in a number of African nations and in the Philippines, poverty and exclusion also lead to harrowing civil wars. The militias involved have no compunction about kidnapping children and using them as **child soldiers** or slaves and prostitutes (Figure 3.20). In some instances, these wars degenerate into **genocides**, which was the case in Rwanda in 1994.

FIGURE 3.19 The war of the powerful uses high-tech machinery that leads to almost total invulnerability

Source: US Department of Defence: Michael Ammons, US Air Force.

Case 3.7 The frenzy of Rwanda

Students beheaded their lecturers and lecturers did the same to their students. Doctors clubbed their patients to death, or were murdered by them. It was 1994, and a wave of violence broke out amongst the seven million inhabitants of Rwanda. Arms, legs, ears and breasts were hacked off with machetes. Refugees hiding in churches were machine-gunned or burnt to death in the thousands by militant gangs and the army.

Rwanda is made up of two tribes – the Hutus and the Tutsis. They had been engaged in armed conflict with each other for years and when the president of the country, a Hutu, was murdered in 1994, tensions exploded to an extent never before seen. It was a conflict between two population groups, based on ethnic hatred, as was later explained. And while this was the case, it was not the entire story.

In the years preceding the great Rwandan genocide, it was among the world's most densely populated nations. However, unlike developed countries with a modern agricultural system capable of feeding its population, Rwanda practiced traditional agricultural methods. In the 1960s and 1970s agrarian production temporarily increased as a result of the introduction of new crops, but the population increased just as quickly – by 3 to 4 percent a year – and it continued to increase even when agricultural production settled. To keep up with the pace of growth, forests were felled and fields planted three times a year with no fallow period.

FIGURE 3.20   The war of the powerless deploys child soldiers, such as this 12-year-old boy who is a member of the ARVN (Army of the Republic of Vietnam). He holds an M79 grenade launcher

Source: U.S. Signal Corps, Archival Research Catalog of the National Archives and Records Administration, USA.

Erosion subsequently caused the fertile top layer of soil to be washed away, with mudslides tearing down hills and the rivers running brown with soil. The growing population meant that plots of ground became ever smaller when they were passed from father to son. Young men without land were no longer able to live by their own means in order to start a family. The population became increasingly dense, and almost everyone went hungry.

In the early 1990s soil deterioration and a period of drought, possibly partly due to global warming, led to food production falling dramatically. In spite of this the population continued to grow. Something had to give, somehow. The army and extremist militant groups incited the population to violence, or forced them to commit such acts, while machetes were bought and distributed on a large scale. The murder of the Rwandan president was the spark, and the ancient hatred that existed between the two population groups was the seam along which this untenable situation burst open.

In around a hundred days it is estimated that 800,000 people were killed. Another two million fled to surrounding countries, with the murders continuing in refugee camps.

After a series of regional wars in the next years, the situation had become sufficiently peaceful in 2004 that a national settlement could be reached. That year saw the start of the International Rwanda Tribunal, under the authority of the United Nations, and those responsible for the genocide are now being charged and sentenced. But it is an impossible task to sentence all those who are guilty – it is estimated that a third of the population participated actively in the murders, mutilations and rapes, whether voluntarily or under coercion (Figure 3.21).

FIGURE 3.21 Kigali, capital of Rwanda: the Rwanda Genocide Memorial in the Ntarama Church, where 10,000 people were murdered on 7 April 1994

Source: d_proffer, flickr.

Questions

- Is the fact that Rwanda is a developing country with a low level of education the reason why this genocide could happen?
- Or – if you are living in a wealthy nation – could something like this also occur in your own homeland, given that the circumstances may one day become comparable?
- Or could it even happen on a global scale?

Civilian victims in countries like Iraq and Afghanistan and the hundreds of thousands of murdered Hutus and Tutsis in Rwanda all demonstrate that, of all these vicious circles of poverty, exclusion, despair, hatred and violence, it is always the same people who suffer the most – the civilians. Driven out of house and home, they flee en masse for unknown

FIGURE 3.22 Refugees, on their way to a refugee camp in Tanzania, are carrying everything they own

Source: Dave Blume, flickr.

destinations (Figure 3.22), frequently to refugee camps in other countries, which in many instances are just as poor as their homelands. Some of them flee to the wealthy countries of Europe and North America, where social exclusion once again awaits for many of them, this time based on mistrust, xenophobia and discrimination. And so the circle is closed for these people too.

The preceding demonstrates that the entire complex of poverty, exclusion and violence is, both at a national and individual level, deeply anchored in the fabric of human systems in the form of a structural flaw. It is impossible to successfully solve just one of these problems while simultaneously ignoring the others. This not only applies to the problems that the impoverished encounter, it also holds for those which the well-off are confronted with, such as the lack of safety and the feeling of losing one's culture through the influx of immigrants. What this means is that it is just as important for the rich as it is for the poor that poverty, discrimination and exclusion are banished around the globe.

3.5 The fabric of man, nature and the economy

Vicious circles: problems that invoke or amplify each other, often recurrently in the form of positive feedback. This chapter has provided a few examples concerning the aspects of people and profit, whereas the previous chapter examined planet and profit. There are countless examples of the three Ps influencing each other. One of these is the Rwandan genocide, where all three of the Ps were associated in a hopeless situation.

People: The population of Rwanda grew exponentially at a very high rate. Thanks to medical facilities, child mortality was lowered and the population doubled in less than 25 years. There were also major differences between the people in respect of power and prosperity (or rather, the degree of poverty).

Planet: Wide scale deforestation took place to make space for agriculture. The fertile soil washed away and the Earth became parched.

Profit: The population increased, the resources for living decreased. Sufficient prosperity would have made it possible to comprehensively modernise agriculture, which might have solved the problem of hunger. But there was little prosperity, and that is why parents needed many children to care for them in their old age. It was impossible to save for the future. And so the families remained large and the population grew rapidly.

This example shows that when the three Ps are under serious threat, a situation can suddenly and dramatically collapse. But there are also less explosive examples that demonstrate how important it is that, where there are issues of unsustainability, the solution takes into account that the three Ps must be balanced. The following case shows how *not* to do this.

Case 3.8 Climate compensation?

Mount Elgon National Park, in the African state of Uganda, has seen trees planted on a large scale in recent years. The intention of the four-million-euro project was to compensate for CO_2 emissions in Western countries. When the project was launched, the area was still largely used as agricultural land, and so the local farmers were involuntarily displaced, receiving cash compensation. This did not go well, as the farmers found themselves unable to start afresh with the money – at best they were able to live off the money for a while, but they could not use it to generate fresh income. Most were unable to obtain new land or a salaried job, although a few were temporarily employed as foresters. In reality, the displaced farmers had only one option, and they took it. They illegally returned to the area and felled many of the young trees. By August 2007, of the three million trees that had been planted, half a million had been chopped down.

This local tragedy was able to happen because people in Western countries had a very one-sided approach to the climate issue. They believed they had found a good solution in Uganda, but they neglected both the traditions and cultural interests of the local population as well as their financial ones. Evidently they did not realise that a pile of money is not the same as an income and a place to live. In other words, *planet* received more attention than *people* and *profit*. The approach was unbalanced.

Fortunately, there are also other examples that demonstrate all the opportunities available when the approach is properly balanced.

Case 3.9   Sustainable cocoa in Ghana

Chocolate brings joy to many. But hardly to the ones who produce the basic stuff – cocoa. The farmers, on several continents, deliver their harvest to big international companies, which are in control of the entire cultivation and transport chain, profiting hugely while leaving the farmers in poverty. They, their women and even their children make many hours, labouring in the plantations, of which the soil gets exhausted.

Or so it was – because things are changing rapidly. All over the world, cooperation is growing between farmers, local organizations, governments and multinational companies.

The largest cocoa purchaser is Mondelēz International, with brands like Milka, Toblerone, Cadbury and Côte d'Or. The latter reminds of the Gold Coast, a former British colony that is now the country of Ghana, one of the members of the ECOWAS that will be the topic of Section 5.4. Indeed, Ghana is one of the largest cocoa suppliers for Mondelēz. For present-day Ghana, cocoa is very important. It is the country's major export commodity, accounting for about 30 percent of Ghana's total export earnings.

Since more than a decade, Mondelēz accepts responsibility for the fate of the farmers and their families. Through its Cocoa Life program, the company cooperates with the Ghanaian government and with local and international non-governmental organizations (NGOs) combined in the Ghana Cocoa Platform, attempting to bring real improvements. Sustainability issues that are addressed in Mondelēz's

$400 million global commitment are e.g. deforestation, crop resilience, community development, gender equality, child labour, adaptations to climate change, and reducing the carbon footprint.

One of the Cocoa Life principles is called 'aligned with our sourcing'. This implies that all members of the supply chain, including the farmers themselves, are seen as active and equal partners. For this purpose, the program pays much attention to agrotechnical and financial trainings for farmers, with an emphasis on empowering women. For children, there are programs dedicated to education and literacy, as a crucial means to eliminate child labour entirely; see Figure 3.23. The program is not organized top-down, as local communities themselves develop a Community Action Plan (CAP) which provides a detailed roadmap for community activation.

Some of the concrete goals of Cocoa Life are:

- Help farmers improve yields and earn higher incomes via the application of good agricultural practices. These should be combined with better access to demonstration parcels and the distribution of improved planting material.
- Enable men and women to work together to transform their communities by developing action plans to improve infrastructure, gender equality and education; build a sense of opportunity and ownership within communities.
- Improve business skills and provide access to microcredit so that farmers can develop additional sources of income and reinvest in their businesses.
- Protect the land and forests in which cocoa is grown to maintain ecosystems and provide viable environments and farming land for future generations.

FIGURE 3.23 Cocoa Life is an attempt to make cocoa beans (centre) not only a source for chocolate but also a financial source for education for all children in the cocoa farming communities

Source: Letizia Piatti, flickr.

Ghana is not the only country where Cocoa Life is active; and Mondelēz is not the only cocoa purchasing multinational that is attempting to operate more sustainably. Many actors cooperate worldwide in the World Cocoa Foundation, with its global CocoaAction strategy. Other involved companies are e.g. Mars, Nestlé, Cargill, Ferrero and Hershey.

Cases 3.8 and 3.9 demonstrate how complex the issues are that sustainable development must solve. Many of these problems amplify or influence each other, and Figure 3.24 shows these influences and interactions. The graphic, even though it might seem complicated, is really only a simplified representation of the actual situation. It is a more complete version of the wickerwork diagram (Figure 2.1) at the start of Chapter 2 – the fabric upon which human society and the economy is constructed, as a component of planet Earth's ecosystem.

Table 3.6 meanwhile contains a few concrete examples of the interaction between various forms of unsustainability. These aside, there are a huge number of other examples one can come up with. In this table, six different kinds of unsustainability (ranging from overpopulation to resources exhaustion) act as *causes* (shown in a top row of the table), influencing each other, as well as *consequences* (shown in the left column), being influenced by each other. As an example: climate change may lead to bad harvests (e.g. through droughts), which causes poverty and hunger. Each of the six kinds of unsustainability in Table 3.6 even reinforces itself; for instance, climate change causes the ice cap of the North Pole to melt; but the ice is highly reflective, bouncing a part of the sunlight directly back into space. When the melting of the ice lowers the level of reflexivity (the 'albedo') of the planet, more and more light will actually reach the surface, and so the climate change reinforces itself – a topic that will be discussed more deeply in Chapter 7.

Both Figure 3.24 and Table 3.6 demonstrate that there is no point in tackling all the part-causes of unsustainability separately – there will be little chance of success. The power of thinking in terms of sustainable development lies in understanding the relationship between the different themes, followed by finding integral solutions that do not cure just the symptoms, but rather the causes. In other words, sustainable development serves as the bridge that links together the themes the world is wrestling with. See Figure 3.25; thanks to this 'bridge' we are able to solve them all.

The bridge symbolises the holistic vision discussed in Section 3.1, through which the different parts of the worldwide ecological, economic and human systems are considered as a single interconnected whole. Figure 3.24 demonstrates both this connection as well as a large number of constituent parts. Investigating these parts in detail is called an **analytical approach**, which is the opposite of the holistic approach. In order to find good sustainable solutions, one must in turn examine the whole system and zoom in on separate components

FIGURE 3.24 (NEXT PAGE)   The various unsustainability issues influence each other in a highly complex manner

Source: Harley D. Nygren, NOAA, 1950; Peter Ellis, 2006, Wikimedia; Jan-Pieter Nap, Wikimedia; UNEP / Topham; Vinod Panicker, Wikimedia; Love Krittaya, 2006, Wikimedia; Mark Knobil, 2005, Wikimedia; Mikhail Esteves, 2007, Wikimedia; Robert R. McRill, 2005, Wikimedia; Marcello Casal Jr., 2006, Wikimedia; Hibernian, 2006, Wikimedia; U.S. Navy: Eric J. TIlford; Sirpa air, Wikimedia; Bernard bill5, 2004, Wikimedia; Rama, 2005, Wikimedia; Mark Knobil, 2005, Wikimedia; Bree, 2006, Wikimedia; SvdMolen, 2005, Wikimedia; Philip Gabrielsen, 2005, Wikimedia; Archivo Gráfico de la Nación (Argentina), 1978; El C, 2005, Wikimedia.

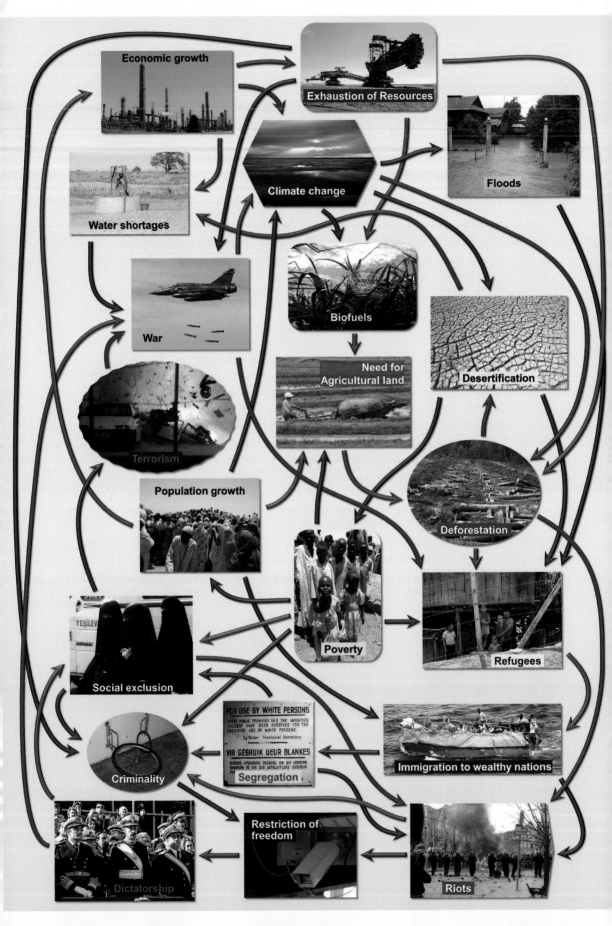

TABLE 3.6 Examples of interactions between types of unsustainability

Consequences	Causes					
	People		Planet		Prosperity	
	Overpopulation	War and violence	Climate change	Environmental degradation	Poverty and hunger	Resources exhausted
Overpopulation	Exponential growth	War refugees	Lower yield	Areas become inhabitable due to environmental disasters	Children to provide in one's old age	Economic refugees
War and violence	Mutual aggression (e.g. Rwanda)	Revenge	Wars for clean water	Resistance by primitive people	Armed resistance	Wars about ore-producing regions
Climate change	Rising production of greenhouse gases	Nuclear winter through radioactive fallout	Change of albedo	Deforestation leads to a decrease in precipitation	Forest fires due to shortage of agricultural land	Combustion of oil, gas, coal, etc.
Environmental degradation	Nature makes way for cities, roads and recreation	Defoliating substances (e.g. in the Vietnam War)	Disruption of the ecosystem	Domino effect due to ecosystem being unbalanced	Habitat loss	Extraction from oil sands
Poverty and hunger	Exhaustion of agricultural lands	Destruction of manufacturing resources and staff	Bad harvests	Reduction in fish catches	Debt burdens through loans	Mines exhausted
Resources exhausted	Ever-increasing number of people sharing resources	Destruction of infrastructure and buildings	Scarcity of fresh water	Loss of natural materials	Loss of timber due to forest fires	More extensive exploitation due to price rises

FIGURE 3.25 Sustainable development is the bridge that connects the themes with which the world is wrestling, making them solvable

and details thereof, then step back once again and look at the big picture. This rhythmic interchange between the analytical and the holistic approaches requires some degree of flexibility, which is no easy task, as many people suffer from the tendency of becoming lost in the details and missing the big picture – not being able to see the forest for the trees, as it were. But it is the very combination of these two approaches that gives rise to structurally sustainable solutions.

A large number of aids and strategies are at our disposal to bring about these solutions, and it is now time to further examine these 'sources of vigour'.

Summary

Chapter 3 examined the flaws in the fabric in the relationship between man and society. The main flaws are

- An imbalance in the Triple P, as a result of which the economy almost always prevails. This is evident from, amongst other things, the fact that multinational companies often exercise greater influence than the democratically elected governments of independent countries; that the GDP is not calculated in a 'green' manner; and that, in the dominant view, humans and the natural environment are considered as components of the economic system, instead of the other way around.
- Another flaw is the economic necessity of continuous economic – and material – growth, which cannot be sustained in the long term.

- The existence of trade barriers and subsidies constitute an impediment to poor nations for economic development. The inequality in the world is also maintained in other ways, thanks to the debt trap and the poverty trap that countries and individuals respectively fall into. There is a direct relationship between these two factors, as Third World poverty results in refugees, a portion of which end up in the wealthy nations. In recent years, this gap has actually become greater rather than smaller.
- One consequence is that people and countries are subject to social exclusion and discrimination.
- Another consequence of the emphasis on economic efficiency is that people become alienated from society, leading to dehumanisation.
- All these factors lead to a lack of safety in the form of criminality, vandalism, terrorism and even war and genocide.

All those flaws detailed in Chapters 2 and 3 influence each other. This makes the complex fabric of the human world extraordinarily difficult to change. But it is not an impossible task, and the first step in the right direction involves understanding the relationships between all the topics of sustainability.

A more detailed summary can be found on the website of this book.

4

SOURCES OF VIGOUR

In this chapter the following topics and concepts will be discussed:

4.1   International organisations
4.2   Ideas and sources of inspiration
4.3   People
4.4   Nature
4.5   Science and technology
4.6   Entrepreneurship
4.7   Students
4.8   The sustainable development goals

A glossary containing all terms in both this chapter and others is available on the website of this book.

Case 4.1   Rio, 1992

On 3 June 1992, 47,000 people gathered in Rio de Janeiro, one of Brazil's biggest cities. They came from 178 nations and counted 108 heads of state and government amongst their number.

This was the **Earth Summit**, the largest conference ever, which saw participants deliberating for two weeks on the future of the planet and of humanity.

The conference had been organised by the United Nations, and bore the official title of the '**United Nations Conference on Environment and Development**' **(UNCED)**. The theme: sustainable development.

One of the outcomes was the **Rio Declaration**, in which a number of basic principles were agreed to, such as:

> *Human beings are entitled to a healthy and productive life in harmony with nature.* (Principle 1)
> *States shall cooperate in a spirit of global partnership to conserve, protect and restore the health and integrity of the Earth's ecosystem.* (Principle 7)
> *The creativity, ideals and courage of the youth of the world should be mobilized to forge a global partnership in order to achieve sustainable development and ensure a better future for all.* (Principle 21)
> *Peace, development and environmental protection are interdependent and indivisible.* (Principle 25)

The summit also saw the drafting of an action plan for the twenty-first century that became known as **Agenda 21**. This bulky document lists a long series of policy goals, towards which the signatory nations promised to work. All nations were called upon to draw up **National Sustainable Development Strategies (NSDS)** for that purpose.

Furthermore 'Rio' also resulted in four international conventions: on climate change, biodiversity, desertification and sea fishing.

Today **Local Agenda 21** projects have been launched in thousands of villages and towns on the basis of the original Agenda 21, through which sustainability projects are undertaken on a smaller scale, closer to the people.

By 2009 108 nations adopted a National Strategy and started to implement it, while another 13 are engaged in developing one. (There are ca. 200 countries in the world.) In 2015, the NSDS received a new impulse due to the launch of the Sustainable Development Goals (SDGs), as will be described later in this chapter.

The UN also set up a new body, the **Commission for Sustainable Development (CSD)**, which provides guidelines on sustainable developments and assists nations in mapping out their policy.

The Earth Summit was a significant '**source of vigour**' for sustainable development, and it did not end with Rio. A decade later, in 2002, another major summit was held, this time in Johannesburg (South Africa) – the World Summit on Sustainable Development (WSSD). During this so-called Rio+10 conference, delegates checked the results achieved thus far and set up new targets.

In 2012, Rio de Janeiro was again the stage for the Rio+20 conference, the United Nations Conference on Sustainable Development (UNCSD).

The previous chapters covered a long list of flaws in the fabric of the systems that are a part of humanity. Fortunately, there are also many positive things, as we can see in this chapter – organisations, people, ideas and technologies that can be deployed for the purpose of sustainable development.

The first part of this chapter deals with major international organisation, and two examples of these will be comprehensively dealt with – the United Nations and the European Union.

Other sources of vigour will subsequently be covered, such as the natural world itself and people, both individuals and groups. We will also take a look at science and technology, which can give us important tools, and companies, which are just as indispensable with regard to sustainable development. All of these can be considered 'sources of vigour for the system'. They are the counterparts to the flaws in the fabric of the system, and they give us hope for the future.

4.1 International organisations

The Rio Earth Summit, detailed in Case 4.1, was a major tour de force on the part of the United Nations. One of the conference's major outcomes was that all the countries recognised the connection between development, the environment and peace, a connection that was then elaborated in the form of people, planet and profit (later: prosperity) by the new UN body, the CSD (Commission for Sustainable Development); see Table 4.1.

TABLE 4.1 Themes of sustainable development, according to the UN Commission for Sustainable Development

Theme	Sub-theme	Theme	Sub-theme
People		**Planet**	
Equality	Poverty	Atmosphere	Climate change
	Gender equality		Depletion of the ozone layer
Health	Food		Air quality
	Mortality	Land	Agriculture
	Hygiene		Forests
	Drinking water		Desertification
	Healthcare		Urbanisation
Education	Level of education	Ocean, seas	Coastal region
	Literacy	and coasts	Fishery
Housing	Housing conditions	Clean water	Amount of water
Security	Crime		Water quality
Population	Population growth	Biodiversity	Ecosystems
			Species
Profit		**Organisational**	
Economic structure	Economic performance	Organisational structure	Strategy for sustainable society
	Trade		International cooperation
	Financial situation	Organisational capacity	Access to information
Consumption and production patterns	Use of natural resources		Communication infrastructure
	Energy consumption		Science and technology
	Waste production and management		Tackling disasters
	Transport		

Source: CSD (2001).

As Table 4.1 shows, the CSD added the issue of 'organisational' to the three Ps, dealing with issues that are concerned with all three of the Ps simultaneously.

There are a great many international organisations that focus on sustainable development or its components. The UN is the biggest of these by far. It was established in 1945, just a few months after the conclusion of World War II, and its core bodies are the General Assembly and the Security Council.

All 192 member states of the UN are represented in the General Assembly. The smaller nations have a relatively large influence in it, due to the fact that there are more small ones than large ones. But the General Assembly is unable to make any decisions with far-reaching consequences, such as imposing sanctions or armed intervention.

The Security Council consists of only 15 members, five of which are permanent ones. These are the United Kingdom, France, the United States, Russia and China. The other ten hold seats on the Council for two-year terms. Each of the five permanent members wield veto power – if even one of them votes against a draft resolution, it is rejected.

In spite of this veto power, which has been exercised on frequent occasions, the body has managed to achieve quite a bit. The Security Council has, for example, decided to deploy armed intervention forces, which it has done on dozens of occasions, such as Cyprus (starting in 1964), Somalia (1993–1995), Bosnia (1997–2004) and Ethiopia (2000–2002).

In 2005, the United Nations and all of its member states adopted the **Responsibility to Protect** (**R2P**) principle, which obliges all national governments to prevent genocide, war crimes, ethnic cleansing and crimes against humanity. In addition to this, the international community also has an obligation: if a state is manifestly failing to protect its populations, the international community must be prepared to take collective action to protect populations. Based on the R2P principle, international interventions have taken place several times, e.g. in the Central African Republic in 2013.

The Security Council has set up a number of courts to try war criminals, like the Rwanda Tribunal and the Tribunal for the former Yugoslavia. New ad-hoc courts will probably no longer be set up, as the permanent **International Criminal Court** (**ICC**) was launched in 2002, with its seat in The Hague. This court convicted or indicted warlords, former presidents and leaders of terror groups for war crimes and crimes against humanity, such as mass murder, rape and massive abuse of children as child soldiers of sex slaves.

The UN has many agencies. A few of these are **UNEP** (the United Nations Environmental Programme); **UNESCO** (the United Nations Educational, Scientific and Cultural Organization); **UNICEF** (the United Nations Children's Fund); **UNAIDS**, which as the name suggests fights Aids and assists its victims; and the **ILO** (the International Labour Organization), which promotes decent work for all adults and combats child labour.

A number of other organisations work in close cooperation with the UN. The **WHO** (World Health Organization) exists to further healthcare, while the **FAO** deals with food and agriculture. The World Bank and the International Monetary Fund (**IMF**) are in turn responsible for the financial aspects of development aid and poverty. The preceding is only a small sample, and the total working field of the UN and related organisations is very large.

In Chapter 3 the UNDP was mentioned, the United Nations Development Programme. The following case provides a picture of how the UN assists development projects in villages and towns on a local scale.

Case 4.2 Cerro Santa Ana

Only a short time ago Cerro Santa Ana, on the outskirts of the city Guayaquil in Ecuador, South America, was a slum. The inhabitants, almost 5,000 of them, struggled to get by and the area had a poor reputation for crime and disease. Nobody went there unless they had to.

Five years later, the suburb is blossoming, drawing 20,000 tourists a week – that is how picturesque it has become (Figure 4.1). The banks of the Guayas River have been rehabilitated and the area is no longer prone to flooding. A sewer system has also been installed, considerably improving the health of the locals. Crime has decreased, and the streets are safe.

Seven years before work started on the restoration of Cerro Santa Ana, an enterprising mayor took over the reins of the city of Guayaquil. Supported by the UNDP and the European Union, he developed the city's entire infrastructure, and roads were tarred, tunnels built and sewer systems laid on. A bus line was created and parks were built. Local companies participated, which saw the average income of bricklayers, carpenters and gardeners rise, with the shopowners' income also rising as a result. The self-confidence of the people increased and a downward spiral was broken.

FIGURE 4.1 The beautifully restored neighborhood of Las Peñas, Cerro Santa Ana, Ecuador

Source: Las Peñas, Cerro Santa Ana, Guyaquil, Ecuador, Wikimedia.

Along the banks of the Guayas River, which no longer floods, museums, shopping galleries, parks and playgrounds were created, all of which attracted visitors from afar.

But the most amazing thing is that all these improvements were introduced at a time when the rest of Ecuador was doing badly, especially in the economic sense. Today Guayaquil is a flourishing city, and Cerro Santa Ana is a colourful neighbourhood. The approach adopted in the last 12 years is used as an example of urban renewal, where people come from all over the world to see how it can be done.

The great thing about the development of Guayaquil and the area of Cerro Santa Ana is that the project was launched at the initiative of the people themselves, and was for a large part undertaken by them too. This is an excellent example of a bottom-up approach. The UNDP and the EU assisted with knowledge and money, but that was all. The inhabitants are proud of their achievements, and that is the primary reason for the project's success.

Questions

- Do you know of any examples of successful projects in your own area that involve sustainable development?
- Have you ever participated in one of these projects?

The UN has spent decades devoting much attention to the relationship between education and sustainable development. This work has been upped from 1 January 2005, which was the date that marked the start of the **United Nations Decade of Education for Sustainable Development**. For the space of a decade, a great deal of focus was placed on arranging education around the world in such a way that the schools and students would be able (both now and later, as graduated professionals) to dedicate themselves to sustainable development.

Another powerful international body is the **OECD**, the Organisation for Economic Cooperation and Development. The OECD counts 35 democratic nations amongst its members, including almost all the wealthy ones. The body focuses on sustainable economic growth and employment, as well as on raising the standard of living in the developing nations.

The European Union

Another example of an international organisation that is very important to sustainable development is the EU – the European Union. Its significance is evident through the following case.

Case 4.3 The row about Iraq

In March 2003 a huge fight erupted between the leaders of a number of Western nations. In the one corner were the United States, United Kingdom and Spain, all of whom believed that it was a good time to start a war against Iraq, while in the other corner were France, Germany and Russia, who were bitterly opposed to it.

The spat between French President Jacques Chirac, German Chancellor Gerhard Schröder and UK Prime Minister Tony Blair was particularly intense and painful, as all three represented a country that is a member of the EU. The EU failed for the umpteenth time to create a unified front in terms of foreign policy.

War broke out against Iraq in that same month. The television and newspapers were naturally packed with news about it, but another story – one at least as notable – did not make it into a single newspaper or feature on a single news broadcast. This was the fact that war *didn't* break out between France, the United Kingdom and Germany.

It might amaze you to read this – why would war be waged between those nations? It would not even occur to anyone, certainly not to Chirac, Schröder and Blair? And indeed, the thought of a war in Europe would not have occurred to these leaders, which is precisely the power that modern Europe is in possession of. You must bear in mind that what we today consider a given has not been around for such a long time.

A telling example can be found by the duo of France and the United Kingdom. Between 1066 and 1800 the French and English kingdoms went to war with each other no less than 33 times. They were at war for over 200 years of that 734-year period – more than a quarter of the time. The average time between wars amounted to less than 17 years. Countless people, both soldiers and civilians, were killed or wounded or suffered from hunger, sickness and poverty. The conflicts did not end in 1800 either, as this marked the start of Napoleon Bonaparte's bloody conquest of Europe.

The United Kingdom and France were no more violent than other European nations, as demonstrated in Table 4.2, which provides an overview of the wars in Europe during an arbitrary 50-year period, just a few centuries ago.

Over this period of half a century 22 wars were waged in Europe, and this list is probably not even complete. Moreover, Table 4.2 only covers the wars fought *within* Europe's borders. The states of Europe also fought a series of wars outside of the continent against each other and other powers, especially in the colonies.

The period between 1800 and 1850 was comparatively peaceful! There were other eras when the bloodshed was even worse.

And now there is the EU, established in 1951 under the name 'European Coal and Steel Community'. It consisted of six members, including France, West Germany and Italy, whereas the United Kingdom and a number of other states joined in 1973. A few expansions later, and the EU in 2013 came to consist of 28 nations and around 500 million inhabitants. However, the United Kingdom is preparing to leave the EU, the so-called **Brexit**, after a referendum in 2016.

TABLE 4.2 European wars, first half of the eighteenth century

War	Period	Belligerent countries and states
Great Northern War	1700–1721	Sweden, Russia, Poland, Denmark, Bremen, Hannover and Prussia
War of Spanish Succession	1701–1714	Habsburg Empire, Great Britain, Dutch Republic, Spanish Netherlands (Belgium), France, Spain, Bavaria, Cologne, Savoy, Prussia, Hanover, Denmark
Camisard Rebellion	1702–1705	France
Kuruc Uprising	1703–1711	Habsburg Empire, Hungary
Bavarian People's Uprising	1705–1706	Bavaria
Russo-Turkish War	1710–1711	Russia, Ottoman Empire
Second War of Villmerger	1712	Swiss cantons
Gorizia Peasant Revolt	1713	Gorizia (Northern Italy)
Jacobite Rebellion	1715–1716	Scotland, England
Austro-Turkish War	1716–1718	Habsburg Empire, Ottoman Empire
War of the Quadruple Alliance	1718–1720	Spain, Holy Roman Empire (i.e. Germany, more or less), France, Dutch Republic, Great Britain
Appell Krieg	1726–1727	East Frisia, Denmark
Corsican Revolt	1729–1732	Corsica, Genova, Habsburg Empire
War of the Polish Succession	1733–1735	Poland, Russia, France, Lorraine, Spanish Netherlands (Belgium), Sardinia, Habsburg Empire, Prussia, Spain
Corsican Revolt	1733–1743	Corsica, Genova, France
Russo-Turkish War	1735–1739	Russia, Ottoman Empire, Habsburg Empire
War of Jenkin's Ear	1739–1741	Great Britain, Spain
War of the Austrian Succession	1740–1748	Habsburg Empire, Prussia, Saxony, Bavaria, France, Great Britain, Dutch Republic, Savoy, Spain
Russo-Swedish War	1741–1743	Sweden, Russia
Transylvanian Revolt	1744	Transylvania, Habsburg Empire
Jacobite Rebellion	1745	England, Scotland, France
Corsican Revolt	1745–1769	Corsica, Genova, Savoy, England, France

Source: WHKMLA (2009)

According to the International Monetary Fund (IMF), the EU's GDP amounts to 16.5 trillion dollars (in 2016; by comparison, the GDP of the US is 18.5 trillion dollars, China's is 11.4 trillion dollars, Japan's stands at 4.7 trillion dollars, India's at 2.3 trillion, and Russia's is 1.3 trillion dollars). The EU is an extremely diverse body, with 24 official languages, more than 50 regional minority languages and three official alphabets (Latin, Greek and Cyrillic). The EU has now existed for over 50 years, and what is really striking is the fact that there has *never been a war between the members of the EU.*

That does not mean that the EU is the reason that war has not been waged between the members. It is rather that there has been an evolution in Europe with a variety of consequences, including peace between the member states and the establishment and growth of the EU. The years since World War II are consequently unique – never before have so many European nations experienced such a lengthy period of peace.

Today the EU has become a leading source of vigour for peace, democracy and human rights. This is evident from a number of things, first and foremost being that democracy is infectious – at least, in Europe it is. Furthermore, human rights follow in democracy's wake. The recent history of Greece, Spain and Portugal bear witness to this. Around the 1970s they were all countries living under dictatorships, with the people oppressed and living in poverty. In part thanks to pressure exercised by democratic nations in Western Europe, all three transformed into democracies between 1974 and 1976 when the regimes were peacefully removed or (in the case of Spain) the dictator died. Greece joined the EU (then still known as the European Economic Community) in 1981, followed by the Iberian nations in 1986. Since joining, the economies of these countries prospered for many years, with the per capita incomes (the GDP) rising to levels approaching those of the rest of the EU, even though they had been considerably less in 1975 – although the financial crisis starting in 2007 showed that their economic position is more vulnerable than that of many other EU nations. Human rights are likewise just as sacrosanct as they are in other EU member states.

Since that time, other countries have also aspired to join the EU. In the wake of the mostly bloodless revolution in the late 1980s and early 1990s, countries in Eastern Europe worked hard to implement democracy, human rights and a modern economy, in part because these are prerequisites for acceding to the EU. By 2004, ten countries had managed to fulfil the requirements and joined the Union, with Romania and Bulgaria following in 2007 and Croatia in 2013. More countries are on the way to membership.

In 2012, the European Union received the **Nobel Peace Prize**. The Nobel Committee unanimously decided this because the EU "for over six decades contributed to the advancement of peace and reconciliation, democracy and human rights in Europe".

Questions

- Has the fact that no wars are fought in the EU nations ever struck you?
- Is it conceivable that the situation might one day change to such a degree that war will once again erupt between countries in Western Europe?
- Is it realistic to believe that war could also be relegated to history in the rest of the world? If you believe it is, how many years would that take? If you believe it isn't, why not?

Three capitals

The trio of people, planet and profit is not only applicable to *the problems*, but can also be used to categorise the *sources of vigour* into groups. The outcome is an overview of **three capitals**: people, nature and the environment, and the economy. Table 4.3 contains examples of how the UN and the EU contribute to these capitals.

The idea of adopting the approach of three capitals is derived from the World Bank. Stock is linked to each capital, making it possible to express in figures how strong or weak a nation or region is in respect of each of these capitals.

The Centre for Sustainable Development Brabant, Telos, created a method for calculating these stocks in the regions of a country. The institute drew up a list of stocks, as shown in

TABLE 4.3 The *people – planet – profit* capitals of a few organisations

	United Nations (and related organisations)	European Union (and Council of Europe)
People	• Unesco • UNDP • UNAIDS • WHO • ILO • UN Population Fund (UNFPA) • Decade of Education for Sustainable Development	• Succeeded in preventing war between member states • European Convention on Human Rights • European Court of Human Rights • European Parliament • Democracy and human rights a prerequisite for membership
Planet	• UNEP • Montreal Protocol for the protection of the ozone layer • Kyoto Protocol combating global warming	• European Environmental Agency (EAA) • European environmental legislation • Ecolabel (overseen by the European Commission)
Profit	• World Bank • IMF • Economic Commissions for Africa, Europe, Latin America, etc.	• Euro • European Central Bank • European Court of Auditors • Economic prerequisites for membership

TABLE 4.4 The three capitals (*people – planet – profit*) according to Telos

People	Planet	Profit
Solidarity	Air	Economic structure
Health	Soil	Infrastructure
Education	Landscape	Capital goods
Living environment	Mineral resources	Labour
Culture	Surface water	Knowledge
Citizenship	Groundwater	Energy and raw materials
Consumption pattern	Nature	

Source: Telos (2004).

Table 4.4. Further details on these stocks can be found in the spreadsheet titled **Three capitals.xls** on the website of this book.

It is interesting to compare this table to that of the United Nations' Commission on Sustainable Development (CSD), which can be seen in Table 4.1. Although they have common ground there are also differences, and it is evident from a comparison that it is no simple task to precisely locate every conceivable topic in one of the three Ps – there are issues that transcend the categories. One of these could be the expertise of a company's staff, which is the knowledge and experience they contain in their heads (people), and which is available to the company (profit). The PPP schedule is consequently not a 'firm' categorisation, but rather a way of thinking that has both benefits and limitations.

4.2 Ideas and sources of inspiration

Chapter 1 described how sustainable development takes place thanks to paradigm shifts. The chapter showed in detail how the paradigm of 'control' makes way in a variety of manners for 'adaptation'. New paradigms, and hence surprising new ways for examining the actual situation, are strong motivational forces for sustainable development. Many of them constitute a new way of expressing changes in the underlying fundamental values of humans, cultures and peoples.

Solidarity

One of the most fundamental values behind the idea of sustainable development is a feeling of solidarity – solidarity between people and also solidarity between people and the natural environment. The previous examples of the United Nations and the European Union are expressions of this feeling of solidarity between nations and between people.

Further scientific insights contribute to the profound shift in values towards this feeling of solidarity. A deeper knowledge with respect to ecosystems and the complex interactions of all their components – including humans – make it clear that in an objective sense we have much stronger ties to our natural environment than was previously realised. Furthermore, our knowledge of the neurology and psychology of people and animals has taught us that our brains, hormones and instincts resemble those of other mammals much more closely than was thought until recently. This knowledge is further amplified by the rapidly increasing learning gleaned from genetics. At the same time we are conscious that evolution means that man not only has much in common with all other living species, but is also directly related to them, a factor that intensifies that feeling of solidarity many have with the natural environment. Then there is also the solidarity one feels with people in far-off countries, which is growing thanks to faster new media and communication channels, including television, websites, email, YouTube, online chatting and Twitter, all of which put people around the entire world in direct contact with each other.

An immediate consequence of this awareness is the growth in international solidarity. People gain something of an understanding of the welfare of others, both those close to home and further away as well as those in the future (inter-generational solidarity). This solidarity is actually the concept behind the Brundtland definition of sustainable development, in that it "meets the needs of the present [generation]", meaning solidarity between here and there, but goes on to state "without compromising the ability of future generations to meet their own needs", meaning solidarity between now and later.

Sources of inspiration

There are many old and new texts that a large number of people consider to be inspiring. These could be ancient tracts, such as the Bible, which urges Christians to be responsible on the basis of stewardship for others and for their environment, or other holy books like the Koran, the Bhagavad Gita or the Tao Te Ching. There are also more recent tracts that express this feeling of solidarity. One moving example is the 1854 address by Chief Seattle, head of the Duwamish tribe of Native Americans. He received a proposal from the American president to sell his tribal lands to white settlers. His response, in the form of a speech, was written down years later by Henry Smith, and one must assume it is not a word-for-word rendering. In the early 1970s, Ted Perry amended the speech for a film called 'Home'. A few excerpts of his version follow:

Case 4.4   Seattle's speech

How can you buy or sell the sky, the warmth of the land? The idea is strange to us. If we do not own the freshness of the air and sparkle of the water, how can you buy them?

We are part of the earth and it is part of us. The perfumed flowers are our sisters; the deer, the horse, the great eagle, these are our brothers. The rocky crests, the juices in the meadows, the body heat of the pony, and man – all belong to the same family.

If we sell you our land, love it as we have loved it. Care for it as we have cared for it. Preserve the land for all children and love it.

Whatever befalls the earth befalls the sons of the earth. If men spit upon the ground, they spit upon themselves. This we know: the earth does not belong to man. Man belongs to the earth.

Source: Perry (1971), cited from Seed et al (1988).

A beautiful contemporary text is the '**Earth Charter**', which was formally launched in 2000. The underlying idea of this tract was proposed by the Brundtland Commission in 1987, but the first major UN sustainability conference in Rio in 1992 did not succeed in getting all participants to agree on a basic declaration on sustainable development. The idea was then taken up by a number of NGOs, including Green Cross International, which was founded by the former president of the Soviet Union, Mikhail Gorbachev. Its further development was supported by the Netherlands after 1994, which is why the official launch in 2000 was held in the presence of the Dutch Queen Beatrix in the Peace Palace in The Hague. The charter was consequently signed by thousands of organisations, including UNESCO, as well as by cities, heads of government, universities and many individuals throughout the world. Case 4.5 offers a few extracts from the Earth Charter.

Case 4.5   The Earth Charter

"To move forward we must recognize that in the midst of a magnificent diversity of cultures and life forms we are one human family and one Earth community with a common destiny. We must join together to bring forth a sustainable global society founded on respect for nature, universal human rights, economic justice, and a culture of peace. Towards this end, it is imperative that we, the peoples of Earth, declare our responsibility to one another, to the greater community of life, and to future generations."

"Humanity is part of a vast evolving universe. Earth, our home, is alive with a unique community of life. The forces of nature make existence a demanding and uncertain adventure, but Earth has provided the conditions essential to life's evolution. The resilience of the community of life and the well-being of humanity depend upon preserving a healthy biosphere with all its ecological systems, a rich variety of plants and animals, fertile soils, pure waters, and clean air. The global environment with its finite resources is a common concern of all peoples."

"Everyone shares responsibility for the present and future well-being of the human family and the larger living world. The spirit of human solidarity and kinship with all life is strengthened when we live with reverence for the mystery of being, gratitude for the gift of life, and humility regarding the human place in nature."

Peace

One of the most striking of paradigm shifts, which is still continuing in large parts of the world, is the view of war and peace. For thousands of years, kings and other royals considered war to be a noble occupation. In 1521 the famed author Niccolò Machiavelli wrote a book under the revealing title *Dell'arte Della Guerra* (The Art of War). A few years earlier he wrote (in *Il Principe*, known in English as *The Prince*): "A prince must have no other objective, no other thought, nor take up any profession but that of war." The objective was hallowed for Machiavelli, who had many followers amongst emperors and kings – if war was beneficial, the question of whether it was ethical was irrelevant.

Even in the nineteenth century the Prussian general Carl von Clausewitz was able to write: "War is a mere continuation of politics by other means." But, ever since the horrors of trench warfare in World War I and the Holocaust of World War II, many have come to understand that war is not so much an acceptable means for pursuing noble goals but rather a horrific and devastating process – the very worst thing that can happen to a country or people. The fact that this turnaround not only affected public opinion but also actual legislation and legal systems is evidenced by the trials of war criminals such as the Nuremburg Trials (1945–1946), the Yugoslavia Tribunal (established in 1993), the Rwanda Tribunal (starting in 1994) and the creation of the International Criminal Court (ICC) in The Hague, the Netherlands, in 2002.

Democracy

Throughout history there have been many kings, emperors and pharaohs that have defended their right to the throne by declaring that God had appointed them. Many of them also considered their subjects to be their personal possessions.

So it was a sensational development when the American colonies, oppressed by King George III of England, formally renounced the monarchy in a declaration, part of which reads as follows:

Case 4.6   The Declaration of Independence

"We hold these truths to be self-evident, that all men are created equal, that they are endowed by their Creator with certain unalienable Rights, that among these are Life, Liberty and the pursuit of Happiness. That to secure these rights, Governments are instituted among Men, deriving their just powers from the consent of the governed. That whenever any Form of Government becomes destructive of these ends, it is the Right of the People to alter or to abolish it, and to institute new Government, laying its foundation on such principles and organizing its powers in such form, as to them shall seem most likely to effect their Safety and Happiness.

Prudence, indeed, will dictate that Governments long established should not be changed for light and transient causes; and accordingly all experience hath shewn, that mankind are more disposed to suffer, while evils are sufferable, than to right themselves by abolishing the forms to which they are accustomed. But when a long train of abuses and usurpations, pursuing invariably the same Object evinces a design to reduce them under absolute Despotism, it is their right, it is their duty, to throw off such Government, and to provide new Guards for their future security."

In other words, the king or the state serves the people, and not vice versa. The Declaration of Independence was inspired by earlier such declarations, including the Act of Abjuration which inaugurated the Dutch Republic in 1581. Over the last few centuries, the concept of the relationship between a country and its government has changed drastically. Democracy, which is based on the ideal that the government serves the people and not the other way around, has taken root in diverse forms across large parts of the world (see Figure 4.2), although not all paths to democratisation are equally smooth. The following case illustrates this.

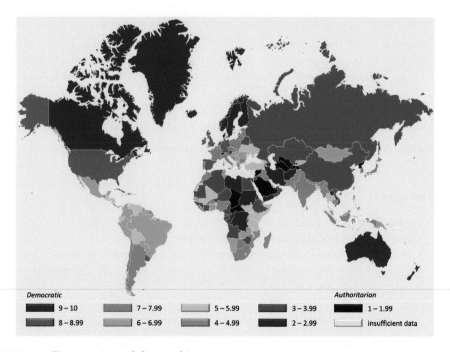

Democratic				Authoritarian	
9 – 10	7 – 7.99	5 – 5.99	3 – 3.99	1 – 1.99	
8 – 8.99	6 – 6.99	4 – 4.99	2 – 2.99	insufficient data	

FIGURE 4.2   Democracies and dictatorships

Source: The Economist, Intelligence Unit: Democracy Index 2015, published in 2016.

Case 4.7   Democracy in Japan and Algeria

The end of World War II was marked by Japan's defeat at the hands of the United States and its allies, after which the country continued to be occupied by the victors. It was only in 1952 that it regained independence, with the Americans imposing a democratic structure. In 1955 the Liberal Democratic Party (the LDP) came to power with a large electoral majority, and proceeded to win every election in the following years. In fact, it became the sole governing party for the next 38 years. The LDP lost its first election in 1993, giving other parties a chance to govern, but between 1994 and 2009 it was once again continuously part of the ruling coalition.

In 1963 Algeria gained independence from France. It soon succumbed to a dictatorship that only waned at the close of 1991 when the first democratic elections were held. In the first round, the Islamic Salvation Front (the *Front Islamique du Salut* – FIS) won by an absolute majority. The FIS intended to transform Algeria into a fundamentalist Islamic state and immediately prohibit democracy once more. The military chose to intervene, cancelled the second round of the elections and outlawed the FIS. The party went underground and became an armed resistance movement. In the civil war that followed these events, some 250,000 people perished.

Japan had never been a democracy before 1945, and had existed for thousands of years as a dictatorship run by an emperor that was worshipped as a divine being. There was much support for this form of government in the country, and Japan did not suddenly become a democracy in 1952, even though the US wanted it to. It became instead a sham democracy, one in which the ritual of an election was performed every few years, which meant little. Algeria in 1991 was not up to democratic rule either when its citizens finally went to the polls in 1991, as quickly became evident when the majority backed a party that wanted to introduce a new dictatorship.

Questions

- If the political party you support had held an absolute majority for 40 or 80 years, would you hope that they won or lost the next election?
- If free and fair democratic elections would result in a two-thirds majority being gained by a party that wanted to abolish democratic rule, should they then be permitted to abolish democracy?

Democracy involves much more than just casting your vote once every few years. True democracy exists in a person's mind, consisting of self-awareness, of freedom and access to information and of the absence of fear of oppression and persecution – i.e. in the mind of

empowered people. It also consists of an active political interest and the participation of both individuals and groups such as NGO's protest movements, trade unions, consumer organisations, neighbourhood committees and many others. And then there is also a respect for the interests of minorities, as the following case demonstrates.

Case 4.8   Democracy in the Netherlands

In 1989 same-sex marriages were still prohibited under Dutch law, as the Court of Appeal in Amsterdam established when a gay couple attempted to enter into a civil union in the city. But the court pronounced at the same time that there was insufficient justification for including this distinction between heterosexual and homosexual people and recommended that the Dutch House of Representatives amend the law. In both the years before and after this ruling, there was intense debate about gay marriage in Dutch society. A wide range of groups and people joined in the discussions – gay rights organisations, church bodies, human rights groups, municipal officials, politicians and people on the street. Opinion polls showed that an increasing percentage of Dutch people were in favour of the right of gay people to get married (see Figure 4.3).

In 1998 a statutory provision resulted in the introduction of registered partnerships for gay people. This was only a small step, and on 1 April 2001 an amendment to the law took effect that allowed all couples to enter into a civil union, whether or not they were of different genders or the same.

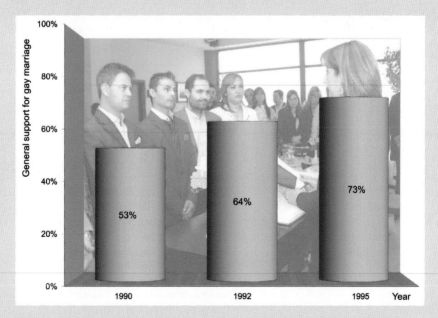

FIGURE 4.3   Percentage of Dutch people in favour of allowing gay marriages

Source: Gaykrant (2005); background photo: Claudio Jofré, Wikimedia.

> In Belgium gay marriages were legalised in 2003, followed by Spain, Canada, South Africa, and more than 20 other countries. In many US states, same-sex marriages were legalised, starting with Massachusetts in 2003 due to a state court decision. The issue remained controversial, and some states refused to introduce same-sex marriages until 2015, when they were legalised throughout the United States due to a ruling of the Supreme Court.

Case 4.8 shows one characteristic of democracy – it is not simply a question of 'the majority rules', but rather a continuous quest for wide support. If possible, this involves finding a **consensus**, an agreement in terms of ideas and concepts that everyone is happy with. If that is not possible, at any rate it involves finding interim solutions that are acceptable to many – the golden mean, ensuring that everyone has the occasional opportunity to get their share.

To reach such a consensus, it is necessary that all important groups are involved in the decision-making process. For the question of gay marriage, this mean that gay rights organisations, the churches and various other bodies had to be on board. They were all **stakeholders**, which means that they all had an interest in one way or another in the outcome of the debate. This active **participation** in the decision-making process by all stakeholders is called **participatory democracy**.

Participation by stakeholders is so essential, not just for democracy but also for the process of sustainable development, that the 'P' of its first letter is sometimes considered to be the 'fourth P', after the Ps representing people, planet and profit.

Table 4.5 provides an overview of the primary stakeholders in a participatory democracy. Individual people fill three roles in the table, as citizens, consumers and professionals. All or

TABLE 4.5 Stakeholders in participatory democracy

Participants	Details
Individuals • Citizens • Consumers • Professionals → (1)	
Groups • Companies • Government institutions → (2) • NGOs → (3) • Churches and other religious bodies • Educational institutions • Care institutions • Expertise centres • Political parties • Trade unions • Courts • Press, radio, television • Once-off demonstrators	(1) *Professionals*: including public officials, artists, doctors, farmers, lecturers, clergymen, economists, traders, imams, lawyers, social workers, managers, military personnel, police officers, priests, psychologists, writers, technicians, nurses, shopkeepers (2) *Government institutions*: including city councils, municipalities, provinces, water boards, ministries, parliaments, advisory bodies (3) *NGOs*: including protest groups, special interest groups, aid organisations, voluntary organisations, sports associations and clubs

most people adopt each of those three roles in turn and, from the perspective of participatory democracy, these are three different points of view, each with their own characteristic questions. These might include:

Citizen

- What type of society do I want?
- What level of freedom is available to me? What security? What assurances for the future?
- What is just?
- What rights and obligations do I have?

Consumer

- What do I want for myself?
- What level of prosperity do I want to attain? More, or maybe a little less?
- What consumer products suit me?

Professional

- What can be done (technically, economically, socially, environmentally, etc.)?
- What can I contribute?
- What is my professional responsibility in that?

Questions

- Do you feel free? Are you free? What is freedom, anyway?
- What assurances do you have for the future?
- What level of prosperity would you like to attain?

Case 4.8 demonstrates that interventional decisions and their successful and peaceful implementation are possible, should a sufficient support basis exist in society. When the gay marriage amendment was adopted in 2000, a large proportion of Dutch people were in favour of it – the time was ripe for the move.

Sufficient consensus. . . when the time is ripe. These are the essential requirements for introducing major societal changes in a peaceful environment. There is a Chinese saying that expresses these characteristics in a notable way: **Wei wu wei**, which might be translated as '**Action without action**'. This sounds contradictory, but it isn't, because the two 'actions' take on a different meaning. The first 'action' represents effective action, truly achieving something. The second represents acting, forcing, pushing through. An action without action could entail swimming with the current in a river instead of against or across it. It is also comparable to pushing somebody on a swing – when you repetitively push them at just the right time, you can get the swing to go very high while consecutively pushing it only slightly. This is action without action. But if you choose the wrong moment to push, maybe when the swing is coming at you, then you slow the motion down and also run the risk of breaking an arm.

Human rights

The European Union is not the only international organisation in Europe. There is also the Council of Europe. This body is larger than the EU, with a membership of 47 nations including Russia and Turkey, and with 820 million people. It too operates as a source of vigour for sustainable development and all its members have signed the European Convention on Human Rights, which guarantees the right to life, the banning of torture, slavery and forced labour, the right to liberty and security, to a fair trial, to respect for privacy and family life, freedom of thought, conscience and religion, freedom of expression and a prohibition on discrimination, amongst other things.

The convention builds on the Universal Declaration of Human Rights, which was drafted by the UN. There is an important difference between the two documents. The UN declaration is impressive but non-obligatory, while the European document has actual legal clout because it is a treaty. Should your rights be violated by the state, as an individual citizen you are able to take the matter to court.

The Council of Europe set up the **European Court of Human Rights** for that specific purpose, through which citizens can bring charges against a country. To understand what that may mean for the relationship between the state and the individual people, it is interesting to compare Case 4.9 and Case 4.10.

Case 4.9   Andrew Jackson and the Seminole Wars

In 1817, American general Andrew Jackson entered the Spanish territory of Florida with an army of nearly 3,000 men. Their mission was to capture Spanish forts at Saint Marks and Pensacola, and to retaliate against the Seminole Indians for harbouring runaway slaves and supporting the British during the War of 1812. After a series of successful attacks, the Spanish quickly ceded Florida to the United States, and the Seminole were pushed from their settlement in Tallahassee into the central part of Florida, or what is now present day Ocala.

Based in part on his military success, Andrew Jackson became President of the United States in 1829. Jackson was involved in efforts to relocate Native Americans from desirable areas in the southern United States throughout his political career, and as President signed the 'Indian Removal Act' into law in 1830. The Act began a series of forced emigrations of tens of thousands of indigenous American Indians to the Western territories. Thousands died of disease, exposure and starvation while making this journey – the Cherokee people called it the 'Trail of Tears.' There was little public outcry against these actions. On the contrary, President Jackson's image is celebrated in statues, paintings and even the American $20 bill bears his likeness (Figure 4.4). Although historians have taken a more critical view of Jackson in recent years, it remains ironic that, if he did today what he did then, he would be sentenced to multiple life sentences by an international court for perpetrating genocide and ethnic cleansing.

Only very recently, protests against Jackson's appearance on the $20 bill were heard. In 2015, a group called Women on Twenties called on the U.S. Treasury to

FIGURE 4.4   President Jackson, depicted on a 20-dollar bill issued in 2009

replace Andrew Jackson's portrait with one of a woman. One year later, the Treasury Secretary announced that in 2020 Jackson's face will be moved to the backside of the $20 bill, to be replaced on the front side by the black female abolitionist leader Harriet Tubman.

That's how it was in those days, on the orders of a 'civilised' nation like the United States. Though it is true that similar atrocities are still committed in some parts of the world, an important distinction is that today there is an outcry and that, in some cases, the perpetrators stand trial for their actions instead of being lionised. The United States and Europe have undergone many changes in that respect, as is illustrated in Case 4.10.

Case 4.10   Chassagnou versus France

Mrs Marie-Jeanne Chassagnou, a French citizen, owned a lovely piece of land with a beautiful natural landscape. Under French law she was obliged, as a landowner, to become a member of the local hunting association. The law furthermore compelled her to allow other members of the association to freely use her land for hunting.

Chassagnou was against hunting on principle and was consequently opposed to the obligation. In 1999 she took the case to the European Court of Human Rights, where she argued that the compulsory membership infringed upon a fundamental human right, being the freedom of association.

The court found in her favour. Although the article Chassagnou invoked was intended to grant people the right to freely establish associations or become members of extant ones, it also meant that people have the right to *not* join an association. The French law was declared invalid by the European court.

Chassagnou is still using her land, and hunting is now banned on it.

Citizens that take their own country to court, and win! That is exceptional, and it demonstrates how the nations of Europe have voluntarily given up some of their independence for the cause of justice.

Views on both democracy and human rights have changed dramatically in both Europe and in other parts of the world. Modern history has shown us that it is truly possible to make giant leaps forward in respect of liberty, democracy and justice for hundreds of millions of people.

The recognition of the rights of the oppressed is not something that simply comes into being of its own accord, and in many cases one requires charismatic idealists who passionately declare their dreams and capture an audience. A great example of this is the African American clergyman, Martin Luther King, who stood up for the rights of people of colour in the United States. In August 1963 he led a march of 250,000 people to the capital city, Washington DC, where he delivered an address that has since become famous. In his speech he asked the demonstrators to resist their oppression in a non-violent way. An extract from his speech follows:

> I have a dream! That one day this nation will rise up and live out the true meaning of its creed: We hold these truths to be self-evident, that all men are created equal.
>
> I have a dream! That one day on the red hills of Georgia, the sons of former slaves and the sons of former slave owners will be able to sit down together at the table of brotherhood.
>
> I have a dream! That one day even the state of Mississippi, a state sweltering with the heat of injustice, sweltering with the heat of oppression, will be transformed into an oasis of freedom and justice.
>
> I have a dream that my four little children will one day live in a nation where they will not be judged by the colour of their skin but by the content of their character.
>
> I have a dream today!

In 1964 a new law was adopted in the US that provided improved protection for the rights of all American citizens. Although the black people of America are still confronted with many issues today, the situation has in any event improved since that time. Martin Luther King received the Nobel Peace Prize in 1964.

Ideals are an essential ingredient in a world where there is still much to improve, and the world would be a much worse place if there were no dreams. A lack of ideals equals a lack of sustainable development.

Questions

- What are *your* dreams?
- What would the characteristics of your ideal world be?

Emancipation and empowerment

When the media discusses emancipation, it almost always relates to the status of women. There is still a great deal to be done in that framework in every country, as can be seen in Table 4.6. Surprisingly enough, Rwanda, which was witness to the massive genocide discussed in Case

TABLE 4.6 Position of women in selected countries

Country	Seats in parliament (in 2016)			Average income (PPP $, 2014)			Senior jobs (2015)
	Men	Women	% women	Men	Women	Women compared to men	% women
Rwanda	29	51	64%	1,612	1,312	81%	34%
Bolivia	61	69	53%	7,140	4,383	61%	35%
Sweden	197	152	44%	51,084	40,222	79%	37%
Mexico	288	212	42%	22,252	10,233	46%	36%
South Africa	231	166	42%	15,737	8,713	55%	30%
Belgium	91	59	39%	50,845	31,879	63%	32%
Netherlands	94	56	37%	61,641	29,500	48%	26%
Tanzania	236	136	37%	2,502	2,320	93%	16%
United Kingdom	457	192	30%	51,628	27,259	53%	35%
Afghanistan	180	69	28%	3,227	506	16%	–
China	2260	699	24%	14,795	10,128	68%	17%
Pakistan	270	70	21%	8,100	1,450	18%	3%
USA	349	84	19%	63,158	43,054	68%	43%
Indonesia	460	95	17%	13,052	6,485	50%	23%
Russia	389	61	14%	28,287	17,269	61%	38%
India	478	65	12%	8,656	2,116	24%	–
Ghana	245	30	11%	4,515	3,200	71%	50%
Brazil	462	51	10%	19,084	11,393	60%	37%
Yemen	300	0	0%	5,412	1,595	29%	2%

The table is sorted according to the percentage of women in parliament. In countries where the parliament has two chambers (a house of representatives and a senate), the figures are according to the house of representatives. Senior jobs are regarded as directors, senior public servants and company managers.

Sources: parliamentary figures: IPU (2016); average income: UNDP (2016); senior jobs: World Economic Forum (2015).

3.7, has the highest percentage of parliamentary representation for women – presently over half of members of parliament are women. In all other parliaments, women are a minority. However, a huge amount has been achieved in the last century, and not just in terms of women's rights. Thanks to a multifaceted process of emancipation, which took off around the 1960s, the level of freedom ad empowerment has increased amongst all groups in Western society. Here are some key issues facing selected groups:

• *Women*: The status of emancipation of women varies widely through the world. In most developed countries, larger numbers of women are employed, their average salaries have increased and so have the number of women in managerial positions. However: the highest scores in Table 4.6 are all found in African countries, as Rwanda has the highest percentage of female members of parliament (64 percent) of all countries in the world. Likewise, in Tanzania, women have the highest average income compared to men (93 percent); and Ghana is the only country where there are just as many female as male directors, senior public servants and company managers: 50 percent each. Heated debate over abortion and women's reproductive rights still exists in the West, particularly in the United States. The treatment of women in some Islamic societies is under increasing global scrutiny.

- *Children*: In 1989 the General Assembly of the UN adopted the Convention on the Rights of the Child. It was ratified by all the member states of the UN, with the exception of Somalia and the US. Under the convention, states are obliged to guarantee the rights of minors as a precedent. These rights include the right to life, to a name and nationality, to a home, to be raised by parents, to medical care, leisure time, play; special protection for, amongst others, adopted children, refugees, handicapped children, minorities, children in armed conflicts, neglected or abused children, children prosecuted for a criminal offence; protection from discrimination, violence, abuse, neglect, economic exploitation, sexual abuse, kidnapping and child trafficking.
- *The youth*: Minors today have much more opportunity to express their opinions through the media thanks to youth magazines, youth-oriented broadcasters and, of course, the Internet.
- *Senior citizens*: The level of freedom of senior citizens, such as those in old-age homes, has increased. Today there are many more public facilities for senior citizens. Age discrimination in job applications has been prohibited by law. Euthanasia is legal in certain European countries.
- *Gays*: Homosexuality is accepted by an ever-increasing number of people – in Western Europe and in many US states, at any rate. Same-sex marriages are permitted in a growing number of countries. But gays enjoy fewer rights in many cultures outside of the West, and countries like Iran, Saudi Arabia, Nigeria and Pakistan have laws providing for the death penalty for same-sex activity.
- *Disabled people*: The number of public facilities for disabled people has also increased considerably, backed by legislation, and there are legal provisions in place prohibiting discrimination in job applications.
- *Minorities*: Although certain racial and ethnic groups have advanced considerably, intolerance exists in every society. Immigrants to Western countries are encouraged to assimilate or face alienation and exclusion. Europe and the United States are seeing waves of anti-Islamic sentiment. However, in many towns mosques and temples are an accepted (by most people) phenomenon, as are Islamic schools. Information is increasingly available in other languages and characters.
- *All citizens*: The sexual revolution played a major role in increasing openness about sexuality. The societal significance of the citizens is continuously increasing, with protest groups and other NGOs translating the notions of a wide range of groups in society and consequently amplifying the **participatory democracy**. In some cases, referendums perform the same role. The people have a great deal more information, not only due to the Internet but also due to the much larger range of periodicals and television stations. The citizens have become more aware and self-conscious in their contacts with professionals like doctors, public officials, politicians and the police. **Depillarization** – the breaking down of religious and sociopolitical barriers – and **secularisation** have resulted in a decline in the social importance of the older and tightly knit groups, allowing people to make more personal choices and decisions. This has also blurred the traditional differences in society, while new differences have arisen (like the youth-adult divide or the native population–immigrant population one). Manufacturers and chain stores are responsive to the increased power of consumers and have emphatically adjusted their policies accordingly.

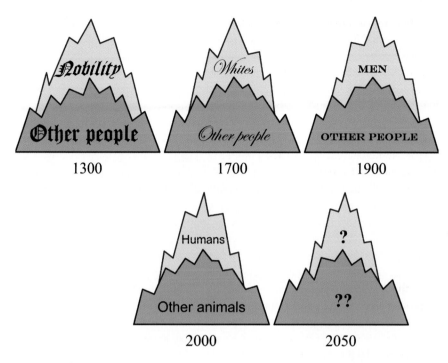

FIGURE 4.5 Shifting views on humanity. . .

The process of emancipation for all of these groups has its foundations in a very gradual paradigm shift, in which the relationships between people, and even the meaning of humanity, has been subject to reconsideration over the centuries, as illustrated in Figure 4.5. The dates in the figure are to some extent symbolic. The fact that the intervening periods are constantly halved symbolises the fact that development is continuously accelerating. Emancipation has led to an increased understanding of freedom and self-awareness amongst the people, which means they have become a very important factor in the field of sustainable development, as the following section will illustrate.

4.3 People

Both the United Nations and the European Union are mammoth organisations, so-called **Intergovernmental Organisations (IGOs)**, to which not everyone feels instinctively tied. Most individuals have little influence upon the policies of such organisations. Yet individuals still have many opportunities for acting as a source of vigour in terms of sustainable development through their actions, their attitude and their choices.

Consumers and citizens

Some types of sustainable development are easy to implement, cheap, and the work involved will hardly change a person's lifestyle. Well-known examples include

- Walking or cycling instead of jumping into the car
- Using green energy, i.e. power generated by sustainable sources

- Declining unnecessary packaging in stores
- Turning off the lights when you leave a room

The results of these actions in respect of sustainable development are meaningful, thanks to the fact that many people are performing them. Other approaches require greater effort and attention, but the effects thereof can also be much greater. A good example can be seen when customers refuse *en masse* to shop at a store that has been exposed as performing actions that the customers consider unacceptable. When the oil company Shell did business with apartheid-era South Africa some decades ago, a large number of people refused to buy gas from Shell gas stations, which had a demonstrable effect on Shell's policies. Today this opportunity exists with regard to companies that sell products that are made using child labour. 'Voting with your feet' is what this action is called – people express their feelings by not buying from these shops.

A relatively new way of contributing to sustainability is to 'repay' the natural world for the piece of environment 'consumed'. This means, for example, that an airline passenger might pay an additional sum, which is consequently used to plant a number of trees somewhere – 'trees for travel'. The fact that this requires careful implementation was demonstrated in Case 3.8, describing that the Mount Elgon compensation project was not exactly a resounding success.

All options listed to date concern purchasing and consumption behaviour – that is, **consumer** behaviour. There is also another type of behaviour that can be demonstrated by people – the responsibility of the **citizen** as a responsible member of society. The role of the sustainable citizen might include:

- Separating garbage
- Donating money to good causes
- Voting for a political party that (in the voter's opinion) heeds sustainable development in the best possible way

NGOs and group protests

In terms of the opportunities open to individual citizens, their ability to act in a sustainable manner increases dramatically when they work together. One can join a group or even start one – there are millions of such groups, ranging from miniscule to titanic. Some are globally known, like Greenpeace, the World Wildlife Fund, Oxfam and Amnesty International. Then there are also countless smaller groups. Local protest committees, residents' associations, the list goes on (Figure 4.6). These groups, from the huge World Wildlife Fund all the way through to the small 'Save the Gopher Tortoise' fall under the title of NGO, '**Non-Governmental Organisation**', to highlight the fact that they are independent of the state (the 'government').

Aside from these formal associations and foundations, there are also many once-off events. An excellent example of this is the Live Aid concert, which was hosted simultaneously in Europe and the US in 1985. A large number of globally famous stars were a part of the concert, which aimed to raise money to fight a famine in Africa. It was said that 1.5 billion people watched the concerts live on television and it raised over a hundred million dollars. In 2005 a similar event was held again, this time much larger as it was hosted on ten stages around the world, including Philadelphia, London, Paris, Berlin, Rome and Tokyo: Live 8 (Figure 4.7).

FIGURE 4.6 Individual people in every country: a huge source of vigour for sustainable development

Source: Luis Miguel Bugallo Sánchez, 2006, Wikimedia; Ferdinand Reus, Wikimedia; Peter Morgan, Wikimedia; PICQ, background blur by Samsara, 2005, Wikimedia; Jesse Nickles, 2004, Wikimedia; Jonathan McIntosh, 2004, Wikimedia; Wen-Yan King, Wikimedia; Christiaan Briggs, 2003, Wikimedia.

Individual people in every country: a huge source of vigour for sustainable development

FIGURE 4.7   Live 8, 2005

Source: Marcel Linke, Wikimedia.

The purpose of the latter concerts was not to raise money but to exercise massive pressure on the G8, which met a few days later to discuss debt amongst impoverished nations and the environment. "Justice, not money!" was the call of the performers and the audience. The pressure resulted in some success, and the cancellation of a number of countries' debts, which had been agreed to earlier, was extended. The G8 countries promised to double development aid but unfortunately the commercial tariffs and trade barriers, which constitute a huge obstacle for the development of poor nations, were not lifted, while tackling environmental issues was transferred forward. But that partial success does still demonstrate that the pressure of public opinion – of the 'normal' person – can really achieve something.

Civil society

The fact that ordinary people can do a lot when working together was amply evident in Eastern Europe in 1989. In East Germany, Hungary, Czechoslovakia and Poland the dictatorial regimes fell like dominoes before peacefully demonstrating citizens. The fall of the Berlin Wall (Figure 4.8) has become symbolic of the incredible army of peaceful citizens. Georgia saw a repeat in 2003, as did the Ukraine in 2004, followed by several Arabian nations in 2011. Peaceful revolutions had taken place even earlier than 1989 – for example, the massive country of India gained independence from the UK in 1947 after the people, led by Mahatma Gandhi, engaged in non-violent protest and resisting the colonial power. Unfortunately, the independence of India and the revolutions in Georgia and Ukraine afterwards led to waves of violence; but the independence processes themselves proceeded mostly peacefully.

Emancipated and empowered citizens, NGOs and peaceful multitudes, together with other active civil groups like charges, schools and peace movements, make up our **civil society**, the 'community of citizens'. Their significance is constantly growing, and civil society today offers a counterbalance to the process of globalisation, through which nations, gigantic international

FIGURE 4.8   Berlin, November 1989: confident demonstrators mount the Wall to compel the East German authorities to open the Brandenburg Gates. As a result, the Communist regime collapsed

Source: Gavin Stewart, flickr.

organisations and multinational companies are gaining increasing influence. Civil society is an essential part of democracy, and it means more than simply casting a vote for a political party once every four years. In part thanks to the Internet, civil society is also becoming more and more international in its actions, and is thus becoming a trans-border **global civil society**. The clout of this group is also growing within the United Nations, with numerous so-called *side events* taking place at the major sustainable development conference in Johannesburg in 2002 (Rio+10), including ones launched at the request of civil society organisations. The same thing happened during Rio+20 in 2012, which again took place in Rio de Janeiro. These side events in fact were entire conferences in themselves, which were officially recognised by the UN and with their outcomes being applied to the 'real' conference. The groups involved were very diverse, from the Women's Development & Environment Organization from Brazil to the Yale School of Forestry and Environmental Studies and from the World Student Community for Sustainable Development (WSC-SD) to the International Youth and Students Movement for the United Nations (ISMUN).

Diversity, cultures and values

Until now the emphasis has been on people working together within civil society. But much vigour is also derived from the differences that exist between people, from **diversity**. It was for this very good reason that Agenda 21 places so much focus on protecting languages, peoples, cultures and religions. Cultures partly exist in different regions of the world, but in part they are also completely intermingled.

Case 4.11 Punks, gabbers and metalheads

Punks are fun-loving, aggressive and have a sense of humour. They are anti-everything (including themselves) and loathe the established order.

Gabbers wear tracksuits, preferably with a bomber jacket, and Nike sneakers. They love *hakking*, a form of rave dancing.

Metalheads detest customs and manners. They could never believe in something as banal as love, and they listen to music in its heaviest and most concentrated form.

Ivy-leaguers like field hockey, branded clothes and fast cars, whereas hippies like flowers, peace and the occasional joint. Goths are easily recognisable by their mystical symbols of runes, crosses and pentagrams, which accompany their black clothes and makeup. They seek out the dark side of the world and humanity.

And then there are the neutrals, the trance-dancers, the straight edgers and the furries. The urbans, the alternatives, the camp club, the grunge set and the adherents of neo-grunge. The valley girls, the bounders, the hip-hoppers, the machos, skaters, johnnies, anitas, fatimas, fakers and wannabes. And of course the provos, nerds, wiggers, skinheads, R&B lovers, rock 'n' rollers and funk aficionados.

The defining characteristics of the groups outlined in Case 4.11 should naturally be taken with a pinch of salt, but behind their external appearances there certainly exists a world of differences. For example, in the way they view the world, or in the way in which they enjoy life – or don't enjoy life, as the case may be. Other differences entail the things a person considers valuable or instead detestable. Each of these groups has their own values and traditions, and taken together, this diversity constitutes a major source of vigour for a society. Just as a type of plant or animal is able, thanks to much genetic diversity, to react flexibly to changing biological circumstances, so does a society possess, through its cultural diversity, a wealth and will to survive that allows it to stay healthy in changing technological, economic and social circumstances. This holds for both the global society and the local ones.

4.4 Nature

Aside from human capital, the natural environment also constitutes major capital. The natural environment supplies us with valuable raw materials, such as iron ore, fresh water and clean air. It gives us our food through the fauna and flora, our building materials of wood and stone, and our energy in the form of oil, gas and coal as well as in the form of wind and solar power, tidal energy and nuclear energy.

Some of those resources are renewable, but many of them are being overexploited. The trick here is to reduce the consumption of these resources to a level where the natural environment is able to replenish whatever is consumed. One example of this is the use of sustainable wood, for which the **FSC certification** was introduced. The FSC, or the '**Forest Stewardship Council**', is an international NGO that supervises the sustainable use of forests and combats the destruction of tropical rainforests.

Other resources are finite and will not be replenished, such as iron ore, oil and gas. There is nothing wrong in principle with using these substances, but there must then be a condition that they are being consumed as a step towards a scenario in which they are replaced by renewable natural resources. Replacing the non-renewable resources with renewable ones is called a process of **substitution**. An example of substitution would involve replacing gas and diesel as a fuel with hydrogen or methanol, which, when extracted from plants, do not contribute to global warming as the CO_2 released was previously absorbed from the atmosphere by those plants – a closed loop.

Nature also gives us knowledge – knowledge of ecological systems, for example, from which we are able to learn how to construct suburbs in an ecologically accountable way, involving the use of natural and low-energy heating and cooling equipment. It also gives us knowledge about medicines, and every year new substances are discovered in plants that can be used to create new drugs or materials. There are still tens of thousands of biochemical compounds hidden in the heart of tropical forests or in the ocean's waters, just waiting to be discovered.

The natural world gives us other things too – opportunities for finding peace, relaxation, recreation, a poetic frame of mind, tourism. **Sustainable tourism** is a form of tourism in which attempts are made to inflict as little damage as possible to the natural environment and the local culture, while simultaneously contributing to awareness on the part of tour operators and their customers, the tourists.

The natural world also protects us. The ozone layer is a good example of this aspect, stopping a large portion of the ultraviolet radiation bombarding Earth from space. Life on Earth – at least, as we know it – would be impossible without the ozone layer. If the ozone layer were to become depleted, cancer and eye diseases would rise dramatically amongst humans and animals.

Last but not least, nature allows for cleaning and recovery. In itself, it is not an issue that we dump our garbage in the natural environment, as much of it is broken down by microorganisms. But it is crucial that certain limits are kept in mind – we should not dump more than the natural environment can digest.

Nature management

There are many ways in which the natural world can be healthily managed and improved. Some of these are of a political or legal nature. Laws and international treaties prohibit or restrict the hunting and fishing of endangered species, while other treaties restrict the trade in threatened species, including the **Convention on International Trade in Endangered Species of Wild Fauna and Flora** (**CITES**). Then there are also various treaties, such as the Bern Convention, dealing with protecting habitats, and the Ramsar Convention, aiming at the protection of wetlands. And there are many others.

Other approaches are of a biological or technological nature, as figure 4.9 illustrates. Breeding programs have been launched in nature reserves and zoos to maintain the populations of rare animals and to ensure there is sufficient diversity within a species so as to prevent inbreeding and the resultant degradation of the gene pool. Fragmented natural environments are connected using facilities such as **wildlife crossings**, also referred to as **ecobridges**, **ecoducts** or **green bridges** (Figure 4.10). In Europe, the **Natura 2000** network works to return damaged ecosystems to their original state and creates protected regions. This network,

FIGURE 4.9 The moors and forest in the Leikeven, a lake in Brabant, the Netherlands, were transformed into agricultural lands around 1950, with Europe suffering from hunger. In
the following decades, overuse changed the wetland drastically and it silted up. The
area has now been returned to nature, the overly fertile soil scraped off. Since that
time, dozens of plants and animals on the IUCN Red List have returned

Source: Niko Roorda.

FIGURE 4.10 Wildlife crossing in the country of Luxembourg, crossing the highway from Brussels
to the city of Luxembourg

Source: Lamiot, 2007, Wikimedia.

which all 28 EU member states are a part of, consisted of 26,000 connected nature reserves in 2010, covering an area of 850,000 square kilometres – 18 percent of the EU's territory.

Thanks to such initiatives, many species are being protected from extinction. In theory, it is even conceivable that certain extinct species can be brought back to life by cloning them. This is only possible if sufficient genetic material is available, which can be introduced into the cells of living animals or plants. In principle, it should be possible to grow adult specimens of the extinct fauna or flora, but this has not met with success to date. There has been talk of performing this process for the mammoth, using samples found encased in ice and frozen, and there was even an actual attempt to recreate the Tasmanian tiger detailed in Case 2.5, but the attempt failed as the DNA was too far degraded.

Case 4.12   De-extinction? The Lazarus Project!

The dodo. The quagga. The woolly mammoth and the flightless, 12-foot-high moa. Could they be brought back to existence? In the University of New South Wales, they think so.

Sydney Morning Herald, April 18, 2015

Scientists from The Lazarus Project are trying to restore Australia's southern gastric-brooding frog. The researchers made a major breakthrough in 2013, growing embryos containing the revived DNA of the extinct frog, the crucial first step in their attempt to bring a species back to life. They used an advanced technique known as somatic cell nuclear transfer to insert dead genetic material from the extinct frog's nucleus into the donor eggs of another species of living frog.

The scientists confirmed the breakthrough late last year when they found DNA from the extinct frog in several cells, proving beyond doubt the DNA was replicating.

The frog, *Rheobatrachus sillus*, is special, as it was the only 'gastric brooding frog', giving birth through its mouth after swallowing the eggs.

A technological approach to protecting fish stock levels in the oceans involves farming the fish instead of catching them in the wild. This **aquaculture** is a fast growing industry: since 2012, for the first time in history more fish is farmed worldwide than cattle. It is a logical step that is comparable to the move from hunting to cattle breeding. However, when farmed fish are fed with fish caught in the oceans, there is little or no gain in terms of the environment.

The development of genetically modified (GM) crops is another method that could contribute to protecting the natural environment. As Chapter 1 showed, altering the genes of cultivate crops could enable them to produce an antibody against certain insects, which means fewer pesticides are required. But the method is not without controversy, and opponents highlight the risks, such as the chance of transmitting newly introduced hereditary characteristics to other plants, which could disrupt the ecosystem in unpredictable ways.

4.5 Science and technology

Aside from the previously mentioned applications for science and technology, many other applications can be used towards sustainable development. Even further, insofar as sustainable development is dependent on technology, it is safe to say that nearly all the problems we are confronted with can – in principle – be solved. One example is global food production – even today there is sufficient food to feed the entire world's population, although in many places the most modern agricultural technology is not being utilised. The fact that, in spite of this, there are still hundreds of millions of people suffering from chronic malnourishment, is not the fault of technology but rather other factors of an economic, political or logistical nature. Although it is true that today's food industry is ruthlessly exploiting the natural environment and is consequently far from being sustainable, this too can be solved using technological means that are largely already available, whereas the remainder can be created within the foreseeable future. As a rule of thumb: when it comes to sustainable development, technology will rarely constitute a barrier. This likewise holds for energy, for example, as in principle it is possible to supply the whole human population with sustainable energy. Unfortunately, many of these sustainable sources of energy are still not anywhere near being competitive in financial terms, making their large-scale implementation impossible for the time being. This economic problem could be solved when the technical yield from generating the energy is improved and the production of energy generators becomes cheaper.

Chapter 7 deals extensively with the energy issue. This section will offer a few examples of innovative technical solutions to issues of sustainability.

Bacteria that clean

Contaminated land can be cleaned by certain types of bacteria. The bacteria could be used to clean land polluted by oil or even heavily poisoned soil. Tetrachloroethylene is one of those poisons that settle in soil, but a specific type of bacteria digests it and actually enjoys it. Thanks to scientific research, certain types of bacteria have been discovered and techniques developed to create those circumstances under which it works optimally.

Vegetable proteins

The fact that our largest source of protein is meat is not good in terms of sustainable development, as Chapter 2 showed. It would be much better if a large percentage of our protein were derived from vegetable sources. Much work is being undertaken to create food that resembles meat but is made from plants, such as soya, or from yeast. This so-called **novel protein food** is already available on the supermarket shelves, but to date meat still sells far better. However, should researchers succeed in getting such foodstuffs to resemble meat more closely – to the extent where the texture and taste are indistinguishable from that of meat, and it would be cheaper – then there is a good chance that meat consumption will largely die out, just as margarine has almost completely replaced butter in many places.

The world's smallest machines

In 1999, Bernard L. Feringa created a molecular rotor blade and got it to spin. Next, he designed a nanocar using a molecular motor: the first man-made engine at nanoscale. These tiny mechanical elements may seem insignificant, but probably they will have a tremendous impact. "In terms of development, the molecular motor is at the same stage as the electric motor was in the 1830s, when scientists displayed various spinning cranks and wheels, unaware that they would lead to electric trains, washing machines, fans and food processors." This was written by the Nobel Prize Committee in 2016, which awarded the Nobel Prize for Chemistry to Feringa and two others. Indeed, expectations are high. How about: robots smaller than blood cells, injected into blood vessels and hunting for cancer cells? Building new materials like medicines, atom by atom? Motors building bridges between brain cells and nanoscale digital equipment?

New vaccines

An entire new generation of vaccines is on the horizon, which might one day be able to completely eradicate major diseases like malaria, tuberculosis and Aids. The first global success on this form was the eradication of smallpox, a disease that wiped out at least 300 million people in the twentieth century alone. The disease itself was wiped out by 1978. There are still occasional reports of a fresh outbreak of smallpox, but so far they have all turned out to be false alarms.

Work is also being undertaken on vaccines that combat addiction to nicotine and drugs like cocaine and ecstasy. Once vaccinated against a substance, your body will contain antibodies that counter the active substances, and smoking tobacco or marijuana or injecting other narcotics will no longer have any effect upon your body or mind. Addiction would be an impossibility.

The vaccines may not be far away. "Anti-cocaine vaccine approved for clinical study in humans", Cornell University reported in August 2016. And a journal called *Biomaterials* reported in November 2016: "The next-generation nicotine vaccine: a novel and potent hybrid nanoparticle-based nicotine vaccine" (Hu et al, 2016).

Questions

- If vaccines combating nicotine and drug addiction were available, would you have yourself treated?
- Do you believe it would be correct to vaccinate all newly born children with these drugs?

4.6 Entrepreneurship

Earlier sections in this chapter were dedicated to humans and at the natural environment as two important sources of vigour – i.e. *people* and *planet*. But *profit* – in other words, the economy – can also make a highly effective contribution to sustainable development. This entrepreneurship firstly relates to companies, both large international ones and small and medium sized enterprises (SMEs). An increasing number of companies are discovering that a concern for sustainable development is not only good for the world, but for the company itself too. Sustainable development can be a highly profitable endeavour, and at the very least can prevent major losses being incurred.

This section does not deal with this topic too deeply, given that the whole of Chapter 8 is devoted to it, and so a few examples will suffice here.

The sustainable use of resources by business and industry is in everyone's interest, including that of the companies themselves. The following case provides a good example of this.

Case 4.13 Sustainable fishing

Unilever is a multinational company that manufactures consumer goods, including foods. In 1996, the company, being the largest purchaser of seafood in the world, became seriously worried about the future of catches, and so it entered into a partnership with the World Wildlife Fund for Nature and the FAO, the UN's Food and Agricultural Organisation, which became known as the Fish Sustainability Initiative (FSI). Unilever undertook to in due course only use fish that was sustainably caught, which means that it is guaranteed that the stocks are not depleted. Together with the WWF they set up a system of certification for fishing companies, the MSC certification program, overseen by the Marine Stewardship Council. Certified fishing companies will only catch fish in accordance with sustainability guidelines, focusing on maintaining and restoring healthy fish populations and ecosystems on the basis of biologically, technologically and socially accepted standards within the frameworks of national laws and international treaties.

The MSC releases an annual 'Fish to Eat' guideline in many languages that lists the species of seafood that are sustainable or less so.

Fisheries, industry and restaurants and supermarkets are increasingly taking the MSC certification into account. In 2016, over 20,000 seafood products were available with the MSC ecolabel in around 100 countries. Nearly 400 fisheries were MSC certified or being assessed.

This case demonstrates the responsibility a company takes with regard to nature and the environment. The question remains, of course, whether a company might do this primarily due to concerns about nature and the environment or also in part to enhance its image amongst customers. But even if the latter is indeed the case, it is still a fact that types of fish that have become rare may be kept from extinction.

One of the aspects of CSR (Corporate Social Responsibility) is that a company looks after its own staff and after its supplying companies. The Case 4.14 details this.

Case 4.14 Fair trade coffee

Utz Kapeh means 'good coffee' in Mayan. It was also the name of an NGO advocating sustainable coffee until 2007, after which the organization changed its name to Utz Certified. The organisation has met with reasonable success, and today a lot of major coffee suppliers buy their beans only if they bear the Utz certificate, including Ikea, Ahold-Delhaize, McDonald's, Burger King, Sara Lee and Asda (a part of Walmart).

The certificate warrants that the rights of coffee farmers are protected and that they are able to work under secure and healthy conditions with access to health-care. It also guarantees that agricultural chemicals are responsibly used and that the natural environment is properly managed.

In 2007, cocoa and tea were added to the certification program. Hazelnuts fol-lowed in 2014.

There are many other ways in which companies can contribute to sustainable develop-ment. Some of these include the use of sustainable energy, and decreasing their consumption of energy, fresh water and natural resources. Developing and selling products that have been designed to be disassembled at a later stage so that the components can be reused and recycled (*design for disassembly*) is another manner: see Chapter 8.

Microcredit

Not only Western companies – big and small – are able to contribute to sustainable develop-ment. One of the most effective ways in which the situation within impoverished nations can be improved is to set up a large number of local businesses.

The previous chapter highlighted the problems that might result from large loans to developing countries. As their debts and the interest owed accrue, these countries can fall into a debt trap, having to pay astronomical amounts to the wealthy nations, the World Bank or the IMF. A very different approach involves issuing small loans, not to states but rather to individuals. There are millions of people in developing nations that dream of starting their own business in order to become economically self-sufficient. They are frequently unable to do that, because they have no access to start-up capital. Many of them cannot get a foot in the door at a bank, as they are unable to provide security for loans simply because they have very few possessions. Today, in a growing number of countries such people are receiv-ing a **microcredit**, or microfinancing – a small loan at a low interest rate. These loans are issued by international aid organisations like Oikocredit and the ICCO, which support local banks for this purpose. One of these is the Grameen Bank in Bangladesh, which has already issued eight million of these microloans. The bank's managing director is Muham-mad Yunus, who pioneered the idea of microcredit, for which he and the bank received the Nobel Peace Prize in 2006.

Thanks to microloans many people have had the opportunity to make both themselves and others economically self-sufficient through their companies. Whereas large international companies adopt a top-down approach to their social responsibility, these new businesses are a good example of the bottom-up approach, with some support received from the outside. What is positive about this approach is that that external support is only temporary, with most new companies quickly ceasing to rely on additional support, in turn forming nuclei around which entire villages or neighbourhoods can develop economically. Another positive aspect is that it contributes to the emancipation of women. Nearly all microloans are granted to women, with one of the reasons for this being that – as experience has shown – these loans have the highest chance of success (Figure 4.11).

Microcredits are not a miracle cure against poverty. In some cases, interests on the loans could not be paid back, and the credits increased poverty, establishing the debt trap on an individual or local level. An investigation of microcredits in Gahan published by the Center for Financial Inclusion (Schicks, 2011) showed that a third of the investigated borrowers were having difficulties to repay the interest. In recent years, the focus therefore is on creating loans with no or a low interest rate.

4.7 Students

Earlier in this chapter, two roles were discussed that people can fulfil in society – that of a *consumer* and that of a *citizen*. A third role, that of a *professional*, was also mentioned. Students are professionals in the making and, while they might still be engaged in their education, nevertheless they are frequently able to make significant contributions to sustainable development, e.g. while undergoing practical training or completing a graduation project. Given that they frequently have the very latest knowledge and insights in their field at their disposal, have much time and are able – often more so than established professionals – to think out of the box, a great number of students are true sources of vigour with respect to sustainable development. This section provides a number of examples.

The first case is characteristic of the successful approach to a typical people problem, that of the imminent social exclusion of a certain group of people.

FIGURE 4.11 The mother in this Kenyan family used a microfinance loan to buy a dairy cow. Proceeds from the milk sales enable her to pay for her children's school fees

Source: USAID.

Case 4.15   Help for Mother Mates

People-to-people service – that is how the Humanitas Association describes its work. The organisation ensures in a wide array of ways that people – generally volunteers – are able to provide support to other people. One of their target groups is women who return to society after spending time in prison and who also have children. These women stand a very high chance of being socially excluded. If they are not assisted, there is an equally high chance that both they and their children will be subjected to long-term poverty and social problems. Faced with this issue, Humanitas launched the Mother Mates project, which has become very successful.

To encourage reintegration in society, the released mothers are counselled by volunteers called 'mother mates'. These volunteers are trained by Humanitas and assisted in providing counselling.

For this purpose, new training material was required. So a group of six students at a Faculty of Social Studies were asked to compile a training methodology that outlined the five themes of the counselling work. These themes included 'psychological, emotional and relational consequences of imprisonment'. Another theme is 'institutions for the assistance of released mothers', such as the social rehabilitation of former convicts and the Youth Care Agency. This collection of materials explaining the themes, compiled by the students, is now the basis of the training programme for these mother mates, enabling to effectively help the mothers and their families. In this way, the students contributed to the ability of these families to fully participate once again in society.

Whereas these students took a social studies course, technology students can also make significant contributions to sustainable development, as the next case shows. Nice about this case is that it depicts how technology can be used to improve the economic and social circumstances of a community in a third world nation.

Case 4.16   Water in Inchanga

Inchanga is a rural area in South Africa, near to the city of Durban. It is a region that has been dramatically afflicted by Aids, with the parents of many young children dead and many orphans being cared for by their grandmothers. A few years back, a group of these grandmothers was given a tract of land to grow food for their grandchildren. The area is fertile and there is a flowing river nearby, but irrigation was undertaken entirely by hand, using buckets the elderly women carried on their heads. This task proved far too strenuous for them, and the older children also had to help, which meant they could not attend school. In spite of their efforts, the land dried out and they were faced with the threat of failed crops.

A number of South African organisations stepped in, together with an NGO, *Church in Action*. Maarten van der Wiel, a student at a University of Technology, was called in to sort out the water issue as a graduation project.

Maarten installed, together with the South African organisations, a water system that contained a hydraulic ram pump to pump the river water to the fields. He started by optimising, from a technical sense, the ram pump, which was created by Biogas Technology Africa, undertaking calculations, computer simulations and field tests until he was certain the pump would fulfil the requirements. The ramp pump is a smart invention, which is perfectly suited to circumstances in a developing region. It is designed in such a way that the energy generated by the river current is used to pump some of that water. This means that the pump does not require fuel to work, and so it can work day and night, in summer and in winter, at 'no cost'. It is also very robust and can run for years without maintenance or spare parts.

The fields, with the new irrigation system installed, now provides sufficient food for over a hundred orphans and their grandmothers. The children have all returned to school and are consequently able to make a future for themselves. They spend their weekends learning from their grandmothers how to grow food, preparing for a time when the elderly can no longer care for them. They are even producing a surplus of food, some of which is given to other orphans and some of which is sold for seeds.

The third case is located at the centre of the intersection between people, planet and profit. So as to render the cultivation of agricultural produce more sustainable, certain standards have been created. These standards are based on a Western perspective. A biology student investigated what this meant for a population group in one of the poorest parts of the world.

Case 4.17 Organic agriculture in north-east India

It is not only the modern Western-style agriculture that is due for change, with traditional agricultural practices in India also being unsustainable and in need of a comprehensive transition.

Agriculture in the north-east of India is largely based on crop rotation, where the land is used for agricultural purposes for a few years and then allowed to rest for a few years, allowing the soil to become fertile once again. This approach to agriculture has been in existence for thousands of years, and would consequently be highly sustainable, except for the fact that the population had mushroomed recently, partly thanks to immigration from neighbouring regions. The population increase compelled farmers to make those periods of rest ever shorter and the land became too intensively used. The soil has become poor and produces less every year, and so the farmers had to make those periods of rest even shorter, leading to its exhaustion. At present both the forests and many species of animals are under severe threat.

An Indian NGO, the Agriculture and Organic Farming Group (AOFG), is advocating the introduction of organic agriculture. There are two advantages to this, being the fact that the land will be sustainably managed and the agricultural produce can be sold on the international market as organic food, bringing in higher prices. Thanks to the increased income, the farmers can live off lower production, sparing the natural environment. But to be able to sell produce as 'organic', the agricultural methods must comply with a standard set up by the International Federation of Organic Agriculture Movements. This IFOAM standard was created from the perspective of Western agriculture, and a number of their requirements are difficult to fulfil by farmers in India, who consider their environment from a very different perspective.

In order to bridge this gap, Natalia Eernstman investigated the background to the Indian values and perspectives on trade for her graduation project at a University of Agriculture. From talks with the Indian farmers, it emerged that one of the problems was that the IFOAM insisted that the valuable nature in forested areas is permanently protected. This was contrary to the practice of crop rotation, which dictated that each stretch of land is used interchangeably for growing crops. Even further, the underlying concept of protecting the natural environment is an alien one to the local farmers. In their eyes the forest is there to be used. A striking illustration of this is that in their language, Thankhul, there is no word for 'nature'.

Natalia tried to find solutions to this and other problems. Some solutions could be found through changing the behaviour of the farmers through, for example, moving to other crops. This required training programmes. But in other aspects it was important that the IFOAM standard was amended, and Natalia proposed that, amongst other things, crop rotation was accepted with IFOAM rules. If her proposals are accepted by IFOAM, this will mean that farmers in non-Western nations have the opportunity to engage in sustainably and recognised organic farming.

The full reports of Cases 4.15 and 4.16 can be found on the website of this book. The cases, together with the reports, demonstrate that professionals and students can be major sources of vigour for sustainable development, if they consistently involve the interests of sustainability in a balanced way in their reasoning, decisions and actions, and consequently undertake their work from a perspective of personal involvement as well as a sustainable attitude.

Questions

- Do you consider yourself to be a source of vigour for sustainable development?
- Compared to others, do you have more or fewer options than average in terms of acting as a source of vigour for sustainable development? Consider yourself both in the present and in the future.

4.8 The sustainable development goals

A major step strengthening the process of sustainable development was set in 2000, at the start of the new millennium. World leaders of all member states of the United Nations met during the Millennium Summit in New York City. A series of concrete sustainability goals were agreed to unanimously. Consequently, these were formulated as the **Millennium Development Goals**, or **MDGs** for short. They were:

The 8 MDGs

1   To eradicate extreme poverty and hunger
2   To achieve universal primary education
3   To promote gender equality and empower women
4   To reduce child mortality
5   To improve maternal health
6   To combat HIV/AIDS, malaria, and other diseases
7   To ensure environmental sustainability
8   To develop a global partnership for development

These very ambitious goals were set to be reached in the year 2015, and so there was a period of 15 years available to realise them. Many of the goals were made more explicit. For instance, goal 1 was formulated as follows:

MDG 1, Eradicate extreme poverty and hunger

1.1: Reduce extreme poverty by half. That is: Halve the proportion of people living on less than \$1.25 a day by 2015, compared to the level of 1990.
1.2: Achieve decent employment for women, men, and young people.
1.3: Reduce hunger by half. That is: halve the proportion of people who suffer from hunger by 2015, compared to the level of 1990.

Many countries have worked hard to realise the MDGs. During the 15 years that were available, it appeared that the rate of success differed strongly between the regions of the world.

The final report, published by the UN in 2015, showed the results. A graphical overview is shown in Table 4.7.

As Table 4.7 shows, some of the goals were formulated in relative terms: 'reduce by half', or 'by 2/3'. They might have a fair chance of being realised completely. Others were expressed in absolute terms: 'universal primary schooling', and 'women's equal representation'. Those goals were harder to fulfil 100 percent.

TABLE 4.7 Situation concerning the Millennium Development Goals (2009)

Region	Africa		Asia				Oceania	Latin America & Caribbean	Caucasus and Central Asia
Goals and Targets	North	Sub-Saharan	East	South-east	South	West			
Including		ECOWAS, §5.4	China, §5.1		India, §5.2				
1. Eradicate extreme poverty and hunger									
Reduce extreme poverty by half									
Productive and decent employment									
Reduce hunger by half									
2. Achieve universal primary education									
Universal primary schooling									
3. Promote gender equality and empower women									
Equal girls' enrolment in primary school									
Women's share of paid employment									
Women's equal representation in parliaments									
4. Reduce child mortality									
Reduce mortality of under-5-year-olds by 2/3									
5. Improve maternal health									
Reduce maternal mortality by 3/4									
Access to reproductive health									
6. Combat HIV/AIDS, malaria and other diseases									
Halt and reverse spread of HIV/AIDS									
Halt and reverse spread of tuberculosis									
7. Ensure environmental sustainability									
Halve proportion without improved drinking water									
Halve proportion without sanitation									
Improve the lives of slum-dwellers									
8. Develop a global partnership for development									
Internet users									
Overall									

Legend:
- Target met or excellent progress
- Good progress
- Fair progress
- Poor progress or deterioration
- Missing or insufficient data

Sources: UN:The Millennium Development Goals Report 2015; UN Statistics Division (2015) Millennium Development Goals: 2015 Progress Chart.

Questions

- Do you think it was wise to formulate such absolute criteria? Would you prefer relative criteria that may be more realistic?
- Or would you rather judge that relative criteria are not ambitious enough; that strong criteria, based on idealistic goals, are necessary in order to get things going?
- If you had the chance to formulate goals for a next policy period of 15 years (2015–2030), what would you choose: relative or absolute goals?
- Can you think of any particular goals you would like to set for 2030?

At the end of the 15-year period, the conclusion was that "significant achievements have been made on many of the MDG targets worldwide". Globally speaking, several of them have been realised. But on the other hand, "progress has been uneven across regions and countries, leaving significant gaps" (UN, 2015). Indeed, Table 4.7 shows that some regions lag behind seriously. This is true especially for Oceania. It is also the case in Western Asia; unfortunately, the situation there has deteriorated further since the UN report was published, due to the wars in Syria and Iraq. Sub-Saharan Africa too has not made sufficient progress. To this region belongs the ECOWAS, the Economic Community of West African States, which is the topic of Section 5.4.

Evidently, the MDGs were never considered as final goals. Even apart from the fact that none of them have been realised in all regions, targets such as 'reduce extreme poverty by half' can never be acceptable in the long run.

In 2015, at the end of the MDGs period, a new set of goals was agreed, again for a period of 15 years (2015–2030). They are called the **Sustainable Development Goals, SDGs**. They are 17 in number, and they are shown in Figure 4.12.

Again, the goals were expressed in more detailed conditions that can be assessed. Here is an example:

SDG 1, No poverty

1.1: By 2030, eradicate extreme poverty for all people everywhere, currently measured as people living on less than $1.25 a day.

1.2: By 2030, reduce at least by half the proportion of men, women and children of all ages living in poverty in all its dimensions according to national definitions.

1.3: Implement nationally appropriate social protection systems and measures for all, including floors, and by 2030 achieve substantial coverage of the poor and the vulnerable.

1.4: By 2030, ensure that all men and women, in particular the poor and the vulnerable, have equal rights to economic resources, as well as access to basic services, ownership and control over land and other forms of property, inheritance, natural resources, appropriate new technology and financial services, including microfinance.

FIGURE 4.12   The 17 Sustainable Development Goals (SDGs)

1.5: By 2030, build the resilience of the poor and those in vulnerable situations and reduce their exposure and vulnerability to climate-related extreme events and other economic, social and environmental shocks and disasters.

1.a: Ensure significant mobilization of resources from a variety of sources, including through enhanced development cooperation, in order to provide adequate and predictable means for developing countries, in particular least developed countries, to implement programmes and policies to end poverty in all its dimensions.

1.b: Create sound policy frameworks at the national, regional and international levels, based on pro-poor and gender-sensitive development strategies, to support accelerated investment in poverty eradication actions.

TABLE 4.8 The 17 Sustainable Development Goals (SDGs)

#	Goal	Description
1	No poverty	End poverty in all its forms everywhere
2	Zero hunger	End hunger, achieve food security and improved nutrition and promote sustainable agriculture
3	Good health and well-being	Ensure healthy lives and promote well-being for all at all ages
4	Quality education	Ensure inclusive and equitable quality education and promote lifelong learning opportunities for all
5	Gender equality	Achieve gender equality and empower all women and girls
6	Clean water and sanitation	Ensure availability and sustainable management of water and sanitation for all
7	Affordable and clean energy	Ensure access to affordable, reliable, sustainable and modern energy for all
8	Decent work and economic growth	Promote sustained, inclusive and sustainable economic growth, full and productive employment and decent work for all
9	Industry, innovation and infrastructure	Build resilient infrastructure, promote inclusive and sustainable industrialization and foster innovation
10	Reduced inequalities	Reduce income inequality within and among countries
11	Sustainable cities and communities	Make cities and human settlements inclusive, safe, resilient and sustainable
12	Responsible consumption and production	Ensure sustainable consumption and production patterns
13	Climate action	Take urgent action to combat climate change and its impacts by regulating emissions and promoting developments in renewable energy
14	Life below water	Conserve and sustainably use the oceans, seas and marine resources for sustainable development
15	Life on land	Protect, restore and promote sustainable use of terrestrial ecosystems; sustainably manage forests; combat desertification; halt and reverse land degradation; halt biodiversity loss
16	Peace, justice and strong institutions	Promote peaceful and inclusive societies for sustainable development, provide access to justice for all and build effective, accountable and inclusive institutions at all levels
17	Partnerships for the goals	Strengthen the means of implementation and revitalize the global partnership for sustainable development

Together, the 17 SGDs and their details like those shown here, define the so-called **2030 Agenda for Sustainable Development**.

As you can see, the new goals go much further than their predecessors, the MDGs. Very new was the fact that the SDGs set concrete targets to be achieved by the rich countries, not only for the developing regions. Examples are SDG 7 (sustainable energy), SDG 12 (consumption and production), and SDG 13 (climate change); they evidently concern all countries in the world.

The last SDG, number 17, is a special one, as it does not set immediate sustainability goals, but rather demands cooperation in order to achieve the other goals. Several items of SDG 17 are directly related to topics that were discussed in the former chapters of this book, such as:

SDG 17.4

Assist developing countries in attaining long-term debt sustainability through coordinated policies aimed at fostering debt financing, debt relief and debt restructuring, as appropriate, and address the external debt of highly indebted poor countries to reduce debt distress.

SDG 17.10

Promote a universal, rules-based, open, non-discriminatory and equitable multilateral trading system under the World Trade Organization.

SDG 17.13

Enhance global macroeconomic stability, including through policy coordination and policy coherence.

Cooperation

Although SDG 17 mainly deals with international solidarity and cooperation, it is also related to cooperation between societal partners, even within regions or countries. This is clearly shown by SDG 17.17.

SDG 17.17

Encourage and promote effective public, public-private and civil society partnerships, building on the experience and resourcing strategies of partnerships.

Several examples of such cooperation have been given in the present chapter. In the three cases of Section 4.7, students work closely together, not only with ordinary people in far-flung corners of the world, but also with the local, national or international NGOs. Earlier in this chapter, Unilever appeared to be working together with the World Wildlife Fund, the FAO and with local fishing companies, while Utz Certified cooperates with multinational companies and local coffee growers. These are examples of **public-private partnerships (PPP)**, through which the boundaries between commercial companies, non-profit organisations and individuals are crossed, enabling cooperation on the basis of parity. Such cooperation is necessary, given that problems caused by unsustainability are frequently extraordinarily complex. In

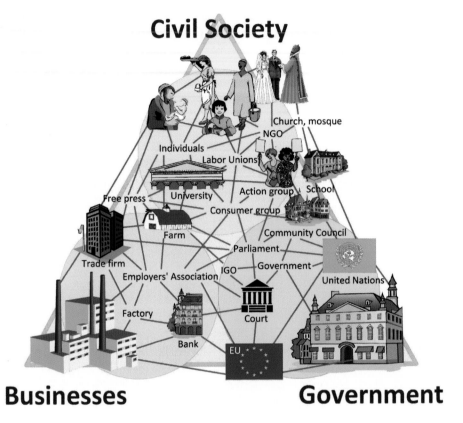

FIGURE 4.13 The triangle of civil society, the corporate world and the state, which can collectively manage transitions for the purpose of sustainable development

many cases, real solutions can only be found through genuine transitions, which lead to fundamentally different ways of thinking and to comprehensively change physical and economic structures. When it comes to guiding these transitions – **transition management** – much research is being undertaken. One thing that has emerged loud and clear from this research is that transition management is impossible if it is only either top-down or bottom-up, simply because many parties must contribute without being coerced but rather do this from a feeling of involvement. Three types of partners, operating together as a **network**, are able to achieve results in this regard (see Figure 4.13) – governments, including intergovernmental organisations; companies, including farmers, banks and the media; and civil society, including NGOs, educational institutions and individuals.

In order to solve major and complex issues of sustainable development, an intensive **interdisciplinary** cooperation is required – in other words, a close cooperation as a team of professionals involved in a wide range of disciplines. But even that is not enough. This cooperative approach must be extended even further, so that not only experts come aboard, but also a range of others who, for whatever reason, are interested parties – stakeholders, such as customers or inhabitants. Such a level of cooperation is referred to as **transdisciplinary**: literally 'beyond the disciplines'. Transition management for the sake of sustainable development is transdisciplinary by definition. This is not always an easy task for professionals, as they are asked to work at an intensive level with others who know little or nothing about their field of expertise. The ability to work together in a transdisciplinary manner might be difficult for many, but it is a very important characteristic for professionals who truly want to contribute to sustainable development.

Summary

There are many types of sources of vigour opposing the flaws in the fabric that were examined in Chapters 2 and 3. These include

- International organisations, including many that are affiliated to the United Nations or the European Union. The Sustainable Development Goals have great significance in the international endeavour towards sustainability.
- Sources of inspiration and of powerful ideas, such as solidarity, peace, participatory democracy, human rights and emancipation.
- People, both as individuals and cooperating within associations, protest groups and NGOs, or more informally in the form of mass movements. Together they make up civil society, which derives its power partly from diversity.
- The natural environment, if properly managed, such as by joining fragmented ecosystems back together.
- Science and technology, which can give us surprising innovations and breakthroughs.
- The corporate world, both the large multinational companies and a large number of small companies, supported where necessary through microcredit.
- The professionals of the future – the students of today who can already make important contributions to sustainability while being trained.

When these sources of vigour work together, such as in the form of public-private partnerships, their combined capacity to generate sustainable development is much greater. Together, they are able to undertake the decentralised management of sustainable transitions.

Chapters 2, 3 and 4 together formed a **SWOT analysis**, in the form of an outline of the weaknesses (**W**) and threats (**T**) in Chapters 2 and 3, followed by the strengths (**S**) and opportunities (**O**) as detailed in Chapter 4.

Based on this analysis, an agenda was introduced for the next decades: the *2030 Agenda for Sustainable Development*, defining the 17 Sustainable Development Goals.

In the second half of the book, programs and methods will be investigated in order to realise this agenda.

A more detailed summary can be found on the website of this book.

PART 2

Solution strategies

The boundaries have been delineated: the flaws in the fabric and the sources of vigour, being the weak and the strong points in the system of human society. The primary flaws and the resultant threats were detailed in Chapters 2 and 3, while Chapter 4 examined the opposing sources of vigour and the opportunities that they create. The relationships between them were unearthed and they culminated in twelve requirements that sustainable development shall have to fulfil. In broad terms, this means the SWOT analysis (strengths, weaknesses, opportunities and threats) has been completed. Now, it is time to see what can be done to institute the package of requirements, which will happen in the next chapters. There are many ways of tackling issues of unsustainability. The global society can progress in very different directions. Such differences that are even more obvious when considered at a regional level. The second part of this book deals with the different directions that sustainable development can take.

Part 2 consists of the following chapters:

5   Here and there
6   Now and later
7   Climate and energy
8   Sustainable business practices

5
HERE AND THERE

In this chapter the following topics and concepts will be discussed:

5.1   China: growth, but not in terms of human rights
5.2   India: high-tech versus rural
5.3   The EU: continent of an aging population
5.4   ECOWAS: explosive population growth in Africa
5.5   Shared responsibility

A glossary containing all terms in both this chapter and others is available on the website of this book.

FIGURE 5.1   A family planning poster along a residential lane in Guangzhou propagates "One child per couple!"

Source: Vladimir Menkov, Wikimedia.

Case 5.1 Too many children

The fine was set at 2,000 yuan – around 200 US dollars. This was a large sum for the Zhou family, who live in Yulin, capital of the Chinese province of Guangxi, given that their monthly income is only 1,200 yuan. The penalty was imposed because they had two children – one more than permitted. Officially, it was not a fine but rather a 'social fostering fee'.

In a way, the Zhou's got off lightly, as stories exist of other families being evicted and pregnant women forced to have an abortion.

Early one morning in a city in the province of Hunan, a tiny body is found beside a highway. It is a newborn girl, dumped by her parents. Perhaps it was their second child. But it might just as well have been their first and, as many do in China, they had hoped for a boy – and so, because they could only have one child, the girl had to go. Cars speed past the anonymous little corpse, splattering it with mud. Nobody stops. They're all in a hurry.

Our studies to date have largely been of the world as a whole. But there are of course major differences between the various parts of the world – between the regions, as they are sometimes called. Regions include China, India, Latin America, North America and Europe, as well as the Arab world or Indonesia. Regions are not strictly defined, and countries such as Egypt and Tunisia might be considered part of the Arab region but are also members of the African Union (AU).

Each region will have its own flaws and its own sources of vigour. These play a role when it comes to determining the types of solutions one adopts for the purposes of sustainable development. As examples, four regions will be investigated in this chapter, making use of the Triple P: people, planet and profit. For each of them, the present state will be described and also the prospects for the future.

There is a good reason why these four regions have been selected: the European Union (EU), China, India, and the ECOWAS, a group of cooperating African nations south of the Sahara. Figure 5.1 shows them clearly. In that graph, the horizontal axis represents the HDI, the Human Development Index, which was mentioned in Chapter 3. The vertical axis shows the average income per capita. There appears to be a clearly visible relation between the two, which is not surprising. The curve depicts the general trend: the higher the income, the higher a country or region is on the HDI list.

Figure 5.2 illustrates that the four regions are characteristic for four different stages of development and prosperity. The EU is an example of a wealthy and developed region. The ECOWAS is at the other extreme, with a low development and much poverty. China and India are in between, both moving upwards.

Besides, the regions have many more differences. Together they offer a good overview of the immense differences, both concerning regional problems and solution strategies in various places in the world.

This chapter puts the emphasis on the dimension of place, of location, of the 'here and now'. The other dimension: time, the 'now and later', will be dealt with in the following chapter.

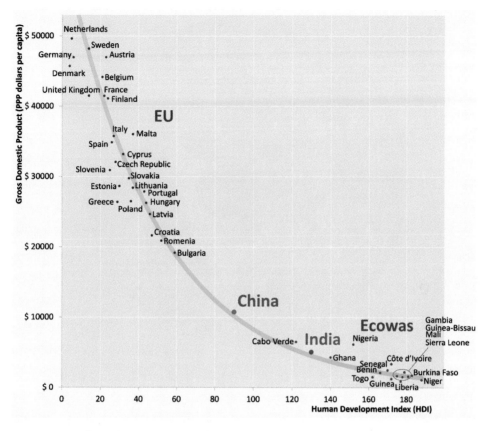

FIGURE 5.2   Relation between GDP and HDI

5.1 China: growth, but not in terms of human rights

TABLE 5.1 China

	Year:	1970	2015	2060
People	Population	809 million	1,376 million	1,277 million
	Birth rate (children per woman)	5.58	1.57	1.8
	Child mortality (up to 5 years)	12%	1.3%	0.3%
	Life expectancy at birth	63.3 years	76.0 years	84.8 years
	Urban population	17%	56%	79%
Planet	Surface area		9.6 million km²	
	Ecological footprint		3.4 ha per capita	
	Biocapacity		0.9 ha per capita	
Profit	GDP (2015 $)	$92 billion	$10,866 billion	
	GDP (PPP$ per capita)		$14,200	
	Income disparity *		13 times	

* Income of the wealthiest 10 percent divided by the income of the poorest 10 percent.

Sources: UNDP (2016), World Bank (2016), Global Footprint Network (2016).

FIGURE 5.3   China

China's history stretches back thousands of years and consists of a patchwork of powerful empires interspersed with periods of fragmentation and foreign dependency – often as a result of invasions (Figure 5.3). This may have been the case when new dynasties came to power in the period between 2200 and 800 BCE, and was certainly true when the Mongols invaded in the thirteenth century AD.

During the seventh century AD, conquests saw the empire grow into a gigantic area that incorporated a vast part of eastern Asia, including the present Siberia, Korea and Vietnam.

The nineteenth century saw other nations becoming increasingly involved in China, with the British empire, France, Germany, Japan, Russia and the United States all occupying pieces of Chinese territory or meddling in domestic administration. These powers employed degrading means, such as the British strategy of importing opium, causing a large number of Chinese to become addicted to the drug. When the Chinese authorities prohibited the traffic of opium as a result of this, the British declared war on China. The British Empire won both the 'Opium Wars' (1839–1842 and 1856–1860), occupying the capital city of Beijing in 1860 and once again legalising opium after the emperor had fled.

The last imperial dynasty fell to a revolution in 1911 when China was declared a republic. Two decades later Japan invaded China in 1937, occupying the country until 1945. The Japanese invasion interrupted a struggle between the governing nationalist party and the communists, which was reignited in the wake of the Japanese departure, culminating in the communists taking power in 1949, led by Mao Zedong. The nationalists fled to the island of Taiwan, where they are still a political force.

The country has been under communist control ever since, and in 1966 Mao announced the start of the Cultural Revolution, which threw the country into a state of chaos. Anything that was – or appeared to be – intellectual was considered 'bad'. Freedom of expression was even more restricted and education, healthcare and the economy collapsed. A civil war broke out that killed millions.

After the death of Mao in 1976, reforms were slowly but surely introduced in the country's economy, giving the free market a chance to flourish. This went hand in hand with increasing openness to other countries. China had previously been very isolated, with few foreigners allowed to enter and the country largely refraining from involvement in foreign affairs. But things have changed drastically since that time.

Two hundred years ago Napoleon said that: "China is a sleeping giant. But when she awakes the world will tremble." We will soon know whether the French emperor was correct, as China has awoken.

People

China is currently the most populous nation on Earth. More than one in every six humans lives in China.

Fifty years ago the population grew at a tremendous rate, as a result of which the **population explosion** became one of the biggest causes of unsustainability and a major factor in determining the Chinese authorities' strategy, starting in 1979, of a **one-child policy**. Families that have more than one child are fined heavily, although in recent years some leeway has been introduced for parents who might, for example, have lost their only child in a disaster. The growth of the population has shrunk considerably (as can be seen in Table 5.1), and experts believe the Chinese population will start to shrink sometime between 2020 and 2060.

The one-child policy is highly controversial and is disputed by human rights organisations and others. Case 5.1 illustrated how the population strategy leads to degrading scenarios, but there are also other consequences, some of which were most likely not anticipated. Because sons are preferred over daughters almost everywhere in China, large numbers of girls are aborted or killed almost immediately after being born. The consequences of this practice are grave, and in recent years ca. 120 boys are being raised for every 100 girls (Source: Zhu et al, 2009). It is estimated that there are 30 million more young males (up to the age of 20) than females, many of whom who will not have a future partner – if they are heterosexuals. This has resulted in a new type of population problem, which hangs like a time bomb over Chinese society. But the fact remains that some highly active policy of stopping the population growth was necessary, and without the one-child policy there would be at least one hundred million more Chinese today.

The one-child policy would have been utterly impossible in a democratic nation. The Chinese government rules the country with an iron fist – it is a dictatorship. There is little respect for human rights. The authorities control the press and television, while the Internet is also subject to censorship. The country is still officially a communist one, although there is little evidence of this in an economic sense.

A shocking event occurred in 1989 when, shortly after the people of Eastern Europe had peacefully overthrown their own communist dictatorships, many Chinese hoped to achieve similar aims. With students at the helm, over a million people started a demonstration on 27 April in Tiananmen Square (the 'Gate of Heaven's Pacification'), Beijing. After some weeks a few thousand students went on a hunger strike.

Then, on 3 June 1989, the army stepped in. The square was emptied with tanks and armed soldiers, during which between 300 and 400 protestors died. Chinese democracy had become even more of a pipe dream.

Questions

- Is the one-child policy a criminal act, should it never have been implemented?
- Or was the policy a necessity, and would the situation in China otherwise have gotten out of control?
- Given the fact that the one-child policy was only possible because China is not a democracy, is this an argument in favour of dictatorship?

Profit

China was a poor nation in the post–World War II years – a standard Third World country. But this gradually changed and, starting in 1978, China evolved towards a market economy. Foreign companies were allowed to set up shop, businesses were permitted to make a profit and Chinese industry was dramatically modernised. The country is a member of the World Trade Organisation (WTO) since 2001. The economy is doing well; very well, to be honest. For years the country's economic growth stood at 8 percent or higher, an extraordinary rate when compared to Western nations. It has a gigantic export base, which is certainly not made up solely of simple products – a quarter of Chinese exports consist of high-tech electronics. At present, China is the second largest economy in the world, and it is expected to become the world's biggest economy sometime in the twenty-first century.

Some of the Chinese people are profiting from this economic leap forward, and the number of people living in conditions of extreme poverty (less than one dollar a day) decreased between 1990 and 2000 from 33 percent to 16 percent. This figure refers to PPP dollars – corrected for inflation – so it really means a great deal in respect of the purchasing power.

The annual growth figures have gone down in recent years, from 10 percent or more in the years until 2011 down to around 7 percent in the second half of the 2010–2020 decade. Nevertheless, the present figures are still high compared to those of the USA and Europe.

But life has not improved for everyone yet, and there is an underclass of factory labourers who are compelled to live in houses or barracks owned by the factory, and buy all their goods from the factory shop. They are forced to work 12 to 16 hours a day, do not earn enough (or earn just enough) to cover the costs of their accommodation and are to all extents slaves of the factories in which they work (Figure 5.4). Many of the products imported by the West from China, such as toys, clothing and computers, are made by this type of labourer. The award-winning 2005 documentary, 'China Blue', provides a harrowing picture of working conditions in such a factory.

FIGURE 5.4   Conditions in Chinese factories are heavy. Workdays of 16 or more hours, without weekends off, are not exceptional

Source: Robert Scoble, Wikimedia.

At the same time many major Western companies are closing down their factories in Europe and the US, dismissing their workers and moving shop to China and other low-wage countries. They frequently have no other option, for if they don't move while their competitors are taking the step, then they run the risk of going out of business.

Case 5.2 The only exit

Foxconn employs over a million young people. Despite the English-sounding name, Foxconn is a Chinese company based in Shenzhen. The employees, who are mostly between the ages of 18 and 24, make telephones, games consoles and computers for Western multinationals like Apple, Dell, Intel and Microsoft.

In May 2010 the entire workforce suddenly received a 20 percent raise. The reason? A desperate attempt by the management to stop a suicide epidemic amongst the workers. For the same reason, the company erected safety nets around the taller buildings and employed a team of councillors.

Whether all these measures will help remains to be seen, given that the background to the suicides primarily involves the inhuman pace of work the employees are compelled to adhere to, together with the incredible amount of overtime. The young workers regularly have only two or four hours of sleep a night for weeks at a stretch, sometimes going without any sleep at all. And then there is also the total lack of a private life, with the workers housed in barracks on the factory grounds and many sharing a room. They hardly have a chance to see family or make friends, never mind starting a family and building up a future. In the months preceding the introduction of those measures by management, the complete lack of future proved a good enough reason for eleven of the workers to choose the only exit still left – suicide. Apple and Dell, both Foxconn buyers, responded with shock, calling for an investigation to be conducted. Those companies might not have been aware that the situation at Foxconn has been typical of many companies in China for years.

The wage increase did not apparently have the immediate intended effect, as barely a week later the 20 percent raise became a 100 percent raise.

Perhaps, though, there is a different interpretation to these issues. Some commentators argued that China generally has a rather high suicide rate of 20 deaths per 100,000 persons annually (*The Independent*, 9 September 2011). In 2010, 14 suicides of Foxconn employees were reported, which is relatively low. Perhaps no suicide epidemic? As to the wage raises: this may be due to China reaching its **Lewisian turning-point**, where a shortage of labour forces leads to a sharp increase of salaries (*China Daily*, 3 June 2010; *The Economist*, 10 June 2010).

In 2016, the company still did not comply with the legal maximum working hours of 49 weekly. The number of suicides at Foxconn has decreased; between 2011 and 2016, eight employees jumped from Foxconn buildings.

Questions

- Do you own any possessions that were entirely or partly 'made in China'? Have you ever checked?

- If you buy items made in China, you might be contributing to a situation in which labourers receive very low wages. But if you don't buy them, then these people might not earn anything at all. What is your best option under these circumstances?

Waste is a significant import for China. The waste trade is gigantic; its size was estimated in 2013 at 400 billion dollars a year. A significant part is imported from Europe, with the Netherlands, Switzerland, Belgium and Germany as the major suppliers: exporting garbage is much cheaper than recycling or landfill. China takes over huge quantities: in 2013 it involved 7.4 million tonnes of plastic, 28 million tonnes of paper and 6 million tonnes of shreaded steel. Electronics waste – actually chemical waste – is shipped too in massive amounts, mostly from the United States, which has not signed the Basel Convention (see Chapter 3).

The Chinese industrial sector uses the waste as a valuable raw material for manufacturing new products. From the perspective of a closed cycle, this is not a bad point, but the fact that the waste problem (including pollution and health risks) is being transferred from wealthy nations to China is a less pleasing aspect.

Planet

The economic development of China has resulted in environmental issues of titanic proportions. The country generates a large quantity of its power using coal, which releases soot and CO_2 and which is retrieved from mines so dangerous that fatal accidents occur on almost a weekly basis. Seven of the world's ten most polluted cities are in China, and 30 percent of the country is plagued by acid rain.

Intensive occupation and agriculture has damaged the natural environment. Tens of thousands of hectares are seriously eroded every year and the forests of China have been dramatically thinned out – a mere 16 percent of the country is still forested. This has threatened a number of major species of animals that are now faced with extinction, the most famous of which is the giant panda.

Deforestation also means soil erosion, with the fertile land becoming parched and blowing or washing away (Figure 5.5). A fifth of China's land has been seriously degraded in this manner, with five billion tons of fertile soil disappearing annually and resulting in dust and sand storms. In 1950 a sand storm would occur once every 30 years, but since 1990 they have been a near-annual occurrence.

Roots can absorb rainwater, much like a sponge might, but eroded and parched land is much less capable of this, and so the deforestation has also increased the chance of major flooding. A deluge in 1996 killed a large number of people and caused 27 billion dollars of damage, with an even bigger flood following in 1998 that affected a quarter of a billion people.

Paradoxically, there is also a continuous shortage of water. So much fresh water is used for drinking, irrigation and industry that one of the country's biggest rivers, the Huang He (the Yellow River), is now dry for much of the year. This destroys the natural environment and hinders shipping, while the high consumption levels of groundwater mean that seawater is flowing inland. Both this and poor irrigation practices means that the land is becoming salinised.

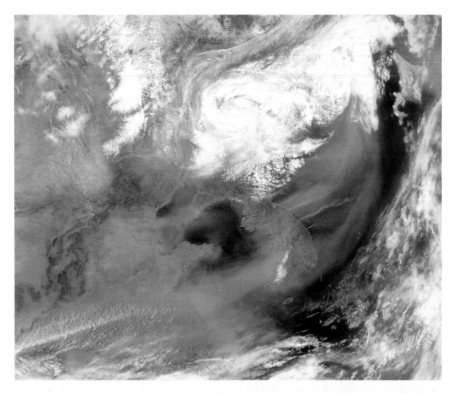

FIGURE 5.5 Sandstorms coming out of northern China. Top: from space, with northern China to the left and the Korean Peninsula in the centre. The white areas are clouds; the yellow ones are sand. Bottom: The sky above Taiwan is overcast with sand from Mainland China

Source: SeaWiFS Project, NASA/Goddard Space Flight Center, & ORBIMAGE; 阿爾特斯, Wikimedia.

Overall water quality is bad, with the water from the major rivers, the groundwater and the coastal stretches seriously polluted by the discharge of waste water by industry and cities. Artificial and natural fertilisers and pesticides for agriculture and aquaculture have also contributed to poor quality of the water – only 20 percent of waste water is treated. The presence of fertiliser chemicals in the water have resulted in **eutrophication**, the overfertilisation of waters that causes algae to flourish and robs the water of oxygen, killing fishes and other organisms.

The damage caused by air pollution and desertification together is estimated at some 100 billion dollars a year – a very large sum when compared to China's annual GDP (see Table 5.1). In recent years the authorities have been serious about the environmental problems and are adopting numerous measures. One of these is a 'Green Great Wall' of trees, planted around the capital city of Beijing at a cost of six billion dollars in order to protect the inhabitants against dust storms. According to Beijing Review (October 2013) this is just the beginning of an even larger project, aiming to create between 1978 and 2050 a green zone with a length of 4,500 kilometres (2,800 miles), on average 1,000 kilometres (600 miles) wide.

Environmental impact reports for all major construction projects have been compulsory since 2003, and the results have been positive, with a number of these projects demolished since 2005 due to excessive environmental damage. China has signed a number of international environmental treaties, including ones related to biodiversity, the ozone layer and the shipping of hazardous goods.

After the huge flooding disaster of 1998, cutting forests is prohibited in China. This is not just unambiguously positive, as the need of wood has not diminished. The import of wood, for instance from tropical Africa, is increasing rapidly – between 1997 and 2010 the volume grew a hundredfold, it is estimated. This means that, just like Western nations, China is transferring a major environmental problem onto other nations.

In 2016 the country signed and ratified the Paris Agreement on climate change, and it is to be expected that China will seriously lower its greenhouse gas emissions; more about this in Chapter 7. A relatively high percentage (almost 20 percent) of the country's energy is already being generated using renewable sources, such as wind and hydropower. However, just as in the Western nations, the problems that China must solve are extremely complex, with every solution having both advantages and disadvantages, as the following case demonstrates.

Case 5.3 The Three Gorges Dam

The generation of a huge amount of electrical power started in 2009. The Three Gorges Dam first cut off the Yangtze River in 2006, resulting in the world's largest reservoir at 600 km long. Since 2012, this mass of water generates 18,000 megawatts of power, sufficient for 160 billion kilowatt hours of power annually: equal to the combined power of twenty nuclear plants. This means a cut of millions of tons of CO_2 emissions into the atmosphere, which is great for the economy and the environment, as well as for the people, as the 300 million people living downstream will be less prone to floods. But there are also disadvantages.

The rising waters forced 1.4 million people to relocate, with 40 towns and an unknown number of villages drowned, while much local nature was also destroyed.

There is a risk of poisonous mud settling on the bed of the dam due to the waste discharged from Chongqing, whose 32 million inhabitants make it the largest city in the country. On top of this, the body of water will mean greater evaporation levels from the river, resulting in the land downstream drying up, the natural environment being damaged, agricultural irrigation coming under threat and an increasing scarcity of drinking water. The fertility of the soil shall decline, because as floods decrease, less fertile sediment is deposited on the riverside fields.

In 2011, the Chinese government admitted that there are some serious problems. The dam appears to cause an increased frequency of earthquakes. Tributaries of the Yangtze River are contaminated with heavy metals such as copper, zinc, lead and ammonium. The many relocated people are facing a lot of social and economic problems. And the dam contributes to droughts downstream, causing a massive loss of harvests.

There is also another ambitious government-run project on the cards, involving rivers in the water-rich south being linked to the northern rivers, which are drying up, through three gigantic canals. It is the largest water-related project ever planned, and food production in the north will gain considerably as a result. But some experts fear that the consequences for the Chinese water resources and the natural environment will be severe, and maybe even also affect the local climate.

Prospects

The Chinese authorities are tackling the grave issues of unsustainability using a completely top-down approach – they are endeavouring to stay in full control of all aspects. 'Control' is the entire leading paradigm, and the methods employed are grand ones – the biggest dam in the world, canals stretching across thousands of kilometres, an unprecedented economic growth that has continued for years, a population policy that is enforced upon citizens numbering over a billion. This is also a nation where dissent is unhesitantly censored, to the extent that even the search engine Google withdrew from China in 2010 after not only its search pages were censored – a move Google accepted – but its websites were also hacked on the orders of the Chinese authorities, according to Google. Facebook, Twitter, YouTube, Instagram and many other sites are blocked by order of the Chinese government.

This use of control has been successful in certain ways – the rate of population growth has decreased significantly, with birth figures well below two children per women, in part due to the one-child policy but also in part due to the rising prosperity of a segment of the people (as will be discussed in greater detail in the following chapter). The only reason why the population is still growing is because a large percentage of the current population is of a fertile age, having been born during the baby boom of the previous generation.

Just a few decades ago a large proportion of the Chinese people were impoverished. Today the authorities have succeeded in dramatically changing this, with living conditions notably improved for many – although certainly not all – of the people. However, there is a flipside to the economic advances, and that is the considerable damage to the environment.

If the current economic growth continues at a high annual rate the consequences will be disastrous for the environment, and even the Chinese economy could stumble as a result of 'overheating'. But this economic growth also means funds for the authorities to tackle the environmental issues. In other words, if the government sticks to a policy that is clearly environmentally minded, the growth in prosperity will actually be the key to improving the environmental conditions. What is also of real importance in this is the fact that China's population growth is low and will come to a halt within a few decades. Paradoxically, this positive development is indebted in part to the restrictions on human rights.

If the Chinese are to succeed in alleviating both poverty and environmental degradation, a balance could be found in which the interests of *people*, *planet* and *profit* are balanced. This means that China might be a prosperous and healthy nation within the not too distant future. Should the country fail in this ambition then China will, together with the presently wealthy nations, continue to contribute to the accelerated worsening of our global environmental problems.

Whether or not the Chinese authorities will be able to maintain the top-down approach in the long term is an intriguing question. In other parts of the world we have repeatedly seen that the population's increasing prosperity developed into a broad middle class that slowly demanded greater civil rights, which in most cases ultimately resulted in democratic reforms and thus saw the control paradigm eroding. At the same time, Western nations are increasingly acknowledging that the forces of nature – including the climate, rivers and spread of nature – cannot be fully controlled, with this approach increasingly giving way to the paradigm of 'adaptation', which is akin to the process of democratisation but which pertains to *planet* instead of *people*. Whether China will move in the same direction remains to be seen.

5.2 India: high-tech versus rural

TABLE 5.2 India

	Year:	1970	2015	2060
People	Population	554 million	1,311 million	1,745 million
	Birth rate (children per woman)	5.57	2.41	1.8
	Child mortality (up to 5 years)	21%	4.8%	1%
	Life expectancy at birth	51.0 years	68.3 years	78.2 years
	Urban population	20%	33%	56%
Planet	Surface area		3.3 million km^2	
	Ecological footprint		1.2 ha per capita	
	Biocapacity		0.5 ha per capita	
Profit	GDP (2015 $)	$64 billion	$2,074 billion	
	GDP (PPP$ per capita)		$6,100	
	Income disparity *		9 times	

* Income of the wealthiest 10 percent divided by the income of the poorest 10 percent.

Sources: UNDP (2016), World Bank (2016), Global Footprint Network (2016).

FIGURE 5.6 India

India, along with China, is one of the BRICS nations (Brazil, Russia, India, China and South Africa), five countries that are rapidly becoming economic giants. And, just like China, India also has a history stretching back thousands of years, with complex cities holding up to 30,000 inhabitants already existing in 3000 BCE. But that is more or less where any similarities with China end.

India has always been surrounded by nations containing numerous peoples and cultures, which is why it has frequently been the stage for the arrival of a new group of people (Figure 5.6). In other parts of the world such an incident would normally lead to the original inhabitants dying out or slowly being assimilated into the new population, but in India it led to strata, with every new conquering people making up a new ruling class that did no mix with the other classes. This is the origin of the **caste system**, which characterises India. The complex caste system is deeply rooted in Hinduism, which is the largest religion in India.

Sometime around 1500 BCE the Aryans arrived in India. They spoke Sanskrit, which is related to European languages, and although it is no longer spoken it is still considered – as Latin is in Europe – to be the 'classical' language of India, especially for texts.

There were subsequent waves of invasions, by the Persians, the Greeks (led by Alexander the Great), the Turks and the Mongols. The Portuguese, Dutch and English fought each other in the sixteenth and seventeenth centuries for control of the subcontinent's ports. The British Empire emerged as the victors and its East India Company and other companies gradually took over ever-larger slices of the gigantic land. The English authorities took over the running of the nation in the nineteenth century.

In the twentieth century India strived for independence, under the inspired leadership of Mohandas **Gandhi** (Figure 5.7), who placed pressure on the colonial power using a strategy of complete non-violence (**ahimsa**: a term expressing a combination of non-violence and respect for all living things). Amongst other things, he challenged the commercial repression of the Indian people. As an example, the indigenous people were prohibited from extracting salt from the sea, as this was a monopoly controlled by the British. Ghandi and thousands of fellow Indians protested by going to the ocean and producing salt, their actions being filmed

FIGURE 5.7   Mohandas 'Mahatma' Gandhi, 1869–1948

Source: www.mkgandhi.org, 1944.

and subsequently shown in cinemas around the world. The non-violent campaign for independence created such an impression on public opinion in Europe that the United Kingdom felt compelled to grant India independence in 1947.

Immediately after independence, long-simmering tensions between the Hindu and Moslem population groups exploded. Millions of people died in the battles that followed, with the country being partitioned into three in 1949 by the secession of Pakistan to the west and Bangladesh to the east. Bangladesh and Pakistan were a single entity until Bangladesh seceded in 1971, with Indian backing. The relationship between India and Pakistan is still a tense one today.

People

As opposed to China, India is a parliamentary democracy, which it has been ever since independence in 1947, although there have been a number of crises, including the assassination of its prime minister in 1984.

The population in India also mushroomed in the twentieth century, but, unlike in China, the growth figures are not declining at any notable rate. Whereas the birth rate might be declining, it is not doing so at a rate (2.1 children for each woman) where the population might stabilise. Forecasters expect India's population to overtake China's sometime between 2020 and 2050 to become the most populous country in the world. One must remember that India is only a third as large as China. A strategy such as the one-child policy in China could never succeed in India because the country lacks the absolute centralised power. Healthcare expenditure is low, as is education, although both are on the rise, and many children do not attend school. Child labour is rife across the nation, with a few hundred thousand children working in cotton plantations while others suffer under dangerous conditions in factories. Many of them are **debt slaves** – they may not be slaves in an official sense but they are not free to leave when they want, as their wages have been paid in advance to their parents, sometimes years in advance. They may only leave once they have paid back all loans. Cotton farmers and other employers profit greatly from this system, as children work more precisely than adults do, they cost less and are more docile, so it is easy to make them work for extended periods. Foreign companies share responsibility for this, as they purchase cheaply grown cotton and other agricultural and industrial products for low sums. But changes are on the horizon, and international organisations like UNICEF and the International Labour Organisation (ILO) are trying to help the children. An increasing number of companies are acknowledging their complicity and trying to change the situation. One of the problems is that when one ensures that children attend school, their families are frequently unable to make ends meet – they need those wages, no matter how paltry the sum. Because of this, people often try to find a solution through a combination of the two, where children can attend school for part of the day and work for the remainder.

Another source of issues is the caste system. The caste system might no longer exist by law, but that has not meant that much has changed in practice. The lowest Indian strata, the **Dalits**, are the **outcastes**, who are known in the West as pariahs or untouchables. The 140 million Dalits are excluded by Indian society, discriminated against in any way imaginable. Foreign aid that was received at the close of 2004 and in early 2005 in response to

FIGURE 5.8   The news of Mayawati's very convincing win was emblazoned across front pages in May 2007

Source: Wikimedia.

the great **Tsunami** that hit the Indian Ocean coasts of Asia and Africa did not reach the Dalits – they were not allowed to receive assistance. Today, however, there are some signs of changes.

Case 5.4   A Dalit in the Uttar Pradesh administration

Few could have predicted it during the 2007 elections in Uttar Pradesh. This Indian state is vast, with a sixth of all Indians calling it home, making it more populous than most nations in the world. Although it forms the heart of the North Indian culture, it is impoverished, with high levels of illiteracy and little public money devoted to welfare and public health.

The results of the May 2007 elections were surprising, with the Bahujan Samaj Party (BSP) gaining an absolute majority in parliament. What made this so notable was the fact that the party was led by Ms Kumari Mayawati, a Dalit. She subsequently became the Chief Minister of Uttar Pradesh (Figure 5.8).

In itself this was not even a notable event, given that she had already headed the state briefly on earlier occasions. But at that time she had led a coalition government, made up of a number of parties. What was different in 2007 was that the BSP gained an absolute majority, as this means that many non-Dalits must have voted for her. Untouchable . . . really?

Profit

Economic growth in India bears some resemblance to that in China, but it got off the ground later and is less powerful. India tried for a long time to develop itself under its own steam and until recently was much less accessible to foreign investment than China, which could be one of the reasons why its economic growth lags behind that of its north-eastern neighbour. Poverty is still a considerable issue and a third of the population live on less than a dollar a day (Figure 5.9).

Strikingly, the income disparity in India is not extreme, with the wealthiest 10 percent having nine times as much income as the poorest 10 percent – lower than in China. This means that the uppermost level of extremely rich people is not as extensive.

Two-thirds of Indians work in the agricultural sector, which is small-scale and relies heavily on manual labour. Agriculture, forestry and fishing together make up a quarter of India's total GDP. The work is vulnerable and is highly dependent on the weather conditions. Although production might have increased greatly in recent years, in times of drought it has sunk by over 10 percent.

FIGURE 5.9 The traditional face of India – farming using man power and animal power

Source: Michael Gäbler, Wikimedia.

Case 5.5   Drought

The rainfall was down by 29 percent in that year, a bad blow as it meant the harvest would be a poor one. And 2008 turned out to be a bad farming year for almost half the districts in India, where the farmers depend greatly on the monsoon rains. They need the rains as many places have little irrigation.

The harvests were poor, as feared, with the rice crop ten million tons less than the preceding year – a 10 percent drop. The price of rice seed and sugar rose dramatically.

Dozens of farmers in the state of Andhra Pradesh could not pay off their loans, which they had taken out to cover the cost of seed, and committed suicide. Others sold their wives and daughters to raise the money, an illegal practice which saw the courts working overtime to reverse the transactions.

Later years brought not much improvement. 2009, 2010 and 2012 again were bone dry years. Partly due to climate change? The droughts still continue:

BBC News, 20 April 2016

"At least 330 million people are affected by drought in India, the government has told the Supreme Court. Authorities say this number is likely to rise further given that some states with water shortages have not yet submitted status reports.

The drought is taking place as a heat wave extends across much of India with temperatures crossing 40C for days now.

An 11-year-old girl died of heatstroke while collecting water from a village pump in the western Maharashtra state. Yogita Desai had spent close to four hours in 42C temperatures gathering water from the pump on Sunday, local journalist Manoj Sapte told the BBC. Yogita's death certificate says she died of heatstroke and dehydration. The pump was a mere 500m from her house, but a typical wait for water stretches into hours.

India is heavily dependant on monsoon rains, which have been poor for two years in a row. The government said that nearly 256 districts across India, home to nearly a quarter of the population were impacted by the drought. Schools have been shut in the eastern state of Orissa and more than 100 deaths due to heatstroke have been reported from across the country, including from the southern states of Telangana and Andhra Pradesh which saw more than 2,000 deaths last summer."

India, like China, is a country that has seen a lot of Western companies relocate to its shores. Many of these companies are involved in high-tech industries, including software. They do not only physically relocate, but also **outsource** activities to India, where only certain divisions of the company move, such as the customer services or accounts departments. The services industry is consequently the fastest-growing source of income in the nation. It is a country of two faces – while a large percentage of the population work in agriculture, often under primitive circumstances, another portion focuses on very modern technology. An impressive example of this is HITEC City, an acronym of Hyderabad Information Technology Engineering Consultancy City. Hyderabad is the capital city of the state of Andhra Pradesh and it is considered the country's second Silicon Valley, after Bangalore. Numerous well-known multinational companies have branches there including Microsoft, IBM, Bank of America, Motorola, Electronic Arts (EA) and hundreds of others.

The Indian IT sector is growing at lightning pace, rising from $1.2 billion in 1996 to $5.7 billion in 2000, $60 billion in 2009, and $147 billion in 2015. It is estimated that it could reach a value of $225 billion by 2020. In 2015 the industry employed 2.5 million people, responsible for 25 percent of the nation's export. The city of Bangalore is dubbed the 'Silicon Valley of India' and is considered as the IT Capital of India. Another city, Hyderabad, contains a huge industrial area called HITEC City, short for 'Hyderabad Information Technology and Engineering Consultancy City'; its nickname is *Cyberabad* (Figure 5.10).

Planet

The population of India is rising fast, as is per capita income. Pressure on natural areas is likewise increasing. At present forests and other natural areas make up some 20 percent of India,

FIGURE 5.10 The modern face of India: the ILabs Oval, one of the more striking buildings in HITEC City

Source: Srisez, Wikimedia.

and the extent and quality is decreasing. Dense natural forests are becoming sparse cultural ones or they are making way for agriculture, and 500 species of mammals and thousands of bird species are being threatened with extinction. Agriculture is increasingly employing irrigation so as to decrease the industry's reliance on rains, a practice that will continue to grow in the next few decades, keeping pace with the population growth. Deep groundwater is the primary source for irrigation – in other words, mineral water. This is not a renewable resource, which can cause serious problems in time. Irrigation is not being professionally undertaken in many cases and much water is wasted while the soil is subjected to increasing levels of salinisation. But things could be different.

Case 5.6   The *johads* of Rajasthan

Rajendra Singh heads the local NGO Tarun Bhagat Singh in the district of Alwar. He is an expert in water management and teaches farmers in Alwar, which is in the state of Rajasthan, what their ancestors already knew – how to contain rainwater in *johads*, using little streams or canals to lead water to underground storage tanks.

The practice no longer existed by the 1970s, and the regional rivers regularly dried out while wells were empty. Not a single tree was still standing.

But things have turned full circle today, and the fields were even green during the drought year of 2008. The wells are overflowing and the water used for irrigation is contained in the ground by the roots of flourishing trees. To achieve this, the rivers were cleaned, traditional small dams were created in numerous places to fill up the *johads* and wells and forests were planted. This all meant that the water which was available in wet periods was retained for times when little rain fell. Not a drop was wasted.

Agricultural and environmental experts now go to Alwar from across India to study Rajendra Singh's approach. Old knowledge that had been lost is thus being re-invoked.

Indian agriculture is complicated by the fact that in a large part of the nation the soil has been degraded to some extent, as can be seen in Table 5.3.

TABLE 5.3 Soil degradation in India

Condition	Area (Mega hectares)	Percentage
Water erosion	93.7	28.6%
Wind erosion	9.5	2.9%
Water logging	14.3	4.4%
Salinity/alkalinity	5.9	1.8%
Soil acidity	16	4.9%
Complex problem	7.4	2.3%
Total degraded area	**146.8**	**44.8%**

Source: Bhattacharyya et al. (2015).

Soil erosion is an international problem, as can be seen from Figure 5.11, but it is especially dramatic in India. Figures 5.12 and 5.13 show soil erosion in India as a result of poorly managed land.

The quality of the air is also worsening, and the concentration of particulate matter in nearly all major Indian cities is higher than permitted by international standards. An increase in sulphur dioxide and nitrogen oxide concentrations has already led to a jump in the number of heart disease and cancer sufferers. The rise in these gases is due to an increase in energy consumption for cars and industry.

Prospects

India has always been a striking combination of extremes, ranging from wholly primitive to extraordinarily modern. Certain regions and aspects of Indian society are comparable to the Middle Ages in Europe, such as the feudal stratification that keeps the Dalits at the very bottom, and the agricultural practices undertaken in many places with simple tools, often by hand. But in other respects India is very much at home in the twenty-first century, although it seems that while the IT industry might appear very high-tech, it is still not sufficiently innovative, with there being few Indian patents compared to international levels. The Indian high-tech industry still follows rather than leads, although there are indications this is changing.

Just as in China, the high levels of economic growth in India result in both positives and negatives. The advances are essential for improving the living conditions of the many impoverished people, and will allow more children to attend schools so that they in turn can improve their own circumstances. But the economic growth is also seriously affecting the environment. To stop this degradation, agricultural methods will have to be employed that are cleaner and much more efficient, growing considerably more food on less land and in such a way that the effects on the natural environment are dramatically cut. This will allow the land to gradually recover from the damage already caused. If this were to succeed, then the

FIGURE 5.11 Soil erosion is not only a major problem in India

Sources: UNEP/GRID, Geneva; International Soil Reference and Information Centre (ISRIC), Wageningen.

FIGURES 5.12 AND 5.13 Erosion caused by rain because no terraces have been created. Bottom: dried earth does not properly absorb the water, creating channels that cause the fertile top layer to wash away

Sources: David L. Van Tassel, Land Institute, Kansas; Jack Dykinga, US Department of Agriculture (USDA).

growing population will have sufficient food while the extant natural environment can be retained and expanded. The country will also have to implement cleaner technology in order to cut back on air pollution.

Major investments are required to achieve all of this, which can only be provided through economic growth. And so India suffers from the same paradox as China does – in order to combat the negative consequences of economic growth, further economic growth is required. This growth is certainly not lacking, but the question remains whether India will succeed in applying that growth to improved social and environmental conditions. Even if it were to succeed, the process will still take decades longer than it will in China, as a result of India's economic growth starting later and increasing at a slower pace as well as the continuing growth in the population.

The preceding will not be implemented by a centralised national economy, as is the case in China, which is inconceivable in an India that is democratic, decentralised and that occasionally suffers from a completely chaotic political structure and culture. The necessary transitions must consequently be implemented through cooperation between countless groups, companies and authorities at every level in the nation. Methods such as microcredit and public-private partnerships are perfectly suited to this approach, while universal education, information and healthcare are essential.

5.3 The EU: continent of an aging population

TABLE 5.4 EU-28*

	Year:	1970	2015	2060
People	Population	441 million	504 million	488 million
	Birth rate (children per woman)	2.34	1.60	1.8
	Child mortality (up to 5 years)	2.9%	0.41%	0.2%
	Life expectancy at birth	72.0 years	80.7 years	87.3 years
	Urban population	66%	75%	85%
Planet	Surface area		4.2 million km^2	
	Ecological footprint		4.80 ha per capita	
	Biocapacity		2.33 ha per capita	
Profit	GDP (2015 $)	$822 billion	$16,180 billion	
	GDP (PPP$ per capita)		$37,700	
	Income disparity**		5 times (Czech Republic) to 15 times (Portugal)	
Nations	Austria, Belgium, Bulgaria, Croatia, Cyprus, Czech Republic, Denmark, Estonia, Finland, France, Germany, Greece, Hungary, Ireland, Italy, Latvia, Lithuania, Luxembourg, Malta, Netherlands, Poland, Portugal, Romania, Slovenia, Slovakia, Spain, Sweden, United Kingdom			

* The 28 nations that have made up the EU since 2013. For comparison reasons, the 1970 data for these 28 nations was also collated, even though they were not all members of the EU at that time. For the same reason, the United Kingdom is still included in the data for 2060, although in 2016 the UK decided to leave the EU.

** Income of the wealthiest 10 percent divided by the income of the poorest 10 percent.

Sources: UNDP (2016), World Bank (2016), Global Footprint Network (2016).

FIGURE 5.14   The European Union (EU)

At the time of Christ, the Romans ruled over the majority of the Celtic peoples in Western Europe, including the Gauls in what is today known as France. Over the centuries the Germanic tribes (Franks, Saxons and others) moved westwards from Eastern Europe, known as the Migration Period (or the 'Barbarian Invasions'), which ended around the fifth century. The Western Roman Empire collapsed in the same period. Sometime around 800 AD Charlemagne, the King of the Franks, conquered a large part of Western Europe. His empire fell apart after his death. This sowed the seeds for modern Europe, as the two largest parts of the empire would later develop into the primary centres of power on the mainland, France and Germany.

In Eastern Europe the migrations continued for centuries, with the region still unsettled by Russian expansion and Mongol and Turkish invasions in the Middle Ages.

Europe frequently considers itself as, more or less, the cultural successor to the classical Greek and Roman civilisations. This was not particularly true in the Middle Ages, when the Arabic world kept that classical cultural heritage alive and further expanded it. The Arabs were repeatedly and viciously attacked by crusades from Western Europe. During the Renaissance, the centre of gravity for modern development moved from the Middle East to Europe. It was from that time on that prosperity started to increase, accelerating even further in the eighteenth century with the advent of mechanisation, followed by industrialisation.

People

Together with the increase in prosperity and the advances of science and technology, the population size increased. This acceleration was tied to an improved healthcare and hygiene, resulting in a decline in child mortality while the birth rate did not immediately follow suit.

The same happened at a later stage in China and in India, and it is presently occurring in Africa, as shall be described later in the chapter.

The biggest population jump in Europe was in the twentieth century. Not even two world wars and the 1918 flu pandemic could dent that growth significantly.

In the aftermath of World War II, the birth rate jumped during the so-called baby boom, which happened at the same time as the start of the intensive economic and political cooperation between European nations, in response to the war. A major motivating factor for this cooperation was the idea that future wars could be avoided if the countries were more closely tied in an economic sense. The history of the EU's expansion can be seen in Table 5.5 and Figure 5.15.

The first form of cooperation only concerned steel production and the coal required for it, and was entirely due to the post-war reconstruction of Europe. The ECSC (European Coal and Steel Community) became the EEC (European Economic Community) in 1957, enlarging its focus to include many other economic aspects, with the biggest one being agriculture. It was at this time that the agricultural subsidies and import duties discussed in Chapter 2 and 3 were introduced, which to this day hinder the development of impoverished nations elsewhere in the world.

TABLE 5.5 History of the EU

Notable events	Year	Accession
The Benelux region is established, a partnership between Belgium, the Netherlands and Luxembourg	1948	
ECSC (European Coal and Steel Community) established	1951	France, Germany, Italy, the Netherlands, Belgium, Luxembourg
EEC (European Economic Community) established	1957	
	1973	Denmark, Ireland, United Kingdom
Directly elected European Parliament	1979	
	1981	Greece
	1986	Spain, Portugal
	1990	East Germany (reunified with West Germany)
The EU (European Union) established	1992	
Customs union (Schengen Agreement)	1995	Austria, Finland, Sweden
Introduction of the euro	2002	
	2004	Poland, Hungary, Czech Republic, Slovakia, Slovenia, Estonia, Latvia, Lithuania, Cyprus, Malta
	2007	Romania, Bulgaria
Treaty of Lisbon, European president	2009	
	2013	Croatia
Brexit referendum: a majority of voters in the UK vote to leave the EU	2016	
Candidate member		Albania, Macedonia, Montenegro, Serbia, Turkey
Applied for membership		Bosnia-Herzegovina, Kosovo
Indicated a desire to join the EU		Georgia, Moldova, Ukraine
Non-EU states with euro as currency		Andorra, Monaco, San Marino, Vatican
Withdrawn application for membership		Switzerland, Norway, Iceland

Members since the 1950's
Members since the 1970's
Idem; aims to leave EU
Members since the 1980's
Members since the 1990's
Members since 2000
Candidate members
Applied for membership
Aims at membership
Possible members

FIGURE 5.15   The genesis of the European Union

When the European Union was established, the treaties that governed it were extended to include matters such as defence, justice, internal affairs and finances. The **Schengen Agreement** brought large parts of the EU together in a customs union, with all citizens entitled to freedom of movement within the Schengen area.

The EU is not a single country. Nor is it a group of 28 independent nations: rather it is somewhere in between. This became palpable to its inhabitants when the common currency, the euro, was introduced in 2002, and when the first president of Europe (more accurately, the President of the European Council) was appointed in 2009.

Not everybody is eager to be part of the multinational community. In 2016, British voters decided with a small majority to leave the EU: the so-called Brexit, mentioned in Chapter 4. Earlier, several countries withdrew their earlier application for an EU membership (see Table 5.5).

Questions

- Do you think that the EU will eventually become a genuine nation, something like the United States of Europe?
- Should this happen, in your view, or definitely not?
- Whatever happens, there will always be a division of powers between the EU as a whole and its separate entities, as is presently the case. This is not really different from the situation in the United States of America. Does this mean that the question of whether the EU will ever become a single country is an irrelevant one?

Population growth in Europe has declined significantly. As children born during the post-war baby boom near retirement age, and there has been a lasting drop in the birth rate since that era, the number of elderly people in Europe is increasing dramatically. Figure 5.16, which shows the **aging** of the population, pertains to the EU-28, the 28 members of the EU that made up the European Union in 2013. Many European countries have responded to the problem of an aging population by raising the retirement age. The extent to which such a move is actually necessary cannot be gauged just on the basis of this aging, i.e. on the decline of the percentage of the working population. Another determining factor in this is the expected increase of the average labour productivity of each working individual, in view of the fact that if a working person ups his or her productivity, then fewer working people will be required. Moreover, the degree to which the retirement age should be raised is dependent on what the people actually desire. If they want prosperity to continue rising in the next few decades, then they will have to give up on retirement plans in order to earn it. But if they are satisfied with a diminished increase of wealth, delaying one's retirement becomes less essential. Greater prosperity or greater welfare? The choice for a growing prosperity is, as opposed to what many tacitly assume, a societal decision and not an autonomous process.

Some believe the problem of an aging population in Europe can be solved by encouraging larger families. But from a long-term perspective this is the least suitable option, because it is essential that the population growth in Europe comes to a halt and subsequently declines, as is expected, in order to restrict the ecological footprint and ultimately significantly shrink it. Aging is nothing more than a temporary issue, which will be solved of its own accord if the population of Europe stabilises in due course. The start of that stability can be seen in Figure 5.16 amongst the younger generations after 2040, in the bottom right of the graphic.

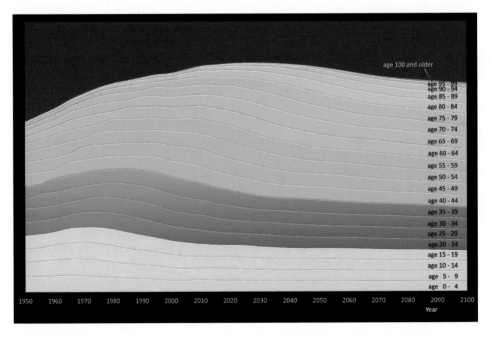

FIGURE 5.16 Aging in the EU-28. Data up to 2014 is established; the remainder involves forecasts

Source: UN Department of Economic and Social Affairs: World Population Prospects, the 2015 Revision.

Many immigrants have flowed into Europe since the 1960s. The first wave of new inhabitants arrived in Europe at the invitation of corporations, who needed cheap labour. These foreign workers and their families aside, there are also many people in Europe from the continent's former colonies and refugees from across the world. Integrating these ethnic minorities has become a problem for society in Western Europe, as Chapter 3 described. At the same time, it is expected that this influx of people will be very important for the European economy in the twenty-first century, as the immigrants shore up the working population and consequently lessen the problem of aging to some degree. This also means that many immigrants end up in the low-valued and poorly paid jobs, which few natives are still prepared to take on. Europe, quite simply, needs the new immigrants. By the way, immigration has been included in the estimates detailed in Figure 5.16.

Profit

Only a tiny amount of Europe's earnings is derived from agriculture – no more than 2 percent. Figure 5.17 shows the comparative figures with China, India and others as well as three African countries (member states of ECOWAS, see the following section). Two-thirds of the European GDP is generated through the service economy, being financial services, healthcare, education, management, tourism, trade, etc.

The total GDP of the 28 EU nations is nearly as high as that of the United States – depending on which exchange rate between the dollar and the euro is employed, which can fluctuate significantly – and about three times that of Japan. But the per capita purchasing

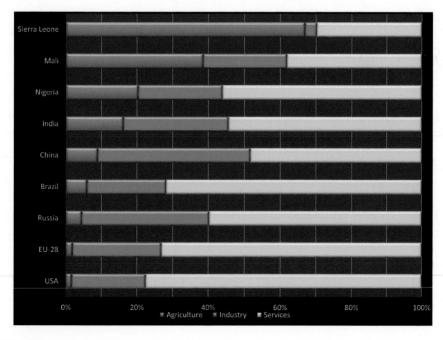

FIGURE 5.17   Composition of the GDP for a number of regions and nations in 2015

Source: CIA World Factbook (2016).

power (the GDP per person in PPP dollars) is much lower than that of the US and Japan, although there are major differences between EU countries in this regard, and the purchasing power of the earliest EU member states is comparable to that of Japan.

The EU plays a much less dominant role in the world than the US does in both economic and military terms. This is symbolised by the fact that world trade is expressed in dollars, although a shift has taken place since the launch of the euro through which the EU is playing a more clear-cut role on the world stage in a financial sense.

The **European Commission**, the EU's 'government', believes the economic comparison to the US and Japan is cause for concern and has engaged in policies to make up the difference. Whether this is a justified move is dubious, given that the GDP of the EU can also be compared to the world outside of Japan and the US, in which case its economy is very sturdy indeed. Moreover, there is also the question of whether the military or economic powers of Europe are the most important indicators for comparing the region to others. In the UN ranking of countries considered to have the best living conditions, the Human Development Index (HDI, referred to in Chapter 3), six European countries are ranked in the Top Ten. Apparently you can be doing very well in a country without having the highest income.

This is partly dependent on the number of hours and years a person might devote to working – which is less in Europe than in the US and Japan and also less than in many poor nations. Whereas this might not be great for the economy, it is agreeable for the people. Further, social security and medical care in the EU are very good when compared to the rest of the world. This is a part of what is characteristic of Europe, and it may be considered as the vigour of the continent. The US author Jeremy Rifkin outlined this strength in his book *The European Dream* (2005) – where the 'American dream' emphasises individual liberty, equality and prosperity, the 'European dream' focuses more on solidarity and participation, equivalence and diversity, quality of life and welfare.

Planet

The first serious environmental disaster in Europe was caused by the Greek and Roman civilisations of antiquity. Forests surrounding the Mediterranean Sea were felled for wood and to free up land for agriculture. The denuded land was subject to erosion and its fertility declined. Large wild animals died out, hunted to extinction or left with no natural habitat.

A notorious environmental hazard in classical Rome was lead poisoning. The Romans clad their aqueducts with lead, and so their bodies absorbed it when they drank the water. The wealthier Romans also absorbed large quantities of lead through wine sweetened with lead acetate. The lead affected the brain and could cause insanity – it could well have been a contributing factor to the downfall of the Western Roman Empire.

In the Middle Ages the natural environment of Western Europe was damaged in a comparable manner to what happened in ancient Greece and Rome. By 1600 many of the primeval forests of England had disappeared, while large animal species such as bears, wolves and aurochs had been wiped out in large parts of the continent. The aurochs, a species unique to Europe, is extinct.

There is an irony in the fact that Europe is presently pressurising countries in the rest of the world to protect their own virgin forests. It's easy for the EU to talk, after its member states had destroyed a large proportion of the original natural environment, granting them land for agricultural, residential and recreational purposes. Furthermore, forests continue to succumb to the logger's axe to this day in Europe, with hillsides cleared en masse to make way for ski slopes. This is countered by recent attempts to preserve the natural environment, the Natura 2000 project that was mentioned in Chapter 4. The present distribution of forests and other areas in Europe can be seen in Figure 5.18.

The large-scale destruction of forests compelled people to move from using wood for fuel to other sources of energy, which in turn led to the intensive use of coal. Around 1700 the first steam engine was powered up in the United Kingdom for the purpose of pumping water out of the coal mines. Between 1770 and 1830 the first industrial revolution took place there, with the rest of Europe following over the course of the nineteenth century.

For the environment the consequences of this industrialisation were dramatic, with coal tar polluting rivers and causing cancer and allergies. The chemicals discharged into surface waters by chemical factories, including those in the rubber industry, did the same. Coal burning released so much soot into the atmosphere that major cities turned black (see Figure 5.19). Smog meanwhile caused an epidemic of breathing problems.

People gradually became aware of the environmental problems. The first protected nature reserves were already created before 1900, but it was only in the 1960s that a forceful environmental awareness came into being. Environmental action groups were launched and governments and industry started to take the issues seriously. Factories installed filters on their chimneys and discharge pipes in order to prevent large emissions of hazardous substances, which is known as **end-of-pipe technology**.

Scientists discovered that the ozone layer was under threat as a result of propellant gases in aerosol cans and fridges. This marked the first time it was realised that people were able to

FIGURE 5.18   Forests and other regions in Europe in 2000

Source: Globalis (2010).

FIGURE 5.19 Thanks to natural selection, the light moth *biston betularia* (top) was superseded in nineteenth century Britain by a dark variation *biston betularia carbonaria* (bottom), which was better camouflaged on soot-covered trees and walls

Source: Olaf Leillinger, Wikimedia.

cause environmental damage at a global scale. At a later stage it was discovered that the same could be said with regard to the rise in atmospheric temperature thanks to the greenhouse effect. It was also noted that major harm was caused by heavy metals like lead, released into the atmosphere through gas, and cadmium in dyes. The consequences of overfertilisation could be seen in the form of the acid rain that affected the forests. Meanwhile particulate matter also appears to be more harmful than was believed until recently.

From the 1970s onwards the most serious environmental issues of the time were tackled in a systematic manner. Air pollution in Europe decreased, thanks in part to catalytic converters fixed to vehicles, surface water quality improved when wastewater was purified and discharges were cut and environmental legislation was tightened up. Laws were also introduced for dealing with chemical waste. In 1993 the EU set up the **European Environment Agency** (EEA), which meant that environmental issues were henceforth largely tackled at a European level.

All in all, the situation with regard to the regional environment on the continent is presently not as bad as it was, apart from the greenhouse gas effect, which will be described later. However, to some extent there is only the appearance of a step forward, as some of the consequences of the European lifestyle are transferred to other parts of the world, as discussed in Chapter 2. The environmental problems caused by industry in China and India are also to some degree a form of transferring the problem, with Europeans buying the products manufactured in those countries, which are cheap thanks in part to the fact that environmental legislation outside of Europe is not as extensive.

Prospect

Europe's environmental footprint is too large, as was already explained in Chapter 2. But there are real chances for improvements, with the continent's population growth being at a low level, coming to a halt within three decades, and the member states are working hard to cut CO_2 emissions. This reduction was initially undertaken on the basis of the Kyoto Protocol, with the basis being the so-called 20–20–20 targets – a once ambitious plan that entailed Europe cutting its greenhouse gas emissions by at least 20 percent, perhaps even 30 percent (compared to 1990) by 2020; obtaining 20 percent of its consumed energy from sustainable sources; and using, through improved energy efficiency, 20 percent less energy than it would if the EU's policies continued unabated.

In 2016, the Paris Agreement on climate change created a new, worldwide effort towards reducing climate change and its effects. In that context, the EU set profoundly more ambitious targets, as Chapter 7 will describe.

The phasing out of agricultural subsidies and trade barriers is on the agendas of many international talks, which could give poor nations the opportunity to improve their trade positions. The same holds for the debts incurred by the poorest of them.

More money is invested in sustainable development in Europe than in other regions, including China, Japan and the US. Although some argue that this is bad for the economy and for global competition, it is not inconceivable that environmental investments will lead to a competitive advantage within some years, as once other regions are compelled to do the same, Europe may have the edge.

Ever since the end of World War II, peace has reigned between the member states of the EU. There were bloody wars in the former Yugoslavia – the low point marked by the

Srebrenica genocide in 1995 – but of the nations that emerged from the fragmented Yugo-slavia, Slovenia has been a member of the EU since 2004, Croatia is set to follow in 2013, Macedonia is a candidate member and Montenegro, Serbia and Bosnia-Herzegovina have applied for membership and are presently negotiating the terms. They are all well on the road to becoming democratic nations, or have already reached this destination, with human rights respected.

The decision-making process within the European Union is frequently a slow process, but what might seem like a weakness is actually one of the organisation's great vigours. Europe holds some 50 nations, over half of which are EU member states, and around a hundred different ethnic groups, each with their own language, culture and customs. Prior to the EU, war had been a common method for exchanging opinions between countries on the continent, but this method of political discourse has now been driven out in most parts of Europe. This marks a true transition, and it is even a very hopeful sign on a global level as it demonstrates *that it is possible to wipe out violent conflict completely*. If such a transition to peace can happen on a continental scale – as Europe, with its bloody history, proves – there is absolutely no reason why it could not happen on a global scale. *World peace – 'war is over' – is possible.*

In light of the preceding it is not a terrible thing that the decision-making process takes so much time in Europe, for this is the price Europeans pay to ensure that the people, groups and nations in their complex corner of the world reach consensus on the course Europe adopts, insofar as is possible, based on support, acceptance and participation. This price is not high when compared to the other option – war. In other words: *please let decision making in Europe be slow!*

The consecutive enlargements of the EU have meant that an increasing number of countries exist on a platform of peace and human rights. Possible future expansions will continue this task. The EU only accepts European nations into its fold, which is why Morocco, which applied for membership in 1987, was rejected, although the country was granted 'advanced status' in 2008, which means it does not have full membership but is still considered more than just an ally.

In recent years, a sense of scepticism has grown in many European countries concerning the EU. Many people experience a large distance to the Union and its bureaucracy, and a lack of democratic control over the EU policies. This has increased considerably during the large wave of refugees entering Europe from Africa and the Middle East starting around 2015. This **European Migrant Crisis** strengthened feelings of nationalism and populism. EU countries had big problems receiving and distributing the refugees. Several countries reintroduced border controls within the Schengen Area or even built fences to keep the refugees out. The human rights policy, for which the EU countries had been strong advocates, were under pressure.

The membership candidacy of Turkey is another test case for the Union. For a number of years, many people in the EU were sceptical about a Turkish membership, and the negotiations flagged. However, as a consequence of a treaty between the EU and Turkey to keep a lot of refugees, especially those from Syria and Iraq (see Figure 5.20), within the Asian country, the candidacy was renewed – at least formally. At the same time, a lot of criticism exists in western countries about democracy and human rights in Turkey, which places the EU leaders for another complicated dilemma.

Treaties like the one between the EU and Turkey may or may not be suitable to solve or soften the refugee crisis on the short term – at least for the EU countries; probably not for the refugees themselves. But it is evident that, on the long term, there is only one real

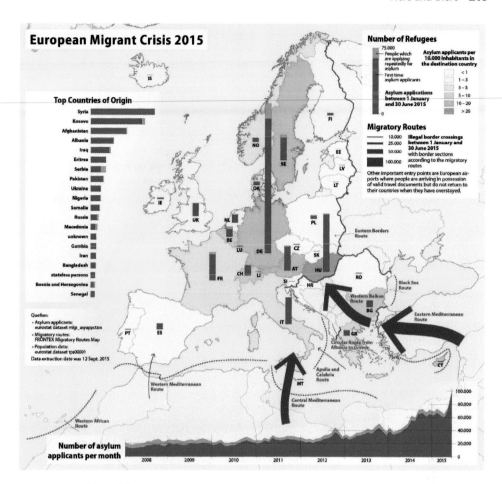

FIGURE 5.20   Map of the European Migrant Crisis 2015

Map created by Maximilian Dörrbecker.

Source: Eurostat, 2015.

solution: making it unnecessary for the citizens of Africa, the Middle East and other trou-
bled regions in the world to leave their homes and try to find a better living as strangers in
strange lands. In other words: to eradicate poverty and war, and to create genuine sustainable development in every country. This is certainly true for the next region to be discussed
here: the ECOWAS.

5.4 ECOWAS: explosive population growth in Africa

ECOWAS consists of 15 nations in West Africa to the south of the Sahara. Just like Europe, it is a
region that contains dozens of ethnic groups and languages with an ancient and complex history.

The first city-states arose around 500 AD, founded by the Hausa, a tribe in the north of
present day Nigeria and Niger. In the following centuries major empires arose under ethnic
groups like the Yoruba and Fulani.

TABLE 5.6 ECOWAS

	Year:	1970	2015	2060
People	Population	120 million	353 million	955 million
	Birth rate (children per woman)	6.70	5.38	3.1
	Child mortality (up to 5 years)	27%	10%	3%
	Life expectancy	43.3 years	55.8 years	67.9 years
	Urban population	19%	45%	67%
Planet	Surface area		5.1 million km^2	
	Ecological footprint at birth		1.30 ha per capita	
	Biocapacity		1.02 ha per capita	
Profit	GDP (2015 $)	$20 billion	$624 billion	
	GDP (PPP$ per capita)		$4,250	
	Income disparity[*]		8 times (Togo) to 20 times (Ivory Coast)	
Nations	Benin, Burkina Faso, Cape Verdes, Côte d'Ivoire, Gambia, Ghana, Guinea, Guinea-Bissau, Liberia, Mali, Niger, Nigeria, Senegal, Sierra Leone, Togo			

[*] Income of the wealthiest 10 percent divided by the income of the poorest 10 percent.

Sources: UNDP (2016), World Bank (2016), Global Footprint Network (2016).

FIGURE 5.21 Economic Community of West African States (ECOWAS)

From the fifteenth century onwards, Europeans began to encroach on the region, starting with Portuguese colonies. Other countries followed, firstly for trade and later to plunder.

Roughly between 1500 and 1800 the region's economy was based primarily on the slave trade, which was not only highly profitable for Europeans but for the African empires too. By 1700 they were selling around 10,000 slaves a year to the European traders, and a total of at least 12 million slaves were shipped to the Americas.

In 1807 the United Kingdom outlawed slavery and the slave trade collapsed, with prices plummeting. After this, most slaves were bought by people in Africa, until the slaves revolted a few decades later, resulting in civil war, destroyed cities and hundreds of thousands of refugees.

The greater part of Africa only fell prey to European colonisation much later than areas in Asia and the Americas, and it was only during the nineteenth century that Africa became the stage for a scramble between France and the United Kingdom to colonise as much land as possible. This was also played out in what later became the ECOWAS region, where Nigeria became the last colony in 1901.

The 15 countries that presently make up ECOWAS came into being as a result of borders drawn by the Europeans. These borders frequently run straight through areas inhabited by a common ethnic group. Of the 15 nations, eight had been French colonies, four had belonged to the British and two were Portuguese.

There was one country that already successfully declared its independence in 1847 – Liberia. This is the reason behind its name, which means the 'land of liberty'. The other nations all gained independence between 1957 and 1975.

The eight former French colonies are called Francophone nations, and the French influence remains strong, while the medium of communication between the peoples is also French. The four former British colonies, including the large country of Nigeria, are called Anglophone nations, with English being the medium of communication between the diverse groups.

Mauritania was once also a member of ECOWAS, but it withdrew in 2000.

ECOWAS was established in 1975 with the original purpose of furthering the economies of the member states. Other goals were added at later dates, including buttressing political stability and finding peaceful solutions to conflicts between the member states. The goals were met with reasonable success, but not always, with conflicts arising on occasion between the nations, particularly about hazy borders. Since 2002, ECOWAS has a Community Parliament and a Community Court of Justice.

On several occasions, the 15 nations intervened in order to guard democracy. Some of these interventions were of a military nature. A joint armed force called **ECOMOG** (ECOWAS Monitoring Group) was deployed in Liberia (1990), Sierra Leone (1997), Guinea-Bissau (1999) and Togo (2005). All of these nations are once again full members of ECOWAS.

Likewise, the membership of Guinea was suspended temporarily in 2009 after a bloody coup, and that of Niger in the same year, when its president changed the constitution to extend his rule. Both countries were readmitted in 2011, after democracy had been restored in 2010 with the help of ECOWAS. Mali's membership was suspended in 2012 after a coup.

In 2017, ECOWAS intervened through political and military pressure in member state Gambia.

Case 5.7 Democracy in Gambia

General presidential elections took place in the Gambia in December 2016. This was extraordinary, because the country had been ruled by dictator Yahya Jammeh for 23 years, after a military coup.

Earlier in 2016, Amnesty International had requested the ECOWAS leadership to suspend the membership of Gambia. "ECOWAS should speak out on the deplorable situation in the country and engage with the Gambian authorities to secure the release of political prisoners. (. . .) If the Gambian government refuses to comply, ECOWAS should consider suspension until Gambia's obligations are met," said Alioune Tine, Amnesty International Regional Director for West and Central Africa. The president of the ECOWAS Commission refused, stating that "there are threats to human rights but condemning them will not help us solve the problem".

Probably president Yammeh expected to win the elections easily, thus safeguarding his rule "for a billion years", as he stated. But after the polls were closed, his opponent Adama Barrow appeared to have beaten him.

Initially Yammeh conceded his defeat. But a few days later he refused to step up, citing 'unacceptable abnormalities' and subsequently announcing he had annulled the result.

This time, the ECOWAS leaders came into action. The governments of Nigeria, Senegal, Mali and several other ECOWAS members warned on 23 December that they would militarily intervene together if Jammeh didn't resign. In the next weeks, presidents of several neighbouring countries negotiated his concession, but unsuccessfully. In the meantime, thousands of Gambian civilians fled from the country.

On 19 January 2017 Adama Barrow was sworn in as the new Gambian president at the Gambian embassy in Dakar, Senegal. On the same day, the United Nations Security Council unanimously approved UNSC Resolution 2337, which expressed support for ECOWAS efforts to negotiate the transition of the presidency. Still, Jammeh did not leave. Then, the ECOWAS troops invaded the country. They were cheered at by the civilians. The small Gambian army did not resist at all. After the suburbs of Gambia's capital Banjul had been reached, the international military force halted for a final round of negotiations.

This time, the dictator stepped down. He was given the opportunity to leave the country for Guinea and afterwards to Equatorial Guinea.

The new president, Barrow, announced that a 'truth and reconciliation commission' would be appointed.

People

West Africa contains some of the most impoverished nations on the planet. The per capita GDP of the ECOWAS region is a mere 5.5 percent of that of the EU. In terms of regional purchasing power (in other words, in PPP dollars), the per capita GDP is somewhat better, at 11 percent of the EU average.

The people adopt a wide range of lifestyles, with many coastal populations living in cities, and a high percentage of people living off agriculture. The Tuaregs, on the other hand, are nomadic and have traditionally lived as herders and traders between West Africa and the Arabic lands of North Africa and the Middle East.

Life expectancy is low, mainly due to the high child mortality rates, while healthcare and hygiene are also poor. In Ghana 80 percent of the population have access to clean water, while in other nations this figure is no more than 50 percent. In some of the countries half the population is malnourished, and between a quarter and a third of children are underweight.

Diseases such as malaria and Aids have ravaged the economy. Malaria-related deaths are especially tragic: there are excellent drugs that, when administered in good time, will generally cure an attack, and yet in reality many African children still die from it. One in six children die before reaching the age of five, with little improvement to this mortality rate being seen over the years.

In 2014 the region was struck by a new disaster: a massive outbreak of the dreaded Ebola disease. From Guinea the deadly infection spread to Sierra Leone and Liberia, and at a lesser scale to Nigeria, Senegal and Mali. The World Health Organization (WHO) declared a 'Public Health Emergency of International Concern'. During two years, the epidemic infected nearly 29,000, killing 11,300 of them: 40 percent. Those are the official data, but the WHO suspects that the real numbers were considerably higher. Before the epidemic was ended in 2016, it had a severe impact on the economics of several ECOWAS states, especially of Sierra Leone, as Figure 5.26 will show.

The birth rate in the ECOWAS countries is high. This is a necessity, in view of the fact that there are no social provisions like state and old-age pension. Elderly people are completely reliant on their children to care for them. This is a risk in itself, given the high child mortality figures, which is why they have to have large families. As a consequence, the population is increasing rapidly. In 1970 the region's population was approximately a quarter of that in the EU-28 – the 28 nations that have made up the EU since 2013 – but by 2000 the population had grown to equal half that of the EU. The population will continue to grow for a long time yet, although at a slower rate, and it is expected that the ECOWAS region's population will exceed the EU's sometime around 2035.

The age distribution of the region's population demonstrates the characteristics of a population explosion. Figure 5.22 shows the example of Guinea, with its base the broadest slice of the pyramid by far. For the purposes of comparison, it is accompanied by a pyramid for Italy. The broadest point for Italy is in the 35 to 44 years old category, identifiable as the group of the post-war baby boomers, also being the approaching wave of people of retirement-age. Guinea will one day experience a comparable situation, as a prelude to a stable age distribution, which Italy might achieve after 2050.

Education in the ECOWAS nations is below standard, with only about 60 percent of children attending school in most of the countries. The number of literate adults varies between 30 percent in a country like Niger and 60 percent in Togo.

Reasonable progress is being made in some ECOWAS states, but it is an unfortunate and frequent reality that the situation relapses dramatically in such nations as a result of violence. Violent conflict is the region's biggest problem, with millions of refugees created as a result of war in the last few decades. Corrupt governments and equally corrupt and violent 'liberation movements' fight each other, with neither side hesitating to recruit child soldiers.

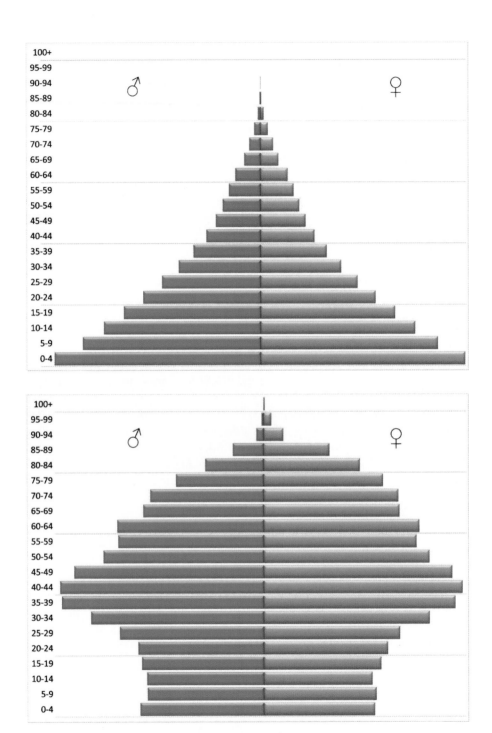

FIGURE 5.22 Two population pyramids: above is the ECOWAS member state of Guinea while below is the EU member state of Italy

Source: UN Population Division (2016).

Case 5.8   Child soldiers in Liberia

In March 2003 Liberian government troops attacked schools and refugee camps, abducting children, some as young as nine. If any resisted they were beaten. The children were housed in military camps, their heads shaved. Some were sold back to their parents but all the others, whose parents were too poor to pay, were armed and sent into battle without any training whatsoever against rebel organisations. Girls were used as sex slaves.

When the mothers of the abducted children demonstrated in the capital city of Monrovia, the defence minister denied that Liberia was recruiting child soldiers. But they certainly were, as Human Rights Watch and Amnesty International confirmed, on the basis of witness testimony.

The Liberian regime was not alone in recruiting child soldiers in the country, with the rebel group Movement for Democracy in Liberia (MODEL) also arming children, as was the Liberians United for Reconciliation and Democracy (LURD), an organisation that was allegedly backed by Sierra Leone, Guinea and the United States.

Child soldiers are deployed by governments and rebel movements in numerous countries in the ECOWAS region. Given the various rebel movements in some nations that are backed by neighbouring countries, one may doubt the level of unity existing between the governments of ECOWAS states.

The level of respect for liberty, democracy and human rights differs from nation to nation, and often from moment to moment. The largest ECOWAS country, Nigeria, which holds over half the region's inhabitants, has been a democracy for a number of years, while Burkina Faso was under a dictatorship until recently. Sierra Leone is meanwhile recovering from a bloody civil war that ended in 2002.

Profit

The ECOWAS region has every opportunity to become a wealthy area. It is rich in natural resources – gold, diamonds, copper, aluminium, phosphorous, uranium, iron ore and many others. Nigeria has large oil reserves, extracted by Shell and other oil companies.

The Sahel, the dry zone bordering on the Sahara, makes up the northern part of the ECOWAS region, where little grows and the inhabitants wage constant war against drought (Figure 5.23). As Case 2.6 illustrated, some progress is being made in this battle. The southern areas are more lush and a large variety of crops are grown there, aimed primarily at the export market.

There are a number of reasons why these countries have little chance of improving their levels of prosperity, with armed conflicts being the primary one. However, the poor infrastructure also plays a role, as does the lack of investment capital, as a result of which the exploitation of the natural resources is largely controlled by foreign companies. As education

FIGURE 5.23 Agriculture in the Sahel involves a constant battle against drought, as seen here in Senegal

Source: UN Photo, Carl Purcell.

is insufficient, local staff are, different from those in China and India, hardly able to move up to responsible positions in the local branches of the foreign companies. This means that industry stays in foreign hands. The foreign companies frequently back the ruling regimes, as they benefit from political stability. The support that the energy company Shell provided to the Nigerian government – which wilfully disregarded human rights in the 1990s – is a notorious example of this.

It is a difficult task for an ECOWAS nation to invest in its own economy, as they are all heavily in debt and are compelled to pay large sums annually in interest and instalments to the wealthy nations – much more than they receive in development aid. Moreover, in the past large parts of that development aid has been appropriated by heads of state, who simply stole it and deposited it into offshore bank accounts. This fact makes the later repayment of interest and instalments on loans an additionally bitter pill to swallow for countries.

The International Monetary Fund (IMF) and the World Bank are playing a part in endeavours to lighten the load of this debt burden. But their approach is a dubious one. Ghana, for example, was offered partial debt relief for sums it had borrowed abroad, but the relief would only be granted on the condition that the country's subsidy for providing clean water to the poorest Ghanaians was withdrawn, for the purpose of giving competitive markets and free trade a chance. Once Ghana accepted the offer, the availability of clean water to its citizens was curtailed.

The export of agricultural products is complicated by the fact that wealthy nations have imposed trade barriers in order to protect their own agricultural industries and by the fact that farmers in the EU, Japan and the US are subsidised. A subsidy for American cotton grow-ers, for example, led to a surplus of cotton, which was sold abroad at prices far lower than production costs, causing global prices to drop dramatically. Unfortunately cotton makes up around half of the income of countries like Benin, Mali and Burkina Faso, leading to many a farmer going bankrupt in the region.

Questions

- Who or what is to blame for the dire situation in West Africa – Europe's colonial past?
- Or is it the fault of the corrupt regimes in these countries?
- Or maybe the debt trap, which is partly a result of interference by the wealthy countries?
- Or is it due to the wars and violence perpetrated by the inhabitants?
- Or the very poorly paid work for multinational companies?
- Could it be the trade barriers and subsidies instituted by the wealthy nations?
- How important is it, to decide who is to blame?

ECOWAS has made efforts to improve the situation through a collective approach. All import duties between the ECOWAS nations have been scrapped and the countries are working on introducing a common currency, much like the euro in the European Union. This has already been achieved in part, with the eight Francophone nations using the same currency – the CFA franc (Figure 5.24). Six other ECOWAS member states are looking to introduce a common currency amongst themselves, the eco. The introduction was postponed several times, because the agreed criteria were repeatedly not met by the six countries.

The ultimate goal is that the two currencies are combined to form a single currency that can be used across the entire ECOWAS region. To further this goal, the West African Mon-etary Institute, headquartered in Accra, Ghana, was launched in 2000 as a precursor to a joint central bank.

FIGURE 5.24   A 1000 CFA franc note

Planet

Large tracts of West Africa were still covered in beautiful tropical rainforests barely a century ago. In 1960 half of Sierra Leone was still blanketed in virgin forest. Today the forests have shrunk to a mere two percent. The forests were felled (Figure 5.25) to give space to the grow-ing population for agriculture and housing and because of the lucrative export market for tropical wood, to China, Western nations and elsewhere. The level of deforestation is not the same throughout West Africa, but all extant forests are shrinking, and the rate at which they are disappearing is accelerating. This has resulted in thousands of animal and plant species being faced with extinction.

The consequences of this are very grave indeed – poor management means that the agri-cultural land is degrading, with fertile soil becoming parched and blown away. The upshot is that desertification marches further and further south from the Sahara. The growing intensity of droughts causes crops to fail and famines to take hold. Much hope now lies in a 'green wall' being built along the edge of the Sahara, as was outlined in Case 2.6.

Yet another problem can be seen in Nigeria, involving the extreme pollution that has resulted from tapping oil reserves. The ground is highly contaminated in many places, the result of 4,000 oil leaks since 1960. Mangrove forests have been severely affected as the soil is so polluted, while gas flares used to eliminate waste gas from oil wells has resulted in heavily polluted air and acid rain.

Even the sea is suffering, endangering those people who consume seafood. The problem is to a large extent due to the fact that for decades both the Nigerian authorities and the oil companies paid little attention to the environment. The picture today is different, as clearly signified by the fine imposed on Shell in 2003 when it was forced to pay 1.5 billion dollars in damages to the Ijaw tribe as a result of damage the company did to the environment and the people's health over a 50-year period.

This process of burning off unwanted gas was outlawed in 1984, and Shell announced it would stop gas flaring in 2008. While it is true that the extent of the gas flaring had been reduced to a third in that year, the practice was certainly still going on, after which the oil company further announced it would invest more funds into further reducing gas flaring, but not to stop it completely.

Prospect

Africa, and especially the sub-Saharan part of it, has long been the world's 'problem child'. Long-term prospects looked not well. The population will continue to grow for many years, which makes it extremely difficult for the region to improve its economic and social condi-tions. At the same time, natural environment in parts of Africa is extremely vulnerable, as the vast and growing deserts demonstrate. The result is that the region becomes overpopulated at an increased rate, which in turn means that conflicts can easily develop into explosions of violence. The genocide in Rwanda in 1994, and the mass murders that have been festering since 2003 in the Sudan (neither of which are part of ECOWAS but both still part of the African problem zone) bear grim witness to this.

Nevertheless, there is not only bad news in this part of the world. The various members of the ECOWAS – and many other African countries – are going through a period of strong economic growth, as Figure 5.26 shows. A few examples: In Nigeria, by far the most popu-lous ECOWAS nation, the GDP had an annual growth form 2000 till 2013 of more than

FIGURE 5.25 Deforestation to make room for agriculture and living space as well as for export has taken on frightening forms in some countries in Africa. The photo shows the *slash and burn* agriculture (*chitemene*) in Zambia

Source: Colalife, Wikimedia.

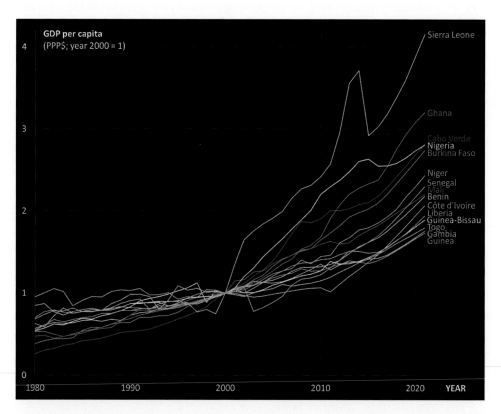

FIGURE 5.26 Relative GDP development of the ECOWAS countries (PPP dollars; year 2000 taken as 1). Data up to 2015 is established; the remainder involves forecasts

Source: IMF: World Economic Outlook Database, 2016.

17 percent every year. This was a real economic growth, as the figures are corrected for inflation. Of course, at the same time the population increased, and the GDP was to be divided
among more people every year. But even when you look at the GDP development *per capita*,
and calculated in PPP dollars, the growth was considerable: more than 7 percent. Per person,
that is; and this is what Figure 5.26 shows. The figure for Sierra Leone in the same period was
even higher: more than 10 percent per capita in PPP dollars.

Figure 5.26 also shows the effects of the Ebola epidemic in the years 2014–2016, which hit
the economies of Sierra Leone, Liberia and Nigeria hard, not only due to illness and death,
but quarantines, bankruptcies and international trade barriers.

For the years after 2016, expectations are high again. Between 2017 and 2021, an average annual growth of the GDP per capita, expressed in PPP dollars, is expected between
2 percent for Nigeria and 7 percent for Côte d'Ivoire. If this happens, the real incomes
of the ECOWAS inhabitants will have improved in four decades (1980 till 2021) with an
average factor of 5.

The continent is rich in natural resources, which can be better employed at present to up
the economies of African nations. Moreover, the continent has a vast cultural wealth, while
large forests still exist that could at least be partially retained if they are properly protected
(Figure 5.27). And it is possible that even the vast Sahara will flourish, if a part of it is used to
generate solar energy, which could be used to irrigate other parts with water. Plans for this
already exist – see Chapter 7.

Just as in Asia, much can also be achieved in Africa through a combination of top-down
strategies run by African states and international organisations and a bottom-up approach by
the people themselves using microloans, amongst other things. On top of this, much can be
expected of private-public partnerships, as the final case of this section demonstrates.

FIGURE 5.27 Africa has a great deal of cultural wealth, such as the Great Mosque of Djenné in
Mali, which is a World Heritage Site

Source: Ferdinand Reus, Wikimedia.

Case 5.9   Healthcare insurance, Africa-style

Volkskrant, 28 March 2008

International recognition for African healthcare insurance plan

An NGO called PharmAccess has received a prestigious award for its 'pioneering vision' for African healthcare. Through the plan African people can get access to healthcare through a collective healthcare insurance.

The prize for a plan to develop the private sector was awarded by the Financial Times and the International Finance Corporation (IFC), a part of the World Bank.

The Minister for Development Cooperation said the award was "a recognition" of the policy. "We are helping thousands of Africans to receive good care through a public-private partnership."

PharmAccess set up the Health Insurance Fund (HIF) last year using a grant of 100 million euros from the ministry. Thousands of people in Nigeria are already insured through the fund.

And the program continues! March 2014: HIF and the governor of the Nigarian state Kwara announced that the state government accepts the financial responsibility for the healthcare costs of all inhabitants with a low income. Kwara (Figure 5.28) has a population of nearly three million people. The insurance program will pay the premium for a considerable part of the population. Around 2018, at least 60% of the people of Kwara should be insured.

FIGURE 5.28   The Nigerian state Kwara

5.5 Shared responsibility

Each of the areas examined previously has been greatly influenced in the last few centuries by the wealthy nations of Europe and North America, and it is not different in other regions, including the Middle East, Latin America and Southeast Asia.

There was a time when Western influence consisted of conquering and oppressing colonies, slavery and waves of immigration, and of displacing or killing local populations. Even the transmission, mostly unintentionally, of infectious diseases has contributed to the wide-scale deaths of the locals.

The invading powers undermined the local populations' traditional and religious concepts and they became culturally uprooted. The consequences of this can still be seen today in almost every part of the world. Nations have become unbalanced and they struggle to find solutions to their issues on their own.

Today's Western influence is no longer exercised through colonialism and slavery, but rather through those debts incurred by the poor nations, the practice of transferring environmental effects, the use of cheap labour for cheap products, backing dictatorial regimes and the cultural damage caused by multinational companies and tourism. But the influence also entails development cooperation and support for the processes of democratisation.

This does not imply that the dire conditions in the poorer parts of the world are caused completely by the wealthy nations – it's not that simple. Some of those causes are due to the poor countries themselves, causing their own environmental problems, waging wars and, given the opportunity, they are just as quick to transfer their problems onto another country. China is a good example of this, importing tropical hardwood so as to save its own forests. However, it is still true that the wealthy nations have caused some of the issues at hand, which creates a **responsibility** in terms of doing something about them.

That is not the end of the story, either. Leaving aside the question of to what extent the wealthy nations are guilty of causing the problems experienced in their poorer counterparts, there is still a moral obligation on the part of prosperous nations and people to do something. The extremes of prosperity that exist between rich and poor cannot be justified by any means, and the fact that people in large parts of our world suffer from the absence of healthcare, education or even something as simple as clean water is unacceptable. Everyone who is able to do something about this situation has a personal and collective responsibility to do something about it.

Questions

- Let's say you are standing on a riverbank when somebody nearby falls into the river. The person cannot swim. You do nothing, you just watch. Soon the victim disappears beneath the surface and drowns. Are you liable to punishment for this person's death?
- Let's say that people are dying of hunger every day in Sierra Leone. You do nothing, you just watch. Are you liable to punishment for those people's deaths?
- Is this a fair comparison?

The wealthy nations have a responsibility towards the people living in poor nations, as do the international companies operating in both the rich and poor countries. So do individual people, by virtue of the fact that they buy products from poor countries or visit them as tourists, and by virtue of the fact that they – unintentionally – transfer the consequences of their lifestyles onto the inhabitants of the poor regions of the world. And also, irrespective of their Western lifestyles, simply because there are people who are suffering on this planet.

Types of responsibility

There are three ways to think about this responsibility.

One of these is the question of *legal responsibility*. Nations and companies have obligations that arise from international laws and treaties, on the basis of which other nations, companies or citizens can use the courts to demand that certain things are done – or not done – or to demand compensation.

Case 5.10   See you in court!

The Pacific Ocean is home to a number of tiny nations, the so-called small island states. They join forces in the international political arena through AOSIS, the Alliance of Small Island States.

Tuvalu is one of them. The country is made up of nine coral islands (Atolls) that only just rise above the sea level, totalling a surface area of 10 square miles (27 square kilometres). It is home to 12,000 people. The highest point on Tuvalu is a mere four meters above sea level, making the nation one of the most seriously threatened by the greenhouse effect. The rising sea level could see the nation wholly or partly sink beneath the waves within a few decades.

In 2002, Tuvalu threatened to take two other nations to court – the United States and Australia, two major sources of greenhouse gases. The plan was to challenge both countries in the **International Court of Justice (ICJ)** in The Hague, and Tuvalu sought out co-plaintiffs for the case, including other island nations in the Pacific and Indian Oceans and in the Caribbean region.

The plan never became reality. But in 2011, another small island state started investigating its options: Palau, consisting of more than 500 islands inhabited by 21,000 people (Figure 5.29). On 22 September 2011, the government of Palau announced a plan to seek an advisory opinion from the ICJ on whether countries have a legal responsibility to ensure that any activities on their territory that emit greenhouse gases do not harm other states. Palau calls upon the so-called **no harm rule**, which is a principle of international law binding states to prevent, reduce and control the risk of environmental harm to other states. The rule has been incorporated in various laws and international treaties. One of them is the **United Nations Convention on the Law of the Sea (UNCLOS)** of 1982, which states in Article 194 paragraph 2: "States shall take all measures necessary to ensure that activities under their jurisdiction or control are so conducted as not to cause damage by pollution to other States and their environment."

FIGURE 5.29 The archipelago of Palau

Source: LuxTonnerre, Wikimedia.

In the ICJ, the 'no harm' principle was successfully applied several times, for instance in 1997 (Hungary v. Slovakia) and 2010 (Argentina v. Uruguay). If Palau really goes to court, it will be the first time such a tiny country sues one or perhaps even many mighty powers of the world.

Another basis for responsibility can be found in *ethical standards.* This entails that people or organisations accept responsibility for a given issue because they believe they ought to do so, even if this is not prescribed by law or treaties. Such a moral obligation is frequently based on a religious, humanist or personal conviction.

Then there is a third form in which the responsibility is simply based on the principle of *humanity* and *compassion.* It is based on a concern for, solidarity with and an emotional feeling for fellow human beings. This was e.g. evident in the immediate aftermath of the 2004 Indian Ocean tsunami, when countries and people around the world felt accountable and offered wide scale assistance.

The rich nations give shape to their responsibility through, amongst other things, development projects, financial aid, military intervention in war zones or through health campaigns, often coordinated by international bodies such as the *International Red Cross and Red Crescent Movement* and *Médecins Sans Frontières* (Doctors Without Borders).

Companies are also increasingly operating within a basic philosophy of corporate social responsibility (CSR), which can involve taking responsibility for poorer nations and their inhabitants. This aspect will be further examined in Chapter 8.

Converting responsibility into action in a positive way is not always an easy task. Well-intentioned assistance has frequently led to harmful side effects. In some cases, these side effects are simply unavoidable, and they constitute a part of a difficult phase on the road to prosperity that cannot be bypassed. An example of this is the fact that improvements have been made in many countries in respect of hygiene and medical facilities, thanks in part to the role played by international organisations. Though child mortality rates have been cut as a result of this – a great achievement – one side effect is a considerable population growth, which leads to scarcity and environmental damage.

Other unwanted side effects of this form of aid might be avoidable. Dishing out free supplies has already sunk many a local company by destroying competition, and financial support to poorer nations has led to vast debt on the part of these countries, a process that could probably have been conducted in a different manner. Developmental aid in this form is not intelligent, and it is being applied less nowadays.

Dilemmas

If everyone in the world always acted responsibly, the world would certainly be much better off. But this is not so easy, as nations, companies and people are constantly faced with choosing between the general interest and their own. This results in a number of tricky decisions, one of which is the following.

The prisoner's dilemma

Once upon a time there were two men who committed an armed robbery. Shortly afterwards they were arrested by the police, and found in possession of two guns, but without the loot. The police could charge them with illegal possession of a firearm, although there turned out to be insufficient evidence to charge them for the armed robbery. The two men were locked in separate cells, preventing them from communicating with each other, and the judge in their case proposed the following to each of them:

1 If both of you continue to deny committing the robbery, you will both be released with a fine for illegal possession of a firearm.
2 If you confess to your involvement, but your buddy doesn't, you'll be released because you were the only one to cooperate.
3 If your buddy confesses to his involvement, but you don't, you'll be sentenced to five years in jail because you refused to cooperate.
4 If you both confess to your involvement, each of you will be sentenced to three years in jail.

This became a difficult choice for both the men who, remember, could not discuss it with each other. Should both keep quiet, then the worst consequence would be that both were fined for illegal possession of a firearm. If only one cooperated with the cops, then he'd be skipping up the garden path, but his buddy would be left holding the baby.

If only they could talk about it! But the cops were stopping any contact. What would be the best solution to the dilemma?

This is the famous **Prisoner's Dilemma**. The problem for each of the prisoners is that they must choose between an action that will benefit both of them (both deny the crime) or an action that will benefit only one of them (confess to the crime), in the hope that the other prisoner does not do likewise (see also Table 5.7). Should both choose in favour of themselves, they both suffer. The dilemma boils down to the following: the best option for all would be to work together, but this is not possible. So the parties instead concentrate on their own benefit, the upshot of which is that the best possible result is not achieved.

There are many scenarios in real life that evoke a similar dilemma, such as in Case 5.11.

Case 5.11 ING bank moves activities to countries with lower wages

"Despite claiming they were restructuring because of digitalisation, it now appears that the ING banking group is also intending to move part of its activities to countries with lower wages. These are mainly in Asia and Eastern Europe.

Based on documents sent to Belgian Unions under the 'Renault law', it appears that administrative functions will be moved to Asia. Part of the risk management activities will be moved to Poland.

ING's restructuring will mean the loss of 7,000 jobs, half of them in Belgium. 'We clearly explained at the start of October that this reorganisation is necessary, as work and work places change. It was always part of the plan', a spokesman for the bank said on Saturday."

Brussels Times, 22 October 2016

In recent years, ING moved more and more jobs to four international centres: the Polish Katowice, Bucharest in Romania, Slovakian Bratislava en Manila in the Philippines. This involved IT jobs and administrative tasks.

In 2015, ING globally had a net profit of more than 4.2 billion euros (US$ 4.47 billion), produced by nearly 60,000 employees. Nevertheless, the bank

TABLE 5.7 The prisoner's dilemma (in brief)

If . . .	. . . I deny	. . . I confess
. . . he denies	I am fined	I am free!
. . . he confesses	I am sentenced to five years	I am sentenced to three years

stated in 2016 that it had to tighten its belt. Reasons were: the low interest rate, heavy competition, and primarily technological developments. With the latest reorganisation, ING hopes to save 900 million euros annually.

In this case ING is one of the 'prisoners', while competing companies are the other prisoners. The dilemma for ING lies in the question of whether or not to move its banking activities from Western to Eastern Europe and to Asia.

As it is, ING may not be happy to make the move – people in Belgium and the Netherlands will lose their jobs, and this is a task no manager is keen to take on. The move to Eastern Europe and the Philippines means that people will be employed there who will most likely have to work for considerably lower wages. Further, environmental regulations in those countries are much less exacting than in Western Europe, so it is possible that ING will cause a great deal more harm once it has moved than before.

Of course, the company does not have to do any of this, and it could simply continue operating in Western Europe, or it could even move to other countries but then pay unusually high wages and adhere to uncommonly strict environmental policy. But the problem is that the company's competitors are shifting their activities to low wage countries as well, where many of them show little respect for reasonable salaries or the environment. So if ING stays where it is, or devotes an inordinate amount of money to wages and the environment in its new locations, it will suffer from an extreme competitive disadvantage. If this results in ING performing even worse, then a lot more people will find themselves unemployed, and those companies that demonstrate less concern for the environment will be much more dominant.

If *all* the chemical companies would decide not to move to low-wage countries, or would decide to up the wages and environmental policies there, then the choice would be an easy one. Then ING could join them and there would have been no objections to operating within the framework of corporate social responsibility. But the moment that even one company does not do this, then the rest – including ING – will be compelled to follow suit or face going bankrupt.

Just like the two prisoners, ING does not have the option of consulting its competitors, because as soon as the financial institutions endeavour to reach joint agreements in respect of wages and fees, they will be guilty of unfair competition. This will immediately raise the ire of powerful international bodies, such as the European Commission, which can impose heavy penalties on the companies.

Another well-known dilemma involves the distribution of scarce resources, including limited ones such as agricultural land, oil and gas, iron ore and aluminium.

The Tragedy of the Commons

In a village of sheep herders all the families jointly own a large paddock, a 'commons' – a common property. For centuries this commons was large and the village was small, so that all the village inhabitants could let their sheep graze in the paddock. But over time the village population increased, and consequently so did the number of sheep, as a result of which the limited size of the paddock became an issue at some point. At this stage it would have be fine if all the herders limited themselves to a certain number of sheep, but it did not work like this. This is because many herders primarily thought only in their own interest, leading them to reason: "If I add another sheep to my present flock, then I have profited to the tune of one sheep. At the same time I do suffer a minor loss, because all the sheep must live off the same land and so all of them have a little less to eat. But I do not suffer that loss alone, as I share it with everyone else. This means that my loss is much smaller than my profit. So let me get myself that extra sheep!"

Because some herders did this, the rest could not be left behind, and every herder did their very best to expand their flocks so they would not suffer from their neighbours' similar endeavours. Of course this could not continue for very long, and the situation ended in tragedy. The commons was overgrazed and stripped, the sheep all died, and the village was left destitute.

This is the '**Tragedy of the Commons**' (first described by Garret Hardin, *Science*, 13 December 1968). All countries use limited resources, but not every country is consuming them at an equal pace. Some countries are very good at buying these resources, and you could disrespectfully refer to them as the 'grabbers'. If every nation were to adopt a modest approach, the world would still be able to continue for a long period with what is now available. But the fact that some countries are 'grabbers' means that others demonstrate the same attitude, so as not to fall behind. Here again, responsible behaviour by everyone appears to be to everyone's benefit. But irresponsible conduct by some provokes others to likewise act irresponsibly, to everyone's disadvantage.

Both dilemmas – that of the prisoners and of the commons – concern communication. The first dilemma arose because communication is impossible or illegal, and while it is possible in the second dilemma, certain parties do not communicate for the sake of their own interest. Misconceived own interest, that is, given that it ends badly for all.

Questions

- What would you do if you were one of the prisoners in the prisoner's dilemma? Why?
- What would you want to do if you were one of the herders on the commons? Would it work?

Good communication, followed by actual cooperation involving everyone, is only possible once all the concerned parties are convinced that their apparent own interests will be, in the long term, detrimental to everyone. Once this point is reached, this is the right time for negotiations and for taking shared responsibility. In the case of sustainable development, this would be the time when international bodies can be decisive, and when international treaties can be concluded.

Consequences

Many forms of unsustainability arose from the fact that decisions were made in an unsound manner. This could be due to excessive concern for, or a misunderstanding of, self-interest – as in the tragedy of the commons – or it could be due to poor communication or the inability to make proper considerations, such as in the prisoner's dilemma. Other reasons might be prejudices, lack of information, or incorrect theories. Another frequent cause for poor decisions is short-sightedness, caused by ignoring available knowledge and insights or by neglecting consequences of decisions – consequences both for the parties involved and for others.

Such neglect could be quite easily remedied using a **stakeholder analysis**. This involves inventorying the consequences of a given decision, both the positive ones and the negative ones – in other words, the advantages and the issues such as damage and inconveniences. Creating such analyses and charting all the consequences are not uncommon. For major construction projects, an **environmental impact assessment (EIA)** has been obligatory in many countries for years. But in many cases the stakeholder analyses concentrate more on the present rather than the future, and where tomorrow does form part of the picture, it tends to be the short-term future rather than the long-term one. Moreover, when the future is considered it is often tacitly assumed that the future will largely resemble the present, give or take a handful of predictable trends – an assumption that has been proved wrong on many occasions.

There are a few directions that help when it comes to taking responsible, more or less future-proof, decisions.

1 Determine the consequence scope

For every decision that has to be taken, consider the possible consequences for the surroundings. The total scope of the surroundings that the decision can have consequences for is called the **consequence scope**. That scope can include people, but in a broader sense it would also concern the natural environment.

For example, when a holidaymaker flies to Thailand, that trip has consequences for the Thai people, for the natural environment of Thailand, for the greenhouse effect, for the people living in the vicinity of the airport our holidaymaker departs from, etc. Should the manager of a company consider moving production from a Western country to India, that decision will have consequences for the workers in the Western country, for their families, and for the economy in both countries involved. It will also have consequences for the environment in India, and for the company's future employees and their families in India. Other consequences include those for the transportation of the products, which in turn will mean consequences in terms of energy consumption and for the environment.

2 Determine the consequences for the entire consequence scope

Once the consequence scope is known, one must try to properly and honestly estimate the positive and negative consequences of the decision for the entire scope. Check whether other people, nature or the environment are not being iniquitously damaged, through which advantages are being gained at the cost of a disadvantage to others – transferring problems. If this is the case, then one must try to amend the decision so as to remove or reduce the disadvantage, or come up with further actions that will compensate for the disadvantages.

The only proper way of determining the consequences for the stakeholders is by consulting with the stakeholders themselves on these consequences. If this is not possible, e.g. because the natural world is a stakeholder which doesn't have a voice, then speak to a representative such as one of the nature bodies.

3 Determine the consequence period

Responsibility not only pertains to the stakeholders of today, but also to those of tomorrow. This is why, aside from a consequence scope, also a **consequence period** has to be considered – the time that will pass before the consequences of the decision are neutralised. The time involved can vary dramatically, from a minute through to centuries. If you were to decide between drinking a cup of coffee or a cup of tea, the consequence period will probably not stretch past 15 minutes, by when you will have drunk your beverage and the outcome of the decision no longer matters. When you select a subject for your internship, then the consequence period might be a few weeks to six months, depending on your choice. But this period could also be much longer if it (a) has an influence upon your entire career or (b) during your internship you exercise a permanent influence on your environment (such as a company) where you perform your internship. This example demonstrates that consequence periods can sometimes last unexpectedly long.

The consequence scope and the consequence period can be symbolically portrayed together as in the image in Figure 5.30, where the space dimension is pictured on the horizontal axis and the time dimension on the vertical one. When dealing with sustainable development, very long consequence periods are frequently involved. One of the determining factors is the scale the decision relates to. A decision to install a solar cell panel to generate green energy has a consequence period of some ten years, after which the solar cells must be replaced. But a decision to install solar cells across and entire nation in order to generate a large amount of energy is a far-reaching one, and may last for 50 years or a century.

4 Determine the consequences for the entire consequence period

Decisions are often made without attention being paid to the total consequence scope. The same applies to the consequence period. Individuals, companies and governments all often make decisions without first consciously considering the long-term or long-distance consequences. People, including heads of government and companies, are inclined to be short-sighted. Numerous examples of this exist. One of them is the application of nuclear energy, which offers advantages for some decades, but may have a consequence period of hundreds of thousands of years, as will be described in Chapter 7. Will the future stakeholders still think the application of nuclear power in the twentieth and twenty-first centuries was a great idea? Maybe they will, maybe they won't. But the point is that this question, which should be a central theme in the discussions, is largely neglected by many decision makers.

FIGURE 5.30   Consequence scope and consequence period

Background photo source: Victor Rocha, Wikimedia.

5 Consider the alternatives

Follow the same procedure used for alternative decisions. Doing nothing – the 'zero option' – is one of those alternatives, for which the consequence scope and the consequence period must also be determined. Then weigh up the consequences of all the possible decisions against each other.

6 Make a good decision

Finally, employ the following directions:

Directions for a good decision

A decision can only be a good decision if:

'Here' and 'There'

1 the consequence scope is determined;
2 the advantages and disadvantages for the entire consequence scope are determined and scrupulously weighed up in consultation with the stakeholders;

'Now' and 'Later'

3 the consequence period of the decision is determined;
4 it is convincingly established that it can reasonably be expected that the people at the conclusion of the consequence period will still think it was a good decision.

It is especially the fourth condition that is rarely followed. Of course, it is often difficult to conjecture on what people at a later stage will think of a decision being made today, but there are methods for investigating this, such as trend analyses, models and scenarios. These methods, which will be discussed in the following chapter, do not offer certainty, but using them is better than not considering the issue at all and moving forward blindfolded.

In this way it becomes possible to take responsibility for decisions and actions. We might not always avoid transferring the consequences of somebody's lifestyle to others. But at least we are aware of this, which enables us to make a fair choice in regard of what is acceptable and what is unacceptable.

Question

- Apply the phased plan just discussed to a decision that you have recently made. Do you arrive at the same result again?

Power creates responsibility

Disparity in the world is not only expressed in the form of difference in welfare, but also in power. Power tends to keep itself going – a person with a great deal of power will generally use it to keep that power and the prosperity it is coupled with.

This is well illustrated by the way in which decisions are reached in the United Nations. As was detailed in Chapter 4, the upper echelons of the UN consist of two bodies. All the nations are represented in the General Assembly, while only a few are represented in the Security

Council. The most powerful countries in the world are permanent members of the Security Council, and they each hold a veto – if even one of them votes against a proposal, it is rejected. The structure is similar to the imaginary story that follows.

The farmer's seven sons

Once upon a time there was a farmer who had a great deal of money, as well as seven sons and a fertile field. But an eternal life he did not have, and one day he felt the end approaching.

He called his seven sons to him and gave them his field and his money. The farmer told his boys to cultivate the field together, but he divided his money amongst them. Each of his sons received five Crowns, except for the oldest, who got 1,000 Crowns. As soon as he had completed this task the farmer let out a sigh and died.

"That's not fair," six of the seven brothers shouted.

"Why not?" the eldest asked. "I didn't steal it, did I? It was given to me. And anyway, if any of you had gotten the 1,000 Crowns you would also have kept it. So that's what I'm going to do – keep it."

And yes, it sounded logical. So each of the brothers selected a piece of the field and readied himself to sow it. . . but there were no seeds left.

So the brothers went to the local farmer's shop and bought seeds. The oldest brother spent 100 Crowns, and the other brothers spent a mere two Crowns each, "because, you know, you've got to keep a little aside for rent and food."

Four months passed and the field was rich with grain. Now it was time to harvest it. The oldest brother kept a quarter of his harvest so that he could have white and brown bread for a whole year, selling the rest of the grain for 300 Crowns – a great profit, but he had worked hard for it, after all.

And then we have the poor other six brothers! They'd all harvested their piece of land, but the yield was not enough to survive off of for even a month. And they'd spent all their money too.

The hungry six approached their oldest brother. Fortunately, he was a nice guy and he gave each of them ten Crowns. But there was one condition – they all had to return in three months and pay him 20 Crowns. This was reasonable, he said, "Because I am helping you after all!"

Three months later the six thin men returned to their eldest brother. "We cannot pay you anything!" they said in despair. "We need the money just to survive, and now we have nothing left!"

But their eldest brother was very philanthropic. "It doesn't matter. In fact, I'll lend each of you 25 Crowns to keep you going.

The six brothers gratefully took the money.

"And now if you all pay me 50 Crowns in three months, everything will be squared," he told them cheerfully. "And look, now you can pay your debt to me!" And he grabbed 20 Crowns from each of the brothers' hands.

However, his siblings weren't stupid. They now realised what he was up to, and they protested, "We'll never be able to do that! If we carry on like this it's only going to get worse."

A major family quarrel broke out. But after 15 minutes the youngest brother came up with a proposal.

"I know!" he said. "Let's set up a committee. Even better, a club of brothers!"

This sounded interesting. "What is a club of brothers?" the others asked him

"In a club we agree together on what is fair," the youngest said, "and if we don't agree then we vote on it. It's democratic!"

All agreed this was a great idea, except for the eldest. "Now wait just a minute," he said. "If we do that the six of you will vote against me every time. Thanks but no thanks."

So the quarrel resumed for another 15 minutes, and in the end they all decided to set up the club of brothers. Decisions in the club would be put to a democratic vote, for which the eldest brother could cast ten votes while the rest had one vote each.

The club of brothers discussed the issue of the six youngest brothers going hungry. A proposal was submitted that all the money the brothers had be redistributed amongst them, with each brother getting an equal share. Well, the proposal was put to vote, and it was rejected by a majority of votes. And so from this point on, it was established that the money had been fairly shared out and that they had all decided this was indeed the case.

But there was one brother who could not stomach what had happened. He got so angry he punched his eldest brother in the nose. The blood sprung out of it!

This was, of course, unacceptable. The club of brothers met to discuss their options, and it was decided that the angry brother could no longer stay.

So he was sent away, to make his own way in the wide world.

But the remaining brothers continued to work the field. And they lived long and happily. Or at any rate, the democratic majority lived long and happily . . .

Power aims to defend itself and stay in place. But there is a flipside to this, which is that one who holds a great deal of power also has a great deal of responsibility in respect of the less-privileged. Many of the readers of this book presumably belong amongst the ruling class in terms of at least two aspects – a large amount of money and possessions when compared to the global average; and, thanks to a good education, higher than average opportunities when it comes to making choices that will influence others' lives.

This means that these readers also have a higher than average responsibility. To the people they manage or are going to manage. To the people who will be their customers, their patients or their pupils. Or to the people whom they will influence through artistic creations. But they are also responsible for those people who are indirectly subjected to the consequences of their choices, and to the natural environment that is influenced by them. In fact, they are responsible for the entire consequence scope and period of their decisions, for what will presumably be a long period of time.

Short and long term

In many cases it is sensible to distinguish between two ways of approaching a problem – combating a problem and eliminating the consequences of that problem. A good example is a situation in which a family congenially shares a lounge while it is raining outside, until one of them suddenly notices that the roof is leaking and water is dripping from the ceiling. Two kinds of action are now required. Firstly, the short-term problem must be solved, which entails placing buckets beneath the leak and mopping up with towels. But that's not the end of the story, otherwise the buckets and towels would become a permanent fixture of the lounge. And anyway, holes in roofs tend to get bigger over time, until the entire roof might collapse. So the long-term problem must also be tackled, which involves somebody getting on the roof and dealing with the cause.

In global politics, the issue of terrorism offers a good example. Implementing security measures is a form of direct action, as is detaining terrorists. Both are short-term solutions – tackling the symptoms but in no sense dealing with the issue. Working to shrink the inequality in the world does the opposite, removing the cause in the long term.

In the world of politics there is strikingly little distinction made between short and long-term solutions. Parliamentary debates on terrorism in many countries regularly deal with limiting civil rights, increasing police powers or the powers of the secret service and the expulsion of foreigners. But the relationship with global inequality is rarely discussed.

The same is evident in discussions on agriculture. Frequently the interests of western farmers are discussed, but hardly ever the one-way traffic of imported feed and the consequences this has for agricultural land elsewhere (the full consequence scope) or for the distant future (the entire consequence period).

This makes it difficult to consider the future consequences of present policy in a realistic and responsible manner. Nevertheless, this is absolutely essential for sustainable development. Actually, there are strong methods available to do this, as will be shown in the next chapter.

Summary

The different regions of the world employ varying strategies for the purposes of sustainable development, depending on the nature of their primary sustainability issues, their political and economic structures and their cultural and historical backgrounds.

- China is successfully tackling population growth through its one-child policy and is making wholesale attempts to solve its other problems through comparable top-down strategies, including those of water scarcity, damage to the natural environment and sandstorms. However, there has only been minor improvement to the working and living conditions in the major cities.
- In the democratic nation of India, where a top-down strategy such as the employed by the Chinese could never work, the growth of the IT industry has become a powerful engine to drive economic development and education. Whereas a section of the stratified population has benefited from this, there is a large rural population that is faced with being left behind. Successful model projects that combine modern and traditional agricultural methods are spreading.
- Population growth in Europe has come to a halt, and the baby boom of a few decades ago means that the aging population is now one of the problems Europe must deal with, as

well as its very large ecological footprint. Amongst the positives of the European Union is the fact it fosters peace, democracy, human rights and solidarity.

- The ECOWAS nations are confronted by a dramatic population explosion, thanks to a combination of improved healthcare and hygiene and an underdeveloped economy and poverty. The region can be improved through robust economic growth, which can in turn lead to a decrease of the birth rate and, ultimately, a stable scenario. Sources of vigour include the economic cooperation the African countries have engaged in, the rich natural resources – which could be used to increase African levels of prosperity to a greater extent than is presently the case – and the cultural wealth.

The diverse sustainability issues that exist today can be solved through collective responsibility on the part of all nations and people. Both the 'prisoner's dilemma' and the 'tragedy of the commons' clearly demonstrate that dialogue and cooperation are essential. Decisions must be made on the basis of both the consequence scope and the consequence period. For the latter, a distinction must be made between short-term solutions (combating the symptoms) and long-term ones (dispelling the causes).

A more detailed summary can be found on the website of this book.

6
NOW AND LATER

In this section the following topics and concepts are discussed:

6.1   Lessons from history
6.2   Prophets, futurologists and science fiction authors
6.3   Models, scenarios and simulations
6.4   Growth models
6.5   World scenarios
6.6   What kind of world do we actually want?

A glossary containing all terms in both this chapter and others is available on the website of this book.

Case 6.1   The future year 2000

By 1990 there will be commercial flights reaching speeds in excess of 6,000 km per hour.

Before 2000, people will be living in cities at the bottom of the sea. Artificial moons, suspended in space, will illuminate large cities.

By 2000 people will be able to hibernate for months, even years.

By the turn of the century computers will weigh no more than 1.5 tons.

In 2000 people will be commuting in their own helicopters.

By 2000, two-thirds of the world's population will earn $1,000 or more.

Poverty will be a thing of the past in the year 2000.

As of 1979, the oceans will be devoid of sealife.

Massive food riots will break out in Western nations after 1980. Famine will hold the entire world in its iron grasp, and four billion people will die of malnutrition between 1980 and 1989.

Life expectancy will have declined to 42 years in the United States by 1980. By 1999 there will only be around 22 million people in the US.

As of 1975 some 40,000 species of animals will die out every year, with a total of one million species extinct by 2000.

By 1995, up to 80 percent of all species of animals will be extinct.

These are just a few of the predictions made between 1960 and 1980 by those specialising in the future.

Sources: Ehrlich (1968), Ehrlich (1970), Myers (1979), Kahn et al (1976), Kahn and Wiener (1967), *Wall Street Journal* (1966).

The unequal distribution of prosperity not only exists between people occupying different regions of the planet, but could also be considered to exist between the people of today and the next generations – i.e. between *now* and *later*. The ruthless exploitation of the natural environment and the exhaustion of non-renewable sources mean we could be faced with a situation in which we make it very difficult for future generations to fulfil their own needs. This could even mean the end of civilisation as we know it – a reality we have learnt from the fates of a number of old, long-gone cultures. The worst example of this might well be that of Easter Island.

After a glance back in time, this section will delve deeply into the future. A range of methods are available for picturing the future, one of which might be simply relying on fantasy, as science fiction authors do, but there are also more scientific approaches for mapping out the future. This is done by futurologists, using resources such as scenarios and computational models. Computer programs also support this exploration of the future.

6.1 Lessons from history

The list of predictions in Case 6.1 demonstrates how hard it is to forecast future developments. From the 1960s through to the 1980s there were many scholars that got it completely wrong. Some of them saw a glittering new world ahead, crammed with exciting technology and human prosperity, whereas others believed the end of our civilisation was nigh.

The year 2000 has come and gone, and new technology has brought us a number of sensational innovations, although they have not brought us much closer to a sustainable society. On the other hand, the end of civilisation is not exactly hovering on the horizon. Or is it?

Before exploring the world far beyond the year 2000, it would be wise to first try and learn something from the lessons of the past. How did past civilisations fare? Why do they no longer exist? Are we still confronted with the same issues that caused their disappearance? The first examination will study ancient Mesopotamia.

Mesopotamia

There is a region in the Middle East, roughly corresponding to the nations of Iraq and Syria today, which was called Mesopotamia in ancient times – the 'land between the rivers'. The region was a cradle of civilisation. Writing was invented here, as were the first-known forms of agriculture, calculus, taxation, history writing, metalworking and astronomy . . . and the wheel, sometime around 3,700 BCE. The land hosted the oldest cities in the world, including Eridu, Ur, Lagash, Kish and later Babylon.

As the region was the first in the world where agricultural methods were employed, a situation arose where much food was available, as opposed to the surrounding areas. Consequently, the entire population was not solely preoccupied with producing food, with a portion now able to choose a different occupation. This was a new development, and some became public officials, whereas others turned to soldiering. The first army in the world was born, which found an easy prey in the surrounding lands. And so a mighty empire came into being – Babylon.

Over the following centuries the nation fared well, very well. The population increased and as a result intelligent methods were required to encourage agriculture. Irrigation was invented and the waters of the two great rivers, the Euphrates and the Tigris, were used to irrigate the lands. Now, river water always contains a small quantity of salt, which is released by the mountains in which rivers have their sources. This salt would normally flow with the water into the sea, where it accumulates – this is why the sea contains salt water. But when river water is used to irrigate lands, the water will evaporate from the land and the salt will accumulate there instead of in the sea. It's an extremely slow process and it is a long time before it becomes noticeable. But in Mesopotamia the lands slowly but surely became salinised.

Soil fertility declined, while at the same time the number of mouths to feed increased. And so a variety of solutions were employed to solve this problem. Instead of wheat, an increasing amount of barley was grown, a crop with a greater resistance to the salt. The fields were no longer used every year, left to lie fallow for certain years so that rainwater could wash away the salt and allow nature to recover to some degree. To compensate this, more and more land was used, which meant that forests had to be felled and surrounding kingdoms were conquered.

The growth in human presence put pressure on the natural environment, with the largest animals dying in rapid succession. The elephant, the lion, the tiger and the rhinoceros all disappeared.

Mesopotamia was, once-upon-a-time, a land of undulating forests, but the space was needed for agriculture and the trees for housing and ships. The forests were decimated and the young trees that could replace the old ones were eaten by large herds of goats. The woods gradually disappeared, with the wind and the rain tussling over the naked Earth. Wide-scale erosion was the result and the fertile top layer of soil – that part that had not yet been exhausted by the intensive agriculture – was blown or washed away, while the remaining Earth, absent of roots, was unable to retain moisture and dried out.

Overpopulation and malnutrition rendered the region vulnerable to disease and invaders, and the situation slowly became untenable.

Present-day Iraq is a country of deserts rather than of subtropical forests (Figure 6.1). It is possible that this is in part due to natural climate change, a factor that is difficult to ascertain. But human activities have certainly contributed too.

Easter Island

There is a tiny island in the middle of the Pacific Ocean – Rapa Nui, the locals call it. Europeans first set eyes on it on Easter Sunday, hence the name. The island has a sad history.

This dot on the map is so isolated that it is a miracle it was ever discovered by people navigating in canoes. But this happened, around 900 CE, when Polynesians arrived on a rich and

FIGURE 6.1 The barren Iraqi desert, well-known from photos and television reports of the Gulf wars, was once the undulating forest landscape of the mighty Babylonian empire

Source: U.S. Marine Corps, Alicia M. Garcia

green island, decked with subtropical forests, palm trees and a great variety of fauna, including 30 species of birds. It was a little piece of paradise.

Almost ten centuries later, the Dutch explorer Jacob Roggeveen became the first Westerner to set foot on the island, in 1722 (Figure 6.2). What he found was a denuded island covered in grass. Not a tree to be found, and a starving population. The largest animals he found were insects. Statues! That's what they found. The Moai of Easter Island (Figure 6.3) are huge. The largest of them is over 20 meters tall – standing next to a block of apartments, it would be peeking in at the fifth floor. More than 200 of these giant statues are dotted around the island.

It was a mystery! How could such a small group of people have been able to erect these giant statues? They had been carved, from their base to their headgear, as one piece out of volcanic rock and dragged for kilometres to their present locations. Some were still sticking out of the rock, half-carved, as if a disaster had suddenly hit the island and halted all work. Others were lying on their sides.

It took a great deal of time to unravel the history of the island, but historians eventually succeeded. When the first inhabitants arrived on Rapa Nui, they encountered so much natural wealth that there was little to do to sustain themselves. With all the time they found themselves with, they were able to occupy themselves with other things, such as sculpting.

But the island's society became more complex as the number of inhabitants increased. The population consisted of 11 or 12 large clans, which engaged in peaceful struggles with each other for power and status. One of the manners of improving one's status was to carve

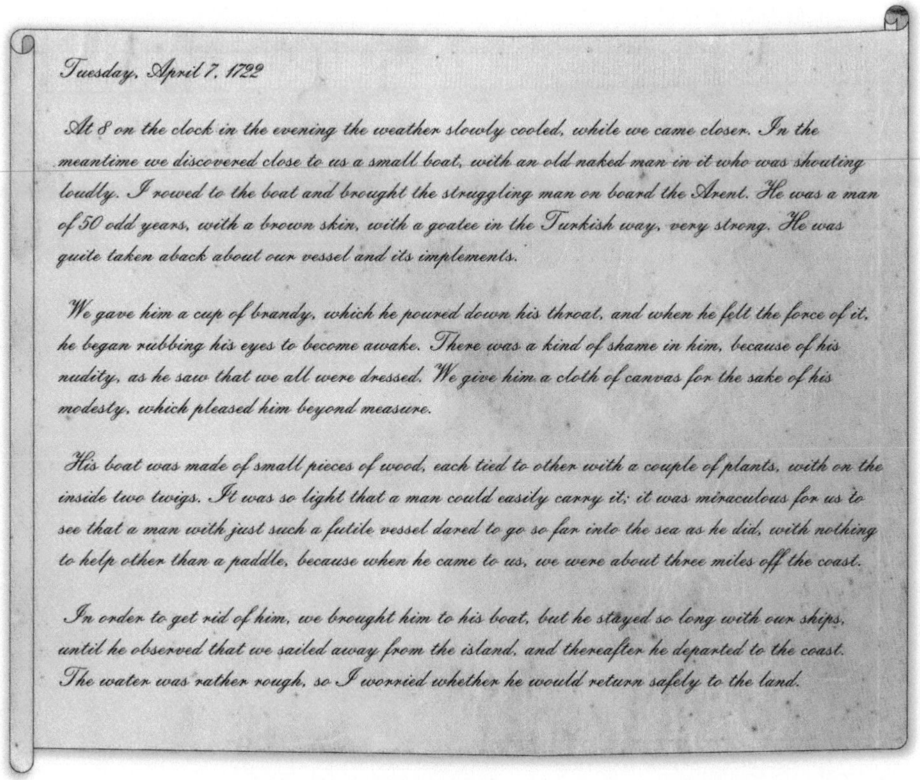

Tuesday, April 7, 1722

At 8 on the clock in the evening the weather slowly cooled, while we came closer. In the meantime we discovered close to us a small boat, with an old naked man in it who was shouting loudly. I rowed to the boat and brought the struggling man on board the Arent. He was a man of 50 odd years, with a brown skin, with a goatee in the Turkish way, very strong. He was quite taken aback about our vessel and its implements.

We gave him a cup of brandy, which he poured down his throat, and when he felt the force of it, he began rubbing his eyes to become awake. There was a kind of shame in him, because of his nudity, as he saw that we all were dressed. We give him a cloth of canvas for the sake of his modesty, which pleased him beyond measure.

His boat was made of small pieces of wood, each tied to other with a couple of plants, with on the inside two twigs. It was so light that a man could easily carry it; it was miraculous for us to see that a man with just such a futile vessel dared to go so far into the sea as he did, with nothing to help other than a paddle, because when he came to us, we were about three miles off the coast.

In order to get rid of him, we brought him to his boat, but he stayed so long with our ships, until he observed that we sailed away from the island, and thereafter he departed to the coast. The water was rather rough, so I worried whether he would return safely to the land.

FIGURE 6.2 When Roggeveen discovered the island the inhabitants had lost all seaworthy vessels, and were left with rickety boats made of straw and twigs tied together, as can be seen from the captain's logbook . . .

Source: Bouwman (1722); background "paper": The Digital Yard Sale

and erect Moai, the statues, which consequently grew ever bigger. Tree trunks were required to move the statues, used like rails over which wooden sleighs were pulled. Wood was also required for houses, boats and as fuel, while many animals were caught for food, including dolphins, fish, rats, birds and seals.

The population grew, until finally it hit maybe 20,000 – far more than the island could sustain. The animals died out one by one, and the land became barren. Plants that were necessary for feeding the populace – such as roots, nuts and palms – became rare and finally disappeared altogether.

And the trees disappeared too, until the very last one was chopped down in a crazed contest between the clans to see who could erect the largest Moai. The statues may also have increased in stature in a desperate attempt to beg for blessing from the gods and ancestors for the dying island. And so, ships could no longer be built with which the people could fish or – even worse – with which they could escape the island for better places. They were prisoners.

FIGURE 6.3 The Moai of Easter Island stare on the bare landscape

Source: Aurbina, 2004, Wikimedia.

Violence broke out. A large number of people were killed in the bloody battles. Some of the Moai were toppled. Few people were left, once Europeans discovered Easter Island. These survivors led a miserable existence, one from which there was no escape.

Other civilisations

The story of Mesopotamia and Easter Island can be heard in many variations and places. The same thing happened in China around 300 BCE, while in Greece it happened around the time of Christ. It was always the same story, with forests decimated for boats and buildings, goats destroying what was left of the environment and the civilisation collapsing.

The Roman Empire collapsed in the fifth century CE, in part as a result of environmental issues. One of these was that the farmers were required to surrender large quantities of grain as part of the war effort, and so ruthlessly exploited the land for centuries. To this day, you will find a barren and abandoned landscape around some old Roman settlements.

The Chaco Anasazi, an American Indian tribe in the state of New Mexico, ruled over an area the size of Scotland in the eleventh century CE. Ruthless exploitation and salinisation due to irrigation meant a decline in the soil's fertility, and the culture collapsed around 1300 CE. The Mayans suffered a similar fate in Central America around 900 CE, as did the Moche and the Tiwanaku in South America, Crete in the Mediterranean Sea, the Kingdom of Zimbabwe in Africa, Angkor Wat in Cambodia and dozens of other civilisations and powerful empires.

And what will become of us?

Questions

- When compared to earlier cultures, our civilisation is incredibly wealthy and powerful. Are we invulnerable? Is it impossible that our culture shall ever end?
- In our present civilisation, do you see symptoms resembling those that caused previous empires to collapse?
- What do you think are the mechanisms behind the collapse of a civilisation? What would people experience?

6.2 Prophets, futurologists and science fiction authors

With the past behind us, it is now time for the future. The biggest question, of course, is whether we are able to avoid the sorry fate of all those civilisations that have disappeared before us. After all, when talking about sustainable development, this is what it's all about. Will our world spiral downwards in the twenty-first century, or will we be able to find a way out of this, leading us to a better world?

Questions

- What do you think will happen – will our technology aid us in making society sustainable?
- Or rather, our understanding of the past?
- Or our predictive powers, and other fresh ways of considering the world?
- Or maybe a combination of all of these?

There are at least three ways of dealing with the future – we can endeavour to predict it, to discover it in advance; we can endeavour to create it ourselves, according to a preconceived plan; or we can simply wait and see what happens.

Simply waiting to see what happens is not a particularly satisfying task for many people. From a viewpoint of sustainable development this is not an attractive option either, as there is a risk that we end up in a future that nobody wants. A future like the one Babylon was dealt, for example. For that reason, the present section will instead examine attempts to know the future before it's here.

Case 6.2 Nostradamus

In the sixteenth century there lived an astrologer by the name of Nostradamus. His fame was widespread in his day, as it still is. He wrote thousands of texts – 'quatrains' – containing mysterious prophecies. Barely a soul can say with any degree of precision what he was actually saying in these writings, and conjecture and guesswork are the order of the day. Some people claim they are able to identify specific historical events in the quatrains, such as the birth of Napoleon and Hitler, the deaths of kings, wars and epidemics.

An example of these alleged prophecies is:
The horrible war which is being prepared in the West,
The following year will come the pestilence
So very horrible that young, old nor beast [will survive],
Blood, fire, Mercury, Mars, Jupiter in France.

Some claim the quatrain predicts the rise of Aids, the 'pestilence' in the second line, with the war referred to in the first line being that between Iraq and Iran in the 1980s. Then again, others believe it refers to the influenza pandemic that immediately followed World War I.

Source: Nostradamus (1554), Quatrain 55 of Century 9; English translation by Charles A. Ward (1891)

Nostradamus is certainly not the only oracle. People who claim they can see the future have been around for thousands of years. They're in the Bible, in Greek antiquity, in the Middle Ages and in our contemporary age. They call themselves prophets, seers or astrologers. As Case 6.2 illustrates, their predictions must be taken with a healthy pinch of salt. Depending on one's personal convictions, one might choose to believe predictions emanating from a certain source. But whatever predictions an individual chooses to believe, for example the Old Testament prophets, they are not likely to provide much useful information on future sustainable developments in the twenty-first century.

Then there is another approach to considering the future, one that is based on creativity and fantasy. Stories of the future can be found in science fiction novels, comic books, films and computer games. Though science fiction authors generally don't endeavour to prophesise the future, their predictive powers are handy when it comes to sounding out and exploring possible futures. This can assist us in considering the consequences of present or conceivable developments, and in starting debates on which futures we might aspire to and which we might shun.

With a polite gesture of respect

He examined his face in the mirror. Once, hundreds of years ago, mirrors were made of silver and glass, he had once heard – very different to today's combination of webcam and monitor. The patterns decorating his face identified him as a Knower, the property of Hitachi ProcterGamble for three years, while the arched forms above his eyes told the world that he had Level 15 Knowledge. This was not enough for the job he now had to do.

He clumsily grabbed a sprayer and drew another two lines above his right eye, hand quivering. For the first time in his life he wished he had learned Writing – it would have made this job much easier! But nobody learnt Writing any more. All done, he now had Level 21 Knowledge.

What he had just done was, of course, highly illegal. If he had been caught, he would have been sublimated, his molecules spread across no less than three continents. To set an example for others.

The excitement made him breathless, the job was really too much for him. He needed greater courage! Fortunately, this was available. He carefully removed the chip from the docking station in his throat. He retrieved another circuit board from his pocket. It looked identical to the first one, but it wasn't. It had cost him a fortune – over 100 gigadollars from the now outlawed Merican government in Deecey. He fumbled it into the docking station and breathed deeply. Courage flowed through his body. Immediately he felt relaxed and confident. It was going to work!

He stood up. The door slid open, the house computer understanding his intentions. He walked outside. It was a pity that the City immediately knew where he was heading, but this was unavoidable. He was momentarily distracted by the commercials on the road-surface, so he almost missed the two passing Neighbours. Just in time he greeted them wordlessly with the Polite Gesture of Respect. They formally nodded their heads in return, showing Affable Friendliness.

Brimming with confidence, he crossed the square in the direction of the Workers' Palace. The Knowledge Bomb in the hip bag of his frock felt heavy.

Historical science fiction can be great fun, such as the Buck Rogers comic strip shown in Figure 6.4, dating from 1929, which takes place in the twenty-fifth century. When it was created, there were no transistors or computer chips, and so twentieth-fifth century technology still used vacuum tubes. In spite of this, they did have SMS capabilities, as can be seen in the bottom right panel.

There is another group of people that are occupied with the future. Through **futurology**, the study of the future, people examine the future in a scientific manner. The success rate varies, it must be said. Sometimes futurologists make sensible predictions, as it turns out at a later stage, while at other times they are very wrong. Case 6.1 illustrates the latter. Futurology employs a variety of methods, one of which is **trend extrapolation**, involving the examination of past developments, 'trends'. When a futurologist assumes that these trends will

FIGURE 6.4 Buck Rogers in the twenty-fifth century, what the future looked like in 1929

Source: Philip Francis Nowlan & Richard Calkins: The collected works of Buck Rogers in the twenty-fifth century AD. Chelsea House Publishers, Chicago 1929–1969.

continue for some time into the future, then he or she could extend, 'extrapolate', this trend into the future, thus making an educated guess on what could happen in the next few years. Figure 5.16, which shows the age distribution of the EU up to 2061, is an example of such a trend extrapolation, this one being drawn up by the European Union's statistical office. The predictions of the economic policy bureaus, which calculate future results of current government policies, amongst other things, is likewise a trend extrapolation, as are the daily weather forecasts.

This is not without its risks, as trends rarely continue for long. Some might last for a while and then start to decline. An example of this is life expectancy in the United States – in the twentieth century the average lifespan steadily lengthened among all groups, but recent reports indicate Americans may be living shorter lives due to increasingly unhealthy lifestyles. Other trends can be capricious and sensitive to fashions. On many occasions, weather forecasts are wrong, and the same applies to attempts by the US Federal Reserve to predict economical developments.

The biggest risk that trend extrapolations run are **trend breaks** – events which (almost) nobody could have seen coming, and that result in radical change. The rise of the Internet is an example of a trend break All science fiction stories preceding 1990 or so, taking place in the twenty-first century or later, are way off the mark, thanks to the fact that Google, email or instant messaging don't feature. A similar hazard can be encountered by futurologists, despite their expertise and experiences. Few of them forecast the severe financial crisis that, starting with the housing crisis in the United States, spread around the world in the second half of the century's first decade, as described in Chapter 2.

But there are also trends that continue for a long period, and could even continue in the face of radical changes. These trends are labelled as **robust**, in that they can take a few knocks. Robust trends in recent years include the increased speed of communications, the growth in the scale of politics and corporations, and urbanisation, the flow of people to the cities. It seems likely that these trends will continue in the present century. But even that is a risky assertion.

Another method employed by futurologists is to relate 'stories', through which they frequently respond to each other and thus build up a picture of the future. Perhaps it would be better to say 'of *a possible* future'. In doing this, futurologists are not very different from many science fiction authors, which is no mere coincidence, given that many science fiction writers are also scientific researchers. Narrative futurology is not per se serious and academic, and it can also involve satire – one that derides leaders for their inability to break trends.

"My fellow countrymen!"

The citizens of this great nation are worried about the rising sea levels around our land, as a result of the so-called 'greenhouse effect'. Especially the predictions doing the rounds that all subjects shall have to flee our nation within 30 years, have caused great concern amongst the population.

Consequently, your Government decided to institute a thorough investigation of this phenomenon. Presently this study is complete, and I am authorised to share its primary conclusions with you.

I am able to set your minds at ease. Let me start by saying that the complete flooding of our nation shall not, as science has told us, take place any earlier than around 2120. Not a single Dutch person will have to leave our beautiful land before then. But not even after that.

Thanks to the achievements of Technology, your Government has drawn up a plan that shall enable us to save our country and people from death by drowning.

In the first phase of this rescue plan, the dunes to the west and north of the nation will be propped up and raised with the aid of dykes. This will be completed by 2060.

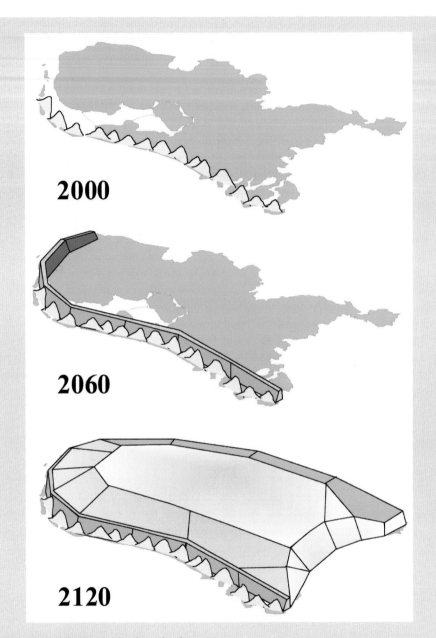

2000

2060

2120

FIGURE 6.5 The Netherlands in the future?

Yet, that is not all.

You will understand that, even in a nation possessing the experiences we have, at a certain time an end will come to the ability to build dykes ever higher. So, when the sea rises above the maximum achievable dyke level, we will be ready to face the situation. Much earlier than this critical moment, a start will be made to expand the greenhouses in the Westland.

In accordance with your Government's plans, these greenhouses (see Figure 6.5) will have reached the size of the entire country by 2120 – just in time for when the sea floods the dykes. By that time the entire country will be covered in glass.

But even then, my countrymen, the Netherlands will not be entirely isolated from the rest of the world. For quite some time after the greenhouse is closed, the country will still be partially dry at low tides. Only after 2150, our country will be submerged 24 hours a day, after which we will maintain contact with other parts of the world by submarine.

For the purposes of that objective, the Government has commissioned some of the largest shipyards in the country to build a few dozen luxury submarines.

As you can see, there is no reason whatsoever for any anxiety on your part. The authorities have the problem firmly under control. You can all rest easy.

A consideration of the future in the form of narratives has resulted in a highly pessimistic view amongst a number of futurologists, with the stories descending into doom-mongering and melancholy. But others are boundlessly optimistic, and these authors assert in their stories that everything will work out of its own accord. Probably, both extremes are viewing the future through tinted spectacles, one through dark glasses and the other through rose-tinted ones. The shade of filter chosen depends on the personality and, maybe, the political inclination of the futurologist.

Dark glasses

First: a look through the glasses worn by the doom and gloom merchants.

This group naturally informs us of those sober prognoses we have all heard before, with warnings that our global society will fall apart as a result of overpopulation, greenhouse effect, pollution, depletion of resources, soils becoming infertile, droughts and salinisation. Such predictions are correct in a certain way, in that these are all real threats – ones that we must work hard to counter.

These also include prophecies of doom about deliberate destruction perpetrated by people – by nations, by terrorist groups or by lone nutcases. An attack involving nuclear weapons is one of the possibilities this group includes, as well as ones with biological weapons, most likely aided by bacteria or viruses constructed in laboratories. The biological version aside, there are also computer viruses that could destroy the global economic system through the Internet.

In recent years there is much talk about the chance of an extraterrestrial body – a meteorite or asteroid – colliding with the Earth and causing a catastrophe comparable to the one that wiped out the dinosaurs 65 million years ago. It is striking that some people suddenly become wrought with fear at this thought, even though the chance of this happening is no greater than it has been in millions of years.

Biologists also fear the chance of a new disease breaking out, which might wipe out a large part of the human race. Indeed, new diseases do appear at intervals, such as Ebola, Aids, SARS and swine flu. As opposed to the chance of us getting hit by a meteorite, the chance of a new pandemic is greater than it once was, thanks to increased population density, greater mobility (not least as a result of exotic holidays) and an increase in contact between people and animals, caused at least in part by our encroachment upon the natural environment.

Then we also have mutterings about completely new threats, ones that could arise from the latest technological developments. Some people fear, for example, that the world could be taken over by artificial intelligence-driven computers and robots that enslave the human race.

Another new technological breakthrough is that of **nanotechnology**, a field in which people are endeavouring to create minute machines, invisible to the naked eye, such as engines, computers, robots and power generators. If scientists succeed in creating these, they might not be larger than a molecule, no bigger than 10 or 100 nanometers (which is where the name comes from, a nanometer being a millionth of a millimetre). These machines would be so light they could float through the air, and they could tackle tasks, either alone or in groups reaching into the millions, such as surgical operations, purifying water, combating bacteria and viruses or building up human tissue, molecule by molecule.

Taking this one step further, if you incorporate into some of them the possibility of copying themselves from materials they seek out themselves, then you have a new form of life, as it were. This form of life could be – just as real life – dangerous if spontaneous errors ('mutations') arise that could copy ('propagate') themselves unhindered and quite literally use all living organisms as building blocks ('food'). Eric Drexler, who has been called the father of nanotechnology, has described this danger as the 'grey goo' problem, in view of the possibility that the entire planet could be reduced to some kind of grey soup composed of trillions of nano-machines within days, in which no life could exist (Source: Drexler, 1986. In 2004 Drexler wrote that he no longer considers the grey goo scenario a danger, but not everyone agrees with him).

The rose-tinted glasses

All these risks and dangers might seem to be major threats, but a number of people are not impressed by them. These optimists adopt the polar opposite view, emphasising those things that are doing well and making good progress.

They believe, for example, that our resources are not running out at all, up until a few years ago happily pointing out that the trade prices for metals and fossil fuels had not risen in the past decades (which would have happened if they were scarce) but had actually decreased. This has changed in recent years, and the prices of many metals and of crude oil have risen considerably, especially as a result of increased demand in Asia. These optimists also highlight the fact that the extractable quantity of oil has not decreased but rather increased, in recent years, in spite of considerable consumption. They are right on this point, as the next chapter will show.

Overpopulation is not an impending threat either, the wearers of these rose-tinted spectacles tell us. In some parts of the world the population is already declining, and other parts will follow within a few decades. This will even happen in areas like the ECOWAS region. At the same time, food production is on the rise at a rate that is faster than the population growth. This is largely due to economic growth and, say these economic optimists, this means that such growth must be dramatically stimulated, as they believe it is the key to sustainable development. Nor are environmental problems an issue, as the well-known eco-optimist Bjørn Lomborg has said (both in his book *The Sceptical Environmentalist*, 1998, and elsewhere). He believes that the figures on the extinction rates of fauna and flora, for example, are greatly exaggerated, with the same applying to environmental problems such as acid rain. Lomborg and others tell us that we should not be so worried about all the issues – after all, countless earlier problems have sorted themselves out, and the same will surely happen with the current batch.

Questions

- Who do you believe are correct, the pessimists or the optimists? Or maybe they're both partly right? Why?
- Are you wearing tinted glasses? If so, are they dark or rose coloured? Or do you believe you are neither optimistic nor pessimistic, merely realistic?
- Do you thing others believe you are wearing tinted glasses? If so, are they dark or rose coloured? Ask others about yourself!

Who is correct, those wearing the dark glasses or the rose-coloured ones?

The first group, the doom-mongerers, are akin to the prophets of doom of old, who in the Middle Ages cried out: "Woe to us all! The end is nigh!" Some of them even seem to take pleasure in our dire future. A number of groups, including some environmental movements, sometimes greatly exaggerate a number of issues at hand, either deliberately or unconsciously. But they are still correct to that extent that a number of the issues are very real issues, are serious and will not disappear of their own accord.

The optimists are likewise partly correct. Advances have been made, while some problems are not as serious as has been suggested. But the idea that all problems encountered previously have sorted themselves out is simply untrue. As appeared earlier in this chapter, it is all too common that fundamental issues are not solved and complete civilisations collapsed like a house of cards. While some pessimists may resemble the prophets of doom of yore, some optimists in turn are like a person sunk into a luxurious armchair, watching the television with a live broadcast of a marathon, and thinking: "See, it all happens of its own accord!" And while he's getting another drink, he is oblivious to the fact that the runners have to give their utmost to make the finish line.

All in all, the situation reminds one of a glass half-filled with water. "It's half-empty," say the pessimists. "It's half-full," say the optimists (Figure 6.6).

FIGURE 6.6 Dark glasses or rose-tinted ones . . .

Source: Peter de Wit, De Volkskrant.

An interesting way in which futurologists give shape to their differences of opinion is through wagers. 'Long Bets' are long-term bets that everyone can take online (www.longbets. org), which include staking money on a challenging assertion. These include:

- At least one person alive in the year 2000 will still be alive in 2150.
- By no later than 2020, solar energy will cost no more, or even less, than energy derived from fossil fuels.
- By no later than 2020, at least one million people will have been killed in a bio-terrorist attack or in a biological accident.
- In 2060 there will be fewer people on the planet than there are today.
- By no later than the year 2100 there will be a world government that is in charge of economic and environmental legislation and controls all weapons of mass destruction.

6.3 Models, scenarios and simulations

A wager like these long bets is a fun way in which futurology can commit itself. The disadvantage, of course, is that the winner is only determined in retrospect – once we are in the future. The same applies to narrative futurologists, trend extrapolation and science fiction, where the truth is only known once we have arrived at that point. This is a pity, and if we want to explore the future from the standpoint of the present, it does not provide much foundation. It is, after all, a fixed characteristic of the future – in principle it is unpredictable, as we can see from the many misses perpetrated by futurologists. This means that sustainable development is inevitably confronted by a wide variety of uncertainties, and the ability to deal with these uncertainties is thus an important aspect for professionals that wish to adopt a future-oriented approach.

In spite of this, futurology has another method that provides a starting point. One could call it 'experimental futurology', given that it envisions the future in such a way that it can be experimented with. In reality, we are not dealing with *the* future here, but rather with *one possible* future. The process involves using a computer and specially designed applications that are called simulation software. The word **simulation** literally refers to 'imitation' and it involves mimicking the real world, or a part thereof, on a computer. Some of this software was designed as a game, with the Sims and SimCity amongst the best known of these. Both those names come from the word 'simulation'. Other simulation packages are intended for more serious purposes, being used to see what the weather will be in the near future, for example, for the weather forecasts that we see and read. Some programs combine both: an example is the game 'Anno 2070', in which the gamer has the option of choosing between an environmental-friendly or a more economically profitable future development (around the year 2070) (Figure 6.7). This choice between *planet* and *profit* gives the program the character of a 'serious game'.

A simulation program uses a **model**, which is a simplified representation of reality. Simulation software is not the only type of model – a plastic kit of an airplane is also a model, just like a map in an atlas is a model of a real country. A photograph serves as a model of the subject pictured, and a series of formulas that collectively detail the orbits of the planets is a model of a planetary system.

The word 'simplified' in the definition of 'model' is very important, as every model, be it a toy airplane, a SimCity landscape or a representation of the atmosphere in weather software, is

FIGURE 6.7   The Anno 2070 computer game

Source: Ubisoft, 2011.

derived from the actual situation by simplifying many of the real aspects. This is inevitable, as a model of the universe that is not simplified in any sense would simply be the universe itself. Reality is simplified through the following:

- shrinking the scale
- omitting surrounding areas
- omitting some of the components
- simplifying other components
- a two-dimensional representation of a three-dimensional scenario (e.g. on a computer monitor)
- simplifying events, the underlying natural laws or the economic or judicial laws

A common error people commit when using models – especially simulation software – is that they forget about the simplifications and draw conclusions about the real world from the simulation results without exercising any caution whatsoever.

The choice of model is the first step when performing a simulation, with the second step involving the selection of a **scenario**. A scenario is the plan for the events that are set to take place in the simulation. The word originally referred to plays – and later, films – to outline the scenes that made up the story, wherein a scenario required that every scene was written out in advance. This is not required for a computer simulation, where the only thing necessary is that the starting situation is determined. The computer then calculates, with the aid of the model, the step-by-step progress of events from that starting point onwards. This is how the future is 'calculated'.

An example demonstrates this. The example is often labelled as the 'prey-predator model'. This model examines the progress of two types of animal – predators and prey, such as foxes and rabbits. The model is instructive as, instead of foxes and rabbits, it could just as well deal with people and their consumption of food and other resources. This allows investigating the consequences of overexploitation.

In its simplest form the model consists of just two mathematical formulas. One of them deals with the increase in the fox population when they eat rabbits, and with its decrease when the foxes die of old age. The other formula deals with the decrease in the rabbit population when they are eaten by foxes, and with its increase through reproduction.

This model is extremely simplified. The genders of the foxes and rabbits don't play a role, nor do the landscape and the grass growth, the change of seasons or the emigration and immigration of the foxes and rabbits to or from other areas. Another thing not included in this model is the role played by chance. Because the chance factor is absent, the future becomes wholly predictable, and once the starting situation is determined – being the starting population of the rabbits and the foxes – the scenario becomes established. Once the computer starts working with this model, it returns a neat and regular graph like the one in Figure 6.8. Repeat the simulation using the same scenario and the exact same graph will be reproduced

Figure 6.8 was generated with the aid of a small computer program called the **FoxRabbit Formula Model**, which can be downloaded from the website of this book. You can conduct experiments using it – change the scenario by selecting different starting populations for the foxes and rabbits, and see the results.

No matter how simple such a model is, it is still of benefit. The graph shows that the fox population increases when there is an abundance of rabbits, and so the peaks on the fox line always come *after* those on the rabbit line – the fox line 'lags behind' the rabbit one. This shows a *periodical* behaviour, i.e. one that is constantly repeated. The way in which this happens is naturally not very realistic – in reality the development will certainly not progress so periodically.

The fox-rabbit model can also be simulated in a different way, which involves representing a landscape in a computer programme in which foxes and rabbits actually exist. In this landscape the foxes roam while hunting for rabbits, as can be seen in Figure 6.9, with the foxes being the bigger dark points and the rabbits the many little ones. This image was created using a different program, the **FoxRabbit Grassland Model**, which can likewise be downloaded from the website of this book. This simulation is considerably more realistic,

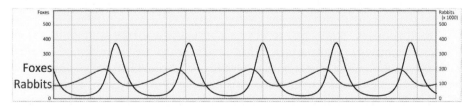

FIGURE 6.8   The Fox-Rabbit scenario. Number of foxes and rabbits over time, according to the Formula Model

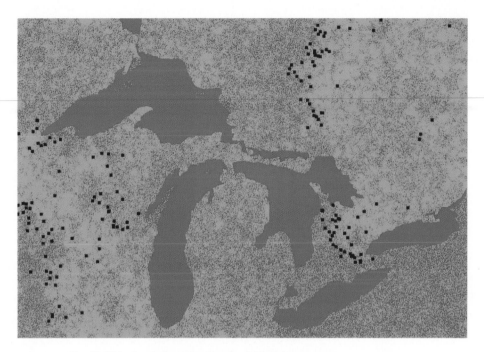

FIGURE 6.9   Fox-Rabbit simulation, the Grassland Model

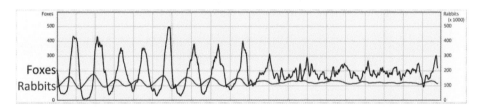

FIGURE 6.10   Same scenario as in Figure 6.8, but a different model. This graph is based on the Grassland Model

thanks in part to the fact that chance does play a role. When the simulation is launched using a given starting situation, the resulting graph will look different to the one in the fox-rabbit model. Repeat the simulation a number of times, using the same starting situation, and the graph will be different every time, as chance is incorporated into the model. An example of such a graph can be seen in Figure 6.10, and more of these types of graphs can be generated using the software.

In Figure 6.10 the waves of the graph correspond roughly to those in Figure 6.8, but the details differ dramatically. In other words, the results are determined not only by the scenario but also by the model that is used. The grasslands model, which is already much more realistic, can be useful when it comes to considering sustainable development. The software allows, for example, to change the foxes' behaviour (see Figure 6.11), which makes them more or less successful at hunting. By studying all scenarios in this way, the consequences of greater or less overexploitation or overpopulation can be examined.

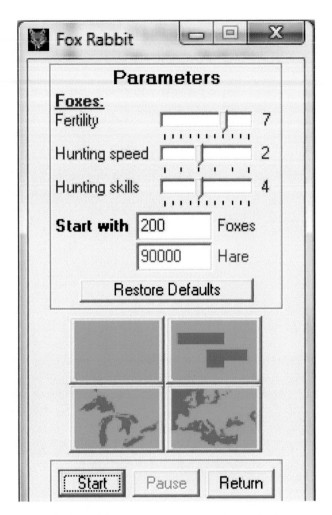

FIGURE 6.11 In the grassland model you can set the properties of the foxes

6.4 Growth models

Using this type of software, it is possible to investigate a very wide range of models and scenarios. These frequently involve growth or shrinkage, which can pertain to populations of people or animals, or maybe bacteria or plants or even – outside of the field of biology – cities, companies, factories or prosperity, profit forecasts or environmental damage.

A study of these types of growth processes shows that there are certain types of growth that are characteristic of many situations. These can be seen in Figure 6.12.

Uninhibited growth

Imagine that a new type of bacteria suddenly appears. This can actually happen if an error – a mutation – occurs when an existing type of bacteria reproduces. Now imagine that this new

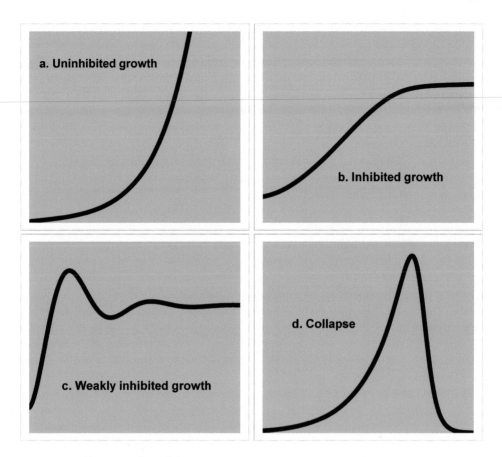

FIGURE 6.12   Four growth models

bacterium is highly successful, splitting in two to reproduce within 15 minutes. A quarter of an hour later, both these new bacteria have again split in two, creating four of them. After another 15 minutes there are eight, then 16 and so on. Those 15 minutes are the **doubling time** of the bacteria, and the increase in the number of bacteria is **uninhibited**, as there is nothing (for now) that could stop that growth.

Uninhibited growth such as this is called **exponential growth**. One receives surprising results when extrapolating the exponential growth trend, as it increases faster than most people would intuitively estimate. Our new bacterium is a good example of this. Within 24 hours, this single one will have become over 16 million bacteria. After another 24 hours there will be 281,474,976,710,656 – almost 300 trillion!

Uninhibited growth can be found abundantly – the human population has been growing exponentially in the last few centuries. To be honest, it has been growing even faster, with the doubling time becoming ever shorter in the twentieth century. In the nineteenth century the human population doubled every 100 years, but the number doubled from 2.5 billion to 5 billion in just 37 years, between 1950 and 1987. At present the growth rate is declining once again, presently with a doubling time of about 50 years.

It is not surprising that the world population is slowing, as it is impossible to continue growing exponentially for a long period of time. This becomes obvious when you examine what the consequences of continued exponential growth would be – through a thought experiment, extrapolating the present growth, with its 50-year doubling time. In the year 2000 there were around 6 billion people on the planet. This implies that by 2300 there would be 384 billion people. In 2740 there will be so many people that every human being will have one square meter of land, including Antarctica and the Sahara. Before the year 2900, there will be standing room only.

In the year 4220 the total mass of humanity will equal that of the planet (Figure 6.13). Can you imagine this – an entire planet made up – from core to crust – only of a gyrating mountain of human flesh and bones?

And should you think that we can solve the problem by colonising other planets: around 7650 the entire Milkyway Galaxy, with its billions of stars and planets, will be made of human tissue. Finally, in 8800 the human mass reaches the size of the entire universe.

The outcome of this little thought experiment is utterly insane, but the strangest thing is that such growth does not seem so high initially. The doubling time used in the preceding calculation is the population's actual doubling time at present, and corresponds to an annual growth of no more than 1.4 percent. This experiment proves that exponential growth is greater than many may think.

Using the **Exponential growth.xls** spreadsheet, one can examine the relationship between the growth percentage, the growth factor and the time required. It can be downloaded from the website of this book.

This does not only apply to the growth of the world population, but to other types of growth as well. Chapter 2 dealt with a number of flaws in the fabric of the human system. One of them is the fact that, in the present economic system, a constant economic growth of 1 or 2 percent a year is essential. Section 2.5 showed that a constant growth of 2.5 percent per annum meant that, in 1,200 years, humanity would be a trillion times as rich as they are today. This outcome, which is again clearly absurd, is the result of an assumed continuing exponential growth. The constant growth by a fixed percentage a year is *identical* to an exponential growth with a doubling time of a number of years. If the annual growth is 1.4 percent, the doubling time is 50 years, while if it is 2.5 percent the doubling time is 28 years. Sustaining such growth for a lengthy period is impossible. Uninhibited exponential growth can last for some time, but it *will* end at a given point, that is 100 percent sure. That end can come in a pleasant way – which is called inhibited growth. Or it can come in a less pleasant way, which will shortly become clear.

Inhibited growth

Let's return to the bacteria, with its doubling time of 15 minutes. In a few days the bacteria will increase enormously. Now imagine that this bacteria is not out in the open but in a sealed container in a laboratory. In this case exponential growth will probably continue for the first few hours, especially if the lab assistant provides them with sufficient food, but at a certain point the effects of the limited space will be noticeable. The growth rate will slowly decrease, the doubling time extends and an actual increase in numbers ceases as the colony of bacteria gradually becomes a constant population. A balance has been reached. This can

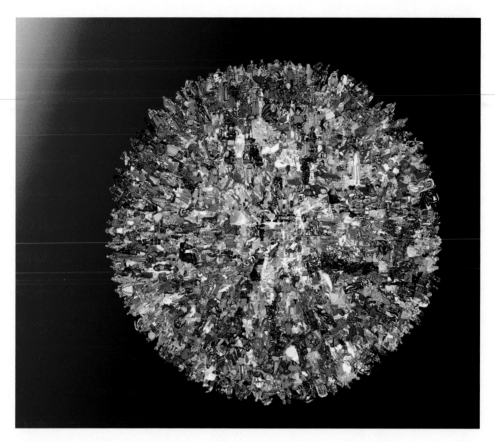

FIGURE 6.13   In 4220, from core to crust the Earth will be made of human flesh. . .

be seen in graph B of Figure 6.12, which shows a **trend shift** from a constant growth to an equilibrium.

This is called **inhibited growth**, also referred to in mathematical terms as **logistic growth**.

Humanity can follow a similar pattern, and it is indeed true that our growth rate is decreasing, with the doubling time in the mid-twentieth century standing at 35 years, whereas today it is around 50 years.

The growth of the global economy has not yet exhibited any signs of slowing down to reach an equilibrium. Its growth rate fluctuates continuously, punctuated by the occasional crisis, during which growth stagnates or even briefly goes into negative figures; but the basic assumption amongst all economists is that the stagnation will once again give way to continued growth. This is a flaw in the economic system – continuous growth is necessary, but it is also impossible to sustain in the long term. Inhibited growth is the result of limits being imposed on a system. This could be limitations to the available space or food or, in a more general sense, limitations to the available resources. Another limitation might be the environment's carrying capacity – increased pollution or degradation of the natural environment can inhibit growth.

Weakly inhibited growth

Inhibited growth is caused by the limitations imposed upon the system. Human population growth could, for example, decline in the wake of a decline in fertility rates, the lack of nutrition or due to the use of contraceptives. Economic growth could also decline if the environment is damaged, which causes profits to decrease. There are many other possible mechanisms that could limit growth.

This does not mean that the limitation always comes on time. The limiting forces may just as well occur at a very late time. If this happens, there is a chance that the growth will 'overshoot' the limits of the system. The deceleration then occurs too late, because of which a period of negative growth (a decline) will have to follow in order to bring the system back within its limits. Graph C in Figure 6.12 demonstrates this. A period like this can be a painful one, and if it concerns prosperity levels that have been overshot, people will have to adjust to lower prosperity levels. It will most likely also imply bankruptcies and rising unemployment.

Weakly inhibited growth could arise if the mechanism that kick-starts the decline is weak and delayed. An example in the real world is the rise in temperatures on the planet as a result of greenhouse gas emissions. This increase can only be remedied if a number of difficult steps are taken in succession. These include:

1   A scientific understanding of the effects of the greenhouse gases
2   A political awareness of the gravity of these effects
3   An effective international political decision-making process
4   Revising production processes and energy consumption and/or planting many trees
5   A decrease in the concentration of greenhouse gases

Taken together, this is a process that will at the very least take decades. This is firstly because of slow decision making on the part of people (steps 1 through 3), followed by the time required to earn back those investments made in the means of production (step 4). At least as important is step 5 – **system lag**, the inertia of the natural process that depletes the greenhouse gases in the atmosphere. This final element is frequently dramatically underestimated. From the moment the cause of a problem is removed, it may take a lot of time before the consequences of it start to decline. Case 6.3 demonstrates this, using a different problem encountered in the atmosphere – the depletion of the ozone layer. Chapter 1 already mentioned the Montreal Protocol (1989), and described how it was an example of a highly successful international approach (see Figure 1.10). Case 6.3 offers some interesting details.

Case 6.3   The ozone layer

The uppermost layer of the stratosphere is called the **ozone layer**, located some 50 kilometres above the surface of the planet. As the name tells, this layer contains a high concentration of ozone (O_3), a special form of oxygen. Ground-level ozone can be dangerous, but it is highly beneficial to us at an altitude of 50 kilometres, where it absorbs a great deal of the ultraviolet (UV) radiation, which causes skin and eye afflictions, including skin cancer.

Humans have produced a number of gases that are useful to us, such as those in aerosol cans and for the refrigerating process in our fridges. Once used, these gases end up being distributed in the atmosphere, reaching a height of 50 kilometres after many years – 10 to 20. These gases deplete the ozone, allowing for an increased amount of ultraviolet light to reach the Earth.

The leading culprit is the **CFCs, chlorofluorocarbons**, which act as catalysers for breaking down ozone. This means that they accelerate the process without being broken down themselves. As a result of this, a small quantity of CFC can destroy a large amount of ozone. The CFCs are broken down by sunlight, but this is a very long process which takes between 50 and 200 years.

The ozone layer is consequently becoming thinner, a process that is happening fastest at the South Pole. Because of this, there has been a 'hole in the ozone layer' since around 1980, covering a region the size of a continent where the ozone has been depleted by up to 60 percent (see Figure 6.14). Eye and skin diseases have increased greatly amongst people and animals in Australia and parts of South America, and people are advised not to suntan. Another 'hole' has been established above the North Pole.

There are two reasons why the ozone problem responds with a lag to any changes. The first is the period of 10 to 20 years between the release of the harmful gases and the time at which they reach the ozone layer. The second is the 50 to 200-year period required for these gases to be broken down. In other words, if we were to completely stop producing these gases at any time, the ozone layer will continue to be depleted for a long time after that.

CFC production has decreased dramatically thanks to the Montreal Protocol, but has not yet come to a complete halt. Under the Protocol, arrangements were also agreed to phase out the production and use of related substances, hydro-chlorofluorocarbons (HCFCs), which also bring harm to the ozone layer. A third group, the hydrofluorocarbons (HFCs), were not brought under an agreement before 2016, as a consequence of the Paris Agreement on climate change, as will be described in Section 7.5.

System lag actually works against us in two ways – at the start and at the conclusion of a damaging process. At the start, it could be many years before damage caused by a human process (see point 1 in Figure 6.15) becomes noticeable (point 2), and at the end because once the cause declines (point 3) it takes many years before the damage itself starts to decline (point 4). The result 'lags behind' the cause, and this **time-lag effect** is deceptive.

The graph in Figure 6.15 resembles the one representing the foxes and rabbits in Figure 6.8, which is no coincidence, as the fox-rabbit model is a good illustration of the time-lag effect.

The same applies to the depletion of the ozone layer, the topic of Case 6.3 that was already mentioned in Chapter 1. There, Figure 1.10 showed the effectiveness of the Montreal Protocol towards the decrease of the production and consumption of CFCs and related substances. This graph is repeated in Figure 6.16, this time not only showing the *cause* (the CFCs) but also the *effect*: the size of the hole in the ozone layer, measured through the years. The red dots in the graph are separate measurements. They vary widely, due to the capriciousness of the weather. But together they establish a trend, represented as a red line. This curve shows a modest decrease in the size of the ozone hole. The slow decrease is rather unsecure yet, thus illustrating the nasty time-lag effect. The atmosphere is expected to take between 50 and 100 years before the hole in the ozone layer above the South Pole has recovered.

As human beings, we frequently neither know nor understand what we are doing. Often we are unable to foresee the consequences of our actions. If we could, and if

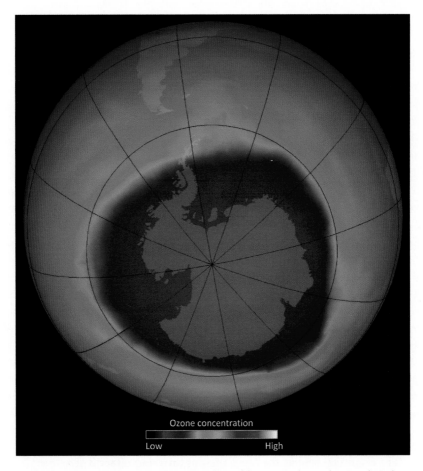

FIGURE 6.14 The 'hole' in the ozone layer (the large blue area) above the South Pole in October 2015, covering the continent of Antarctica (purple)

Source: NASA Visible Earth, NASA Scientific Visualization Studio, Goddard Space Flight Center.

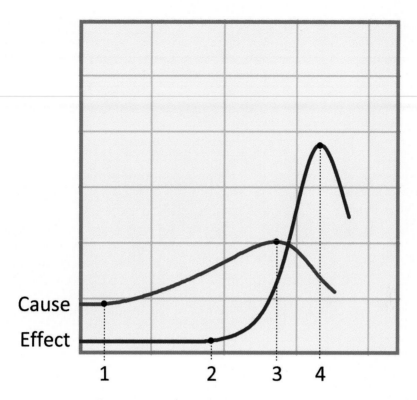

FIGURE 6.15   Time-lag effect – the result lags behind the cause

we were able to **anticipate** in good time – i.e. take action at an early stage in order to combat the damage caused – then the decline in growth would always be represented by graph B (Figure 6.12). But, given the fact that this is not the case, reality often resembles graph C more closely.

Collapse

But reality does not always resemble graph C either, and there is a risk that the inhibition is so weak and so slow that the system severely overshoots and something gives. This causes the entire system to collapse, as can be seen in graph D.

This book has already covered examples of such a **collapse**. The 1987 stock market crash on Black Monday was one of these. Consequently, the form of graph D (Figure 6.12) mirrors that of Figure 2.12 in Chapter 2 – look at the 'bubble' followed by 'Black Monday'. The consequences of the 1987 crash remained limited as a recovery quickly got off the ground, but the 1929 crash was much worse, and the global economy only took off once again after a world war.

Much more dramatic were the collapses witnessed in ancient Babylonia and on Easter Island, as outlined earlier in this chapter. These civilisations were completely lost. A collapse on this scale is not uncommon, as a combination of overpopulation and overexploitation,

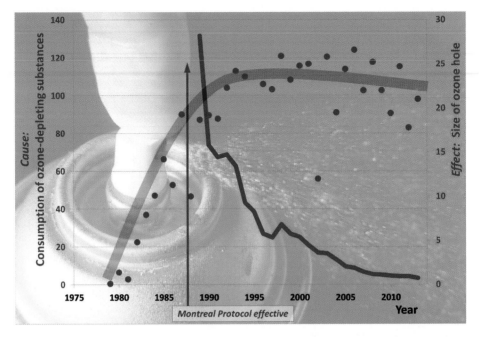

FIGURE 6.16 Time-lag effect for the ozone layer – the use of CFCs (cause) and the extent of the 'hole' in the ozone layer (result)

Sources: CFC use: UNEP GEO Data Portal, 2016. Extent of the ozone layer: NASA Goddard Space Flight Center, 2016; background photo: Andrew Magill.

sometimes amplified by external causes such as climate change or attacks, repeatedly led to disasters causing the system to permanently disintegrate.

When a collapse happens on this scale, it cannot be called a trend *shift* from growth to equilibrium, but rather a trend *break*, in which the growth inverts radically to become a process of rapid shrinkage. The economy collapses, production freezes, the number of people decreases drastically within one or a few generations because of famine, war, pandemics and declining birth rates. Governments are ousted, nations disappear and chaos reigns.

Warnings that our present civilisation is at risk of this happening are nothing new. As early as 1798, Thomas **Malthus** already wrote about the danger of an exponential growth in the population ('*An Essay on the Principle of Population*'). He pointed out that, sooner or later, the growth in food production would come to a halt, which could have disastrous consequences.

If we wish to avoid the same sorry fate that so many earlier civilisations suffered from, we shall have to change a great many existing trends. Some of these can gradually be changed, in the form of trend shifts, while others will have to be more radically altered in the form of self-elected trend breaks. Trend breaks *will* come. If we do not select and control them ourselves, they will come in undesirable and uncontrollable forms. An examination of future scenarios for the entire planet makes this clear, as the following section will show.

6.5 World scenarios

A large number of models have been developed for the purposes of studying our future. The United Nations, for example, uses models to chart the expected growth of the global population. When creating such models, many issues are naturally simplified, otherwise they would be impossible to generate. Assumptions are made about future developments, such as economic growth, possible new discoveries of metals, oil and other resources, as well as new technological developments. Different scenarios can be generated through adjusting the assumptions, and so some scenarios result in a higher population growth than others. Standard practice is to represent the results using a 'high', 'medium' and 'low scenario', as can be seen in the UN example in Figure 6.17.

For the purposes of comparison, a scenario of uninhibited growth is included in Figure 6.17, which is (fortunately) not realistic. The 'high' scenario is based on the 'Upper 95' estimates of the UN's World Population Prospects published in 2015; likewise, the 'low' scenario is based on the 'Lower 95' estimates.

All of these scenarios share the same curve in the twentieth century, which is logical as this part represents the past, which is already known.

Also added are the 'medium' scenarios based on earlier UN Prospects: of 2002 and 2012. It is striking that, through the years, the medium expectations are getting higher and higher. In 2002, it was expected that the world population would peak around

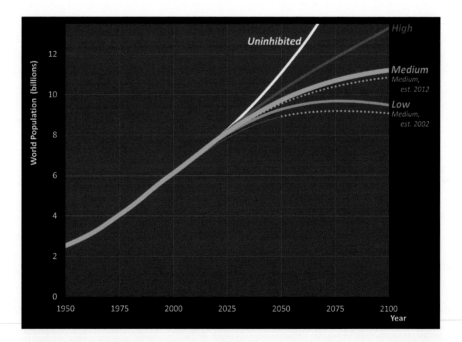

FIGURE 6.17 World population: prospect until 2100

Source: UN Population Division, Department of Economic and Social Affairs (UN DESA): World Population Prospects (2002, 2012, 2015).

2075. Current forecasts do not even expect a maximum before or around 2100, which is not very good news. The corrections are mainly due to an unexpected high population growth in Africa.

With the aid of a model such as this one it is possible to examine '**what if**. . .' questions. 'What if the natural environment can take more than we thought?' 'What if we have an Aids vaccine within a decade?' These and any other relevant questions can be studied. Such assumptions are translated into scenarios, calculated in the form of simulations, and the results are examined. This allows us to develop a picture of the future − or rather, of one possible future.

Aside from investigating growth forecasts for the entire world, the UN's growth models also allow us to examine those for a region. Figure 6.18 contains the graphs for the four regions that were dealt with in the previous chapter, with the section to the left covering the past and that on the right dealing with a possible future. A medium scenario has been used for each of the regions.

It is interesting that the four lines in Figure 6.18 fit together like pieces of a puzzle, as if they are part of the same development, just at different stages. Take first the ECOWAS curve, and next the India, China and EU lines in succession and place them side-by-side, overlapping slightly. This will provide a graph resembling that in Figure 6.19, which is not coincidental, as the four regions are undergoing a process within which a number of the processes correspond to each other. This development can be considered as a '**standard scenario**'.

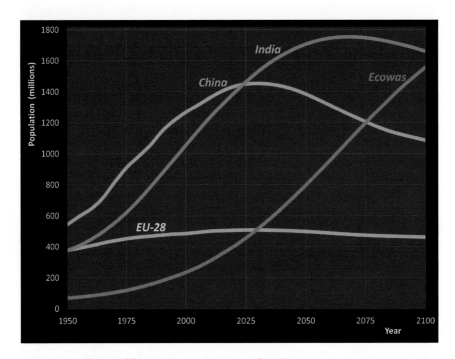

FIGURE 6.18   Population of four regions: prospect until 2100

Source: UN Population Division, Department of Economic and Social Affairs (UN DESA): World Population Prospects (2015).

The 'standard scenario'

The 'standard scenario' has already played out – partly or wholly – in many places, in many forms and at many speeds. In general, the development roughly goes as follows.

The story that Figure 6.19 tells starts off in prehistory, and in the far left of the graph the people are still subsisting from gathering edible plants and dead animals, as well as from some hunting. The fertility rate – the number of children per female – is high, but there is little population growth as the infant mortality rate is also high as a result of disease and accidents, amongst other things. This is actually fortunate, as only very few people following this lifestyle can live off the land – no more than a couple on each square kilometre.

And so it takes a long time, maybe even thousands of years, before the population reaches a density where it becomes impossible to continue this way of living, and once that point is reached, famine becomes an issue. This necessitates a new lifestyle, which is either invented or adopted from neighbouring regions – agriculture (**A** in the graph).

The shortage of food declines thanks to agriculture. The new lifestyle makes it difficult to maintain a nomadic existence, and so permanent homes are built. New health issues arise, such as contagious diseases due to larger groups of people living together. At the same time, the fertility rate increases, pushing up population growth. The introduction of agriculture is far from idyllic, as farmers have to work much harder than hunter-gatherers and dependency on weather conditions increases – there is always the chance of failed crops and livestock diseases!

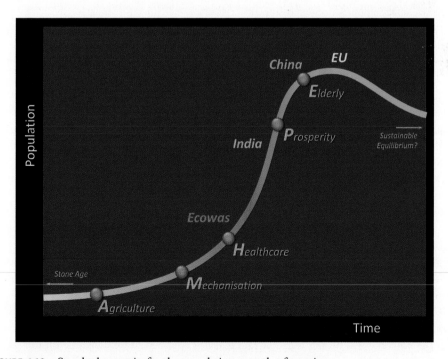

FIGURE 6.19   Standard scenario for the population growth of a region

Agricultural productivity increases where this transition is successful and, because more people can survive per square kilometre through agriculture, the population can grow unabated for a time. Over the course of hundreds or thousands of years, villages and towns come into being, and the population density continues to rise. In due course, agriculture itself proves insufficient to feed all the mouths, despite innovations such as the plough and the use of draught animals.

And so mechanisation (***M*** on the graph) is introduced at a certain time. Windmills are amongst the oldest forms of this mechanisation. This is followed by industrialisation. In Europe and America, it is now the nineteenth century. Coal becomes the main source of energy, with oil employed next. Artificial fertilizers are introduced in agriculture. But the population growth is still not dramatic, as both the fertility rate (the birth-index) and infant mortality are still high. In spite of this, the population is considerably larger than it was before, because the growth is exponential, as can be seen by the characteristic shape of Figure 6.19 (to the left of ***H***), which is comparable to graph A in Figure 6.12.

Hygiene and healthcare improvements and vaccination then result in a radical change (***H*** in the graph). Infant mortality decreases greatly. But the birth-index does not significantly follow. This is logical, as there are still no centrally organised provisions for old age, such as pensions. Adults need their offspring to care for them when they become elderly. Besides, there is little or no opportunity to restrict the number of births, with contraceptives not yet existing (in nineteenth-century Europe) or not widely available (in the twentieth-century ECOWAS region).

This results in the population skyrocketing – the graph suddenly becomes much steeper between ***H*** and ***P*** – and there is a population explosion, a baby boom.

Meanwhile, education also improves and the population's level of knowledge increases. Together with industry, this leads to increased prosperity (***P***), which allows for pensions to be introduced, taking the pressure of having many children off the parents. The fertility rate decreases, and the population explosion slows down.

The combination of a fast-growing population and increasing prosperity ups the pressure on the environment. Ever greater areas of land are subjected to cultivation, for which the natural environment has to give way, while dumping and industrial discharge spoil the habitat.

Once the population growth slows, the baby boom generation starts to mature and a large group of people reach retirement age while far fewer children are born. This means that a region is confronted with an aging population, i.e. with an increasing percentage of elderly people (***E*** in the graph).

A point is ultimately reached when the population starts to shrink instead of grow. This is already the case in a number of European countries, including Italy.

One can envision many variations to this 'standard scenario'. For China, ***M*** and ***H*** are much closer together than they are for Europe, which means the population explosion occurred relatively early. Another feature for China is that the decline in the population growth has not only been due to increased prosperity but also to intervention by the authorities. In another region, Russia this time, the deviations are different – the population is shrinking even though the people have not peaked in terms of prosperity. Russia does not fit well into this standard scenario as it is beset by a long-term economic downturn, with many Russians no longer optimistic about their future.

What happens after the ***E*** on the graph? Will Malthus prove correct, and will our civilisation collapse, or will we be able to attain a sustainable equilibrium? We do not yet know what the outcome will be, but it can be said that it is a rare event for a civilisation to reach a point of equilibrium. Of all the civilisations that have ever existed, some fell apart in a calm and peaceful manner before reaching **E**. Others are still developing and have not yet reached that point. Only a very few have found a stable balance. These cultures, which had abandoned issues such as population growth and overexploitation, were mostly in small areas – generally isolated islands – where no technology comparable to that of today was developed. Our civilisation, the stage at which it finds itself and the global nature of things, together constitute an 'entirely new experiment' in world history.

In order to find out what *might* happen next, we can once again turn to models and simulations.

PopSim

You can create an experimental future yourself. On the website of this book, software is available called **PopSim**, which stands for **Population Simulation** (Figure 6.20). It can be used for studying a wide variety of scenarios, including the standard scenario, which can be run for a low, medium and high version. The differences between these are striking. You can also study the effects of positive and negative feedback, uninhibited and inhibited growth, higher and lower birth rates and a one–child policy, amongst other things.

The Club of Rome

In 1968 a group of concerned scientists set up a think tank called the **Club of Rome**, which has made many contributions in terms of considering the future.

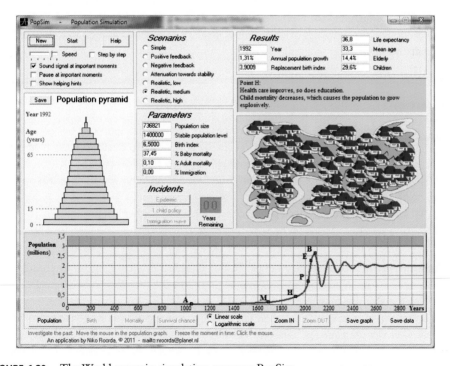

FIGURE 6.20   The World scenario simulation program PopSim

One of their reports is the book ***Limits to Growth*** by Meadows et al. It was published in 1972. It had a great impact upon politics and public opinion, as it marked the first time that the results of calculations using scenarios and simulations were made available to the general public.

The Meadows model, called World3, is an extensive one. It endeavours to include all possible factors that will influence future human developments. These include the depletion of resources, economic growth, population, literacy, environmental damage, the chance of finding fresh oil sources, distribution of prosperity and any other you might care to mention.

A number of updated editions have appeared since 1972, the last one in 2004. In the 2004 edition, 11 different scenarios are calculated. A number of these are based on the assumption that little or no policy changes will be implemented on a global level. All of these scenario's end dramatically, as the global human society collapses in the course of the twenty-first century. It is striking that in those scenarios in which many additional resources (such as oil) are assumed to be discovered between the present and two decades hence, the future is not rosier but is actually worse. The reason behind this is that the discovery of additional resources means that we can continue to perpetrate overexploitation for longer, which means that, when things finally go wrong, they will go wrong in a much bigger way.

Other scenarios are based on the assumption that there will be drastic changes, involving trend breaks introduced in a planned and controlled manner, based on transitions – in other words, profound changes to the system. In these scenarios, it appears to be possible to evolve towards equilibrium. That is, towards a society that no longer overexploits its resources and is able – according to the model – to continue to exist indefinitely: a sustainable society.

Two of the eleven scenarios can be seen in Figure 6.21, with 'scenario 2' demonstrating a less-pleasant future involving global collapse and 'scenario 9' demonstrating a sustainable one. Three graphs are included for each scenario: one for some *people* aspects, one for *planet* and one for *profit*. For the purposes of orienting yourself, it is best to first examine the curve of the population graph.

Questions

- In the People graph in scenario 2, a rapid decline in population can be seen from around 2040. Could such a rapid decline be solely due to death as a result of old age? If not, what other causes of death could play a significant role?
- Imagine that scenario 2 should come true. What chance do you think you have of being there?
- Which is more probable, scenario 2 or scenario 9, or neither?

Unfortunately, it is common for people to not understand what it means to consider the future using scenarios. A large number of people think that the Meadows model actually entails prophecies, and that the disasters are announced as inevitabilities. It is with relief that they comprehend that the story since 1972 (when the model was first published) has not followed the grimmest scenarios contained in 'Limits to Growth'. 'Meadows was proved wrong!' they cry.

But the reality is that Meadows has been proved neither right nor wrong, as the World3 model makes no predictions – it only calculates scenarios. The benefit of these is that it aids

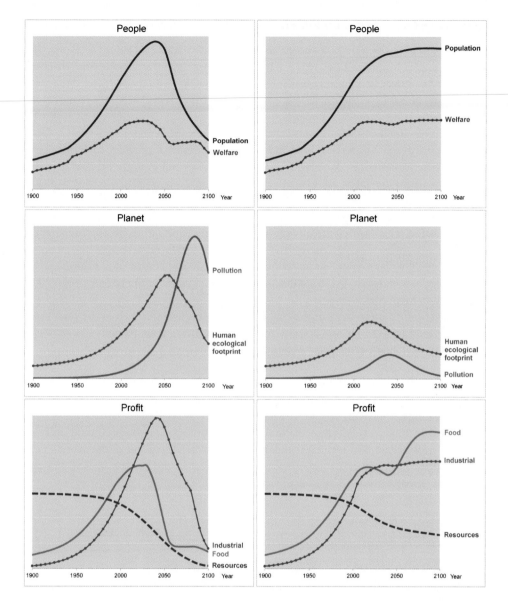

FIGURE 6.21   The World3 model by Meadows et al. A number of *people, planet* and *profit* aspects are shown for scenario 2 (left) and scenario 9 (right)

Source: Meadows (2004).

us in considering the possible consequences of our lifestyle, enabling us to make intelligent decisions that will allow us to avoid the grimmer scenarios and work towards creating the world we want.

For the investigation of several possible directions into which our world may develop in a sustainable way, a huge research program has been undertaken. This is the Millennium Eco-system Assessment, which is covered in the next section.

6.6 What kind of world do we actually want?

A vast amount of research into the threats and opportunities available to our planet was conducted. In the **Millennium Ecosystem Assessment**, some 1,360 academics from 95 countries worked together. This possibly makes it the largest scientific study ever. The first reports were released in 2005, and its conclusions corresponded largely with the results of models for the future such as the Meadows model.

The Millennium Ecosystem Assessment, or simply the Millennium Assessment (MA), focused primarily on the services that the natural environment provides to humanity, of which 24 were identified; see Table 6.1.

One can see in the Table 6.1 that most services have declined in the recent past. This is often the result of the progress we have managed to attain through modern technology amongst some of these services, all relating to food production. What this means is that there is a **trade-off** in which agriculture, livestock farming and aquaculture are intensified at the expense of most other services. A serious aspect is that this trade-off takes place in an unbalanced manner. The increase of certain services is mostly for the benefit of the inhabitants of the wealthier nations, while the decline is mostly at the expense of the poorer people, most of all in sub-Saharan Africa.

This trade-off demonstrates that the transfer of problems from the rich to the poor is not incidental, not merely by chance, but a systematic event. It is a flaw, a weaving fault, deeply integrated in the fabric of the global system.

The MA report provides many examples of the way in which most of the services derived from ecosystems are declining. The planet's ecosystems have changed faster than ever before in the last 50 years as a result of human activities, and it has resulted in the diversity of life on Earth decreasing considerably and, for the most part, irreversibly. For example, in the 30-year period between 1950 and 1980, more natural land was transformed into agricultural land than in the 150-year period between 1700 and 1850. Moreover, 20 percent of the world's coral reefs are dead, with another 20 percent severely damaged. In the last few decades, 35 percent of the mangrove forests have disappeared, while the natural circulation of water has

TABLE 6.1 The 24 services provided by ecosystems, according to the Millennium Assessment

Provisioning services		Regulating services		Cultural services	
Food: Agriculture	Δ	Air quality	▼	Spiritual and religious value	▼
Livestock	Δ	Global climate	Δ[1]	Beauty	▼
Fisheries	▼	Regional and local climate	▼	Recreation and ecotourism	–
Aquaculture	Δ	Water circulation	–	**Supporting services**	
Hunting/gathering	▼	Erosion	▼	*Not included by MA, as*	–
Fibre: Timber	–	Water and waste	▼	*these do not directly benefit*	
Cotton, flax, silk	–	purification		*humanity*	
Firewood	▼	Diseases	–		
Species diversity	▼	Plagues	▼		
Drugs, chemicals	▼	Pollination	▼		
Clean water	▼	Natural risks	▼		

Δ = *increased,* ▼ = *declined in recent years*

[1] *This does not mean the climate has improved, only that the absorption of carbon dioxide has increased*

Source: Millennium Ecosystem Assessment (2005).

been seriously disrupted, with humans retaining three to six times as much water in artificial reservoirs as flows through all the rivers. Water extracted from rivers and lakes for domestic, industrial and (especially) agricultural purposes has doubled in quantity since 1960, resulting in a number of them drying out completely. The Aral Sea serves as the worst example of this. Meanwhile, the rate at which species of plants and animals are becoming extinct has been a thousand times higher in the last few centuries than it was in prehistoric times. The MA confirmed earlier studies that 10 to 30 percent of mammals, birds and amphibians are currently threatened with extinction.

There are even indications that the changes to the ecosystems increase chances of *non-linear* reactions. (The notion of non-linear processes will be explained in Chapter 7.) This might even mean that the system suddenly undergoes dramatic changes, resembling those in graph D of Figure 6.12: collapse, the strongest kind of non-linear behaviour, an unpredictable trend break. This can lead to disastrous consequences, some of which are already perceptible, such as the sudden outbreak of epidemics, abrupt changes to the water quality, the existence of 'dead zones' in coastal waters, the collapse of the fish population or even changes in a regional climate.

MA scientists also confirmed Meadows' findings that the present problems we are faced with are set to get much worse if no changes are introduced to policies on a global level. One of the reasons for this is that the consumption of the services provided by the ecosystems will increase greatly if nothing changes. The international GDP will be three to six times its present levels in 2050, the MA expects, and under current policies that will have to be largely provided by the natural environment. And so there exists an extraordinary incentive for introducing large-scale change. This demonstrates that there is an urgent need to devote all our efforts and powers to work towards sustainable development.

Extensive improvements are feasible, the MA concluded. The scientific program developed a variety of scenarios that could lead to such improvements. Each of the scenarios will

> . . . involve significant changes in policies, institutions and practices that are not currently under way. Many options exist to conserve or enhance specific ecosystem services in ways that reduce negative trade-offs or that provide positive synergies with other ecosystem services.
>
> *(Source: Millennium Ecosystem Assessment, 2005)*

In other words, such improvements are only realisable through grand changes in the system, and with the cooperation of many parties, from politicians to industry, from education to science, etc. Contributions are required by many professionals for this, especially those with higher education who occupy positions of responsibility, as well as their successors – the students of today.

The four MA scenarios

The four scenarios studied by MA were each labelled with a name, as can be seen in Table 6.2. Like scenarios that were covered earlier, these are not prophecies, but possible futures that humanity could opt for. Combinations of these are naturally also possible, as well as thousands of other scenarios, including the one of 'continuing the current policy', which would lead to gigantic problems.

Figure 6.22 gives an impression of the expected population growth for all four scenarios. It must be remarked that the prognoses are based on UN populations model of around 2005;

TABLE 6.2 The four scenarios of the Millennium Ecosystem Assessment

		Focus →	
		Focus on economy	*Focus on environment*
Scale →	Global	**'Global Orchestration'** A globally connected society based on free trade and economic liberalisation • Waiting for environmental problems to become apparent • Strong approach to reduction of poverty and inequality • Investments in infrastructure and education *Result:* ○ Greatest economic growth ○ Smallest population growth ○ Little improvement to the environment	**'TechnoGarden'** A globally connected society relying on environmentally responsible technology • Proactive approach to environmental problems • Rapid technological headway • Technology used for environmental management *Result:* ○ Relatively high and rising economic growth ○ Average population growth ○ Strong nature and environment
	Regional	**'Order from Strength'** Fragmented world concerned with security and protection • Waiting for environmental problems to become apparent • Regional markets • Little focus on public provisions *Result:* ○ Lowest economic growth ○ Highest population growth ○ Environment in poor state	**'Adapting Mosaic'** Political and economic activity focuses regionally on present ecosystems • Proactive approach to environmental problems • Strong local institutions • Local approach to environmental problems *Result:* ○ Low economic growth, increases later ○ High population growth ○ Strong nature and environment

Source: Millennium Ecosystem Assessment (2005).

if the four scenarios would be calculated a decade later, they would no doubt render significantly higher outcomes. For comparison reasons, the three UN scenarios (high, medium and low) of 2015, shown in Figure 6.17, are repeated in Figure 6.22; and the UN 'low' scenario of 2002 is also shown. Together, they give an impression of the level of change that should be applied to fit the four MA scenarios with present insights. All in all, this means that the absolute heights of the four MA curves are not very relevant, but their relative levels certainly are.

The assumption for two of the four MA scenarios is that globalisation will continue at full steam: 'Global Orchestration' and 'TechnoGarden'. Nations will cooperate on an increasing basis, whereas the corporate, scientific and educational communities will become increasingly internationalised. In the one scenario, 'Global Orchestration', the economy is leading, with free trade amplified on a global level and trade barriers and subsidies – which have caused so much harm to the poorer nations – abolished. This will benefit prosperity in all nations, thereby causing poverty to decline and the population growth to ease. Economic growth is high and the ecosystems are heavily damaged.

Meanwhile, in the other globalising scenario, 'TechnoGarden', much focus is placed on the environment. Science and technology are given a great deal of room so that resources are used

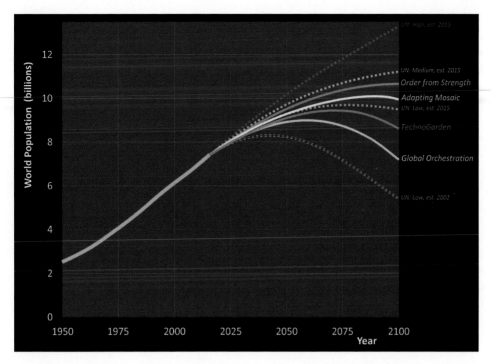

FIGURE 6.22   The growth of the world population, according to the four MA scenarios

Source: Millennium Ecosystem Assessment Synthesis Report (2005).

with much greater efficiency. Economic growth is lower in this scenario, but because the eco-systems are less affected, it starts to increase at a later stage. Population growth is also average.

Both of the other scenarios assume that globalisation will decline, with less international cooperation and greater regional protection. Thus, the trade barriers in the scenario 'Order from Strength' are more likely to increase as regions move to protect their own products. These barriers will also increase for reasons of security, and so border controls are intensified as a mark of this fear. Less attention is paid to environmental problems in this scenario, and economic growth is at a zenith due to the stagnation of international trade. Because poverty continues to be a major issue, a dip in the population growth will be a long time coming, and so the global population will increase.

Under the 'Adapting Mosaic' scenario, regionalisation does not arise as a result of fear and protection, but rather for the purpose of gearing the situation in each region to the local cir-cumstances. An energetic local approach to environmental problems will mean good results on a local level. Initially, this will be at the expense of economic growth, but that will increase at a later stage thanks to the resilience of the local ecosystems.

Using computer-modelling techniques, calculations have been made about how these scenarios might turn out in the future. For each of the 24 services derived from an ecosystem, it has been established whether they will improve, remain the same or decline. The results can be seen in Figure 6.23. For example, in the 'Global Orchestration', three services will improve in the wealthy nations, while four will decline and the remainder stay more or less the same. Under the same scenario, six services will improve and eight will decline in the impoverished nations.

The graphs in Figure 6.23 show that 'Order from Strength' will, in particular, lead to the environmental problems the world is confronted with becoming much worse, especially in the poor nations. In these countries, the problem is emphatically that poverty is a major cause of environmental damage, simply because the people are unable to allow themselves to adopt a sustainable lifestyle. The 'TechnoGarden' and 'Adapting Mosaic' scenarios will lead to the highest improvement in terms of the environment.

Whether or not one of the four scenarios will ever become reality, depends on the policy choices that must be made by those in power on our planet. This could be the G20, for example, the leaders of the most influential nations. The future will in all likelihood not consist literally of one of these four scenarios, but rather a combination of them, and probably combined with a large dose of 'Continuing the current policies' – a scenario that is easy to anticipate. The MA scenarios demonstrate that we are dealing with fundamental choices. What kind of world do we actually want? A highly globalised world or rather one consisting of separate regions that retain a great deal of their uniqueness, either as a result of fear of all that is strange, or thanks to cultural vigour? Or maybe a world in which poverty is rapidly eradicated, or one where nature and the environment fare better at an accelerated pace? According to the MA scenarios, these two desires are not properly compatible, so what would be the best choice? Or might we come up with a scenario in which both aspects improve together?

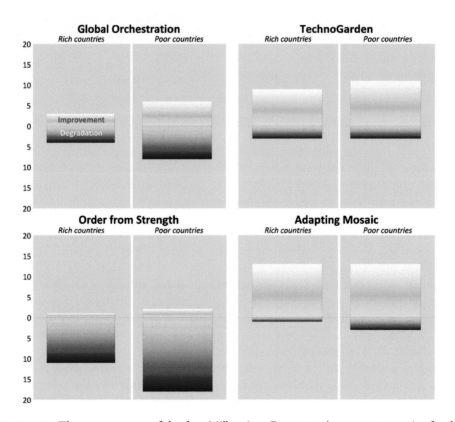

FIGURE 6.23   The consequences of the four Millennium Ecosystem Assessment scenarios for the 24 services provided by the natural environment

Source: Millennium Ecosystem Assessment (2005).

Questions

- What do you consider to be more urgent – combating poverty or improving the environment?
- Would you prefer globalisation to continue, or would you rather live in a world of independent regions?

Sustainable development is a question of choices. Choosing for a better world or for one that will go downhill. Choosing for *which* better world we want. Sustainable development also means: thinking and acting on the basis of a comprehension of the future. And it means: cooperation between nations – top-down cooperation between governments, companies, science and technology; bottom-up cooperation between responsible citizens. Professional and interdisciplinary cooperation between economists, lawyers, engineers, teachers, artists, scientists, care workers and many others. And it also means cooperation on a trans-disciplinary level between professionals and civil society.

The following two chapters will go into a bit more detail for a number of topics, as these are leading when it comes to determining the direction where the world will be able to develop sustainably. The first issue to be covered is the unsustainability problem that at present might be the biggest threat for the future of human society and of the natural environment – climate change.

Summary

Over the course of human history, many civilisations have disappeared, often as a result of forms of unsustainability such as overexploitation and overpopulation. In examining whether our present global civilisation could be similarly afflicted, a number of tools are available:

- The pronouncements of prophets and science fiction writers have no predictive value, while those of futurologists tend to be wrong.
- The expectations of optimists are generally too rosy. Those of pessimists can only be considered to be realistic if policies remain unchanged.
- Scenarios can be created on the basis of models that can be worked out through simulations.
- There are a number of different growth models, including uninhibited growth, strongly or weakly inhibited growth and collapse.
- In reality, combinations of these types of growth occur, which can be brought together to make up a world scenario. The ECOWAS region, India, China and the EU all fit into this scenario.
- The model provided by the Club of Rome provides diverse scenarios, some of which lead to collapse while others lead to sustainable development. The model allows for making policy choices.
- The same applies to the scenarios provided by the Millennium Ecosystem Assessment, which make the choice of the world in which we want to live the central point of focus.

A more detailed summary can be found on the website of this book.

7

CLIMATE AND ENERGY

In this chapter the following topics and concepts will be discussed:

7.1   The phenomenon: temperatures rising
7.2   The cause: the greenhouse effect
7.3   The consequences: from the rise of sea levels to crop failures
7.4   Solutions: technology and lifestyle
7.5   Political and economic instruments

A glossary containing all terms in both this chapter and others is available on the website of this book.

Case 7.1   Student project – a zero-energy building in the Alkmaar shopping centre

The city of Alkmaar, the shopping precinct of Overstad. Offices and apartments are to share a large 60-meter-tall building (Figure 7.1). There will be a restaurant on the uppermost floor and a parking garage in the basement, and the whole lot is going to consume a lot of heat and lighting. Office and kitchen appliances also eat up a large amount of energy, and so it is reasonable to expect the total power bill for the occupants and users to be extensive. But it's not. The grand total is set to be *zero* euros a year.

This might seem impossible, but it really can be done, as three students from a School of Architecture proved in 2005. For their graduate project, Tjeerd Hellinga, Randy Sinnema and Jan Davelaar designed the entire building. The job was commissioned by the Alkmaar municipality, which wanted to kickstart the Overstad shopping precinct, and the students relied on the latest concepts for energy generation and consumption. They naturally designed the building so that there would be minimum heat loss in winter, but they took this a step further, and in summer the building accumulates as much heat as possible using solar thermal collectors, which it stores deep underground. This heat is used in the winter to warm up the office and apartment space.

The design also utilises sustainable energy in another manner – with the upper half built around a set of gigantic wind turbines, which can generate a large amount of power. These turbines generate half of all the energy required for the building.

This office and apartment block is a so-called zero-energy building. Though these buildings still require energy sourced from the national power grid during certain times of the year, they return just as much back to the grid at other times, so that when one looks at the annual average, they do not require any energy to be supplied from outside.

The three students received a national award for the best graduate project.

Of all the issues that result in unsustainability, the problem of climate change is without doubt the most serious. It is a worldwide threat to people, cities, economies, cultures and the natural environment. Any future sustainable developments shall have to devote much focus on solving the climate problem, because without finding a sound solution to this, there is little point in advancing other types of sustainability – it would be like swimming against the tide.

FIGURE 7.1 An artist's impression of the zero-energy building in Alkmaar; the aperture containing the wind turbines can be easily seen

Source: T. Hellinga, R. Sinnema, J. Davelaar: 'Final Report WindInholland', Hogeschool Inholland, March 2005.

Responses to climate change are, by necessity, complex, consisting of a very wide range of solutions. This is inevitable, as both the causes and the consequences of climate change themselves are extremely complex. Some of the methods focus on changes we will have to implement in respect of that degree of climate change that can no longer be avoided. Others are intended for the purpose of annulling the underlying causes, which are largely found in our global addiction to fossil fuels – oil, gas, coal, etc. This addiction is a deep-seated flaw in the fabric of the world's human society. Some of the solutions are technical in nature. Others are rather economic or political, and the methods employed – as well as their combinations – are partly determined by the future world we consider the most desirable. What this means is that there are many choices to be made, and in order to make a well-founded choice, it is first necessary to develop a clear picture of what exactly is going on. Consequently, this chapter starts by examining the causes and the background to climate change, followed by an overview of the primary consequences. Next sections will take a look at the range of solutions on offer, one of which was illustrated in Case 7.1.

7.1 The phenomenon: temperatures rising

Changes to the climate are difficult to demonstrate, because the climate is a kind of average for the weather over a large number of consecutive years. The weather itself is generally rather capricious, which means that when it is warmer for a few consecutive summers or winters this does not immediately mean that the climate is changing. However, evidence of rapid climate change is highly convincing.

Climate change is caused by the **greenhouse effect**, which has been a factor on this planet, in the form of a **natural greenhouse effect**, for billions of years, long before humans existed. This phenomenon means that the temperature on Earth is considerably higher than it would otherwise be, which is of great benefit to life, including human life. But human activity since the Industrial Revolution, over and above this natural greenhouse effect, has resulted in an **anthropogenic greenhouse effect** (anthropogenic meaning it is caused by humans). The temperature on this planet is rising at an accelerated rate, as can be seen in Figure 7.2, in which the temperature of the last 166 years is charted, expressed as a difference with the average temperature between 1961 and 1990.

When we map out the temperature fluctuations over an even longer period, as in Figure 7.3, it becomes even clearer that something exceptional is happening.

The coloured line represents the average annual temperature over 15 centuries, and the black curve shows the trend over this period. The graph first exhibits the warmer period that the Earth went through during the Middle Ages, followed by a colder period lasting a few centuries – also called the Little Ice Age. Both these periods bear witness to the fact that the planet undergoes fluctuations to the average temperature due to natural causes. The current rise in temperatures could even seem to be part of these natural fluctuations, but there is an important difference – it is not just that the temperature has reached levels in recent years that were not even experienced during the Middle Ages, but the rate at which the temperature is presently rising is faster than ever before. The trend line has never been this steep, indicating that more is going on than just a natural variation.

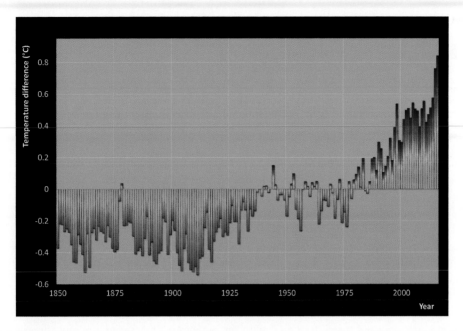

FIGURE 7.2   Variations on the average global temperature between 1850 and 2016, compared to the average temperature over the period 1961 to 1990

Source: Met Office Hadley Centre for Climate Science and Services, London, 2016

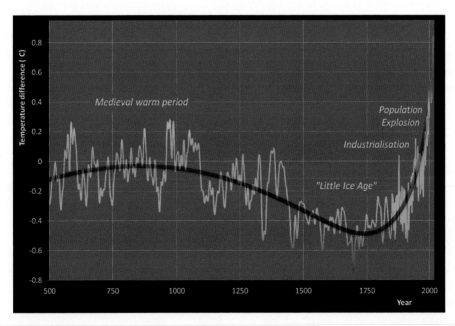

FIGURE 7.3   Variations in the average temperature on the planet since 500 CE, compared to the period between 1961 and 1990

Note: The average worldwide EIV (error-in-variables) land temperature is used; the trend line has been added.

Sources: Mann et al (2008); Met Office Hadley Centre for Climate Science and Services, London, 2016.

7.2 The cause: the greenhouse effect

The Earth's atmosphere is transparent, and visible light can pass through it with relative ease. If this were not the case we would live in perpetual darkness, as the sunrays would not be able to reach the surface of the Earth. But the sun does penetrate, and the result is that the planet is warmed up. This heat must once again be released, otherwise the planet would get ever-hotter and have disappeared in a puff of gas a long time ago. Our world discharges its heat by also radiating heat into space. This is not just light we can see but rather mainly infrared light. So long as the Earth is emitting as much heat as it receives from the sun, the temperature on the planet is constant, this aside from the seasons and the whimsy of nature.

Temperature fluctuations are caused in many different ways, such as long-term changes to the sun's intensity, changes to the Earth's orbit around the sun, continental drift, volcanic activity and changes to the ocean currents. The Medieval Warm Period and the Little Ice Age (Figure 7.3) were caused by these factors, as are the bigger ice ages that have afflicted the planet.

The climate change we are presently experiencing is a result of the greenhouse effect. While the atmosphere contains a number of gasses through which visible light can pass, infrared light does not travel through it with the same ease. These gases, the most significant of which are water vapour and carbon dioxide (CO_2), ensure that the Earth cannot easily lose its heat, and so the temperature on the planet is higher than it would have been if those gases were not present. This is what we know as the greenhouse effect. The average temperature on the Earth is around 15 °C (60 °F). Without the natural greenhouse effect the temperature would stand at 17 °C below zero (1 °F), and life as we know it could not exist.

We have been pumping out extra **greenhouse gas** (**GHG**) since around the start of the Industrial Revolution – primarily carbon dioxide, which is released when humans and animals burn up food in their bodies, as well as when we burn wood and fossil fuels, like lignite, coal, oil and natural gas. When our bodies do this, oxygen (O_2) is absorbed and carbon dioxide (CO_2) is produced as part of a biological cycle, as plants are simultaneously performing the exact opposite system – absorbing CO_2 and producing O_2, using solar energy. This cycle provides an equilibrium. But because we are burning fossil fuels on a large scale, this balance is disturbed and the amount of CO_2 in the atmosphere rises. At the same time, other gases are discharged into the atmosphere, which contributes to this anthropogenic greenhouse effect, the most prominent of which can be seen in Figure 7.4. The term '**radiative forcing**' relates to the extent to which the various substances influence the balance between the incoming rays from the sun and the outgoing heat ('radiation') and thus 'force up' the temperature on Earth.

Halocarbon production, including CFCs, has been successfully phased out as a result of the Montreal Protocol that was mentioned in earlier chapters, aimed at protecting the ozone layer.

Ozone (O_3) has two opposing effects – a negative radiative forcing of the ozone in the **stratosphere** (a higher layer of the atmosphere), which lowers the temperature, and a larger positive forcing in the **troposphere** (the lower part of the atmosphere). The net effect is the ten percent shown in Figure 7.4. The damage to the ozone layer in the stratosphere by CFCs thereby contributes to the greenhouse effect.

Methane (CH_4) is a very hazardous greenhouse gas, and while there is much less of it in the atmosphere than CO_2, the per-molecule radiative forcing is many times greater. There are a number of ways in which methane is released into the atmosphere, one of which is by

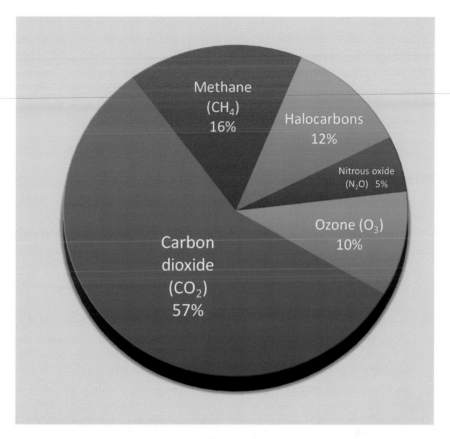

FIGURE 7.4   The primary 'long-lasting' greenhouse gases and their contribution ('radiative forcing') to the anthropogenic greenhouse effect

Source: IPCC (2007).

livestock – this being the gases produced by cattle and other herbivores. Much methane has
been stored in ancient marshes and peat bogs over millions of years in places like the Siberian
tundra and on the ocean floor. When the temperature rises, there is a chance that the frozen
regions of the planets may thaw and the ocean beds start to move, releasing large quantities
of methane and quickly pushing temperatures up even further. The methane stored in the
ground and on the ocean floor are like a time bomb that, should it explode, will have disastrous consequences.

Correlations and cause-consequence relationships

It seems one can rapidly conclude that as long as greenhouse gases increase in the atmosphere,
the temperature on Earth will continue to rise, and so the one causes the other. Or does it?

Unfortunately, this process is not as simple as one might think. Firstly, Figure 7.3 contains
a fair number of uncertainties – temperatures were not measured in the Middle Ages, so the
figures in the graph for that period are based on indirect evidence, such as the size of trees'

growth rings. There is also uncertainty with respect to the concentration of greenhouse gases in the air, with levels from the past being based on measurements taken from tiny air bubbles trapped in glaciers, for example. These measurements are, to a certain degree, also uncertain.

Even if we set these uncertainties aside, it is still not a given that the increase of greenhouse gases causes the temperature to rise. It is all too common that – by way of oversimplification – when two phenomena occur at the same time, the one is believed to be the cause of the other.

Questions

- Children in America spend less time outside and more time indoors. The percentage of American children who are obese has increased. Has the former caused the latter?
- We brush our teeth more frequently than a century ago. Besides, the costs of dental surgery are much higher than they were a century ago. Should we consequently stop brushing our teeth?

It has been relatively well established that a positive **correlation** exists between the concentration of greenhouse gases and the temperature on the planet – a connection through which both simultaneously increase. But this factor does not automatically prove that the increased levels of greenhouse gases *cause* the rise in temperatures. Scientific debate has raged intensely for years on the question of whether this **causal relationship** (or **cause–effect relationship**) actually exists, and much scientific research has been undertaken, including by or on the orders of the **Intergovernmental Panel on Climate Change (IPCC)**. Today nearly all experts agree that the anthropogenic greenhouse gas effect is the actual cause of the rise in temperatures. The primary reason for this is that it is becoming increasingly evident that the rise in temperature in recent years is no longer due to coincidental weather fluctuations – the rise has been too rapid and too widespread. The second reason for this conclusion is because the scientific models that are used to calculate the anthropogenic greenhouse gas effect are becoming increasingly powerful and complete, thanks in part to the increase in computational power, and the results of the computer-made predictions correspond with increasing accuracy to the actual situation.

Feedback

The models upon which the computer-based calculations of the greenhouse effect are based are very complex. This is necessary, as there are many factors that influence this effect. One of these is the presence of water vapour, which is just as significant as a greenhouse gas as carbon dioxide. Though it is true that humans are responsible for a direct increase in the evaporation of water, thanks to the construction of dams, this additional water vapour is not of great importance in relative terms. But there is also an indirect increase, as the rise in temperatures has caused water to evaporate from the oceans at an accelerated rate, which in turn is causing the temperatures to also rise at an increased rate. This is an example of positive feedback – the greenhouse effect drives up the evaporation of water and the evaporation of water raises the level of the greenhouse effect. They drive each other up, as illustrated in Figure 7.5.

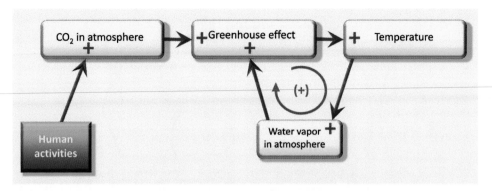

FIGURE 7.5   The evaporation of water causes a positive feedback for climate change

Water vapour is just one example of dozens involving feedback loops, and a number of the most significant can be seen in Figure 7.6. Loop 1 again shows the positive feedback for vapour. Loop 5 shows the release of methane that was discussed earlier, also in the form of positive feedback. The left part of Figure 7.6 (loop 6) shows that the growth of plankton is responsible for a *negative* feedback. Plankton consists of microscopically sized plants and animals. The plants ('**phytoplankton**') convert, just as plants on land do, carbon dioxide into oxygen. The rise in carbon dioxide levels in the atmosphere means that its concentration in the oceans will likewise rise, which acts like fertiliser for the plant plankton, causing it to grow and consequently convert more carbon dioxide into oxygen. This decreases the greenhouse effect, which is why the phytoplankton is considered to be a '**carbon sink**' – where carbon dioxide is stored.

To the right in Figure 7.6 another example of *positive* feedback is visible. The rise in temperatures is causing the polar ice caps to melt. These ice caps play an important role, as they reflect sunlight. This is one of the reasons why much of the sunlight that hits the Earth is not absorbed, with around 30 percent of sunlight being reflected directly back into space. This ability to reflect the sun's rays is called the **albedo**, which was mentioned briefly at the end of Chapter 3. The greater the albedo, the less solar energy is absorbed. But the melting ice caps mean that the albedo is also decreasing, and a greater amount of sunlight is heating up the planet. This once again amplifies the greenhouse effect.

The size of the Arctic ice cap is decreasing significantly, as seen in Figure 7.7. This size has always shown a lot of variation through the months and the years. Partly this is seasonal, as the ice caps are at their smallest towards the end of the northern summer in September. (For the purposes of a fair comparison, both the photos in Figure 7.7 were taken at the same time – in September – in different years.) Other natural variations are a result of fluctuations to the weather patterns. But the current shrinking of the ice cap is far stronger than a natural variation. It is impressive, and it is expected that the North Pole will be entirely ice-free in summer within a few decades.

Because of the large number of positive and negative feedback loops that influence the greenhouse effect, the computational models are very complex. In spite of this – or because of it – the results are increasingly closer to the changes measured in the real world. A few of these results are contained in Table 7.1. The table demonstrates the outcome, for example, if carbon dioxide was the only greenhouse gas and its concentration levels would double. If

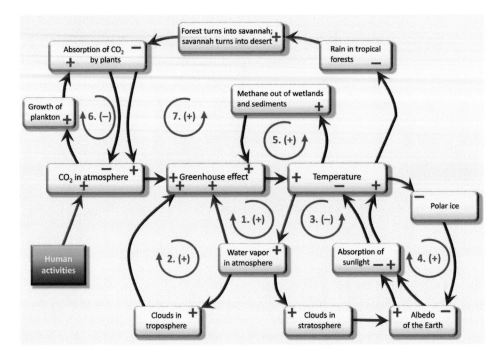

FIGURE 7.6 Various forms of positive and negative feedback for climate change

Based on information from: Houghton (2004).

no feedback would occur, the temperature would rise by 1.2 °C. When the feedbacks are taken into account, the temperature rises by 2.5 °C, and if the consequences of the other greenhouse gases are taken into account, then the temperature would rise by between 2 and 6 °C over the course of the twenty-first century. That might not seem like a great rise, but if the temperature were to *decrease* by the same amount, our planet would once again be locked in an ice age.

7.3 The consequences: from the rise of sea levels to crop failures

Before taking a look at a number of the consequences of climate change, it is important that we first examine the degree to which these consequences can – or cannot – be forecast and calculated.

Linear and non-linear consequences

The extent to which the greenhouse effect will be responsible for climatic changes is difficult to predict, as described earlier, thanks to a number of feedbacks that make the changes extraordinarily complex. So, it is no surprise that it is much more difficult to state realistic expectations when it comes to possible consequences, including rising sea levels, changes to wind patterns and the increase or decrease of rainfall.

The many feedbacks mean that the atmosphere can respond to a temperature increase in unexpected ways. This is what is called **non-linear processes**. Many people intuitively

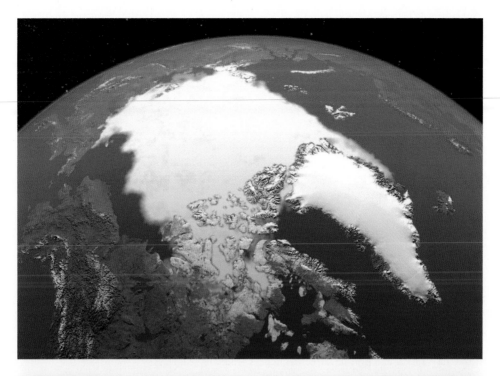

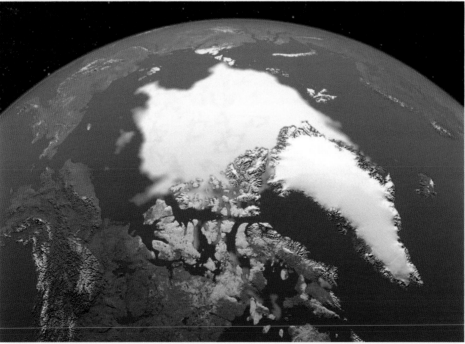

FIGURE 7.7 The Arctic ice cap is shrinking – the top image dates from 1979, the bottom one from 2015

Source: NASA/Goddard Space Flight Center Scientific Visualization Studio.

TABLE 7.1 The effects of the greenhouse effect on temperatures

	Temperature	Temperature difference
Average temperature on Earth	15 °C	
Without a natural greenhouse effect	–17 °C	–32 °C
With CO_2 levels doubled, sans feedback	16.2 °C	1.2 °C
With CO_2 levels doubled, with feedback	17.5 °C	2.5 °C
Due to anthropogenic greenhouse effect, up to 2100	17 to 21 °C	2 to 6 °C
By way of comparison:		
Warm period compared to an ice age		5 to 6 °C

Source: Houghton (2004).

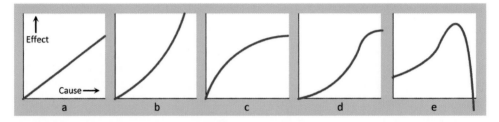

FIGURE 7.8 Linear and non-linear consequences – only (a) is linear

assume that causes and their effects are connected to each other in a *linear* manner. Should we, for example, apply this to the rise of the sea level due to the rise in the temperature, this would mean that the sea level would rise by a fixed amount for every degree that the temperature increases, maybe 10 or 20 centimetres for every degree Celsius or Fahrenheit. If this were the case, the rise in temperature would be *directly proportional* to the rise in seal levels. Chart this, and the graph would like the one in (a) of Figure 7.8, being a straight line (which is what '**linear**' means).

But in reality, causes and effects are rarely linked in a linear manner, which means the comparative graphs of them might rather resemble graph (b), in which unexpectedly powerful effects occur as the causes become greater; graph (c), in which the effects increase at a slower rate than would have been expected; or graphs (d) or (e), in which the effects depend on the causes in a more complex manner. Graph (d) demonstrates a trend shift, while (e) shows a complete trend break where an unexpected effect occurs, in which an increasing cause may initially trigger an effect, but this effect stops or even becomes negative as the cause continues to rise. This is a *rebound effect* (see Section 1.1).

The significance of linear and non-linear effects can be better understood through an example. If you pour some water into a straight glass (glass (A) in Figure 7.9), the glass will fill up to a given height. Pour twice as much water into it, and the water level in the glass will be twice as high. Pour three times as much water, and the water level will triple in height. The effect (the water level in the glass) is thus directly proportional to the cause (the amount of water you poured into the glass). If you were to interpret this graphically, you would get graph (a) in Figure 7.8.

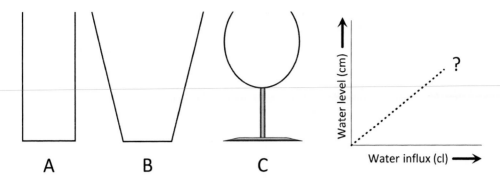

FIGURE 7.9   Pouring water in glasses: in glass (A) the water level rises linearly, but not so in glasses (B) and (C)

When pouring water into differently shaped glasses such as (B) and (C) in Figure 7.9, they will not be filled in a linear manner, and the graph for glass (B) will look roughly like graph (c). But should you continue to pour water into glass (A), this will not be linear either. Once the water reaches the edge of the glass, the water level will no longer rise but remain constant, as the added water flows away. You have then reached a **system boundary**; the line in the graph is sharply angled – a trend break – and continues horizontally. Another trend break could occur if you are not using cold water, but boiling hot water, and the glass cannot take it. If the glass shatters when the water has almost reached the brim, then another type of system boundary has been reached – the system falls apart, the water flows off, while the trend break takes on the form seen in graph (e) in Figure 7.8.

People often intuitively expect real-life phenomena to act in a linear manner, and this is indeed what happens in a number of cases. Should you, for example, double your speed while driving a car, air resistance will also double, but as you approach 80 kilometres (50 miles) an hour, air resistance will increase at a much more rapid rate than your speed because vortices will become an issue. At that speed, air resistance will no longer behave linearly, and the graph will look something like graph (b).

There are many other situations where there is an intuitive assumption that the world will act in a linear fashion, and this does not only hold for your average person, but business leaders and politicians too. One notorious example is the idea that we can solve congestion by creating more roads or traffic lanes, which in reality will encourage the use of cars, and will most likely not – or barely – reduce the problem. The real world rarely acts in a linear fashion.

Feedbacks, such as those influencing the greenhouse effect, are a source of non-linearity. Positive feedback causes the reactions to amplify, as can be seen in graph (b). Conversely, negative feedback weakens the reaction to change, which might give rise to a graph like graph (c). Many forms of positive and negative feedback are involved in the greenhouse effect, and so the reaction could resemble graphs (d) or (e), or be even much more complex.

The **biosphere**, which consists of the Earth's atmosphere, the continents and oceans, is a so-called **complex system**, containing properties that cannot be derived from the properties of the individual components, and which acts in a way that is difficult or even impossible to predict. When certain system boundaries are exceeded in a complex system, **chaotic behaviour** could occur, and whatever happens is totally unpredictable. A number of examples have already been studied, where such chaotic behaviour arises because system boundaries were exceeded:

- the 1987 Black Monday crash (Case 2.2, Chapter 2)
- the frenzy in Rwanda in 1994 (Case 3.7, Chapter 3)
- the Easter Island tragedy (Section 6.1)
- 'scenario 2' of Meadows' World3 model (Section 6.5)

The complexity of the biosphere implies that the ultimate effects of climate change, such as rising sea levels, are extremely different to compute, all the more because little is as yet known on where the boundaries of this system lie.

Rising sea levels

The increasing temperature influences the **sea level** in at least three ways. The first one is that the oceans' waters expand due to the rising temperature. Next, the polar ice caps and glaciers around the world are melting. The melting of the Arctic ice cap does not influence the sea level, as it is floating ice. But landlocked ice – such as the ice sheets of Greenland, Antarctica and on mountain tops – is not floating, and if it melts it does raise the sea level. On the other hand, a larger amount of water will evaporate because of the rising temperatures, which will mean increased precipitation around the world. The portion that comes down in the form of snow on landlocked ice will build it up. To date it is not 100 percent sure which effect is presently stronger – the shrinking of glaciers due to melting or their expansion due to the increased precipitation – but evidence accumulates that the ice sheets of Antarctica, Greenland and mountain glaciers all show a net decrease of their volumes, each contributing to rising sea levels, and at a growing pace.

Should the Greenland ice sheet ever entirely melt, the sea level would be raised by some six metres, with disastrous consequences in view of the fact that around half of the human population live in coastal regions. If all the Antarctic ice were to melt, then the oceans would rise by 60 metres or more. The chance of this happening is extremely unlikely. However, there is a mechanism that could cause the Greenland ice sheet to disappear at an accelerated rate. Meltwater is seeping straight through the ice onto the rocky surface of Greenland, from where it flows into the ocean like an underground river. It is conceivable that these rivers could act like a slide, down which large sections of the Greenland glaciers slip into the Atlantic, after which they drift southwards with the currents until they are melted (Figure 7.10). The likelihood of this mechanism cannot be determined, but if it happens it will serve as an example of a trend break that will cause the global human system to 'disintegrate', much like a glass that breaks.

Even in the absence of such dramatic events, the sea will still rise, although it is relatively uncertain by how much. The oceans rose by 10 to 20 centimetres in the twentieth century and estimates for the twenty-first century range from 20 centimetres to over a meter. This will be problematic for countries with low-lying coasts, such as the Bangladesh (with a population of 160 million) and the Netherlands (17 million), both of which are amongst the most densely populated nations in the world. But those set to suffer the worst are the small island states like

FIGURE 7.10   Huge icebergs broke off the Collins Glacier (Antarctica), which some predict could disappear within a few decades

Source: Jeffrey Kietzmann, US National Science Foundation.

Tuvalu, its highest point a mere four meters above the sea level. In the long term – over the course of a few centuries – the sea level could gradually rise by many meters, submerging large parts of many nations.

Warmer and warmer

Indeed, it gets warmer, as Case 7.2 shows.

Case 7.2. "NASA & NOAA data show: 2016 warmest year on record globally"

NOAA (United States National Oceanic and Atmospheric Administration), January 18, 2017

"Earth's 2016 surface temperatures were the warmest since modern recordkeeping began in 1880, according to independent analyses by NASA and the National Oceanic and Atmospheric Administration (NOAA).

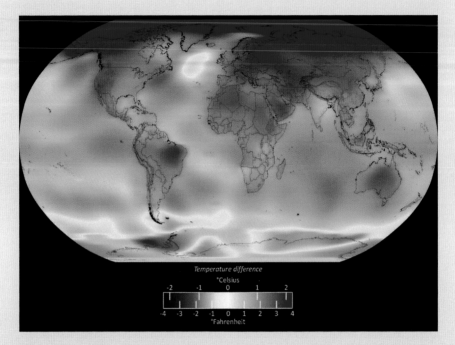

FIGURE 7.11 Temperature differences averaged over the years 2012–2016, compared to the average of 1880–1899

Source: NASA/Goddard Space Flight Center Scientific Visualization Studio. Data provided by Robert B. Schmunk (NASA/GSFC GISS).

Globally-averaged temperatures in 2016 were 1.78 degrees Fahrenheit (0.99 degrees Celsius) warmer than the mid-20th century mean.

This makes 2016 the third year in a row to set a new record for global average surface temperatures.

The 2016 temperatures continue a long-term warming trend (see figure 7.11), according to analyses by scientists at NASA's Goddard Institute for Space Studies (GISS) in New York. NOAA scientists concur with the finding that 2016 was the warmest year on record based on separate, independent analyses of the data.

The planet's average surface temperature has risen about 2.0 degrees Fahrenheit (1.1 degrees Celsius) since the late 19th century, a change driven largely by increased carbon dioxide and other human-made emissions into the atmosphere.

Most of the warming occurred in the past 35 years, with 16 of the 17 warmest years on record occurring since 2001. Not only was 2016 the warmest year on record, but eight of the 12 months that make up the year – from January through September, with the exception of June – were the warmest on record for those respective months. October, November, and December of 2016 were the second warmest of those months on record – in all three cases, behind records set in 2015."

Capricious weather

The weather is not only heating up, it's becoming less predictable, too. In general, thanks to global warming there is simply more energy in the atmosphere, and this has to be released somehow. In the form of hard rain. Crashing thunderstorms. Or major hurricanes.

Case 7.3   Katrina

One of 2005's most destructive hurricanes was Katrina, a category 5 hurricane that passed directly over the large metropolis of New Orleans in the southern United States. The city is located on both the coast and the banks of a river, and is protected from both by levees (dykes). A large part of New Orleans is below sea level, and the huge rains that Katrina brought flooded sections of the city. This was followed by a number of levees breaking and most of the city flooding.

Authorities started to evacuate over a million people at a very late stage. Within days of the flood many were still being picked out of the flooded city, which was threatened with outbreaks of disease and where buildings above the waterline were on fire – impossible to extinguish as there was no power. Bodies floated on the water and over 1,300 people died. Financial damage reached a hundred billion dollars.

Much scientific debate surrounds the issue of how a rise in temperatures will affect the incidence of tropical cyclones. (Hurricanes, cyclones and typhoons are the same phenomenon. They only differ in the location: hurricanes occur in the Atlantic and Northeast Pacific Oceans; in the Northwest Pacific they are called typhoons; and in the South Pacific and Indian Oceans they are cyclones.)

On paper, there are reasons for expecting hurricanes to become more common, given that the seawater will warm up – this heat is feeding storms and allowing them to reach cyclonic proportions. In practice, it looks like the total number of hurricanes is not increasing, but the percentage of major ones on a scale of Katrina is on the rise. This means that, although it is impossible to say that an individual hurricane like Katrina is caused by climate change, but the number of such cyclones is higher than they once were (Figure 7.12).

A hurricane's power is indicated by a number between 1 and 5 (the 'Saffir–Simpson Hurricane Scale'), with the destructive power of a force 2, 3, 4 and 5 hurricane is respectively

FIGURE 7.12 Hurricane Katrina caused unprecedented damage in 2005, largely flooding the city of New Orleans

Source: NASA Visible Earth, NASA Scientific Visualization Studio, Goddard Space Flight Center.

10, 50, 100 and 250 times as powerful as a force 1 hurricane, and a force 5 hurricane such as Katrina sees wind speeds exceeding 250 kilometres (155 miles) an hour. A study published in 2015 indicated that the number of hurricanes of at least force 4 had significantly increased in nearly all ocean sectors in the last decades: see Figure 7.13.

Wind patterns

In Chapter 5 it was explained that 2016 was an extremely dry year in India (Case 5.5), when the monsoon failed to appear; just as in 2008, 2009, 2010 and 2012. The monsoon is a wind, caused by the difference in temperature between land and sea, which normally blows from the ocean onto the land in the summer months, bringing much rain with it. The rise in temperature as a result of the greenhouse effect does not affect all parts of the globe in the same way, and this results in wind patterns changing around the world. Some parts might be afflicted with more rain while others will actually receive less, with exceptionally long periods of drought occurring. This leads to deforestation, soil erosion and desertification.

Once in every three to seven years, an extraordinary weather phenomenon occurs called **El Niño**. For reasons not yet fully understood, the patterns of wind and sea current patterns over and in the Pacific Ocean, respectively, change, influencing the weather in large parts of the world. In South America it is warmer and wetter, which has resulted in floods, whereas on the other side of the Pacific Ocean it has become much drier – from Indonesia through

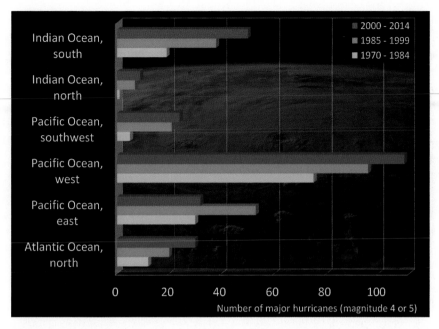

FIGURE 7.13 Number of major hurricanes (magnitude 4 or 5) between 1970 and 2014

Source: Klotzbach and Landsea (2015); background photo source: NASA International Space Station.

to Australia, with crops failing and famine threatening. Ocean currents also change, with fish dying out and South American fisherman struggling to survive. El Niño is itself not caused by the greenhouse effect, as the phenomenon has been around since at least the early twentieth century, and maybe much longer. But it appears as if the greenhouse effect is intensifying it, with consecutive El Ninos occurring more frequently in recent decades and the scope and consequences being greater than they once were. In the 1997–1998 period, El Niño was blamed by the Food and Agriculture Organization (FAO) for flooding in 41 nations and extreme droughts in 22, and causing tens of billions of dollars in damage.

Case 7.4   Smoke above Sumatra

In the year 2015, here it was again. . . The forests on the Indonesian island of Sumatra were burning, just as in previous years. Smoke clouds rose into the sky, so large that they could be seen with the naked eye by astronauts on the International Space Station. The forests burnt for months, as they did in all years of the last two decades, with air pollution in surrounding nations so thick it caused tears. The city-state of Singapore was covered by a thick layer of smog, and a state of alert was declared in Thailand and the Philippines.

The fires were probably started by **slash and burn** farmers, trying to clear new land by burning off the forest after their own lands were exhausted through intensive cultivation.

Satellites detected fires burning in southern Sumatra since early September. Scientists monitoring the fires expected the fires to continue burning until the monsoon rains arrive at the end of October. However, they cautioned that the dry season could be unusually long in Indonesia this year, because of the strong El Niño in the Pacific Ocean.

In several years, a state of emergency was declared in Malaysia due to the suffocating smoke. Schools, offices and companies were shut. Flights were cancelled and billions of dollars were lost in the absence of tourists.

The increasing prevalence of droughts, rains and tropical cyclones are all phenomena that can be calculated to some degree using computer-based climate models, even though they cannot be forecast using the software. But there are also potential rebound effects for climate change that are a great deal more complex.

Ocean currents

Although it is far from certain, it is possible that there will be at least one remarkable consequence of the greenhouse effect, which is that Western and Northern Europe will actually become *colder*. The underlying reason can be found in the massive currents in the ocean, as seen in Figure 7.14. Warm water flows from the Pacific and Indian Oceans into the Atlantic Ocean. This water, flowing northwards to the region of Greenland, is known in the Atlantic as the **Gulf Stream**. In the north it sinks deep down into the ocean, flowing along the bottom of the ocean back south and to the other oceans, forming a cycle. This current, the

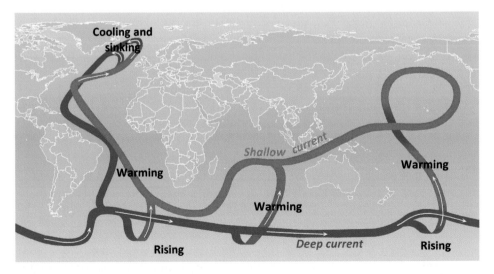

FIGURE 7.14   The thermohaline circulation, with the Gulf Stream as its Atlantic leg. Surface currents are in orange, with deep-sea currents in purple

Source: IPCC (2001); background image source: Thesevenseas, Wikimedia.

thermohaline circulation – also called the 'Great Conveyor Belt' – brings a great deal of warmth to Western and Northern Europe and ensures the nations in this part of the world have a temperate climate. Areas in Canada at the same latitude that are not warmed by this current experience a climate resembling that of the far north of Norway.

The 'engine' that drives this current is located near Greenland. Over the course of the lengthy voyage through the oceans a great deal of water evaporates, and so the remaining water becomes much more salty. Salt water is heavier than fresh water, having a higher density, and by the time the water arrives off the coast of Greenland this difference in densities has become so great that it sinks to the bottom of the ocean, driving the entire current.

But now the polar ice caps are melting, as are the glaciers covering Greenland, all introducing a large amount of fresh water into the seas. This fresh water mixes with the salt water in the Gulf Stream and, its density reduced, the tendency of the water to sink to the bottom will decrease. This means that the thermohaline circulation might weaken, or even come to a complete stop, at some point in the future. In past eons, long before historic times, this has happened repeatedly, so it is not inconceivable it may happen again. If it does, the warmth carried from the tropics to the northern regions will decline, causing the tropical areas to heat up and Northern Europe to cool down. It is difficult to predict by how much the temperature in Europe might drop, and it is even difficult to predict whether the circulation would actually stop. There are some indications in recent years that the Gulf Stream is weakening, but they are as yet not convincing.

The consequences of a declining or absent ocean current would be very serious. The economic damage caused if major world ports in the global north were to freeze shut for a part of the year, as the ports in the north of Norway do, would alone be incalculable.

This potential trend break in the thermohaline circulation is an example of a rebound effect resulting from the greenhouse effect. It is also an example of positive *and* negative feedback – in the event of a decline or absence of the circulation, the temperature in the tropics will rise, which is positive feedback, while in the northern latitudes it will decline, which is negative feedback. For the northern regions the situation will resemble graph (e) in Figure 7.8.

Significance for the natural environment, humanity and the economy

The range of the changes resulting from the greenhouse effect has far-reaching consequences, even if all those sudden and drastic trend breaks do not occur. Of great significance is its influence on the ecological footprint, a significant part of which consists of the so-called **carbon footprint**, as can be seen in Figure 7.15.

The extent of this is determined by the amount of the world's surface required to absorb CO_2 emissions in the forests, marshes, steppes and other environments. Young forests are especially important in this process, as older forests absorb little or no additional CO_2. The carbon footprint is so large that if we could manage to reduce it to, say, just 20 percent of the present value, the entire global footprint would be less than the biocapacity of the planet. As Chapter 2 showed, generating sustainable power in parts of the Sahara could play a role in causing other parts of that desert to blossom. In the present chapter, with respect to the ecological footprint, sustainable energy appears to play a far greater, even a worldwide role. This means that replacing energy derived from fossil fuels with sustainable forms of energy plays a crucial role for the entire process of sustainable development. As long as this substitution is not

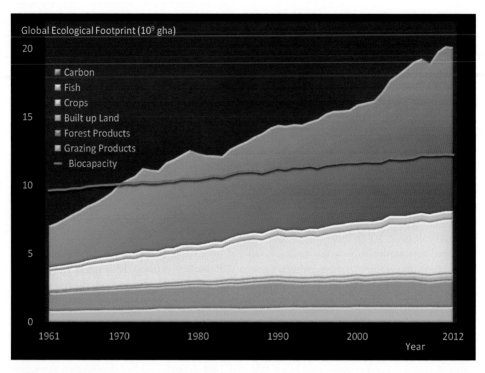

FIGURE 7.15 The 'Carbon Footprint': the effect of climate change on the global ecological footprint

Source: Global Footprint Network (2016).

introduced on a large scale, and the climate thus continues to change unabated, there will be further consequences for the natural environment. A few of these have been described already. Others include the disruption of biological equilibriums and climate migration.

Case 7.5 The polar bear

Scientific Name: *Ursus maritimus*
  Common Name: *Polar Bear*
  Kingdom: *Animalia*. Phylum: *Chordata*. Class: *Mammalia*. Order: *Carnivora*. Family: *Ursidae*.
  Red List Category: *Vulnerable* A3c ver 3.1.
  Justification:
  Loss of Arctic sea ice due to climate change is the most serious threat to Polar Bears throughout their circumpolar range. We performed a data-based sensitivity analysis with respect to this threat by evaluating the potential response of the global Polar Bear population to projected sea-ice conditions. Our analyses included a comprehensive assessment of generation length for Polar Bears; development of a standardized sea-ice metric representing important habitat characteristics for

the species; and population projections, over three Polar Bear generations, using computer simulation and statistical models representing alternative relationships between sea ice and Polar Bear abundance.

Our analyses highlight the potential for large reductions in the global Polar Bear population if sea-ice loss continues, which is forecast by climate models and other studies (IPCC, 2013). Our analyses also highlight the large amount of uncertainty in statistical projections of Polar Bear abundance and the sensitivity of projections to plausible alternative assumptions.

Across six scenarios that projected polar bear abundance three generations forward in time using the median and 95th percentile, the probability of a reduction in the mean global population size greater than 30% was approximately 0.71.

The median probability of a reduction greater than 50% was approximately 0.07.

Red List, International Union for the Conservation of Nature (IUCN), 2014.

The climate zones in the world are shifting – the weather in the northern parts of the world will slowly but surely start to resemble the global south, while the south will in turn become drier. Nature adapts to these changes, but not always at sufficient speed, and plants and animals that once only lived in subtropical zones, e.g. in Mexico or southern Europe, are **migrating** to regions at higher latitudes. These species include the wasp spider, the (poisonous) oak processionary and the melodious warbler. Invasive plant species, which have gained a foothold in the western United States, such as cheatgrass, spotted knapweed, yellow starthistle, tamarisk, and leafy spurge, are expected to spread. Other species are simply disappearing as the temperature rises (such as the threatened polar bear), disrupting carefully balanced ecosystems. Germs also migrate, including the virus that causes the bluetongue disease amongst sheep.

Climate change also results in major changes for humans. Should the sea level rise by a considerable amount, the consequences will be dramatic for the hundreds of millions – maybe even billions – of people that are forced from the present coastal regions. But even if this does not happen, large groups of people will still have to abandon their familiar surroundings, with some people suffering from drought and desertification, and others from flooding, cyclones or failed harvests and catches. This process is already well on the way, and in the last decade or so there have been more **climate refugees** than war refugees – between 25 and 50 million in 2007, with various estimates expecting this number to rise to 150 million by 2050.

In 2006 a comprehensive report was released of a study undertaken for the British government, the 'Stern Review', which examined the economic consequences of climate change. The report's conclusions were impressive, stating that many major cities, almost all of which are located on coastlines, would be threatened by flooding, harvests would fail more frequently, ocean life would die out en masse and extreme weather would wreak enormous damage. The total economic damage could run up to 30 percent of the GDP of the entire world, exceeding that caused by World War II. And if non-linear consequences start to prevail, then the risk would even exist that the global economy collapses into chaos, the consequences being incalculable. Stern asserted that these dramatic results were only avoidable if a powerful international adaptation policy is implemented. The commission calculated that an annual investment of one percent of the world's GDP would be required for this.

Around the same time as the Stern Review, a documentary dealing with the climate problem was released by the name of 'An Inconvenient Truth', by the former US vice president, Al Gore. The film, and the book of the same title, created a deep impression on heads of government and the general public in most Western nations, and reinforced international debates on comprehensive changes to policy. It resulted in Al Gore receiving the 2007 Nobel Peace Prize together with the IPCC. In the same year, the film received an Oscar for best documentary.

The precautionary principle

This section detailed a wide array of possible consequences of the greenhouse effect. Some of them have gradually become pretty certain, such as the increase in temperature and the rising sea levels. Others are likely, including the rise in drought and deluges of rain. The increase of powerful tropical cyclones and the changes brought by El Niño can also be attributed to the greenhouse effect with a reasonable degree of certainty. It is far from certain that the thermohaline circulation will stop, but if it happens, the consequences will be disastrous.

In spite of all of this, there are still people that doubt whether the whole thing is actually true. These 'climate sceptics' assert that the risks are highly exaggerated, with some even doubting that there is such a thing as an anthropogenic greenhouse effect. One camp of this group states that the climate is not changing. Another says the changes are due in full to external factors, such as an increase of solar activity.

In the meantime, billions of dollars, euros, pounds and yen are spent around the world on measures to combat global warming, with a multiple of these sums planned for further use in the next few decades. What if, the sceptics ask, all that expenditure is futile?

For those who ask this question, there is a counter-question: have they taken out fire insurance for their homes? They most likely have. Why? Because they know for a fact that their houses will catch fire within a few years? No, of course not. Nobody knows for sure whether something like that will happen, aside from those who might decide to become a home-based pyromaniac. We take out insurance because there is a *chance* that there may one day be a fire, and because, should this happen, the *consequences* would be disastrous for the occupant. We take out insurance as a precaution.

Many other things are done on exactly the same grounds – we all have locks for our front doors, cars and bikes, not because we are certain that something will get stolen, but just because such theft is a real possibility. Many people have health insurance because they might be faced with medical expenses, and also legal expenses insurance in case they ever find themselves embroiled in a legal conflict. Moreover, a climate sceptic's home might have a lightning conductor or a fire escape, all as a precaution for covering those potential events that are not a foregone conclusion. Even pension payments or life annuity paid by people not yet retired fall under this, because who knows for certain that they will ever be using that pension? Figure 7.16 contains many other examples of precautionary measures.

Society as a whole has also engaged such precautionary measures, including vaccinations against epidemics, such as Tamiflu to combat the flu, emergency generators, dyke and tsunami monitoring, storm surge barriers, air-raid shelters, emergency supplies, disaster plans, disaster teams and emergency facilities.

And then we have the greenhouse effect. Nearly all experts agree that it is a real issue, that it is the most serious of all our environmental problems, and that the damage experienced to date is only the start. But imagine that there was space for reasonable doubt – would it then

FIGURE 7.16 Those who believe it is wrong to spend money on measures combating climate change for the reason that it is not yet fully established as fact, probably do not have any of the things shown in this photo either

Source: Niko Roorda.

be wise to adopt a wait-and-see attitude, to only act when it was absolutely certain what would happen? There is every chance that, so long as we do indeed wait and see, it will be far too late to take sensible steps and that the consequences will be titanic, both in a human and a financial sense.

This is why we apply the **precautionary principle**: while it is impossible to say that the whole scenario is a certainty, the possible outcomes are dramatic, and so we do not sit and wait for them. Any investments made in stopping the climate change that might later prove unnecessary are of much less consequence than what will probably be the colossal consequences of taking no action whatsoever. And so we are working on solutions for the climate problem in many places and ways. In Section 6.3 it was already stated that thinking and working in a future-oriented manner inevitably goes hand in hand with many uncertainties. The precautionary principle is a sensible point of departure in this.

7.4 Solutions: technology and lifestyle

Chapter 4 already stated that there are either no or few issues of unsustainability for which no technological solutions are available, or will soon be available. The same holds for climate change. These technological solutions can be divided into two groups – ones that combat the symptoms and ones that combat the underlying causes. In the former case these entail learning to live with the consequences of climate change, insofar as these have become inevitable due to a long-term lag effect. This means that, even if we did stop all greenhouse gas (GHG) emissions today – which is not the case – the consequences of climate change would continue for at least half a century until a new equilibrium is reached. The relationship between combating the symptoms and the far more important elimination of the causes can be compared to the situation of the leaking roof in Section 5.5, in which the same relationship exists between catching the water and repairing the roof – solutions for the short term and for the long term respectively.

Learning to deal with the consequences of inevitable climate change means that something must be done at all levels. For example, to deal with the rising sea levels we will have to raise the dykes – or evacuate the population. The increasingly capricious weather means we require bigger reservoirs of clean water, facilities to withstand cyclones, improved irrigation for dry regions, and improved drainage for regions that become wetter. In anticipation to a possible wave consisting of maybe 150 million climate refugees, all measures will have to be engaged that, on the one hand, attempt to prevent this deluge from happening and, on the other, assist and accommodate them.

This chapter will not deal too deeply with combating the systems in this manner, but rather concentrate on tackling the causes. There are a variety of possible technological solutions for this, all of which shall have to reinforce each other. This entails making energy consumption more efficient, employing sustainable sources of energy, using less energy through lifestyle changes and dealing with the residues of combustion – in other words, storing CO_2.

Fossil fuel reserves

We are faced with a climate problem because fossil fuels are being extracted from the Earth, which in turn release greenhouse gases through their incineration into the atmosphere. This is a form of one-way traffic. In one location – the ground – there will eventually be a shortage once oil and gas are depleted, and in another location – the atmosphere – there will be a surplus, as outlined in Chapter 2. A part of Figure 2.5 is repeated here in the top half of Figure 7.17, as the outlined form of one-way traffic is crucial.

Opinions differ in respect of a possible shortage on the supply side. However, to date the global **fossil fuel reserve** has always been increasing, and never decreasing. This appears to be miraculous, especially when one considers how much oil, gas and coal we have consumed. But the reserves depend on four factors: new discoveries of fossil fuel fields, technical extractability, economic extractability and political decisions.

New discoveries are being made regularly. In recent decades, this usually occurs in ocean floors. Especially the area around the North Pole is becoming more and more important, as the

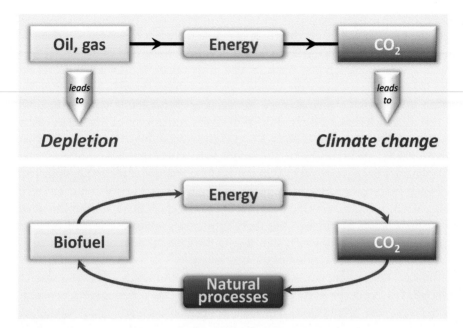

FIGURE 7.17   Use of fossil fuels. Top: one-way traffic (as seen in Figure 2.5); bottom: a closed cycle

polar icecap melts away and the fossil fuels under the Arctic Ocean become available; ironically, this is yet another positive feedback loop reinforcing climate change, not even mentioned in Figure 7.6. A political struggle as to which countries own these reserves has burst out.

At the same time, **technical extractability** has increased due to new technological developments. For example, since it has become possible to extract oil from the seabed, the global reserves have increased drastically.

At least as important is the **economic extractability**. Oil, natural gas, coal and ore are considered to be economically extractable when they return a net profit, i.e. when the gains are higher than the costs for extracting them. The economically extractable reserves of oil and gas have been increasing for many years, partly due to the technological improvements in the extraction process. They also depend on the price of crude oil on the world market, which has been highly volatile in recent years, as will be described in the next section.

Lastly, the amount of reserves depends on political decisions, that is to say: the willingness or refusal of governments to exploit fossil fuel fields that cause great risks or damages. This refers to reserves for which the extraction and transportation cause serious hazards, e.g. in arctic conditions.

Case 7.6   The Exxon Valdez

The giant tanker was following a northerly route, with a load of 200 million tons of oil. The Exxon Valdez had made many voyages in the three years since it had been launched, and they all proceeded without a hitch until that one time in 1989.

In the freezing waters off the coast of Alaska there is a treacherous reef below the surface close to Prince William Sound. An error on the part of the captain saw the tanker hit this *Bligh Reef*. With its side ripped open, a tsunami of oil flowed into the sea: estimates vary between 42 and 144 million litres (11 and 38 million gallons). Thousands of animals were immediately killed – 250,000 sea birds, 2,800 sea otters, 300 harbour seals, hundreds of eagles and dozens of whales, as well as millions of fish. And even though a large-scale rescue operation for the animals was launched, the number of victims multiplied in the following months.

There have been worse oil spills in terms of the amount of oil that has escaped, but what exacerbated the misery of this particular disaster was that it occurred in ice-cold temperatures, which meant that the oil could not be rapidly broken down by bacteria. Large portions of the sticky substance sank to the seabed, which it continued to pollute for years, and despite the cleanup operations, there was a complete long-term disruption of the ecosystem.

The local population, consisting mostly of Native Americans, was also severely affected. Fishing became impossible and almost all the fisheries went bankrupt, as did a number of industries. The local population became impoverished, and one despairing mayor committed suicide. The multinational Exxon, owner of the Exxon Valdez, was sentenced to pay a fine of five billion US dollars. After an appeal filed by Exxon, in 2008 the fine was lowered to 500 million dollars.

In reaction to the spill, in 1990 the US Congress passed the Oil Pollution Act (OPA). This law prohibits any vessel that, after March 22, 1989, has caused an oil spill of more than 1 million US gallons (3,800 cubic metres) in any marine area, from operating in Prince William Sound.

In 1998, Exxon started a legal action against the US government, demanding that the Exxon Valdez should be allowed back into Alaskan waters. The company claimed that OPA was actually a bill of attainder, a regulation that was unfairly directed at Exxon alone. In 2002, a Court of Appeals ruled against Exxon.

As of 2002, OPA had prevented 18 ships from entering Prince William Sound. The act also set a schedule for the gradual phase in of a double hull design, providing an additional layer between the oil tanks and the ocean. Although such a double hull would probably not have prevented the Valdez disaster, a Coast Guard study estimated that it would have cut the amount of oil spilled by 60 percent.

Meanwhile, in 1990 the tanker was repaired and sailed once again under a new name, the *SeaRiver Mediterranean*. In August 2012, it was beached at Alang, India and dismantled.

Huge damages are also caused by the extraction of *oils sands* and *shale gas*, both of which are highly disputed. **Oil sands** are a mixture of sand, clay and water, saturated with petroleum in the form of natural **bitumen** or **tar**. They are found in many countries, such as Kazakhstan and Russia. In Canada too, where it is extracted at a large scale, in a way that completely destroys large natural areas, expelling native Canadian communities. **Shale gas**, hugely available in many countries, and extracted intensively in e.g. the USA, is deeply hidden natural gas that is gained through **fracking**, a process in which liquid is injected at high pressure into subterranean rocks, crushing them and releasing the gas. Fears exist that this process will contaminate the soil and the groundwater with toxic chemicals, use lots of water in water-deficient regions, cause blowouts due to gas explosions, and induce earthquakes and subsidences. Indeed, in Oklahoma and several other US states earthquakes have been reported as a result of fracking.

In spite of all these increases of reserves, there will no doubt come a time – if we continue extracting them – when the total reserve of extractable fossil fuels on the planet will no longer increase and reach a maximum, after which it will decline: anything else would be physically impossible. For oil, this moment is called '**peak oil**', also known as the **Hubbert peak**. Peak oil has been predicted many times. In 1974, M. King Hubbert predicted that it would occur in 1995. Around 2000, predictions for peak oil varied between 2005 and 2050. On several moments, some experts estimated that peak oil had already been met. Anyway, there is little doubt among experts that it will happen somewhere before 2050.

Whatever will happen to reserves and exploitation of fossil fuels, it is evident that this is only relevant for the supply side of Figure 7.17 (top section), not for solving the climate change issue. So, other solutions are needed.

Energy extensification

One of the available solutions is **extensification**, which pertains to decreasing energy consumption using smart technologies that will lead to greater efficiency. This implies that we continue on our present course, but we do this using an intelligent approach, allowing us to achieve the same results while using less energy. For buildings, for example, this would include insulating the walls and roofs and using double-glazing. In the best-case scenario, this results in **zero-energy buildings** like the one in Case 7.1. For power stations, we could convert to **cogeneration plants** (also known as combined heat and power, or **CHP** power stations), through which the heat created when generating electricity is used to heat offices and homes, for example. When it comes to cars, they can be made more aerodynamic, reducing wind resistance, new materials can be utilised that are both lighter and stronger and the engine can be designed to be a great deal more efficient. The **hybrid car** uses smart technology, containing both an internal combustion engine and an electric motor. The first hybrid car was able to travel a distance of over 20 kilometres on one litre of gas, i.e. 50 miles per gallon (US) or 60 miles per (imperial) gallon (UK). By comparison, a standard car will get you about half as far, and some of the biggest SUVs don not even get three kilometres on a litre of gas. Fully **electric cars** can be even more energy efficient; but for them as well as for hybrid ones, the contribution to sustainable development depends on the way the electric energy is generated in the first place: sustainably or not? And so, the difference in efficiency can be large between cars, and are set to become even larger.

However, all these attempts at extensification fall way short, and more drastic measures will still be required.

Sustainable energy

There are many different forms of **sustainable energy**, almost all of which use solar radiation. Solar energy can be utilised directly either with the aid of solar cells, i.e. **photovoltaic cells (PV cells)**, that generate electricity; or with solar thermal collectors, which concentrate and use the heat generated by the sun, delivering **concentrated solar power** (CSP). Images of both can be seen in Figure 7.18 (top row). Solar radiation is utilised indirectly through the

a. Solar cells (photovoltaic cells)

b. Solar collector (parabolic dish)

c. Windmills

d. Hydroelectric power (dam)

e. Wave energy generators

f. Biomass

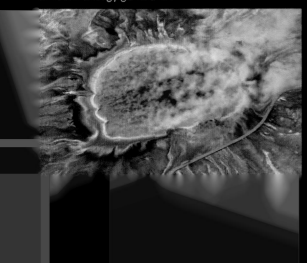

FIGURE 7.18   Eight kinds of sustainable energy

Source: Walmart Stores; Xklaim, Wikimedia; Kim Hansen, Richard Bartz, Wikimedia; ccfarmer, Wikimedia; Jumanji Solar, flickr; Ton Ruikens, flickr; Jim Peaco, National Park Service; Nova Scotia Power.

energy in wind and water currents, captured with the aid of turbines and dams (Figure 7.18, second row) or wave power generators (on the left of the third row). Another indirect form of solar energy is the use of biofuels (on the right of the third row).

There are also sustainable sources of energy that do not find their origins in solar radiation. One of these is the heat released by the Earth itself, which in most places is hidden deep beneath the planet's crust from where it can be raised using water. In some places this heat is released directly onto the Earth's surface, such as the hot geysers in Yellowstone National Park in Wyoming, US (Figure 7.18, bottom left) and, of course, through volcanoes. Tidal power (bottom right) relies on oceanic tides driven by the gravity of the moon and the sun.

Each of these sources of energy has its own advantages and disadvantages. Dams take up a great deal of space, forcing people from their homes. They also increase the evaporation rate of scarce fresh water, thus contributing to droughts, and some of them cause earthquakes. Wind turbines meanwhile require a great deal of material, and much energy is also devoted to their manufacture. Moreover, the amount of power they generate fluctuates as dramatically as the weather, and they impinge upon the landscape. Another factor often said to be a disadvantage is the frequency of birds colliding with them, with recent estimates in the United States standing at 20,000 to 37,000 bird fatalities a year. While this might seem like a large number, it is small compared to the millions of birds that die in other ways every year, including traffic collisions.

Underground CO_2 storage

Aside from the introduction of sustainable energy, another solution being explored for the surplus of CO_2 shown in the top part of Figure 7.17 is to store the carbon dioxide underground. Trials with this **carbon capture and storage** (**CCS**) are being performed in regions where the ground contains hollows and porous sections from which the natural gas was pumped out. The research focuses on whether these gaps can be filled with CO_2. It is not yet clear if the technique can be employed on a large scale and significantly contribute to solving the climate problem. Essentially, the underground storage of CO_2 is a typical end-of-pipe solution that does nothing to take away the causes of the greenhouse issue. Moreover, it involves a number of disadvantages, and not everyone believes that this form of storage would be entirely risk-free. Inhabitants of towns where trials were planned, have protested strongly and – in several cases – successfully: they fear that stored gases may someday escape, spread around their villages, push away the oxygen and suffocate the inhabitants.

But maybe there are other ways.

Case 7.6   Storing carbon dioxide underground by turning it into rock

Science Daily, November 18, 2016

A study, reported in *Environmental Science & Technology Letters*, has found that within two years, carbon dioxide (CO_2), injected into basalt, transformed into solid rock.

First, lab studies on basalt showed that the rock, which formed from lava millions of years ago, can rapidly convert CO_2 into stable carbonate minerals. This evidence suggested that if CO_2 could be locked into this solid form, it would be stowed away for good, unable to escape into the atmosphere.

But what happens in the lab doesn't always reflect what happens in the field. So, starting in 2009, researchers with Pacific Northwest National Laboratory and the Montana-based Big Sky Carbon Sequestration Partnership undertook a pilot project in eastern Washington to inject 1,000 tons of pressurized liquid CO_2 into a basalt formation. After drilling a well in the Columbia River Basalt formation and testing its properties, the team injected CO_2 into it in 2013.

Core samples were extracted from the well two years later, and the research team confirmed that the CO_2 had indeed converted into the carbonate mineral ankerite, as the lab experiments had predicted.

Because basalts are widely found in North America and throughout the world, the researchers suggest that the formations could help permanently sequester carbon on a large scale.

From the original source, McGrail, B.P. et al. (2017)

Following post-injection monitoring for 2 years, cores were obtained from within the injection zone and subjected to detailed physical and chemical analysis. Nodules found in vesicles throughout the cores were identified as the carbonate mineral, ankerite Ca[Fe,Mg,Mn]$(CO_3)_2$. Carbon isotope analysis showed the nodules are chemically distinct compared with natural carbonates present in the basalt and in clear correlation with the isotopic signature of the injected CO_2. These findings provide field validation of rapid mineralization rates observed from years of laboratory testing with basalts.

Biofuels

Another approach, which really does tackle the problem of one-way traffic, is to close the cycle using vegetable fuels – as the bottom part of Figure 7.17 illustrates. Figure 7.18 shows one of the crops that are used as a source for **biofuel**: the fruits of the *jatropha*. Sugar cane, linseed, corn and other crops are also used, but the disadvantage of this is soon obvious.

Case 7.7   EU votes to scale back on biofuels linked to deforestation

Mongabay News/Jeremy Hance, April 28, 2015

The European Parliament voted overwhelmingly today on a new cap on biofuels derived from edible crops, which critics say not only compete with feeding a growing global population but also contribute to deforestation and release unacceptably high levels of greenhouse gas emissions. The new legislation sets the cap on edible food crop biofuels – such as palm oil, corn, rapeseed, and soy – at seven percent. Currently, the EU set a 10 percent target for transport fuels will be so-called "renewable" by 2020.

"Let no one be in doubt, the biofuels bubble has burst," said Robbie Blake, a campaigner from the Friends of the Earth Europe. "The EU's long-awaited move to put the brakes on biofuels is a clear signal to the rest of the world that this is a false solution to the climate crisis. This must spark the end of burning food for fuel."

A decade ago biofuels were touted as one among many solutions to climate change. However, research since then has increasingly argued that many biofuels may actually emit more greenhouse gases than fossil fuels due to deforestation and land use change. In addition, deforestation linked to biofuels for Europe has potentially led to biodiversity loss, land conflict, labor issues, and indigenous right issues in places as far away as Indonesia, Brazil, and Tanzania.

Under the new legislation, biofuel companies will still not have to take into account greenhouse gas emissions from **indirect land use change (ILUC)**, which refers to the fact that biofuel development often unintentionally pushes deforestation into new areas. However, companies will have to estimate emissions from ILUC and report it to the European Commission in a bid to improve transparency.

The fact that biomass is in direct competition with food contributes to rising global food prices, and may even contribute to political instability in food-deficit countries. Additional land is needed for agriculture and thus increases the already overly large ecological footprint. Much work has gone into finding solutions to the problem. The so-called first generation biomass relied primarily on crops that directly compete with agriculture for human consumption. **Second generation biofuels** include waste from forestry and agriculture, such as wood chips and straw from corn and grain. The third generation is focused on a very different universe – the oceans with their algae. This is not illogical – not just because this removes the competition with agriculture, but also because the greenhouse effect stimulates algae.

Nuclear fission

Then, there is also the option of nuclear energy. To be more precise, *two* options – **nuclear fission** and **nuclear fusion**.

All nuclear power plants today use nuclear fission, with uranium or plutonium serving as the source of energy. There are a number of disadvantages associated with these power plants, one of which is the possibility of materials and technology being stolen and used for terrorist attacks – atomic weapons, poison attacks (aside from being radioactive, plutonium is also highly poisonous) or attacks on the nuclear power plants. There is also a chance of accidents occurring.

Case 7.8 Fukushima, 2011

It was the strongest earthquake ever recorded in or near Japan. The Tōhoku earthquake of Friday 11 March 2011 had a magnitude of 9.1, and it hit the island nation from 70 kilometres outside the coast of the Oshika Peninsula. The earthquake was the first disaster, but not the last in those weeks.

A giant tsunami was the second disaster. Waves with heights up till 40 metres (133 feet), raised by the earthquake, stormed the Japanese coasts, destroying everything it met up to 10 kilometres (6 miles) inland. The earthquake moved Honshu, Japan's main island, 2.4 metres (8 feet) eastward and shifted the Earth's axis 10 to 25 cm (4 to 10 inches). But that was still not all.

The third and biggest disaster followed when the tsunami hit the large coastal Fukushima Daiichi Nuclear Power Plant (Figure 7.19). The plant was designed to be earthquake-resistant – at least, that was what experts stated. But apparently, the possibility of a tsunami was largely overseen. Immediately after the quake, the plant, with six nuclear reactors, was shut down automatically, which disabled the cooling system of the reactors. Unfortunately, the tsunami destroyed the emergency generators for the cooling system. Consequently, reactor 4 quickly overheated due to decay heat from the fuel rods. In the next days, more reactors became overheated, leading to nuclear meltdowns of reactors 1, 2 and 3; a nuclear accident that severe had never before happened anywhere in the world.

FIGURE 7.19 The Fukushima Daiichi Nuclear Power Plant during the nuclear incident. Reactor 1 to 4 from right to left; reactors 2 and 3 are on fire

Source: Digital Globe, Wikimedia.

Several explosions occurred between 12 and 15 March, releasing giant clouds of radioactive materials into the air.

In the next weeks and months, there was no safe way to cool the reactors, and so water from the ocean was used. Large quantities of radioactive substances such as iodine-131 and caesium-137 were released into the Pacific Ocean. Fisheries were prohibited. Radioactive iodine-131, exceeding safety limits for infants, were detected at 18 water-purification plants. Radioactive materials were detected in food, including spinach, tea leaves, milk, fish and beef, produced up to 320 kilometres from the plant.

The combined disasters forced 470,000 people to be evacuated, 154,000 due to the nuclear accident. Five years later, 174,000 evacuees still remained. Financial damages are estimated at US$ 100 billion, not counting healthcare spending and reduction of life expectancy.

The Fukushima disaster was the second that was given *Level 7*, the maximum event classification of the International Nuclear Event Scale. The first one was the Chernobyl Incident.

Chernobyl, 1986

On April 26, 1986, one of the reactors in the Chernobyl nuclear power plant in Ukraine blew up. An enormous radioactive cloud was blown into the atmosphere and spread across Europe. The first international warnings that something was wrong came from Swedish scientists, who reported that they had recorded radioactive fallout. Throughout Europe, agricultural animals were stabled and outdoor produce and plants that were contaminated had to be destroyed. The impact on the people living in the vicinity of the power plant was much worse, and it is estimated that 600,000 people were infected by radiation, with around 4,000 presumed to have died as a result – some of them very soon after the disaster and some years later as a result of radiation sickness.

The explosion occurred at the exact moment that a number of safety systems were disconnected for tests. A combination of mechanical and human errors resulted in the cooling water heating up, followed by a dramatic rise in temperature and pressure. The reaction rate increased tenfold and the fuel rods melted. Pipelines and the roof were torn open and the heavily radioactive steam escaped into the atmosphere.

The reactor was finally sealed off using concrete poured from helicopters a few weeks later, an operation that resulted in a number of the pilots later succumbing to radioactive disease and death.

The power plant had four reactors and, once the damaged reactor was sealed off, the remaining three were simply started up again. The entire power plant was only shut down in 2001 following international pressure. The city of Chernobyl and the surrounding region are abandoned.

Even the Chernobyl disaster was not the first major nuclear accident. In 1957, the nuclear reactor at Windscale (now Sellafield in the UK) caught fire, and substantial amounts of radioactive fallout were released into the surrounding area. In 1979, the Three Mile Island nuclear reactor near Harrisburg, Pennsylvania (US) had a core meltdown. One hundred and forty thousand pregnant women and preschool age children were evacuated, as radioactive gases were released into the atmosphere.

There has been intense debate for decades, both among scientists and politicians as well as by protest groups and the general public, on whether nuclear fission can be considered a form of sustainable energy. In a literal sense, it certainly is not, given that its source of energy – uranium – will one day run out and is thus not indefinitely available. There is much uncertainty on the point of 'peak uranium', which is the time when the global economically extractable reserves no longer increase but decline. Estimates for peak uranium differ hugely, varying between 40 to 70 years (European Commission, 2001) and 100 to 8,500 years (OECD, 2003 and IAEA, 2008). The high level of uncertainty is due to a number of factors. One of these is the fact that there are vast reserves of uranium at low concentrations, which are not economically extractable today but could be if the technology improves and the global market price of uranium rises. Moreover, there is a chance that new fuel can be created from used fuel. Nuclear power plants only use one of two uranium isotopes, U-235, and the much more common but unusable U-238 can be converted in breeder reactors into plutonium, which can be used to drive the nuclear power plants.

Besides, experiments using thorium as another nuclear source are taking place. As thorium is much more available in the Earth's crust, it will lengthen the availability of nuclear energy sources greatly. Should these technologies be deployed on a large scale, nuclear fission could be a source of power for centuries or even millennia – the exact length of time depending on how intense consumption is. If, as has been proposed, nuclear power was to adopt a central role in tackling the climate issue, then it will have to contribute much more power than it presently does, drastically cutting the time for which fission material will be available.

But there is another problem when it comes to nuclear fission. In certain respects, it resembles fossil fuels in that Figure 7.17 (top part) could also apply to uranium. This is because, leaving aside the potential of breeder reactors, the power generated by nuclear power plants constitutes one-way traffic. This means that we are not only faced with possible shortages on the input side, but also with a surplus on the output side, in the form of **radioactive waste**. This waste is made up of depleted fission material, and of the remains of demolished nuclear power plants and other materials used in the process that have become radioactive. These waste products contain low to medium radiation levels, which means they must be treated with great care and continue to pose a danger for decades or centuries. The fuel rods are meanwhile highly radioactive, and continue to be lethal for tens of thousands to a million years.

Experience with decommissioning nuclear power plants is slowly growing. One of the first decommissioned reactors was the Main Yankee power plant in the US. It was commissioned in 1972, but was declared unsafe in an investigation in 1995, with so many risks identified that it became too expensive to repair. The power plant was demolished between 1997 and 2005 at a cost that was more than double the original construction price. The same applies to other nuclear power plants that have been or are scheduled to be decommissioned, where the costs are estimated to be a number of times higher than the construction costs. Most power plants that no longer produce electricity are still waiting to be dismantled.

Storing radioactive waste is still a problem with no real solutions. All the waste generated to date is still being provisionally stored, awaiting a viable solution. One idea is to store the waste deep beneath the Earth's surface in geologically stable areas, so that the material will not have to be constantly monitored. But these safe areas are hard to come by. In the United States, Yucca Mountain was considered as an option (Figure 7.20). However, the University of Colorado established that the region is prone to earthquake activity, which means the waste could escape into the groundwater at some stage and disperse in an unpredictable manner. In 2011, the US government ended the federal funding for the site. In 2012, a commission of the US Department of Energy (DOE) expressed urgency to find a consolidated, geological repository. As such a site has not yet been found, all nuclear waste is still stored temporarily.

A fundamental problem is the extremely long period for which the radioactive material continues to be hazardous. It is near impossible to guarantee that any region will remain geologically stable for a million years, which is why there has been much protest against the suggestion of storing the radioactive material in an inaccessible location and ceasing to monitor it ('**stewardship cessation**'). Many scientists argue that it should be stored aboveground for at least a hundred years so that the safety can be continuously controlled.

FIGURE 7.20   Much doubt has existed about the safety of using Yucca Mountain as a repository for nuclear waste since it was discovered that the Bow Ridge fault line is located close to it. This means that there is a chance of earthquakes occurring. In 1992, an earthquake struck a mere 20 kilometres away

Source: United States Department of Energy.

All these issues also meant that there are problems when it comes to calculating the true cost of nuclear power. The cost estimates per kilowatt-hour rarely take sufficient account of the dismantling costs of the nuclear power stations, especially in light of the fact that these are frequently much higher than was originally thought. Meanwhile, the costs of continuously monitoring the material for at least a century, and possibly for ten thousand years or more, are either systematically underestimated or ignored entirely. Budgeters have little other option, as nobody can possibly know what price tag a work hour or technical equipment may carry in 50, 800 or 20,000 years. The wheel was only invented some 6,000 years ago. . .

Nuclear power can be considered as an example of transferring the problems caused by our present lifestyle to future generations. The consequence period when it comes to nuclear power is very long indeed, which means that using the rule of thumb for proper decisions (see Section 5.5) is extremely important in this case. What might people think in the year 20,020 or in the year 200,020 if they still had to secure nuclear waste that was generated in the year 2,020? This is assuming that they are capable of doing so, as it is conceivable that in 50 years or 2,500 years or at any other time a crisis erupts that is of such a scale that humanity is no longer financially or technically able to deal with aged radioactive waste.

Questions

- What is more serious – the climate problem or the disadvantages of nuclear power?
- Or is this an unfair comparison? If not, why not?
- Do you think we can accept responsibility to do something that might pose a danger for people a hundred thousand years in the future?

Nuclear fusion

Aside from nuclear fission, there is also nuclear fusion – the same process the sun uses to create its energy (Figure 7.21). At present there are no nuclear fusion reactors providing us with power, and it will likely be some time before we see one, as the technology is still being developed. Within a nuclear fusion power plant, a *plasma* is created. This is a gas in which the pressure and temperature are so high that hydrogen nuclei fuse to become helium. The temperature required for that to happen is 150 million degrees Celsius (270 million °F) and, given that all materials will vaporize at that temperature, the plasma is held in magnetic fields.

A few fusion reactors are already operational, but they use more power than they generate. The first power station designed to provide energy, ITER (International Thermonuclear Experimental Reactor), is presently being constructed in Cadarache in France. The experimental project is being funded by the EU, the United States, Japan, Russia, South Korea, China and India, and it is a gigantic task that will take dozens of years to complete. But should it succeed, we might be able to solve the energy problem using nuclear fusion, as it is not fuelled by a hazardous and scarce radioactive substance but by hydrogen – one of the two elements that make up water – and the product of the fusion is helium, a completely harmless inert gas. Generating energy by 'burning' water? It might sound like a fairy tale, but it is possible, and sometime after 2025 ITER will start to deliver power. If the experiment succeeds, of course.

But nuclear fusion is not perfect either – it produces low and medium level radioactive waste because the released neutrons irradiate the walls of the plant.

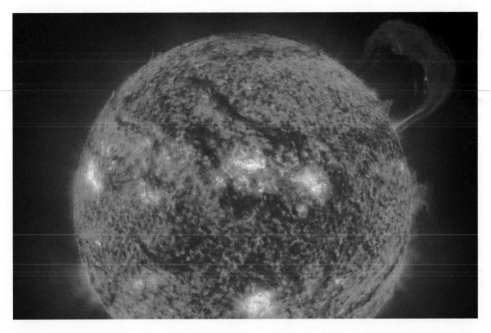

FIGURE 7.21   The plasma in an experimental reactor, in which the process of nuclear fusion takes place, reaches a temperature of around 150 million degrees Celsius, ten times as hot as the sun's core

Source: SOHO (ESA & NASA).

Transportation

All the concepts examined up until this point involve *generating* energy. But there is also a second issue related to energy, and that is its *transport*. Cars, airplanes and ships all run on fuel, almost exclusively gasoline, diesel, natural gas and so on – all of them fossil fuels. These make up a significant part of the CO_2 emissions, a factor that shall have to change. This means that within a few decades most vehicles will no longer run on fossil fuel. A range of alternatives exists, which differ in the degree to which a large-scale system change is required – from minor adjustments through to a true transition.

The simplest adjustment involves the step from fossil fuel to biofuel. Little will have to change for this, with drivers continuing to fill up with liquid or gas at gas stations, just as they have always done. But if many nations move to biofuel, this will create fresh problem, as described earlier. A slightly more comprehensive substitute would be hydrogen, also a great fuel, which can be obtained by splitting water into its two components, hydrogen and oxygen, in power plants. The oxygen escapes into the air, and when the hydrogen is burned in the engine using oxygen in the air, water is once again created, closing the cycle. No CO_2 is created in the process, which provides a very good solution, but one that does require extensive changes. Today's car engines cannot run on hydrogen, and their fuel tanks cannot store it. Gas stations do not provide hydrogen either, and so the automobile industry, the fuel suppliers and infrastructure will all need to change over. If this change is completed on a sufficiently large scale, it will lead to a **hydrogen economy**.

While the preceding solutions are all based on internal combustion engines, the electric car marks a complete departure. The electric car has proven to be a good alternative, even for long-distance travel, as the range of the present top models has reached 500 kilometres (300 miles). On the other hand, it still takes a lengthy time to charge the batteries; the latest technology has reduced the charging time to around 30 minutes – still too long to 'quickly fill up' but short enough to combine charging time with a cup of coffee en route. This means that, if the electric car is going to be widely used, traffic could take one of two possible directions. On the one hand it is conceivable that technological developments see the charging time even more drastically reduced, which would mean that we can continue to drive as we always have. On the other hand, if this technology will remain far off for a long time, we will have to adjust to a different way of long-distance travel, where we deliberately plan for longer breaks. In the latter case, more sustainable driving leads to a behavioural change amongst consumers. This will also be the case if it becomes a habit to plug in your car at home at night – then you'll rarely have to recharge at a 'filling station'.

Other solutions also exist for the present problem of our reliance on fossil fuels for vehicles, but they are all somewhat more comprehensive and have greater consequences in terms of our lifestyles. An obvious one is a large-scale increase in the use of bicycles and public transport, especially trains and metros, which do not have to carry their own fuel. This will also contribute to a reduction of other problems of unsustainability, as there will be less road congestion, noise and emission of damaging particulate matter. The use of space, which is scarce in many countries, will also be cut.

Lifestyle changes

The following alternative is even simpler – travelling less. Options for this include decreasing the distance between workplaces and homes, or setting up virtual workstations at home, as well as cutting distant vacations, maybe substituting them with vacations in virtual reality. This not only relates to transporting people, but goods too. A large amount of fossil fuel could be spared if foodstuff production, for example, became more localised. This does of course require behavioural changes on the part of consumers, who are accustomed to products that are flown across half the world to arrive as fresh goods in their locations.

The question of whether consumers will engage en masse in behavioural change goes beyond transport alone. It also concerns the acquisition and use of energy-hungry luxuries, such as jacuzzis and second homes. This sort of behavioural change means cutting consumption. You can also cut consumption through using equipment more sparingly, by turning off lights when you leave the room and by not leaving televisions and other apparatus on standby.

Sceptics of these types of solutions point out that the contribution to solving the climate issue is minimal, in part because only a few percent of the population will truly permanently change their behaviour. And while it is true that it is difficult to convince large groups of people to change, there are examples of real successes. For example, millions of people in Western countries have freely opted to move to **green power** – electricity generated using sustainable energy – even when it was more expensive than the alternatives. Another success story is separating garbage, with nearly entire populations depositing their bottles in bottle banks and separating paper and kitchen waste from other refuse.

There are various ways of convincing people to adapt to a more sustainable attitude. Action groups, authorities, educational institutions and companies can all engage in campaigns to inform people and provide them with a greater understanding of the situation, appeal to their conscience or simply guide them towards sustainable behaviour through advertising. The cost of sustainable behaviour can also be cut, or the price of unsustainable behaviour can be increased – either by way of natural market developments or through subsidies and taxes.

Perhaps the primary method makes use of technological devices, tempting people to behave sustainably by making it easy and pleasant. Should we not succeed in convincing people to switch off the lights when they leave a room, sensors can be installed that switch off the lights when the room is empty or if there is sufficient daylight; such equipment is being installed in many buildings. No more light switches! Another well-known example is to install a flush stopper on a toilet, so that it is easy to use less water when flushing. And once vegetable-based meat substitutes are created that cannot be distinguished from the real thing and could even be cheaper, a mass move to this product would be incredibly positive for sustainable development. These examples demonstrate that there is a close relationship between technology and human behaviour.

Questions

- Do you deliberately opt for ways of cutting consumption, e.g. of energy?
- Do campaigns that focus on sustainable behaviour influence you? For a long time?
- Do you think that a behavioural change amongst people can make a real contribution to the climate problem?

The question of whether comprehensive behavioural change is necessary for sustainable development has met with a wide array of responses. As yet it seems that a much more sustainable global society can be created through multiple approaches, with or without far-reaching changes to our lifestyles. So, the implementation of these changes is at least in part a matter of choice. New technology will play a major role in all of the approaches, but whether it will also have the opportunity to do so to a sufficient degree, and in time, depends on the policymakers and decision makers – i.e. on politicians and business leaders.

7.5 Political and economic instruments

In May 1992, an international agreement called the **United Nations Framework Convention on Climate Change (UNFCCC)** was made. A month later, the framework was opened for signing and ratification during the UNCED, also called the 'Earth Summit', or simply 'Rio', as this first major UN conference on sustainable development was hosted in Rio de Janeiro (see Chapter 4).

The UNFCCC itself was not a breakthrough towards solving the climate crisis. But it was the beginning of a long and complicated political process that is still going on and will no doubt continue to do so for many years.

One of the results is that the signing parties – 196 countries and the European Union, by December 2015 – meet annually in a **COP**, i.e. a **Conference of the Parties**, the first of which was in 1995 in Berlin.

Two years later, in 1997, COP3 took place in Japan, in the city of Kyoto. There, the first international treaty on climate change was adopted: the **Kyoto Protocol**. The signatories to the protocol undertook to cut carbon dioxide and methane **emissions**, as well as four other greenhouse gases (GHGs), by 5.2 percent of 1990 levels by 2010. This was a major promise, as emissions had been expected to increase considerably by 2010 in the absence of the Kyoto Protocol.

In spite of this fact, the 5.2 percent was just the first step, and emission would ultimately have to be reduced by a much larger margin. The percentage arrived at was an average – nations with high CO_2 emission levels in relation to their populations (see Figure 7.22, showing the levels of 2013) agreed to cut emissions by a larger margin. So, for example, the EU – which at that time consisted of 15 nations – undertook to cut greenhouse gas emissions by 8 percent from 1990 levels sometime between 2008 and 2012.

Unfortunately, Kyoto appeared of a limited significance, as not all countries were prepared to ratify it, including Australia and the United States. Other countries did sign it, including China and India, but were not obliged to reduce emissions at all, because – when calculated on a per capita basis – their proportional contribution to the greenhouse effect was not large.

Moreover, it was not until 2005 that the protocol entered into force, when there were enough signatories after Russia decided to sign. Australia joined the list of signatories in 2007; but by that time the final year of the protocol – 2012 – was already on the horizon, and the groundwork was being laid for a follow-up convention that was intended to impose much heavier requirements.

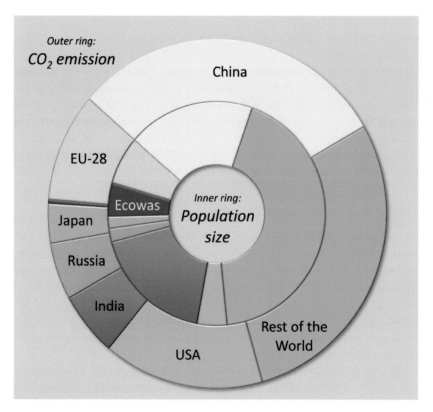

FIGURE 7.22 CO_2 emissions by a number of regions in 2013, compared with their populations (inner ring)

Sources: CDIAC (2016); UNDP (2016).

These talks led to COP15 in Copenhagen in 2009, where it was hoped that international agreements would be reached that would suffice for the next few decades. Some nations, including Japan and the EU, were prepared to undertake major emission cuts on the condition that others followed suit; it was a classic case of the *Tragedy of the Commons*, see Section 5.5. But, as the media described it, the conference descended into chaos. No consensus had been reached on binding decisions by the last day. The final outcome was the **Copenhagen Accord**, which merely contained a number of observations, recommendations and non-binding resolutions. The Copenhagen Accord stated that it was very important to limit the rise in temperature to 2 °C above pre-industrial levels, to prevent climate change from running wild. It also recommended that a climate fund should be established, which should make 100 billion dollars annually available as of 2020, to enable developing countries to mitigate emissions. However, it was not stated where that money was supposed to come from. In Copenhagen, no new emission reductions were imposed upon nations from 2012 onwards, i.e. after 'Kyoto', and thus not one single measurable result emerged from the conference.

One may wonder: why does it appear to be so immensely difficult to reach a really effective international agreement on the climate issue, which is so quintessential to a safe and sustainable future? This may seem odd, when it is compared with another issue related to the atmosphere: the ozone hole, briefly discussed in Section 1.3 and more deeply in Section 6.4. The Montreal Protocol, the international treaty of 1989, was highly successful – although, as described, a complete restoration of the ozone layer will take at least the entire twenty-first century.

The Montreal Protocol however just had to deal with the production and use of chlorofluorocarbons (CFCs) and hydrochlorofluorocarbons (HCFCs). They were relatively easy to replace; they were no pillars of the global economy, so the interests of countries and most companies were not significantly harmed. The climate issue, on the other hand, is related to the production and consumption of fossil fuels, which is a multi-billion-dollar market, fundamental to the world economy: the world is 'addicted to fossil fuels', as is often stated. Five of the ten largest multinational companies are in the oil and gas business (in 2016), considering their revenues. Perhaps as a consequence of this, the scientific and political debate has long been influenced by 'climate skeptics', in spite of overwhelming scientific proof; the debate may continue for many years.

After 'Copenhagen', i.e. COP15 in 2009, it was not until COP21 in Paris, 2015, that an important next step was set. By that time, the Intergovernmental Panel on Climate Change (IPCC) and many other experts had concluded that even a limitation of the global average temperature rise to 2 °C was not good enough; in order to avoid havoc, it should instead be limited to 1.5 °C above pre-industrial levels – an even harder objective, considering the temperature rise that had already taken place.

During COP21, the **Paris Agreement** was negotiated by representatives of 195 countries, and adopted by consensus on 12 December 2015. The agreement stated that it would enter into force (and thus become effective) only after 55 countries, together producing at least 55 percent of the world's GHG emissions ratify, accept, approve or accede to the agreement. The agreement became open for signature by Parties to the UNFCCC on 22 April 2016, after which a thrilling period of about half a year began. During that period, many countries ratified or otherwise formally accepted the agreement. After both China and the USA – the two biggest GHG emitters, see Figure 7.22 – formally joined on 3 September 2016, and the European Parliament ratified for itself and its 28 member nations on 5 October, both starting conditions were met. The agreement entered into force on 4 November 2016.

The Paris agreement has three interrelated goals. As the agreement formulates it:

a) *Mitigation*: 'Holding the increase in the global average temperature to well below 2 °C above pre-industrial levels and to pursue efforts to limit the temperature increase to 1.5 °C above pre-industrial levels, recognizing that this would significantly reduce the risks and impacts of climate change';
b) *Adaptation*: 'Increasing the ability to adapt to the adverse impacts of climate change and foster climate resilience and low greenhouse gas emissions development, in a manner that does not threaten food production';
c) *Finance*: 'Making finance flows consistent with a pathway towards low greenhouse gas emissions and climate-resilient development'.

In short, this means: (a) to restrict temperature rise, (b) to learn to live with the consequences of the unavoidable temperature rise and (c) to make it financially feasible and to help those who suffer the severest consequences and are not able to help themselves.

The goals of the Paris Agreement were certainly not yet sufficient. UNEP, for instance, stated that the emission cut targets would result in a temperature rise by 3 °C above pre-industrial levels. The agreement was largely seen as a first step that needed improvements in future deals, but yet an important one, as for the first time *all* major GHG emitting countries have signed and ratified. However, another major weakness of the treaty was that it was based on promises without a binding enforcement mechanism, i.e. no specific penalty gradation or fiscal pressure (e.g. a carbon tax) to discourage bad behaviour. A lot of work had yet to be done.

The first opportunity for a genuine improvement was already there on 15 October 2016, ten days after the conditions were met for the Paris Agreement to enter into force. For the Montreal Protocol on the ozone layer issue, a new treaty had become necessary. The Protocol had banned CFCs and HCFCs; the two groups of substances were phased out, as they were highly detrimental to the ozone layer. As one of the substitutes, another group of substances was widely applied: hydrofluorocarbons (HFCs). This was not really a major improvement, because not only do these also harm the ozone layer; besides, just like the abandoned CFCs and HCFCs, they contribute significantly to climate change, in spite of their low atmospheric concentration, as their per-molecule radiative forcing is extremely high.

During a conference in Kigali (Rwanda), an amendment of the Montreal Protocol was made, agreeing to a gradual 90 percent reduction of HFC production and consumption. It is estimated that this phasing-out alone reduces the global average temperature rise with 0.5 °C.

In November of the same year, right when COP22 took place in Marrakech (Morocco), a new US president was elected, who was known to be opposing actions against climate change. In June 2017, the new US president announced to withdraw his country from the Paris Agreement. In an immediate reaction, the other two major GHG emitting powers, China and the EU (see Figure 7.22), agreed to speed up and coordinate their efforts to reduce emissions. This is one reason why the consequences of the US leaving 'Paris' may perhaps not be very severe. Another reason is that global political treaties may be quickly decreasing in importance, as will be explained next.

Regional reductions and plans

It was no coincidence that the Paris Agreement was ratified by all major GHG emitting countries. Around 2016, the consequences of climate change had become painfully obvious in many parts of the world. So, a lot of countries felt the need to act drastically, and were designing or executing thorough plans, e.g. China (the biggest GHG emitting country), Japan, Brazil, India, and others.

And so did the EU. The European Union has for many years taken the initiative to set emission reduction targets and to realise them: through binding regulations; through agreements with industry, agriculture and aviation; and through economic instruments.

The initial emission reduction by the EU-15 (the 15 nations that were member states before 2004), which was promised under the Kyoto Protocol, was set to be reached somewhere between 2008 and 2012. But the target was achieved already during 2007, even by the larger EU-27: see Figure 7.23, showing data for the EU-28.

In the same year, 2007, the EU member countries agreed to set more ambitious goals, formulated in the so-called **20–20–20** package. In 2009 the agreement was enacted in legislation that was binding for all EU members. The package consisted of three targets, to be realised in 2020: to cut greenhouse gas emissions by at least 20 percent, perhaps even 30 percent, compared to 1990; to obtain at least 20 percent of its consumed energy from sustainable sources; and to increase energy efficiency with at least 20 percent.

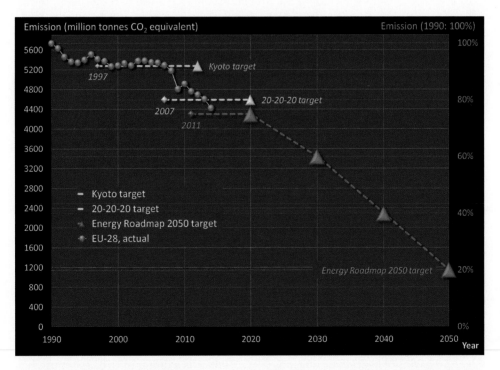

FIGURE 7.23 Emission of greenhouse gases by the EU-28 nations, 1990–2014. Targets for next decades are also shown

Source: EEA (2016).

The 20 percent emission reduction was already realised and surpassed in 2014, as Case 7.9 shows.

Case 7.9   EU greenhouse gas emissions at lowest level since 1990

European Environment Agency (EEA), www.eea.europa.eu/ highlights, 21 June 2016

European Union (EU) greenhouse gas emissions continued to decrease in 2014, with a 4.1% reduction in emissions to 24.4% below 1990 levels, according to the EU's annual inventory published today by the European Environment Agency (EEA).

The figures come from the EU annual greenhouse gas inventory submitted to the United Nations. In absolute terms, greenhouse gas emissions have decreased by 1383 million tonnes (Mt) in the EU since 1990, reaching 4282 Mt of CO2 equivalents in 2014.

The reduction in greenhouse gas emissions over the 24-year period was due to a variety of factors, including the growing share in the use of renewables, the use of less carbon intensive fuels and improvements in energy efficiency, as well as to structural changes in the economy and the economic recession. Demand for energy to heat households has also been lower, as Europe on average has experienced milder winters since 1990, which has also helped reduce emissions according to an analysis linked to the inventory.

Other findings:

- The overall reduction of 24.4% in greenhouse gas (GHG) emissions, 23% including international aviation, was accompanied by a 47% increase in gross domestic product (GDP).
- GHG emissions decreased in the majority of sectors between 1990 and 2014. Emission reductions were largest for manufacturing industries and construction (-372 Mt), electricity and heat production (-346 Mt), and residential combustion (-140 Mt).
- Not all sectors were able to reduce emissions. Road transport, responsible for the largest increase in CO2 emissions, grew by 124 Mt from 1990–2014, and 7 Mt from 2013–14.
- Emissions from international transport (aviation and shipping), which are not included in national totals reported to UNFCCC, also increased substantially between 1990 and 2014 (93 Mt).
- Emissions of hydrofluorocarbons (HFCs), which is a group of GHG gases used in the production of cooling devices such as air conditioning systems and refrigerators, also increased (99 Mt).

- EU GHG emissions were cut by 185 Mt between 2013 and 2014 (4.1%). The reduction in emissions was mainly due to lower heat demand by households due to the very warm winter in Europe. The increase in non-combustible renewables, particularly from wind and solar power also contributed to lower emissions in 2014.

  Source: Annual European Union greenhouse gas inventory 1990–2014 and inventory report 2016.

Combining the 47 percent GDP growth (from 100 percent to 147 percent) between 1990 and 2014 with the 24.4 percent emission reduction (from 100 percent to 75.6 percent), this actually amounts to nearly *doubling* the CO_2 efficiency (147 percent divided by 75.6 percent) in 24 years. While this was realised, the European competitiveness on global markets did not suffer significantly, even while other economically powerful nations and regions acted much less on emission reduction. This proved an important conclusion:

A significant GHG emission reduction did not destroy the economy, even in times when the costs of sustainable energy were higher than those of fossil fuels.

Approaching the 20 percent emission reduction target, in 2011 the EU set new goals for the next decades in the **Energy Roadmap 2050**. It was concluded that a reduction by 2050 of 80 to 95 percent was needed, to be realised fully by domestic actions, i.e. not by transferring emission processes to other parts of the world.

Analyses indicated that a cost-efficient pathway to an 80 percent reduction in 2050 called for cuts of 25 percent in 2020, 40 percent in 2030 and 60 percent in 2040, all compared to 1990 emissions. (These targets are shown in Figure 7.23 in green.) This pathway requires an annual reduction in emissions (compared to 1990) of approximately 1 percentage point in the decade up to 2020, 1.5 percentage points in the decade up to 2030 and 2 percentage points in the remaining two decades up to 2050.

Cap and trade

One of the tools the EU introduced to realise the emission targets, is a system of **emission allowances**. This system, called **EU Emissions Trading System (EU ETS)**, compels industrial and trade sectors that produce a large amount of greenhouse gases to pay for these emissions. The EU originally introduced the system so that the corporate world would comply with the Kyoto promises of its own accord in the free market.

The ETS system goes through four phases.

Phase 1 (2005–2007) was seen as an orientation phase, a pilot, characterised as 'learning by doing'. Only emissions from power generators and energy-intensive industries were covered. When the system was introduced in 2005, around 5,000 European companies received a supply of EU emission allowances (**EUA**) free of charge, collectively adding up to 2,200 million tons of CO_2 equivalent a year. Companies that exceed the allotted total had a number of options: they could purchase additional emission allowances from other companies that had a surplus of them; they could devote funds to sustainable energy, decreasing their CO_2 emissions; or they could downscale their production levels in order to cut emissions. They could also pay penalties, although these were very costly: €40 per ton.

EU ETS is a '**cap and trade**' system. The reasoning behind it is that the total quantity of EUAs would gradually decrease over the years: the 'cap'. Trading in these allowances, which would get increasingly scarce, would in turn become more and more profitable. In early 2005, when the system was launched, the value was around €6 per ton, but this soon increased to about €30 per ton within seven months: see Figure 7.24.

It emerged during 2006 and 2007 that the system was not operating according to plan, mainly for two reasons.

First, it became clear that too many allowances had been issued to companies across the EU. This widespread availability caused the prices to plummet.

Second, the EUAs for one year could be saved by companies to be spent in a later year. But it was decided that at the end of phase 1, in December 2007, such a transfer to phase 2, starting in 2008, was not allowed. Thus, approaching the end of phase 1, the trading value of the allowances went down sharply to around 0.5 euro per ton of CO_2: the yellow line in Figure 7.24.

Phase 2 (2008–2012) coincided with the target period of the Kyoto Protocol, during which the EU wanted to cut emissions with 20 percent. At the start, three non-EU countries joined the ETS system: Norway, Iceland and Liechtenstein, bringing the number of participating countries to 30. At the same time, the penalty for surplus emissions was brought to €100 per ton.

This time, having learned from the experiences of phase 1, companies were able to transfer their allowances from phase 2 to the next phase.

The phase started with a severely curtailed number of allowances. Initially, the prices at which the allowances were traded were high, again up to €30 per ton. But in 2008 the economic recession struck hard. As the industrial activities shrunk, emissions shrunk too, and the

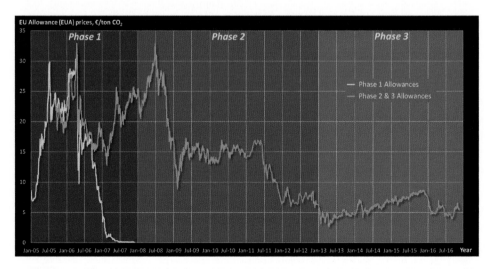

FIGURE 7.24 Prices of EU Allowances (EUAs) from the beginning in 2005 to the end of 2016
Sources: EEA (2012), Investing.com (2016).

total number of allowances again became excessive. Prices dropped to around €15 per ton. After new legislation, attempting to remove a significant percentage of EUAs, was rejected by a majority of the EU ETS members, prices went down even further to less than €10 euros, making the system hardly effective.

Phase 3 (2013–2020) is scheduled to end with the deadline of the 20–20–20 package. As Croatia entered the EU in 2013, it also entered the ETS system, bringing the number of participating countries to 31.

At the start of this phase, a major change was introduced: 57 percent of all allowances were auctioned, whereas nearly all allowances were freely allocated during phases 1 and 2. The percentage of auctioned allowances is increased annually.

More gases and sectors are included in the system; one of them is the aviation sector (since 2012). Besides, the total number of allowances is decreased annually with 1.47 percentage points (based on 1990 emissions).

Millions of allowances were set aside: they were dedicated to the **New Entrants Reserve** (**NER**), aiming at funding the deployment of innovative renewable energy technologies and carbon capture and storage.

In order to reduce the surplus amount of EUAs due to the economic crisis, the European Commission first took a short-term measure by '**backloading**', i.e. postponing the auction-ing of 900 million allowances until 2019–2020. By doing so, the commission was able to take time for a long-term solution, which was introduced in the form of a **Market Stability Reserve** (**MSR**). Starting in 2019, surplus EUAs will dynamically be allocated to this reserve, including the backloaded 900 million. Through this flexible mechanism, the EU expects to be able to keep the ETS system effective during phase 4.

Phase 4 (2021–2030) is planned to contribute to a 40 percent GHG emission reduction, being one of the milestones of the Energy Roadmap 2050. Annually, the number of allow-ances will be reduced with 2.2 percentage points.

The history of the EU ETS shows that the trading of emission allowances is a complicated process. Many mistakes were made; many lessons were learned. Nevertheless, it is estimated that the European ETS contributed significantly to the achieved GHG emission reductions.

In other parts of the world, expectations are similar. Following the EU, ETS systems have also been implied in New Zealand, Tokyo (and on a voluntary basis also the rest of Japan), South Korea, and several US states and Canadian provinces.

After ratifying the Paris Agreement in 2016, China announced that an ETS will start for the entire nation. The country already experimented with an ETS in certain regions. India and several other countries are studying the introduction of an ETS.

Competitiveness of sustainable energy

Whether or not the ETS scheme contributed significantly, the successes of the emission reduc-tion strategy of the EU proved, as said, that this can be done without losing competitiveness, even when sustainable energy prices are higher than fossil fuels. It is evident that this is all the more true when solar, wind and water energy become cheaper than energy from coal, oil or gas.

Costs of the latter are dominated by the global prices for crude oil. These prices have been highly volatile in recent years, as Figure 7.25 shows.

Theoretically, the crude oil prices should go up dramatically when peak oil is approaching, as the supplies would become scarce. Actually, the price did indeed rise sharply several times

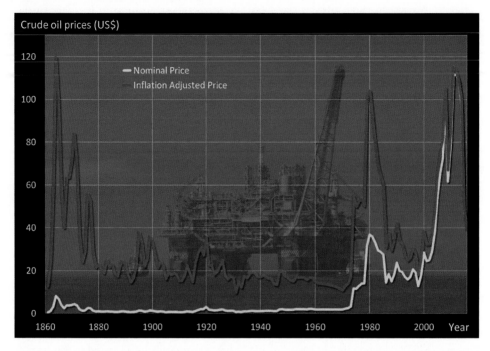

FIGURE 7.25   Crude oil prices from 1860 to 2016. 1861–1944: US Average. 1945–1983: Arabian Light. 1984–2016: Brent dated

Source: Chartsbin.com; background photo source: Agência Brasil / Divulgação Petrobras.

in the last decades; and some announced that peak oil was near. But so far, prices went down again. This makes it very hard to predict those prices in future years and decades.

It is exactly this volatility of the oil prices that causes problems to oil companies and industry. Businesses generally don't appreciate such uncertainties; this alone could make sustainable energy more attractive.

Various forms of sustainable energy have become competitive with fossil fuels in recent years. Figure 7.26 shows the price ranges for several kinds of energy in 2015. The figure clearly shows that, generally speaking, sustainable energy does not cost more than fossil energy anymore.

This becomes even more significant with the aid of Figure 7.27, which shows that there is no volatility whatsoever in the prices of the most relevant kinds of sustainable energy. Instead, they consistently go down at a rapid pace, caused by improving technologies and by growing markets that enable mass production: yet another example of positive feedback, this time reinforcing sustainable development.

It is to be expected that it will not take long before fossil energy has become unattractive worldwide, as it will both be more expensive and more uncertain at the same time. It is no wonder that energy suppliers are in search of ways to invest heavily in sustainable energy projects, as Case 7.10 illustrates. If such projects are successful, solving the climate crisis may perhaps depend less and less on international treaties like the Paris Agreement, and more on market development. Sustainability will simply outcompete fossil.

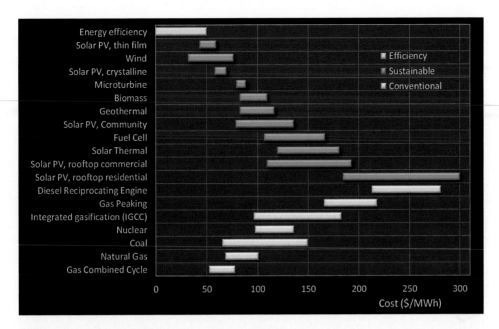

FIGURE 7.26 Costs of several kinds of energy in 2015

Source: Lazard (2015).

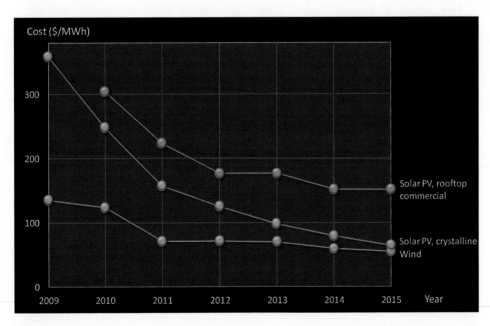

FIGURE 7.27 Development of average prices of some kinds of sustainable energy between 2009 and 2015

Source: Lazard (2015).

Case 7.10 Sahara power

2009

TREC, the Trans-Mediterranean Renewable Energy Cooperation, launched a very ambitious plan. TREC was an initiative of the German wing of the Club of Rome, together with universities, power companies and others in the entire **EU-MENA** region: that is, Europe, the Middle East and North Africa.

Why not use large parts of the Sahara as a power generator? They all wondered. Putting their money where their mouth was, they set up a foundation called Desertec: short for Desert Technology.

Shortly before, calculations had been published, estimating that the entire world could be provided with all necessary electrical energy if only a section of 254 by 254 Saharan kilometres was used for the production of solar power. (Later, this calculation appeared to be too optimistic.) This square is shown in Figure 7.28, as well as smaller squares for more limited regions.

The involved parties estimated that an investment of €400 billion ($472 billion) until the year 2050 should suffice to produce enough sustainable energy for the entire EU-MENA area.

FIGURE 7.28 Map of the ambitious Desertec plans

Source: Desertec Foundation (2011).

Plans were made for a huge power grid, connecting all EU-MENA countries. Existing sustainable power plants were studied. Experiments started, as well as negotiations with governments of involved countries.

Great benefits for Africa and the Middle East were expected: a permanent source of income from energy, large-scale employment and the gaining of expertise within the nations' own borders. Plus: sufficient power for desalinating large quantities of saltwater, allowing the desert to flourish.

2012

The Desertec programme comes close to a halt. Several problems have arisen. One of them is the political instability of countries in the Middle East and North Africa. Another is the fact that prices of sustainable energy have gone down drastically due to an increased production, causing European countries to expect they will be able to produce all energy they need within their own territories. Besides, a lack of trust has arisen between participating regions: African partners fear that mainly European countries will benefit financially form the programme.

Most of the 17 partners of the cooperation step out, including Spain, Bosch and Siemens, leaving only German RWE, Saudi Acwa Power and China State Grid. Consequently, ambitions are scaled down. Smaller projects are still carried out in Tunisia, Morocco and Algeria, now supported by the Africa Development Bank.

2016

Morocco: The *Ouarzazate* solar power station is going to be a large concentrated solar plant, with a capacity of 580 MW. An area of 2,500 hectares (6,178 acres) will be covered with CSP technology (concentrated solar power), as in Figure 7.18 (top right; see also figure 7.29). Energy will be stored daily in heated molten salt, allowing for production of electricity into the night. Phase 1 has been completed and is connected to the Moroccan power grid; it enables storage for 3 nightly hours; phase 2, to be completed by 2018, will stretch this to 8 hours. In addition, an 80 MW photovoltaic power station will be constructed.

Algeria: The *Hassi R'Mel* integrated solar combined cycle power station is less ambitious. It was already completed in 2011. The plant combines a 25 MW CSP array, covering an area of 18 hectares, together with a 130 MW combined cycle gas turbine plant.

Tunisia: The *TuNur* project will be the first CSP project that exports solar energy from Africa to Europe. It consists of a 2.25 GW (2,250 MW) CSP power plant in the Sahara, plus a 2 GW high-voltage, direct current (HVDC) submarine cable from Tunisia to Italy, north of Rome. From Italy, the energy will be transported to other European countries such as Germany, Switzerland, France and the United Kingdom.

FIGURE 7.29 Massive CSP (Concentrated Solar Power) is not only raised in Africa, but also in America, as this huge Crescent Dunes Solar Power station near Las Vegas proves

Source: Amble: Crescent Dunes Solar Energy Project.

Summary

Climate change is possibly the most serious cause of unsustainability.

- It is quite certain that the Earth's temperature is increasing at a record rate.
- The cause of this can be found in the increased concentration of certain gases in the atmosphere, causing an anthropogenic greenhouse effect. This is a very complex process, due to the presence of numerous feedbacks.
- Climate change results in a number of consequences that provisionally seem to be still more or less linear, such as rising sea levels and melting land and polar ice. But non-linear processes may also occur, which are difficult or impossible to calculate. Climate change has a great impact upon the global ecological footprint.
- Insofar as uncertainty still exists as to the cause and scope of climate change, it is wise to employ the precautionary principle.
- Technological solutions are either abundantly available or will be available within the foreseeable future. Whether nuclear fission is one of these solutions is a debatable point. A number of these solutions are coupled to a behavioural change amongst consumers.
- Political instruments have been agreed, as well as combined political-economic instrument, to implement these technical solutions, including treaties and emission trading systems.
- Economically, it is to be expected that sustainable energy will outcompete energy from fossil sources within years or a few decades.

A more detailed summary can be found on the website of this book.

8

SUSTAINABLE BUSINESS PRACTICES

In this chapter the following topics and concepts will be discussed:

8.1   Corporate social responsibility
8.2   Corporate governance
8.3   Sustainable products and services: towards a circular economy
8.4   Future-oriented entrepreneurship
8.5   The sustainably competent professional

A glossary containing all terms in both this chapter and others is available on the website of this book.

Case 8.1   Randstad aids VSO

It was one the many projects undertaken by VSO. Every year since 2012, a European expert works for a number of weeks on a voluntary basis in Bangladesh in the village of Burridhanga, contributing to improvements of the water management. This is very important work, as many years of drought have led to food scarcity. The volunteer, sent out by an organization called VSO, coordinates the work of local youth organisations. Together they constructed a system of rainwater tanks and pipes, and also a community center, and a biogas installation running on manure form the cows in and around the village.

Randstad is one of the world's largest temporary employment agencies. Starting in 2004, the commercial company entered into a joint venture to help VSO. VSO, short for Voluntary Services Overseas, is also a large employment agency, but it is not-for-profit, focusing on experts that are sent on a temporary basis as volunteers to impoverished nations. There is a great need for Western experts in developing nations, who can be temporarily utilised for overseeing projects that are undertaken by local workers. These are managers, technicians, teachers, healthcare workers and social workers, as well as farmers, environmental experts and biologists, or accountants, lawyers, IT specialists and any other field you can think of. In North America and Europe there are thousands of well-educated people who are highly motivated to perform such work for a time – many of them would gladly exchange their daily occupation for a few months to work as a volunteer in a developing nation. The companies that employ them are also often glad to cooperate.

This is where Voluntary Service Overseas comes in to act as a broker. The charity is in touch with local organisations in dozens of developing nations, and examples of their work include the establishment of a Waiting House for pregnant women in Cambodia, health and sex education to prevent HIV/Aids in southern Africa and China, psychotherapy in disaster zones, and improving education (for girls in particular) in Zambia and Namibia. The project in Bangladesh too is carried out in cooperation with a local organisation, the ngo Gram Bikash Kendra.

Finding the right experts for the work is no simple task, and it is for this purpose that Randstad's expertise has been used to support VSO. The Randstad staff is tasked with finding suitable volunteers for VSO projects, who have both the appropriate knowledge and experience. Randstad also works with companies that employ specific types of experts that VSO has an urgent need for. This allows a growing number of companies to contribute their staff for the purpose of combating poverty and aiding development around the globe.

In the final section of the previous chapter, the role was highlighted played by national governments and international cooperation with regard to finding solutions to the climate problem. But, whereas finding political agreement appeared to be a highly complicated process, it appears to be increasingly likely that commercial developments will play a major role in solving the crisis.

The final chapter of this book will examine more possibilities companies have to contribute to sustainable development. An increasing number of companies are actively doing this, for a wide range of reasons. One of these might be that they believe this is the right way to do business. Others may express concern about the future of society or of the company itself, and yet others could simply see an opportunity for profit in doing so. Companies could also contribute to sustainable development because the state helps to create a situation in which companies are, to a greater or lesser degree, forced to operate in a more sustainable manner. The introduction of CO_2 emissions trading, as discussed in the previous chapter, serves as an example of this.

Chapter 8 will deal with the various ways in which companies can engage in sustainable business practices, examining the various underlying motives for doing so and the effect in terms of profitability. Finally, the chapter will look at the role of the individual professionals in a corporation, and at the competencies expected of them in their field, both today and in the future.

8.1 Corporate social responsibility

Case 8.1 deals with a company doing something it does not automatically *have* to do. The support Randstad gives VSO is not one of the company's core activities and presumably provides no returns. The same applies, to a greater or smaller extent, to other companies engaged in **corporate social responsibility (CSR)**. But there are companies for which sustainable development is part of their very essence – their raison d'etre – in their **mission**, their **corporate mission**.

Case 8.2   The Body Shop

Since the Body Shop started in 1976, the company adheres to five basic principles. One of them is *Support Community Trade*, which means that they engage in fair trade with local groups in all parts of the world. The locals are guaranteed a fair income, and the company works together with them on the basis of equality. Local development projects are also supported, such as HIV/Aids education, schooling, preservation of culture and women's rights.

Another one of these principles is *Against Animal Testing*. The Body Shop guarantees that no products are sold in its shops that are tested on animals, and that they do not even contain any ingredients that have been tested on animals since 1991. The company is a signatory to the Humane Cosmetics Standard and is actively engaged in having animal testing for body care products outlawed in the EU, the US and in other countries.

The third principle is *Defend Human Rights*. The company has undertaken campaigns for political prisoners and against domestic violence and child labour. Every year it devotes millions to good causes.

The fourth ethos is *Protect our Planet*. The company's factories make almost exclusive use of sustainably harvested timber (FSC certified). The Body Shop works together with Greenpeace to stimulate the use of sustainable energy. Where possible, natural ingredients are used that are manufactured in an ecologically responsible manner.

The final one is *Activate Self-esteem* – the Body Shop states you must not only be good to others and to your environment but also to yourself. You can be proud of yourself without employing artifice (such as cosmetic surgery), and The Body Shop's products will help you to do this. This philosophy is a good example of how idealistic and commercial objectives can be combined.

In 2006 the Body Shop was bought by L'Oréal, after which it was feared that the acquired company would have to abandon or weaken its principles. In 2017, however, L'Oréal planned to sell the Body Shop to Natura Cosmeticos, a Brazilian multinational retail chain with equally sustainable principles.

The Body Shop releases an annual 'values report', detailing the ways in which the company has worked on these five principles. The 2015–16 report describes a new commitment called 'Enrich not Exploit'. Writing about CSR, the values report explains: "While we maintain these values today, they are less distinctive in 2016 than in 1976. It is time to move on. The key challenge facing The Body Shop at this milestone anniversary is how to orient ourselves in the new global landscape so we can achieve our aim of being the world's most ethical and truly sustainable global business." The report then goes on with describing a series of concrete goals, linked to the Triple P, which are described as: 'Enrich our People', 'Enrich our Planet', and 'Enrich our Products', titles that exhibit a smart combination of ideals and commercial interests: a philosophy that illustrates: commerce and sustainability don't have to be opponents.

Some of the concrete targets the Body Shop set for the year 2020 are:

Double our community trade programme from 19 to 40 ingredients and help enrich communities that produce them.

Ensure 100 percent of our natural ingredients are traceable and sustainably sourced, protecting 10,000 hectares of forest and other habitat.

Power 100 percent of our stores with renewable or carbon balanced energy.

Publish our use of ingredients of natural origin, ingredients from green chemistry and the biodegradability and water footprint of our products.

The first two cases in this chapter outline a great many ways in which companies can engage in CSR, and there are plenty more. A number of attempts have been made to place all these approaches in a table of sorts, one of which is included here as Table 8.1. Categories B through G on the left show a stakeholder analysis for companies – individuals and parties that, in one way or another, have a positive or negative interest in what the company does. The environment (or the natural world) and society also fall under this. This stakeholder analysis is incomplete, as there are many other stakeholders, such as those people living in the environs of a company building and NGOs, protest groups, educational institutes, consumer organisation or maybe the spouses and children of the employees, local and national authorities, trade unions or professional associations. The list goes on. They could all benefit or suffer as a result of a company's actions, e.g. by creating employment or cutting staff, by manufacturing high- or low-quality products, by purchasing raw materials or semi manufactured products, or by discharging substances into the environment, creating noise, providing local assistance, supporting associations, paying taxes and dozens of other things.

As a corporate philosophy, CSR is still relatively young, but it is growing at lightning pace. The S&P Dow Jones Index – the primary stock market indicator – is an example of the focus on it, with its '**Dow Jones Sustainability Index**' (**DJSI**), managed together with RobecoSAM. This index lists many multinational companies that are clearly operating with corporate social responsibility in mind. On the World Index, there are 24 industry groups, such as: Consumer Durables & Apparel (no. 1 in 2016: LG Electronics, Korea); Banks (#1: Westpac Banking Corp, Australia); Energy (#1: Thai Oil); Health Care Equipment & Services (#1: Abbott Laboratories, USA); and Household & Personal Products (#1: Unilever, Netherlands).

The DJSI World Index is based on the largest 2,500 companies in the Dow Jones Global Total Stock Market Index (DJGTSMI). It covers about 300 companies, which are the top-ten

TABLE 8.1 Examples of CSR topics

Category	Principles and policies (e.g. formal policy declarations)	Management system	Performance (generally quantitive data)	Public reports (e.g. annual reports, special reports, websites)
	Examples of topics			
A. Ethics	• Policy on bribery and corruption	• Assigning ethical responsibilities	• Political donations	• Description of ethical programs
B. Society	• Human rights policy in sensitive countries	• Consultation with society	• Activities in local communities	• Involvement in society
C. Management	• Code on corporate governance	• External inspection	• Management rewards	• Shareholders and voting rights
D. Customers	• Customer satisfaction • Marketing	• Responsibility for safety in production	• Quality certification	• Customer interests
E. Staff	• Health, safety • Child labour	• Profit sharing • Equal opportunities	• Education and training • Staff satisfaction	• Program for staff welfare
F. Environment	• Environmental policy declaration	• Environmental care system • Cutting emissions	• Power and water consumption • Greenhouse gas emissions	• Emissions
G. Suppliers	• Non-discrimination • Working hours, wages	• Human rights • Checking compliance	• Forced labour at suppliers	• Code of conduct for suppliers
H. Controversial topics	**Environment** • CO$_2$ generating products • GM organisms • Bioindustry	**Controversial products or services** • Alcohol, tobacco • Weapons • Pornography	**Controversial actions** • Animal testing	

Source: SiRi Group (2006).

percent regarding economic, environmental and social criteria. There are regional indices as well, e.g. Europe, Nordic, North America and Asia Pacific.

Being included in the index contributes to a company's reputation, while being suddenly removed from it will have the opposite effect.

Case 8.3   Volkswagen AG to be removed from the Dow Jones Sustainability Indices

New York and Zurich, September 29, 2015

Effective October 6, 2015, Volkswagen AG (VW) will be removed from the Dow Jones Sustainability Indices (DJSI). A review of VW's standing in the DJSI was prompted by the recent revelations of manipulated emissions tests.

Per the published and publicly available methodology for the DJSI, potential problematic issues relating to any DJSI component company automatically trigger a Media & Stakeholder Analysis (MSA), which examines the extent of the respective company's involvement and how it manages the issue. Following the MSA, the Dow Jones Sustainability Index Committee (DJSIC) reviews the issue and decides whether the company will remain in the index, based on DJSI Guidelines.

In VW's case, the DJSIC reviewed the situation and ultimately decided to remove the Company from the DJSI World, the DJSI Europe, and all other DJSI indices. The stock will be removed after the close of trading in Frankfurt on October 5, 2015, thus making the removal effective on October 6, 2015. As a result, VW will no longer be identified as an Industry Group Leader in the "Automobiles & Components" industry group.

Source: RobecoSAM (2015)

Volkswagen's removal from the index was not the first one. Every year, a couple of companies are removed. Most of them simply disappear because other companies surpass them. Thus, Intel, British American Tobacco and Samsung had to leave in 2016, making room for Royal Dutch Shell, Adobe Systems and Nissan.

But sometimes a company is deleted because of manifest misbehaviour. Like Toshiba Corporation in 2015, just like VW. And BP, in 2010, because of a fire that broke out on April 20, 2010, on the Deepwater Horizon oilrig in the Gulf of Mexico, which led to the largest oil spill the world has ever seen (Figure 8.1).

An estimated ten million litres of oil flowed into the sea every day for months, swamping the southern coast of the United States. It emerged from subsequent investigations that both safeguards against fire for the oilrig as well as attempts to deal with the problem during and after the disaster left much to be desired. BP suffered enormous damage in financial sense and to its reputation. Angry citizens boycotted BP gas stations and the company's removal from the DJSI contributed to its rapid stock market devaluation.

The DJSI aside, there is also the **World Business Council for Sustainable Development** (**WBCSD**), set up in 1991, through which over 200 international companies in more than 30 countries consult on CSR from a people-planet-profit perspective. As of 2006, there

FIGURE 8.1   April 2010. Ships try to extinguish the flames aboard Deepwater Horizon, which had capsized and by this stage was largely submerged. Eleven people were killed

Source: US Coast Guard.

has been the European Alliance for Corporate Social Responsibility. CSR is clearly mushrooming, and there are numerous reasons behind its growth.

Motivations for CSR

One reason for corporate social responsibility is the great amount of power wielded by customers. When it comes to most companies, this is not so much due to efforts at advertising or building up a good image – there are even companies who prefer not to highlight their social projects, fearing that consumers might think they're only doing it for show. Conversely, there is of course a risk that companies which avoid corporate social responsibility will develop a poor reputation and, as with the 2010 BP drama, a negative image can be disastrous. Another well-known example is the controversy generated when Google agreed to provide Internet service in China under the condition that it adhere to the Chinese government's censorship laws. Though the company itself was not violating freedom of speech, it was working together with a government that did. An incident like this can adversely affect a company's image, and the damage can last for years. Almost all companies are well aware of the power of the civil society, i.e. the combination of consumers, the media, critical citizens and protest groups. The combined consumers' power is illustrated by Table 8.2, a part of the magazine of a consumers' organization.

TABLE 8.2 Example of a CSR assessment in a consumer magazine

Corporate social responsibility in banana production

Banana brand	Environment			Social aspects					Transparency	
	Environmental policy	Use of pesticides	Other environmental measures	Verification and certification	Labour rights	Inspection for labour rights	Communal and economic development	Final checks and certification	Involvement in Consumers' Association inspection	Voluntary public reports
Bonita	□	□	□	–	–	–	–	–	□	–
Chiquita	+	+	+	+	+	□	□	□	□	+
Consul	+	+	+	+	+	□	□	□	□	+
Del Monte	□	□	□	–	–	–	–	–	–	□
Dole	+	□	□	+	+	□	□	–	+	+
Ekoke Max Havelaar	+	+	+	+	+	+	+	+	+	+
Fyffes	+	+	□	–	+	□	□	–	+	–
Turbana	□	□	□	–	–	()	+	–	–	□

\+ Complies with Consumers' Association requirements
□ Partial compliance   Consumer magazine April 2004, pg. 49
– Non-compliance
() Insufficient information
Source: Consumer Guide (2004).

The power of the customer is one of the reasons behind corporate social responsibility. Should the primary reason for this endeavour be a company's image, then we can call this 'window-dressing', although this is rarely the sole reason. A wide range of motives could play a role, and in detailing them **Maslow's hierarchy of needs**, a well-known model for detailing the motives of individuals, can also be applied to companies, as in Figure 8.2. Some motives relate to protecting the existence of the company, while others involve window-dressing. But there are also motives that concern the sincere intention of being something that is good for society.

Questions

- Do you think the primary aim of Randstad and The Body Shop is window-dressing, or maybe securing the company's existence or increasing profits? Or are their motives rather sincerely intended to make a positive contribution to society?
- Could it be a combination of all these motives for the companies, and if so, is that a bad thing?
- What would be the case for the majority of companies?

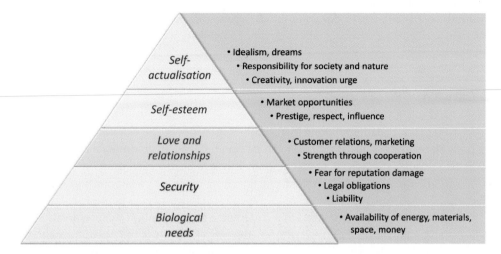

Self-actualisation
- Idealism, dreams
  - Responsibility for society and nature
  - Creativity, innovation urge

Self-esteem
- Market opportunities
- Prestige, respect, influence

Love and relationships
- Customer relations, marketing
- Strength through cooperation

Security
- Fear for reputation damage
- Legal obligations
- Liability

Biological needs
- Availability of energy, materials, space, money

FIGURE 8.2   Motives for CSR according to Maslow's hierarchy of needs

Source: www.5thpillar.org.

From shareholder to stakeholder

The traditional image of a commercial, listed company is that there is ultimately one group of interested parties involved, and these are the shareholders, or in America the stockholders: the collective owners of the company. As long as they make a good profit on their shares every year they are satisfied, and it means the company has **shareholder value**. But, according to the rapidly spreading CSR concept, a paradigm shift is occurring, known as '*from shareholder to stakeholder*', and in recent years the term **stakeholder value** has also been bandied about. A company holds this latter value if it not only provides something for the shareholders but also for the other interested parties (stakeholders) too. It is not uncommon for there to be a conflict of interest between the shareholders and the other stakeholders, with shareholders frequently focusing on the short term (high stock prices and quick prices) while society prefers to fight for long-term goals, such as employment and a healthy environment. The stakeholder value is, from the point of view of society, the reason why a company exists and can continue to exist – because it contributes something to society.

Questions

- Think of a company you are familiar with. What exactly does that company contribute to society?
- In your opinion, are there sufficient reasons why that company exists, and why it should *continue* to exist?
- Do you know of any companies that have insufficient reasons for existing, ones that we could do just as well without?

To date it might seem as if CSR only played a role in the very large companies, but this is not true, as the following case proves. It involves a company that is an **SME**, a small- or medium-sized enterprise. In this company they have considered who the stakeholders are, based on a stakeholder analysis. And they're doing something with it too.

Case 8.4 "Pizza Fusion"

Making pizza. . . can it be done in a sustainable manner? The Florida-based company Pizza Fusion is proving that it can be done, taking environmental and social issues seriously. In addition to its company mission, Pizza Fusion even has its own environmental mission, which reads:

> "Pizza Fusion is committed to a sustainable future through the preservation and improvement of the environment with all aspects of our operations and existence. We strive to improve the social, economic and environmental well-being of the world through:
>
> - *The support of sustainable business by seeking out environmentally conscious vendors and suppliers to partner with*
> - *Our commitment to environmental education to raise awareness for more sustainable approaches to living and business*
> - *Educating the general public on the importance of sustainable living through ecological community service, consumer education and environmental mentoring*
> - *Lobbying for political action to support a more sustainable future*
> - *The support of organic agriculture*
> - *The continuous evaluation of our ecological impact in our endless pursuit to minimize our environmental footprint"*

While providing a menu featuring organic pizzas, salads, sandwiches, wines and beer, Pizza Fusion makes deliveries using hybrid vehicles that consume less fossil fuel and emit less carbon into the atmosphere. The company offers employees who work more than 20 hours a week health insurance – quite a rarity among foodservice businesses in the United States. Pizza Fusion makes pizza in energy-efficient buildings constructed to LEED standards (Leadership in Energy and Environmental Design). The pizzeria is a commercial success – it is growing from an SME to a large company, expanding into California, Colorado, Connecticut, New Jersey, and Ohio, with new locations on several American college campuses.

8.2 Corporate governance

Pizza Fusion explains its policy on sustainability on its website, and The Body Shop releases a values report every year, both of which are examples of a new openness demonstrated by modern companies. An increasing number of companies are being frank about their actions, explaining them to the public, not only taking responsibility for them, but also accounting for them – they are **accountable** for their actions. In Table 8.1 it consumes the entire right column. These annual reports are often called a 'social report' or a 'sustainability report', and they can be downloaded off the websites of almost all major as well as many smaller companies. Standards have been developed for these reports, which indicate how such a report can be constructed in a systematic manner, allowing for the reports from different companies to be compared to each other. The best-known standard is the **Global Reporting Initiative (GRI)**, an international organisation for the standardisation of CSR reporting. When companies publish internal information it is known as **transparency**, and this openness towards employees, governments, NGOs, the press and society in general is considered one of the most important elements of CSR – let everyone see what you are doing. Many companies use the term **ESG** for this, which stands for **environmental, social and governance** issues – a triptych that is closely related to the Triple P.

Accepting responsibility and being held accountable – these are things that not only concern commercial companies, but are just as applicable to non-profit organisations such as governments, schools and care institutions.

Case 8.5 Dealing with child abuse

A few years ago it was established, in one modern hospital, that cases of child abuse were almost never recorded. This was striking, as in other hospitals this was a regular occurrence – cases of physical or psychological abuse, sexual abuse or negligence, mostly by the children's own parents. It was unlikely that there was much less abuse in the area served by this hospital than there was in the rest of the country. Therefore, it was obvious that the hospital staff were not succeeding in exposing it.

Most doctors and nurses, including the accident and emergency unit, were not concerned – an out of sight, out of mind attitude. But a small group of staff members believed things had to change. They set up a work group. An in-house course for the staff was developed. How does one recognise child abuse? When does a broken arm, bruises, burns, scars or damaged genitalia indicate abuse? How do you recognise a parent's lie, such as 'She fell down the stairs!'? What do you do if you suspect child abuse? All these things were dealt with in the course.

A fair number of doctors and nurses resisted, fearing extra work, furious parents, possible legal consequences and their own fears and emotions. But the work group persisted, with support from the hospital board, and an increasing number of their colleagues became enthusiastic about the issue. Today, a few years later, cases of child abuse are identified every week. Every year around a hundred children are rescued from a violent family situation, and some of them from death.

This case demonstrates something else that is of interest – bearing social responsibility is not just the job of a company as a whole, or of just its managers. In Case 8.5 the institute was clearly failing with regard to what society could expect of it, something that a small portion of the staff refused to accept and subsequently took measures to remedy – successfully. They demonstrated an essential characteristic of professionals acting in a sustainable manner and, in weighing up the official directives issued by their employer and their own consciences, they opted for the latter – their own personal responsibility. Acting responsibly is thus also the job of *every* individual member of staff, or in any event it should be.

Should the management and workers of a company have such competences and use them in their actions, then corporate social responsibility is deeply ingrained in the nature of that company. Running a company in such an accountable and transparent way is called '**corporate governance**', which might literally merely refer to running a company, but in reality comes closer to the idea of decent management. Good corporate governance includes integrity and transparency, proper control, accountability, and preventing the extravagant remuneration of top executives.

Another controversial theme is corruption. In many countries, companies and citizens can achieve little when dealing with authorities unless managers or public officials are bribed. This is a thorny issue, for if you refuse to accede, there is a very good chance that what you want will simply not happen – a passport, a permit to buy a house or office building, an export permit, etc. For companies this is a typical example of the prisoner's dilemma – should every single company refuse to engage in corruption, these practices would soon disappear, but if just a few companies pay a bribe, then the rest can choose between following suit or shutting the company's doors for good. However, in India a successful counter-assault has been devised.

Case 8.6   You get zero rupees!

India Times, Rishabh Banerji, March 18, 2016

"On 22 April 2011, I took an auto to Chennai Domestic Airport to board a flight at 10:40 AM. The auto I was traveling on was stopped at the entrance of the Airport and I was asked to walk with my luggage all the way to the domestic airport. It was a long walk from the entrance and as I had my luggage, I asked the policeman the reason for him to stop all the vehicles at the entrance. I got a very "standoffish" reply from him saying that he is not the person to be questioned and he is simply following the instructions given to him by the Airport manager. I got out from the auto and handed over a Zero Rupee Note to him, explaining that he can use it when someone asks him for a bribe, such as when he needs to get an electricity or water connection for his residence (Figure 8.3).

He looked intrigued by the note and I went on to tell him that when he hands this Zero Rupee Note to any authority he would get his services without having to pay the bribe; and if there is some resistance or unwarranted delay he can contact the address indicated at the back of the Zero Rupee Note and action would be taken right away. I told him that we have chapters in all the districts of Tamil Nadu

FIGURE 8.3   Zero rupees

Source: 5th Pillar (2016).

and also in major cities in India, and we would inform the vigilance department if we receive the complaint from the public and follow up on the action.

The policeman said that the auto can go inside and drop the passenger in the Domestic Airport entrance. This is a victory for the Zero Rupee Note and I feel happy to know that we are able to get our rights without having to indulge in confrontation and by just handing over a Zero Rupee Note and creating awareness that we have an organization to back up against corruption and bribery."

The organisation 5th Pillar has been set up in India to combat bribery and corruption. They have printed and distributed millions of Zero Rupee notes, mainly through schools and universities. The notes bear the statement: "I promise to neither accept nor give bribe." The organisation hopes to print at least another 200 million banknotes – one for every Indian family. High-resolution versions of them can also be downloaded from their website.

The initiative was imitated in other countries too, and on the http://zerocurrency.org website you can download banknotes for zero American, Canadian and Australian dollars, UK pounds, Euros, Russian roubles, Turkish lira, Chinese renminbi, Japanese yen and over a hundred other currencies, as Figure 8.4 shows.

The **Caux Round Table**, an international network of senior managers at major companies, spend time considering the principles of corporate governance. They discuss social guidelines for the corporate world, and in their vision CSR is based on two basic ethical principles. The one is a Japanese term, **kyosei**, which means: living and working together for the common good enabling cooperation and mutual prosperity to coexist with healthy and fair competition.

FIGURE 8.4 That's a lot of zero money . . .

Background photo source: Vincenzo Reina, flickr.

The other principle is **human dignity**, a principle under which the sacredness or value of each person is an goal in itself, not simply as a means to the fulfilment of others' purposes or even of a majority.

One of the founders of the Caux Round Table was Frits Philips, who spent years as the head of the board of the eponymous Philips company. He explained the principles of CSR as follows:

> "Firstly, we must enter into an open dialogue and learn to listen more closely to each other, where we are not overly concerned with reaching consensus but rather with understanding each other. Secondly, we must strive for true friendship and trust. Thirdly, consider the fundamental ethical issues, and allow yourself to be guided by clear values and an understanding of responsibility. And finally, do not make assertions about what others ought to do, but rather propose personal actions in the different organisations and environments that you are a part of."

8.3 Sustainable products and services: towards a circular economy

It is great when companies accept responsibility, but that also raises the question of how they could do this in practice, should they manufacture products or provide services and want to do so in a manner that takes the interests of the environment and sustainable development into account.

Products

When it comes to **sustainable product development**, a great deal of knowledge and experience has been acquired. A significant and fundamental insight is that, as a manufacturer, one does not in reality create one product, but rather a *product life cycle*. This entails questions such as: where do the raw materials come from? How are they transported and what are the consequences thereof? How do the consumers of the produced goods use them? How much waste is created and where is it stored?

Much research is required, even for simple products, to respond to such questions. A notable example of this is a can of soda, shown in Figure 8.5. The entire history of this can of soda, or of any other product, is called the **ecological rucksack** of the product, with the idea behind the rucksack being that a person holding it in his or her hands is in essence holding much more than just that product – including a stockpile of resources, a large quantity of manufacturing processes and transportation, including oil, natural gas, human labour, the discharge of gasses into the atmosphere and liquids into the rivers and oceans, and many other things are all part of the package.

The rucksack of the can of soda can be seen in Figure 8.6. The illustration in reality is still far from complete, as it primarily examines the origin of the can, and does not consider other materials, such as the printing ink, the cardboard for the boxes or the plastic for the crates. And the schedule barely considers the waste flows that arise at almost every production step. A number of these can be guessed, such as the conversion of one ton of bauxite into half a ton of aluminium oxide – what happens to the other half ton?

Questions

- If you follow the steps in Figure 8.6, do you get a rough idea of all the waste created in the process?
- What would this mean to you, the next time you drink a can of soda?

FIGURE 8.5   Can with rucksack

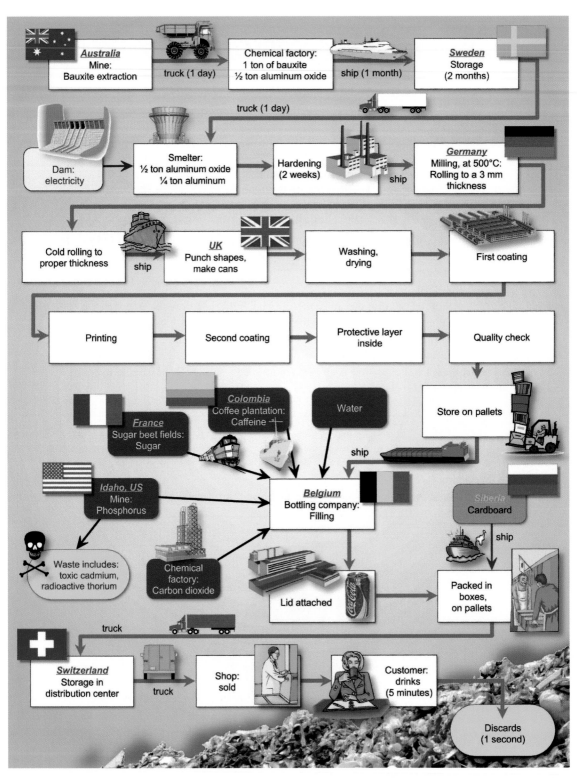

FIGURE 8.6 In the 'rucksack' of a can of soda

Data derived from: Womack and Jones (1996); Hawken et al (1999).

A knowledge of the content of this rucksack is the first step towards sustainable production. The next step would involve furthering that knowledge so that it can be used to calculate the steps to consumption. A much-used system for this is the **life cycle assessment (LCA)**, through which we endeavour to calculate in full the impact of a product, including the depletion of stocks, the damage to the environment, the influence on the greenhouse effect and many others. This calculation is undertaken for the entire **life cycle** of a product, from the extraction of the raw materials, through the production process and the consumption by the consumer, until the phase in which the product is recycled, reused or discarded. All these effects can be expressed in a points system, '**eco points**', with the aid of a method called the '**Eco-indicator**'.

Case 8.7   The LCA for two coffee makers

An LCA was undertaken for two coffee makers in order to compare the environmental impact of each one. The results are displayed in Figure 8.7. When only manufacturing is taken into account, the aluminium coffee maker is worse for the environment than the plastic one: more eco points. But when the entire life cycle is taken into account, it is the other way round. Of all the environmental damage caused by the apparatus, the power consumed when making coffee is by far the greatest – much greater than any effect during the production process. The aluminium model has a thermos flask for the coffee, while the plastic one uses a warming plate, which consumes more power.

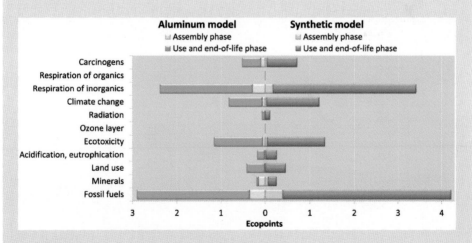

FIGURE 8.7   LCA comparison of two coffee makers

Source: Pré (2007).

Try it yourself

A program can be downloaded from the website of this book, called **EPU.exe**. Using this software – a *serious game* – the reader can undertake simple product design, based on a simplified version of the eco points system, under the name 'environmental pollution unit' (EPU: see Figure 8.8).

Towards a circular economy

Sustainable product development, making use of rucksacks and LCAs, is a first step towards a fundamentally new global economic system, called '**circular economy**'. The process from traditional economic activities towards circularity is happening right now, and it is set to profoundly change the way we do business.

The principles of a circular economy are shown in Figure 8.9. Fundamental to the circular paradigm is the 'two cycles' principle: the '**Technical Cycle**' (also called a 'Technological Cycle' or a 'Technology Cycle') and the '**Biological Cycle**'. They can be applied to all kinds of products, varying from dairy products that are consumed as food, other agricultural products such as wooden shelves, to technological equipment containing many components made of metal, plastics and other materials. You can also think of combinations, like food products contained in a plastic package.

An example of a product going through the double cycle is shown in Figure 8.9 as a yellow 'figure 8': the archetypal shape of a circular economic process. The yellow line may e.g. be related

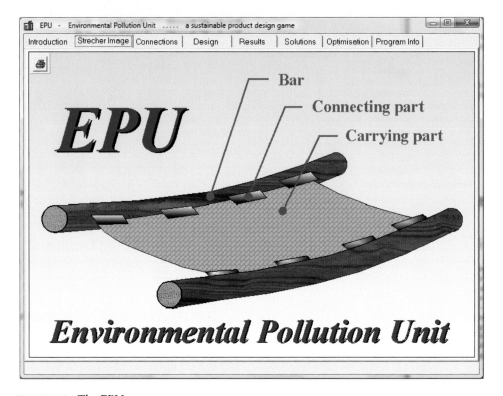

FIGURE 8.8   The EPU program

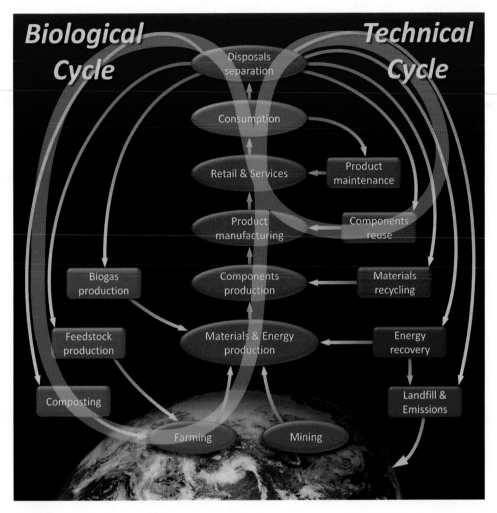

FIGURE 8.9   The two cycles of a circular economy

to a bamboo rod, which is used as a component of a piece of furniture that is sold by a retailer, used by a consumer, and after some time disposed. Continuing through the technical cycle, the furniture may be disassembled after which the bamboo rod is reused for another product. Next, if it is again disposed, it may be composted, on the condition that it was never painted or otherwise chemically preserved. After the compost is used for farming, the double loop is closed.

Actually, a circular economy is much more than just closing loops. The transition from a traditional to a circular economy can be seen as consisting of a number of steps.

1 Waste is a resource. Instead of attributing a negative value to our disposals and throwing them away, we become aware of their positive value. They are collected, separated and used wherever possible. Even more so: not only are the disposables reutilized, they are so at the highest achievable quality, as Figure 8.9 illustrates. For the technical cycle, a **waste hierarchy** is applied. The highest level in this ranking is: try to keep the product in use as long as possible, based on maintenance and repairs. When this is no longer possible (technically or economically), the components are taken apart and reused for new products – if possible.

There are exceptions, where it is not desirable to keep products or components in use as long as possible. A counter example are cars that were produced decades ago, as they will be consuming lots of energy and producing highly polluting emissions: it may be much better to replace them with entirely new cars. Another example: using throwaway paper cups is not necessarily worse than using pottery, as washing those after use takes heat and clean water; which of the two is ecologically more sound, depends on the circumstances, as LCAs have shown.

2 Design for disassembly (DFD). In order to increase the options to reuse entire components – the second level of the waste hierarchy – the product is designed so that its parts can be taken apart without damaging them. Of course, whether this is possible depends on technical demands regarding quality, safety, health aspects, etc. For instance, it means that – if acceptable – parts are not glued or welded together but screwed or clicked. Laminates, e.g. of paper and plastic layers for food packaging, were to be avoided until recently, as they could not be separated after use; however, new technologies have brought new options for this.

If component reuse is not possible or desirable, the next level in the waste hierarchy is, to recycle the materials. The components are shredded or molten, the materials are separated (or vice versa) and used for new products. In some cases, the materials don't return to the original quality, and they have to be **downcycled** to lower-quality products.

If even that is no longer possible, the last option is **energy recovery**, which means that the waste is burned: at high temperatures, to avoid emission of toxic gases. The remainder may end up as landfill or as emissions into the atmosphere or surface water, which is the worst possible outcome, as it causes the cycle to open up instead of being closed.

3 Substitution. Instead of using one-time materials, renewables are used, contributing to the ability to close material loops. New, sensational developments in materials technology allow for thrilling innovations.

4 New technologies. The same is true for other kinds of technology, allowing the use of less materials (*dematerialisation*) and energy, not only during manufacturing but also while products are used. Nanotechnology and biotechnology are good examples. Another nice example is the 3D printer, which allows products to be made on demand and **just in time (JIT)**, avoiding wasting valuable materials.

5 Integral chain management. There are only a few manufacturers that directly control the entire life cycle of their products themselves. In reality, almost every company deals with suppliers, intermediaries and shops. Most companies were not traditionally occupied with the entire chain, focusing primarily on only two of the links – manufacturing and sales. This is changing rapidly, with companies trying to control not only the quality of their own production and sales processes but also those in the other phases of the life cycle of their products.

If cooperation is arranged between the companies that are involved in the various phases of the chain, including the disposal phase, integral chain management leads to a **Cradle to Cradle (C2C)** approach, resulting in closed loops. Case 8.8 offers a nice example.

At the same time, the real costs of a product are calculated. Aside from the technical and environmental LCA, there is also an economic model called **Lifecycle Cost Analysis (LCCA)** that calculates the complete cost price of a product, including the maintenance and repair costs and those involved in the removal, disassembly, reuse and recycling or discarding thereof. Whereas LCCAs not always include environmental consequences, related methods do, such as **Whole-Life Cost**.

6 From product to service. When companies stay involved in the products they manufactured, even in the consumption phase and the disposal phase, the relation with products and with customers changes. The producer stays responsible for malfunctions, even in a legal way, and in several sectors also for collecting the disposed products: see Case 1.5. The customer, on the other hand, stays dependable on the producer or at least of the retailer, for maintenance and repairs, and for returning the product at end-of-life. It is only natural that their interaction is changing from a one-time contact to a permanent mutual relation.

For photocopiers, this has been so for many years. The copying equipment usually was not bought and sold but leased. For cars and mobile phones, this is increasingly the case. In the Business-to-Business (B2B) world, the same is true for many kinds of machinery. A major consequence is that the customer actually does not pay for a *product* but rather for a *service*. A car leasing company does not provide a car but *mobility*. If the car malfunctions, that's not the customer's problem but the producer's: the garage has the obligation to repair immediately or else to deliver another car, so that the customer can continue moving.

A good B2B example is "pay per lux," a principle that was developed by Philips in collaboration with architect Thomas Rau. According to this principle, as a company, you don't buy lamps but rather light. (Hence the name: "lux" is a measure for luminance or brightness.) That is to say, Philips designs the illumination scheme in the laboratories and offices of a customer based on the customer's needs. Philips installs the armatures and lamps. Philips also pays for the electricity, replaces failing lamps and adapts the lighting when the company changes. In other words, Philips is no longer a product seller but a service provider.

There are many advantages. The customer, a company paying 'per lux', doesn't have to take care of the lighting anymore since the service provider guarantees that everything works. In the past, some people used to say that light bulbs were produced in such a way that they would fail sooner rather than later ('planned obsolescence'); otherwise, the light bulb industry would not make enough money. With the new approach however, planned obsolescence is unthinkable because if the lights don't last, the only one suffering is the provider itself. The provider also has an advantage: Instead of one-time contract while selling lamps, the provider now establishes an ongoing connection with customers, who will stay as long as they are satisfied.

7 Biomimicry. Closed loops were not invented by humans; they have existed for hundreds of millions of years. Actually, our imitation of natural processes, *biomimicry*, may go far beyond just closing loops.

Natural environments consist of many interrelated loops, together forming a complex ecosystem. In the same way, the human world consists of many different and interrelated processes; closing all material loops will be just as complex, as they influence each other in many ways, e.g. due to scarcity: of raw materials, energy, production capital, customer money, customer attention, etc. Therefore, terms like 'life cycle' and 'chain management' are not strong enough to describe what is needed, as they seem to suggest that product cycles are one-dimensional processes without external links. In reality, it would be better to replace 'cycle' with 'network' or even better: 'system', thus speaking of 'network analysis' or even 'system analysis'.

Optimising not just one-dimensional cycles but real networks is highly complicated. Biological ecosystems – which are *ecological* systems – developed in the course of millions of years thanks to evolution. Human ecosystems – which are *economic* and *social* as well as ecological systems – have arisen during processes that may have some resemblance to evolution, but really is fundamentally different in many aspects. Although we can learn a lot from studying nature, we cannot afford to wait for slowly evolving economic processes to gradually become sustainable all by themselves – if they would ever do that. Instead, designing our agricultural and industrial processes cleverly, to make them link with each other efficiently, is a main task of sustainability science. This requires a new way of thinking – a paradigm shift – and a profound systemic transformation, a *transition*.

8 Systems thinking. For the purpose of such a transition, new theoretical and technological developments have become available in the last decades, to fulfil the complicated task of transforming the economy. Nowadays, we possess tools like *complexity theory*, *game theory*, simulations, self-learning neural networks, virtual reality, the ability to handle big data, and more. These are strong tools that help us to think in a genuinely integrated and holistic way, at a complex and systemic level. Together, these and other methods and ways of thinking will help us to make the transition towards a circular economy.

This transition is the one that was announced in Section 3.1, telling about bringing the Triple P in balance. If successful, it will bring the P of 'profit' in better harmony with the Ps of 'people' and 'planet'.

Case 8.8   The suppliers of Philips

The electronics company Philips has a huge number of suppliers and business relatives, totalling 40,000. The company purchases over 15 billion euros in acquisitions from them every year, amounting to two-thirds of total turnover. The contracts the company has signed with them are based on the 'Philips Supplier Sustainability Declaration', which includes CSR demands, e.g. a list of substances and materials that are not permitted. Every supplier must sign the agreement, which means that each of them declares that they are acting in a sustainable manner; and, on top of that, demands the same from their own suppliers. And Philips checks on compliance too: through 'Supplier Sustainability Audits' by independent external organisations. Any company not complying with the sustainability requirements is granted the opportunity to remedy these errors, but should that not happen within a given time then the company will lose its Philips contract. In order to assist the suppliers, Philips provides training courses in sustainable business practices in e.g. China, India, Brazil and Mexico. Companies wishing to supply Philips can also assess themselves through a *self-assessment* method.

Philips itself acts as a role model. In the four years from 2011 till 2015, energy consumption in manufacturing decreased with 20 percent. In the eight-year period between 2007 and 2015, GHG emissions decreased with 58 percent, water consumption with 32 percent, release of hazardous substances with 93 to 100 percent.

Philips is also a strong performer when it comes to the people aspect. Soon after it was founded in 1891 the company became well known for taking care of its employees and their families through education, health and pension schemes, which was highly unusual at that time – and still is, in many companies. One of the children of that tradition is the soccer club PSV (Philips Sport Association).

Philips does not use child labour. The proportion of women at executive levels is not excellent, but improving: from 5 percent in 2005 up to 10 percent in 2008 followed by 18 percent in 2015. (Overall in 2015, 35 percent of all Philips employees were female.)

The services industry

There are also other fields that deal with variations on integral chain management, which are not focussed on manufacturing tangible products but rather on providing humanitarian services. This includes areas such as healthcare, education, banking, and public administration, or public servants, amongst others. The primary purpose of an integral approach in the services sector is not to cut environmental damage but rather involves focusing on another aspect of sustainability – human dignity. The life cycle involved here does not consequently involve that of a can of soda but that of a human being, or of a family, a class of schoolchildren or a municipality. Instead of integral chain management, this might involve **integral healthcare**, for example, which concentrates on coordinating all facets of healthcare, both the medical and psychosocial ones.

Case 8.9   The patient who receives the doctors

The Orbis Medical Centre has adopted a new approach to healthcare. In many hospitals it is the patient that visits the specialists, and if a person has to see three specialists and the meetings cannot be coordinated, then he or she shall probably have to visit the hospital on three separate days, and thus have to take three different days off from school or work. But things work differently with Orbis, where a patient has a personal consulting room where the specialists come to see him or her, one after the other in immediate succession, where possible. 'The patient is the point of focus,' is the concept.

Patients that are hospitalised all have a computer on their bedsides, where they can see their complete medical files, allowing them to always control their own treatment plans. What often happens in most hospitals is that, should a number of physicians be involved in dealing with a variety of complaints, they are not even aware of each other. This could result in drugs being prescribed that cannot be combined. In Orbis every doctor is kept informed of everything that is done to a patient.

Scheduling for physiotherapy and, where necessary, counselling is started immediately after surgery, and patients undergo an initial session the very next day. The Orbis Medical Centre demonstrates what emancipation really means – in this case, for the patient.

Approaches such as that in Case 8.9 mean that people are not treated like 'medical objects' but like real humans. In the same manner, a paradigm shift has occurred in many educational institutions from the 'teacher is the point of focus' to 'the student is the point of focus', so that the learning processes and methods of individual students have become the determining factor for how the teaching takes shape. Under this method, it is not only the education in the present school or university that is of concern, but the chain as well – kindergarten, primary school, secondary school, university, career, retirement. The processes of learning do not cease once official education is concluded, and the phrase **'life-long learning'** is the educational equivalent of integral chain management for manufacturing companies.

8.4 Future-oriented entrepreneurship

One of the motivations behind sustainable business practices in Maslow's hierarchy of needs, as shown in Figure 8.2, is the urge of creativity and innovation. These are important forces for sustainable development and are indispensable to sustainable transitions. Bright and imaginative entrepreneurs – in many cases young and just starting off – contribute to a sustainable future through surprising innovations. One could label this approach 'future-oriented entrepreneurship'.

Case 8.10   Meet the meat: 3D printed – or even lab-cultured?

Cnet.com, 26 February 2013

3D printed meat: it's what's for dinner

3D printing has been used to create running shoes, medical implants, and, to the delight of firearm enthusiasts, a .22 calibre handgun. So why not a 3D-printed steak for the grill?

Billionaire investor Peter Thiel's philanthropic foundation plans to announce today a six-figure grant for bioprinted meat, part of an ambitious plan to bring to the world's dinner tables a set of technologies originally developed for creating medical-grade tissues.

The recipient of the Thiel Foundation's grant, a Columbia, Missouri-based startup named Modern Meadow, is pitching bioprinted meat as a more environmentally-friendly way to satisfy a natural human craving for animal protein. Co-founder Andras Forgacs has sharply criticized the overall cost of traditional livestock practices, saying "If you look at the resource intensity of everything that goes into a hamburger, it is an environmental train wreck."

"Modern Meadow is combining regenerative medicine with 3D printing to imagine an economic and compassionate solution to a global problem," said Lindy Fishburne, executive director of Breakout Labs, a project of the Thiel Foundation. "We hope our support will help propel them through the early stage of their development, so they can turn their inspired vision into reality."

BBC News, 5 August 2013

A hamburger of £215,000

The world's first lab-grown burger has been cooked and eaten at a news conference in London. Scientists took cells from a cow and, at an institute in the Netherlands, turned them into strips of muscle that they combined to make a patty. Researchers say the technology could be a sustainable way of meeting what they say is a growing demand for meat.

The burger was cooked by chef Richard McGeown, from Cornwall, and tasted by food critic Josh Schonwald. Upon tasting the burger, Mr Schonwald said: "The mouthfeel is like meat. I miss the fat, there's a leanness to it, but the general bite feels like a hamburger."

Prof Mark Post, of Maastricht University, the scientist behind the burger, remarked: "It's a very good start." The professor said the meat was made up of tens of billions of lab-grown cells. Asked when lab-grown burgers would reach the market, he said: "I think it will take a while. This is just to show we can do it."

Sergey Brin, co-founder of Google, has been revealed as the project's mystery backer. He funded the £215,000 ($330,000) research.

Stem cells are the body's 'master cells', the templates from which specialised tissue such as nerve or skin cells develop. Most institutes working in this area are trying to grow human tissue for transplantation to replace worn-out or diseased muscle, nerve cells or cartilage. Prof Post is using similar techniques to grow muscle and fat for food.

He starts with stem cells extracted from cow muscle tissue. In the laboratory, these are cultured with nutrients and growth-promoting chemicals to help them develop and multiply. Three weeks later, there are more than a million stem cells, which are put into smaller dishes where they coalesce into small strips of muscle about a centimetre long and a few millimetres thick. These strips are collected into small pellets, which are frozen. When there are enough, they are defrosted and compacted into a patty just before being cooked.

The Guardian, 5 August 2013

How the world's costliest burger made it on to the plate

"Cows are very inefficient – they require 100g of vegetable protein to produce only 15g of edible animal protein," Post told the Guardian before the event in London. "We need to feed the cows a lot so that we can feed ourselves. We lose a lot of food that way." With cultured meat, scientists can make meat production more efficient because they can keep all the variables under control. They also do not need to slaughter any cows.

The human appetite for meat means that 30% of the Earth's usable surface is covered by pasture land for animals, compared with just 4% used directly to feed humans. The total biomass of our livestock is almost double that of the people on the planet and accounts for 5% of carbon dioxide emissions and 40% of methane emissions – a much more potent greenhouse gas.

Different methods of growing meat in labs will have different impacts on the environment, and Post said early indications were that his lab meat reduced the need for land and water by 90% and cut overall energy use by 70%.

> **Questions**
>
> - Would you eat this type of cultured or printed meat if it was available in shops?
> - Do you believe it is ethically responsible to utilise nature in this way?

Survival of the company

There are also other reasons why companies adopt future-oriented business practices. Figure 8.2, Maslow's pyramid for business, shows concerns, e.g. about the availability of raw materials, as well as opportunities, including market opportunities. A significant number of companies consider sustainable development important simply because they perceive that if society cannot be sustained, neither can the company. However, some companies are more preoccupied with their future than others.

Case 8.11 Future-proof?

The future is uncertain, especially in the midst of transitions. This is certainly true for the information technology revolution, and has been for several decades, in which some companies saw the opportunity to anticipate radically to the changes, while others were less inclined.

Xerox

In 1938, the very first photocopy was generated in a New York laboratory. The first photocopier appeared in 1949. The process, called 'xerography', was owned by a company that called itself the Xerox Corporation from 1961 onwards, describing itself as 'The Copying Company'.

But the company did not stop there. Beginning in 1970, Xerox also investigated computer technology. As computers were starting to conquer the world, Xerox realised at an early stage that there would come a day when computer monitors and hard drives would largely replace the role of paper documents. If that were to happen, the use of photocopiers would decline and this would ultimately – maybe only after decades had passed – spell the end for the Xerox Corporation.

This perspective of the future resulted in the company adopting a drastic change of course in the 1990s, when it launched a new image and officially called itself 'The Document Company'. On top of photocopiers, the company placed a larger focus on products and services for digital information and documentation.

Xerox was ready for the future.

Kodak

Now, here's the story of the Eastman Kodak Company.

1888: The Kodak company is founded by George Eastman and Henry A. Strong.

1975: Eastman Kodak dominates the US market for photography, commanding 85 percent of camera sales and 90 percent of film sales.

Also 1975: Kodak develops the very first digital camera. *But it is dropped, as the company fears it will threaten Kodak's own chemical photography business.*

1994: Apple introduces the innovative QuickTake digital camera. Although it carries the Apple label, it is produced by Kodak, which proves that Kodak's digital knowhow is up to date.

2000: In the years around the start of the new millennium, Kodak does not develop a digital photography strategy. The company believes that its core business, traditional film, will not be threatened by the digital technology.

In the same years, Sony, Nikon and Canon start flooding the market with digital cameras.

2004: While in the midst of a hasty U-turn towards digital technology, Eastman Kodak announces it will shed 15,000 jobs. A year later, the number is raised to 27,000. Its stock value plummets; see Figure 8.10.

2010: Kodak rapidly used up its cash reserves. Most of its revenues now come from patent licensing to competitors.

2012: Eastman Kodak is declared bankrupt. In an attempt for a restart, its photographic film, commercial scanners and kiosk divisions are sold.

2013: Next, many of its patents are sold as well, for more than half a billion dollars. In August, the company emerges from bankruptcy after also abandoning personalized imaging and document imaging. In October, it returns to the New York Stock Exchange (NYSE), as Figure 8.10 shows.

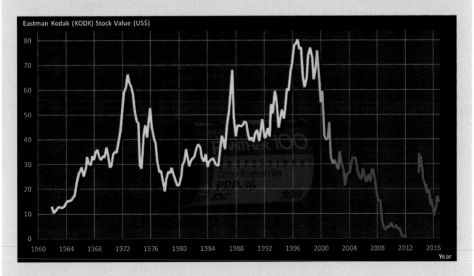

FIGURE 8.10 Stock values of Eastman Kodak, from 1962 to 2016

Source: Yahoo! Finance, 2016; background photo: Vincenzo Reina, Flickr

In the twenty-first century, hardly anyone still buys old-fashioned rolls of film. Kodak started to move too late, years after young computer companies had already conquered the digital photography field, leaving no niche for Eastman's company.

Kodak was *not* ready for the future.

Ready for the future in good time – that is only possible if you anticipate that future, if you look far into the future and act accordingly. Xerox anticipated the future, while the chemical-based photography companies were less successful in that endeavour. Companies that do not sufficiently anticipate the future run the risk of missing the boat and consequently struggling to survive. A good way to compel yourself, as an entrepreneur, to anticipate the future is to ask yourself: why would my company still exist in 25 years? The answer to that involves the question of whether you will still have something to offer society in a quarter of a century – whether, by that time, your company still has stakeholder value. In reality, every single company should pose that question at regular intervals; and if, like Xerox, the conclusion is that there is a good chance the company will lack any stakeholder value in 25 years, then it is time to reconsider the company's purpose. Why did it start? What is the company mission at present? Who are we as a company, anyway? What could the mission become, for stakeholder value to exist in 25 years?

Much is demanded of companies in such a situation. **Redefining the company mission** (from *copying company* to *document company*, for example) is a difficult task for many, if not an impossible one, requiring much flexibility and the ability to think outside of the box. And one also needs a great deal of courage to take on uncertainties. Companies – sometimes even entire sectors – that fail to do this run the risk of disappearing, just like the professions and sectors listed in Table 8.3.

Questions

- If you work in a company, or study in one (an educational institute is also a company, even if it is perhaps not-for-profit), or maybe even own a company, what are the reasons for the company's existence?
- Why would that company still exist in 25 years? What will it contribute to society at that time? Will society still require that contribution in 25 years?

TABLE 8.3 Professions and sectors under threat

Largely extinct (in the Western world)	Clog makers, millers, bridge keepers, shepherds, shoe repairers, eel fishermen, knights
Threatened	Photochemical companies, printing companies, desktop publishers, paper industry, music industry, paper ticket sellers, local grocery stores
Possibly soon to be threatened	Typists, train drivers, driving instructors, cashiers, translators, livestock farmers, the infantry, money printing companies

8.5 The sustainably competent professional

A future-oriented approach requires people who are creative and who have the capacity to be innovative. Meanwhile, corporate social responsibility needs staff that has a sense of responsibility and a social consciousness. An integral approach, focusing on the entire life cycle of both people and products, also helps in thinking outside of the box, while corporate government needs managers and staff that are not afraid to publicly state what they are doing – not only the good side, but also the less-good aspects of their work. A fair number of competences are demanded of the current and future workforce of a company, government or education or care institute, from the perspective of sustainable development. And this is not all, as a truly sustainably competent professional is also able to take on the impossible: weigh up those things that cannot be weighed up. The following case – an imaginary email exchange – will illustrate what this means.

Case 8.12   Weighing up the unweighable

From: *Marianne@BackelBioChem.com*
To: *Ralph@BackelBioChem.com*
Sent: Thursday, June 01, 2013 11:07 AM
Subject: Re: Problem with green bacilli

Ralph,
I was shocked by your statement. You are acting in a highly unprofessional way – do you know that you are endangering the entire company with these types of messages? We have signed contracts for the delivery of our bacilli to 30 cities, including Mexico City and New Orleans! We cannot afford to lose that money, or would you rather that we fire 1,300 people next month? Because that will be the result. And what about our share price? It will plummet, believe me, and we can easily go bankrupt. What you have stated is far from certain, so what do you want me to do? I can hardly blow up the entire damn company because of a damn rumour!
It's simple – next week we will release the green bacilli. We are going to break down the soot in the air. You cannot stop this, and I PROHIBIT you from saying anything about it to anyone.
Marianne
– – Original Message – –

From: *Ralph@BackelBioChem.com*
To: *Marianne@BackelBioChem.com*
Sent: Thursday, June 01, 2013 9:38 AM
Subject: Problem with green bacilli
> Dear Marianne,

> Things don't look too good here. A foreign bacteria was found in the blood of the two lab

> assistants who suffered liver infection. Further studies have shown that the bacteria
> are probably a mutated version of our own 'green bacilli'. This means that the green
> bacilli can possibly change spontaneously into a type of bacteria that can be hazardous
> to people!
> What struck me is that both my ill colleagues have a very rare blood type – Duffy
> negative – which only people of African origin have. Both the lab assistants are
> African Americans, which means that the mutated green bacilli only affect black people!
> And so, while we might have created green bacilli that can break down the soot in the
> air – a commercial breakthrough, as you told the press last week – there is still a
> flipside. If people are getting sick as a result of it we cannot deploy it, surely?
> I acknowledge that I am in part at fault. I should have extended the lab tests. We might
> then have uncovered the problem in time. I accept all responsibility for this, and I am
> prepared to state this to the media in person. However, now that we know what could
> happen, we cannot release the green bacilli into the atmosphere. Once it is released
> and it starts to reproduce, it will be too late to do anything. I trust you see my point?
> Ralph

This (imaginary) company, BackelBioChem, has created a very attractive innovation called 'green bacilli', which could apparently break down soot in the atmosphere. This would be a major contribution to combating particulate matter, which is released by industry, traffic and agriculture and constitutes a nasty threat to our health. It can also damage the economy, in part because a number of countries prohibit the construction of roads and buildings in regions where the concentration of **aerosols** (particulates) is excessive. BackelBioChem's invention is an extraordinary opportunity for the company that could mean a great deal of money. But, according to Ralph's email, there is another side to their creation – a possibility, although not a certainty, that the bacilli could cause liver disease.

When free choice was possible, the logical response would be to first undertake further studies before releasing the bacilli into the air. But the circumstances no longer allow for free choice, and if its release is postponed there will be mass dismissals and, says Marianne, the company could go belly-up. But on the other hand, should the bacilli be released and result in fatalities, and the company was aware this could happen, this could likewise result in bankruptcy and mass dismissals (this might be why Marianne responded angrily – she simply did not want to know). The situation is rife with risks, and things can always go wrong, irrespective of the path one chooses. Choices will have to be weighed up between completely dissimilar interests, between issues that are in reality **unweighable**. A decision must be made concerning an impossible dilemma – to postpone or not to postpone.

Questions

- What is the greatest concern – a solution to the problem of soot, the dismissal of 1,300 people or the chance that an unknown number of people *might* fall ill?
- Do you agree with Marianne that Ralph is acting unprofessionally?

There are further issues concealed in the BackelBioChem dilemma which have already been looked at previously in this book.

Cause and effect (see Section 7.2): Ralph is being very simplistic if he immediately states that it is a certainty ('... *the mutated green bacilli only affect black people!*'), that the liver infection the two lab assistants are suffering from has been caused by the spontaneous mutation of the green bacilli. This may be probable, but only further investigation can demonstrate whether it is true. The same holds for Ralph's assumption that only people with 'Duffy negative' blood (which is real, and is almost only found in people of African origin) are susceptible to the problem. This is a fallacy, a logical error, in which he confuses suspicions with facts. Marianne also commits a comparable fallacy when she says that Ralph is acting unprofessionally – stating this as fact while in reality it is simply an opinion. The ability to distinguish between facts, assumptions and opinions is a very important competence for sustainably oriented professionals.

Discrimination (Section 3.2): could it be possible that Marianne's decision to continue with the process is due in part to the fact that only black people are endangered?

Stakeholder analysis (Section 5.5): who holds an interest in this issue, in both a positive sense (such as company profits and public health) and a negative sense (such as the chance of a population group falling ill and possible dismissals)?

The *consequence scope* and *consequence period* (Section 5.5): how far do the consequences extend in terms of space and time? Could the mutated bacilli also spontaneously come into being in the outside world (*in vivo*, and not just in the laboratory, *in vitro*), and if they could, would they eventually spread around the globe? Could the bacilli ever be eradicated?

Uncertainty: although it is by no means certain that the liver infection was caused by the mutated bacilli, a decision still has to be made, *as not deciding is still deciding* – if you decide to postpone releasing the bacilli, many people will have to be dismissed. Whatever a person does do or does not do will always have consequences.

Precautionary principle (Section 7.3): if it is suspected that releasing the bacteria will result in extremely grave consequences, it might be better not to take the risk. This is what Ralph is arguing, but Marianne dismisses this point. Who is correct?

Taking responsibility (Section 5.5): the company clearly has a number of different social responsibilities in this issue, but not just the company:

Conscience (Section 8.2, Case 8.5): every one of the employees concerned also has an individual responsibility, including Ralph. Marianne imposes a duty of confidentiality upon him. What is he to do? Will he become a **whistleblower**, ignoring his duty of confidentiality and informing the outside world, even if the consequences of doing this could be grave for him personally? The question for him is which carries the most weight – the order from his superior or his own conscience?

Being accountable, transparency (Section 8.2): will the company finally inform the public of the problem, either in the short or the long term? What are the consequences of doing this? What are the consequences of *not* doing this?

Taken together, these add up to a fair number of aspects that make up the complex problem presented in Case 8.12. Fortunately, most issues that a company's staff are confronted by are less complicated, although it is not unusual that highly trained professionals have to deal, at some point in their career, with situations wherein aspects are difficult to weigh up against each other. This is true for every field, irrespective of whether the players are managers, engineers, healthcare providers, teachers, public officers, farmers, biologists or any other professional. At such crucial times, it boils down to making the right choices, which requires a wide range of competences. A number of these have already been listed in the context of Case 8.12, and we can find more from the preceding chapters. All these competences, which a professional requires to operate in a sphere of corporate social responsibility and contribute to sustainable development, are summarised in the so-called **RESFIA+D** model, which consists of six general competences related to sustainability ('R' through 'A'), all of which are further elaborated into three part-competences, as can be seen in Table 8.4. Aside from the general competences, one can also identify competences for sustainable development that are specific for each separate discipline, which is where the '+D' comes in.

The importance of sufficient sustainably competent professionals in all disciplines

The number of companies and institutions that are actively devoted to CSR and sustainable business practices are growing quickly, but in a certain sense this is accidental. This is because, for most companies operating with sustainability in mind, it is largely a lucky coincidence that people are employed in decisive areas of the company who are concerned about environmental degradation, poverty or declining resources, and who have resolved to do something about these problems. Of course, it is great that these people exist, but in the long term this is simply not good enough. What society really requires is that *every* company, and also every public institution, school, healthcare institute or NGO, operates in a socially responsible and future-oriented manner. If we are to achieve this, we cannot leave the issue of whether professionals adopt a sustainable approach up to mere chance. The means to achieve this is through education. If all vocational and university level courses, as well as all primary and secondary education, contribute to their students developing a sustainable attitude, then it will no longer be simply accidental whether or not companies and public authorities engage in sustainable policies. Moreover, if all graduates were to have the knowledge, understanding and skills required for converting this attitude into deeds, an unstoppable, society-wide process of sustainable development will arise.

Working towards such a goal is not a luxury. There is no truth in the idea that higher education can be of a decent quality if it does not pay attention to social responsibility and sustainable development. Global threats such as climate change, the degradation of biodiversity, desertification and the chance of dislocation and absolute chaos in developing countries as well as the very real possibility of hundreds of millions of refugees around the world – and not just in poor nations – are of such a serious nature that we, as human beings, cannot allow

TABLE 8.4 RESFIA+D: professional competences for sustainable development

Competence R: Responsibility A sustainably competent professional bears responsibility for his or her own work. *In other words, the sustainably competent professional can . . .*	See Section:	Competence E: Emotional intelligence A sustainably competent professional empathises with the values and emotions of others. *In other words, the sustainably competent professional can . . .*	See Section:
1. Create a stakeholder analysis on the basis of the consequence scope and the consequence period	5.5	1. Recognise and respect his or her own values and those of other people and cultures	4.3
2. Take personal responsibility	8.2	2. Distinguish between facts, assumptions and opinions	8.5
3. Be held personally accountable with respect to society (transparency)	8.2	3. Cooperate on an interdisciplinary and transdisciplinary basis	1.3, 4.8
Competence S: System orientation A sustainably competent professional thinks and acts from a systemic perspective. *In other words, the sustainably competent professional can . . .*		**Competence F: Future orientation** A sustainably competent professional works and thinks on the basis of a perspective of the future. *In other words, the sustainably competent professional can . . .*	
1. Think from systems: flexibly zoom in and out on issues, i.e. thinking analytically and holistically in turn	3.5	1. Think on different time scales – flexibly zoom in and out on short- and long-term approaches	5.5
2. Recognise flaws in the fabric and sources of vigour in systems; have the ability to use the sources of vigour	Ch. 2–4	2. Recognise and utilise non-linear processes	7.3
3. Think integrally and chain oriented	8.3	3. Think innovatively, creatively, out of the box	8.4
Competence I: personal Involvement A sustainably competent professional has a personal involvement in sustainable development. *In other words, the sustainably competent professional can . . .*		**Competence A: Action skills** A sustainably competent professional is decisive and capable of acting. *In other words, the sustainably competent professional can . . .*	
1. Consistently involve sustainable development in his or her own work as a professional (a sustainable attitude)	4.7	1. Weigh up the unweighable and make decisions	8.5
2. Passionately work towards dreams and ideals	4.2	2. Deal with uncertainties	6.3
3. Employ his or her conscience as the ultimate yardstick	8.2	3. Act when the time is right, and not go against the current: 'action without action'.	4.2

Plus: **Disciplinary competences** for sustainable development (differs for each course, discipline or profession)

them to be ignored. The same is true for impending shortages of fossil fuels, uranium, iron ore, copper and many other minerals. We can solve all these issues, provided we get all hands on deck. Or, to put it differently, for sustainable development we need the graduates of *all* disciplines. If the question exists, whether or not sustainable development should constitute a part of all higher education, this is actually the question of whether we are going to look forward to a healthy future, or to one involving global collapse.

This naturally does not mean that every graduate has to be a full expert on sustainability. It will be more than sufficient for every professional to gain, within the space of a few years, a certain amount of general competences related to sustainability, as detailed in Table 8.4, and also to acquire a few more specific tools within their own fields in the form of knowledge, understanding and skills.

To promote such a situation, higher education courses can impose their own requirements on students. Cases in Section 4.7 and at the start of Chapter 7 offer examples of projects undertaken by students that contributed to sustainable development in a sublime manner. We do not have to expect that every student will deliver such projects, but they should be required to submit projects that fulfill certain basic conditions. A few of these are listed in Table 8.5, all derived from the competences in Table 8.5. They deal partly with requirements that can be imposed in advance on internship and graduation projects, and partly with the characteristics against which project reports can be retrospectively tested. Both of these can be included in the internship and graduation rules, so that students will know exactly what is expected of them.

Throughout their careers, graduates will in many cases end up in a position where they take on responsibilities. This could entail being responsible for students, patients or the elderly, or being responsible for staff, expensive equipment, major investments or hazardous experiments. Many students are not yet aware of this future responsibility.

Students graduating in medicine, however, have already been made aware that they will have a large degree of influence in other people's lives as professional practitioners. When they

TABLE 8.5 Example of a checklist for sustainability requirements for an internship or graduation project

Explicit project prerequisites:	Report can also be retrospectively assessed on the grounds of:
R1: Creating a stakeholder analysis; determining consequence scope and consequence period for the project and its conclusions	E1: Respect shown for one's own values and those of others
R3: Taking personal responsibility for one's own work and conclusions	E2: Drawing a clear distinction between facts, assumptions and opinions
S1: Zooming in and out, adopting both an analytical and holistic perspective	E3: Proper inter- and transdisciplinary cooperation (where applicable)
S3: Thinking integrally and with a chain process in mind	F2: Non-linear processes have not been conceived of as linear
F1: Zooming in and out – focusing on both the short and the long term	I1: Sustainable attitude has been clearly rendered
F3: Thinking innovatively, creatively and outside of the box	I2: Personal involvement, or even passion, has been demonstrated
A2: Determining the degree of certainty or uncertainty in terms of the information and the conclusions	I3: One's own conscience has been used as a yardstick
	A1: Issues were weighed up in a defendable manner
	A3: Actions were undertaken at the proper time

are awarded their degrees they take a solemn pledge, the **Hippocratic Oath**. A similar pledge for other graduates might not be a bad idea, and it could read as follows:

A Pledge

I promise that in my work I will consistently consider the consequences of my actions for society and for the environment, both today and in the future. I shall, before making decisions and whilst making them, conscientiously assess issues. I shall not undertake any actions geared towards harming people or the natural environment. I shall use my education, talents and experiences in order to make a contribution to a better world through sustainable development.

I accept that I am personally responsible for my choices and actions, and I promise that I will be held publically accountable for my work by everyone for whom that work holds consequences. I shall not appeal to the fact that I acted on the instructions of others.

I promise that in my work I will not only make an effort for my own interests and my career, but also for my dreams and my ideals. In this I shall respect the values and the interests of others.

I understand that there will be times in the course of my career when it will be difficult to do what I am now promising to do. I will adhere to this pledge, even in those times.

Sources: This pledge has borrowed, inter alia, from the Pugwash Declaration, Student Pugwash USA 1995; INES Appeal to Engineers and Scientists, International Network of Engineers and Scientists for Global Responsibility, 1995; the Hippocratic Oath, KNMG (the Royal Dutch Medical Association) and the VSNU (the Association of Universities in the Netherlands), 2003.

Questions

- What is your response to the fact that all doctors (must) take a pledge upon graduating?
- Do you have any idea what your work might entail in a decade or three, and what responsibilities you will then be bearing?
- Do you think the work of a doctor involves greater responsibilities than your work as a professional (in the course of your career)?
- If all your fellow students take the pledge when they graduate, would *you* be prepared to follow suit?
- Or would you even take the initiative, and propagate the idea to others?

One chance only

It looks as if the twenty-first century is set to be a unique period in world history. In the wake of the population explosion of the previous century, which is still continuing today, we are now in the middle of a technological explosion that is still accelerating, thanks primarily to IT.

This has created opportunities, and also risks. If we all put our shoulders to the wheel, we will be able to create a global society in which many of us can thrive. If we don't, we will ruin that opportunity. We have one chance and one chance only. At least, that is the assertion of the astronomer Fred Hoyle. In his 1964 book 'Of Men and Galaxies' he wrote:

> "It has often been said that, if the human species fails to make a go of it here on Earth, some other species will take over the running. In the sense of developing high intelligence this is not correct. We have, or soon will have, exhausted the necessary physical prerequisites so far as this planet is concerned. With coal gone, oil gone, high-grade metallic ores gone, no species however competent can make the long climb from primitive conditions to high-level technology. This is a one-shot affair. If we fail, this planetary system fails so far as intelligence is concerned. The same will be true of other planetary systems. On each of them there will be one chance and one chance only."

If we have enough well-trained professionals who have the proper competences to introduce sustainable development, we will be able to grab that chance in this very decisive period that will make up the next few decades. The most important of all the competences is the ability to uphold ideals and nurture dreams – to have the passion to devote your entire being to these dreams, not losing them in a slow-but-sure process but instead holding onto them and nurturing them throughout a lengthy career. If we have enough professionals that, at the very least, have this competence, then sustainable development will be a success story. Another well-known author, T.E. Lawrence (better known as Lawrence of Arabia, 1888–1935) said the same in 1922 in his book *The Seven Pillars of Wisdom*:

> "All men dream: but not equally. Those who dream by night in the dusty recesses of their minds wake in the day to find that it was vanity: but the dreamers of the day are dangerous men, for they may act their dream with open eyes, to make it possible."

Summary

Companies can contribute to sustainable development in a variety of ways:

- Through CSR, through which a number of principles and motivations entailing responsibility can be employed as a point of departure
- By operating transparently and being held accountable on the basis of corporate governance
- By means of providing sustainable products and services based on an integral approach
- Future-oriented business practices, taking into account the expected and unexpected developments, including social trends, technical innovations and decreasing natural resources

A professional who wants to contribute to sustainable development requires a number of special competences. Education plays a special role in this, in part through imposing requirements for sustainability upon student performance. Graduates could, when concluding their higher education, take a pledge in this respect.

A more detailed summary can be found on the website of this book.

BIBLIOGRAPHY

5th Pillar (2016): "5th Pillar". New York/New Delhi/Singapore, http://5thpillar.org.

Bender, A. (1992): "Meat and Meat Products in Human Nutrition in Developing Countries". FAO Food and Nutrition Paper 53, Rome.

Bhattacharyya, R. et al. (2015): "Soil Degradation in India: Challenges and Potential Solutions". *Sustainability*, 7, 3528–3570. DOI:10.3390/su7043528.

Bouwman, C. (1722): Scheepsjournaal van Kapitein Cornelis Bouwman van de Arent, Rotterdam Municipal Archives, published in: F. E. Baron Mulert (ed.), "Scheepsjournaal, gehouden op het schip Tienhoven tijdens de ontdekkingsreis van Mr. Jacob Roggeveen, 1721–1722", in: "Archief. Vroegere en latere mededeelingen voornamelijk in betrekking tot Zeeland uitgegeven door het Zeeuwsch Genootschap der Wetenschappen", 1911, 52–183.

CDIAC (2016): "Carbon Dioxide Information Analysis Center", http://cdiac.ornl.gov.

CIA (2016): "World Factbook 2016", CIA, www.cia.gov/library/publications/the-world-factbook.

Clarke, R., and King, J. (2004): "Atlas of Water". Earthscan, London.

"Consumer Guide" (April 2004): Consumer Association, The Hague.

CSD (2001): "CSD Theme Indicator Framework, Commission on Sustainable Development", www.un.org/esa/sustdev/natlinfo/indicators/isdms2001/table_4.htm.

Desertec Foundation (2011): DESERTEC EU-MENA Map: Sketch of possible infrastructure for a sustainable supply of power to Europe, the Middle East and North Africa (EU-MENA), https://commons.wikimedia.org/wiki/File:DESERTEC-Map_large.jpg

DJIA (2010): "Dow Jones Industrial Average", www.djindexes.com.

Drexler, E. (1986): "Engines of Creation". Anchor Books, New York.

EEA (2012): "Data and Maps, European Environment Agency", www.eea.europa.eu/data-and-maps: EUA future prices 2005–2011; EUA future prices 2008–2012.

EEA (2016): "Data and Maps, European Environment Agency", www.eea.europa.eu/data-and-map.

Ehrlich, P. (1968): "The Population Bomb". Ballantine, New York.

Ehrlich, P. (1970): "Eco-Catastrophe". Harper & Row, New York.

Eurostat (2015): "Online Database, European Commission", http://epp.eurostat.ec.europa.eu/portal/page/portal/eurostat/home.

FAO (2003, January 26): "Countries Around the World Should Be Concerned About 'Mad Cow Disease' and Should Take Action to Reduce and Prevent Risks", www.fao.org/WAICENT/OIS/PRESS_NE/PRESSENG/2001/pren0103.htm.

FAO (2016): "AQUASTAT Main Database".

"Fortune 500" (2016): http://beta.fortune.com/fortune500/2016.

"Fortune Global 500" (2016): http://beta.fortune.com/global500.

Freedom House (2016): "Freedom of the World 2016. Anxious Dictators, Wavering Democracies: Global Freedom Under Pressure".

Gaykrant (2005): "Gaykrant online", www.gk.nl.

Global Footprint Network (2009): "Ecological Footprint Atlas 2009", http://pthbb.org/natural/footprint.

Global Footprint Network (2016): "Datatables", www.footprintnetwork.org/en/index.php/GFN/page/footprint_for_nations.

Globalis (2010): Interactive world map, http://archive.is/globalis.gvu.unu.edu

Hawken, P., Lovins, A., Lovins, L.H. (1999): "Natural Capitalism – Creating the Next Industrial Revolution". Earthscan, London.

Houghton, J. (2004): "Global Warming – the Complete Briefing". Cambridge University Press, Cambridge, UK, 3rd ed.

Hoyle, F. (1964): "Of Men and Galaxies". University of Washington Press, Seattle.

Hu, Y., Smith, D., Frazier, E., Hoerle, R., Ehrich, M. and Zhang, C. (2016): "The Next-Generation Nicotine Vaccine: A Novel and Potent Hybrid Nanoparticle-Based Nicotine Vaccine". *Biomaterials* 106, November, 228–239.

IMF (2016): "IMF Data Mapper 3.0". International Monetary Fund, www.imf.org/en/Data.

Index Mundi (2016): "Country Facts", www.indexmundi.com.

INES (1995): "INES Appeal to Engineers and Scientists, International Network of Engineers and Scientists for Global Responsibility". International Network of Engineers and Scientists for Global Responsibility, Berlin.

Investing.com (2016): "Carbon Emissions Futures Historical Data". www.investing.com/commodities/carbon-emissions-historical-data.

IPCC (2001): "Climate Change 2001 Synthesis Report". Intergovernmental Panel on Climate Change, Genève.

IPCC (2007): "4th Assessment Report, IPCC Working Group 1". Intergovernmental Panel on Climate Change, Genève.

IPCC (2013): "Climate Change 2013: The Physical Science Basis". Contribution of Working Group I to the Fifth Assessment Report of the Intergovernmental Panel on Climate Change. Cambridge University Press, Cambridge, UK.

IPU (2016): "PARLINE Database on National Parliaments". Inter-Parliamentary Union, www.ipu.org.

Jehoel-Gijsbers, G. (2004): "Sociale uitsluiting in Nederland". Sociaal en Cultureel Planbureau, The Hague

Kahn, H., Brown, W., and Martel, L. (1976): "The Next 200 Years". Morrow, New York.

Kahn, H., and Wiener, A. (1967): "The Year 2000, a Framework for Speculation on the Next Thirty-Three Years". Palgrave Macmillan, New York.

Kirchner, J.W., and Weil, A. (2000): "Delayed Biological Recovery From Extinctions Throughout the Fossil Record". *Nature* 404 (6774), 177–180.

Klotzbach, P.J., and Landsea, C.W. (2015): "Revisiting Webster et al. (2005) After 10 Years". *Journal of Climate* 28, October, 6221.

KNMG (2003): "Hippocratic Oath". KNMG & VSNU, Utrecht.

Lan-Huong, L., Thi-Hoa, B., Van-Thanh, D., and Thi-Thanh-Nga, N. (n.d): "The Current State on Water Quality, Eutrophication and Biodiversity of West Lake". http://wldb.ilec.or.jp/data/ilec/WLC13_Papers/others/48.pdf.

Lawrence, T.E. (1922): "The Seven Pillars of Wisdom". Oxford University Press, Oxford.

Lazard (2015): "Levelized Cost of Energy Analysis 9.0". www.lazard.com.

Leakey, R. (1995): "The Sixth Extinction – Patterns of Life and the Future of Humankind". Doubleday, New York.

Lomborg, B. (1998): "Verdens sande tilstand"; English translation: "The Skeptical Environmentalist: Measuring the Real State of the World", Cambridge University Press, 2001

Maddison, A. (2001): "The World Economy: A Millennial Perspective". OECD Development Centre, Paris.

Mann, M.E., Zhang, Z., Hughes, M.K., Bradley, R.S., Miller, S.K., Rutherford, S. and Ni, F (2008): "Data Files Being Part of 'Proxy-Based Reconstructions of Hemispheric and Global Surface Temperature Variations Over the Past Two Millennia." *Proceedings of the National Academy of Sciences* 105(36).

McEvedy, C., and Jones, R. (1978): "Atlas of World Population History". Penguin, New York.

McGrail, B.P., et al. (2017): "Field Validation of Supercritical CO_2 Reactivity With Basalts". *Environmental Science & Technology Letters*. 2017, 4 (1), pp 6–10.

Meadows (2004): "World3–03 Computer Program, Being Part of: Donella Meadows, Jorgen Randers and Dennis Meadows: 'Limits to Growth, the 30-Year Update'". Chelsea Green, White River Junction, Vermont (USA).

Millennium Ecosystem Assessment (2005): "'Synthesis Report' and 'Summary for Decision Makers'". Island Press, Washington, DC.

Myers, N. (1979): "The Sinking Ark: A New Look at the Problem of Disappearing Species". Pergamon Press, Oxford.

NASA (2010): "NASA Goddard Space Flight Center", www.nasa.gov/centers/goddard/home/index.html.

National Oceanic and Atmospheric Administration (2011, January 12): "2010 Tied for Warmest Year on Record", www.noaanews.noaa.gov/stories2011/20110112_globalstats.html.

Nostradamus (1554): "Quatrain 55 of Century 9"; English translation by Charles A. Ward (1891). Perry, Ted: movie 'Home', 1971.

Pizza Fusion (2001): www.pizzafusion.com/.

The Poverty Site (2016): "United Kingdom: Low Income and Ethnicity". www.poverty.org.uk/06/index.shtml.

PRB (2016): "World Population Data Sheets (2001–2015)". Population Reference Bureau, www.prb.org.

Pré (2007): "Simapro 7.0, Based on EcoIndicator 99". Pré Consultants, www.pre.nl/simapro.

Pugwash (1995): "Pugwash Declaration". Student Pugwash, USA, Washington D.C.

Rai, N., Henshaw, C., and Moffett, S. (2011, June): "Food Prices Posing Risk to Poor Nations". *The Wall Street Journal*. http://online.wsj.com/article/SB100014240527023044323045763711812550 14642.html.

RobecoSAM (2015): Press release, September 29, 2015.

Schicks, J. (2011): "Over-Indebtedness of Microborrowers in Ghana: An Empirical Study From a Customer Protection Perspective". Center for Financial Inclusion, Brussels.

Seed, J., Macy, J., Fleming, P., and Naess, A. (1988): "Thinking Like a Mountain: Towards a Council of All Beings". New Society Publishers, Philadelphia, PA.

SiRi Group (2006): "Dutch Sustainability Research: Research Methodology". SiRi Group, Zeist.

Stanley, S.M. (2016): "Estimates of the Magnitudes of Major Marine Mass Extinctions in Earth History". *PNAS*, published online before print October 3, 2016, DOI: 10.1073/pnas.1613094113.

Telos (2004): "Monitoring van provinciale duurzame ontwikkeling: De duurzaamheidsbalans getoetst in vier provincies". Telos, Tilburg.

UN (1999): "'The World at Six Billion', Table 1: 'World Population From Year 0 to Stabilization'". United Nations, New York.

UN (2015): "The Millennium Development Goals Report 2015", United Nations, New York.

UN DESA (2002): "Online Statistics". UN Department of Economic and Social Affairs: Population Division, New York.

UN DESA (2012): "Online Statistics". UN Department of Economic and Social Affairs: Population Division, New York.

UN DESA (2015): "Online Statistics". UN Department of Economic and Social Affairs: Population Division, New York.

UN Population Division (2016): World Population Prospects 2016 Revision, http://esa.un.org/unpd/wpp/Excel-Data/population.htm. United Nations, New York.

UNDP (2015): "Human Development Report 2015". United Nations Development Programme, Brussels.

UNDP (2016): "Human Development Report: Online Database". United Nations Development Programme, Brussels, http://hdr.undp.org/en/statistics/data.

UNEP (2016): "GEO Data Portal". United National Environmental Programme, Nairobi.

UN Statistics Division (2015): "Millennium Development Goals: 2015 Progress Chart". United Nations Statistics Division, New York.

UN Statistics Division (2016): "National Accounts Main Aggregates Database". UN Statistics Division, New York

Vié, J. C., Hilton-Taylor, C., Pollock, C., Ragle, J., Smart, S., Stuart, S., and Tong, R. (2008): The IUCN Red List: A Key Conservation Tool. In: J.-C. Vié, C. Hilton-Taylor and S.N. Stuart (eds): "The 2008 Review of The IUCN Red List of Threatened Species". IUCN Gland, Switzerland.

VROM (2001): "Vijfde Ruimtelijke Nota". Ministerie van VROM, Den Haag.

Wall Street Journal (1966): Quoted in Montgomery, D.C. et al (2015): "Introduction to Time Series Analysis and Forecasting", 2nd Edition, Wiley, 2015

WCED (1987): "Our Common Future: Report of the World Commision on Environment and Development". Also known as the "Brundtland Report". Oxford University Press, New York.

WHKMLA (2009): "Encyclopedia of Wars". Zentrale für Unterrichtsmedien, www.zum.de/whkmla/military/warindex.html.

WHO Global Health Observatory (2015): "Global Health Observatory (GHO) Data", www.who.int/gho/mdg/environmental_sustainability/en.

Wilson, E. O. (1992): "The Diversity of Life". The Belknap Press of Harvard University Press, Cambridge, MA.

Womack, J., and Jones, D. (1996): "Lean Thinking: Banish Waste and Create Wealth in Your Corporation". Simon & Schuster, New York.

World Bank (2010): "Health Nutrition and Population Statistics", http://databank.worldbank.org/ddp/home.do.

World Bank (2016): "World Bank Open Data", http://data.worldbank.org.

World Economic Forum (2015): "The Global Gender Gap Report 2015".

Zhu, W. X., Lu, L., and Hesketh, T. (2009): "China's Excess Males, Sex Selective Abortion and One Child Policy". *British Medical Journal* 2009; 338: b1211.

INDEX